Fuzzy Modeling and Genetic Algorithms for Data Mining and Exploration

The Morgan Kaufmann Series in Data Management Systems

Series Editor: Jim Gray, Microsoft Research

Fuzzy Modeling and Genetic Algorithms for Data Mining and Exploration

Earl Cox

ELSEVIER

AMSTERDAM • BOSTON • HEIDELBERG • LONDON
NEW YORK • OXFORD • PARIS • SAN DIEGO
SAN FRANCISCO • SINGAPORE • SYDNEY • TOKYO

Morgan Kaufmann Publishers is an imprint of Elsevier

MORGAN KAUFMANN PUBLISHERS

Publishing Director	Diane D. Cerra
Acquisitions Editor	Rick Adams
Publishing Services Manager	Simon Crump
Project Manager	Dan Stone
Developmental Editor	Emilia Thiuri
Editorial Coordinators	Corina Derman and Mona Buehler
Cover Design	Yvo Riezebos Design
Cover Image	Getty Images
Composition	CEPHA Imaging Pvt. Ltd.
Technical Illustration	Dartmouth Publishing Inc.
Copyeditor	Daril Bentley
Proofreader	Phyllis Coyne Proofreading Services
Indexer	Lucie Haskins
Interior Printer	The Maple-Vail Book Manufacturing Group
Cover Printer	Phoenix Color

Morgan Kaufmann Publishers is an imprint of Elsevier.
500 Sansome Street, Suite 400, San Francisco, CA 94111

This book is printed on acid-free paper.

Library of Congress Cataloging-in-Publication Data
APPLICATION SUBMITTED

ISBN: 0-12-194275-9

For information on all Morgan Kaufmann publications,
visit our Web site at www.mkp.com or www.books.elsevier.com

Printed in the United States of America

05 06 07 08 09   5 4 3 2 1

Contents

Part I   Concepts and Issues

■ ■ ■ Chapter 1
Foundations and Ideas 3

▪▪▪ Chapter 6
Fuzzy SQL and Intelligent Queries   149

▪▪▪ Chapter 7
Fuzzy Clustering   207

■ ■ ■   Chapter 11
       # Genetic Tuning of Fuzzy Models   483

Preface

This is a book about using fuzzy logic and evolutionary strategies — primarily genetic algorithms—to explore the structure of data, understand patterns in data, and create rule-based models from these patterns. As a general approach to exploring and modeling data, it is neither a book on data mining nor a book on expert or decision support systems. Rather, its goal is to provide project managers, business analysts, knowledge engineers, and system developers with a broad spectrum of concepts underlying the use of fuzzy systems and genetic algorithms.

These two technologies are complementary in many ways. Fuzzy systems provide an extraordinarily rich way of representing and manipulating a wide universe of diverse business, industry, policy, and technical data. Fuzzy-logic-based clustering, query, and rule-based systems have a richness and a breadth of representation that are difficult, if not impossible, to achieve using corresponding technologies based on crisp or Boolean logic. Genetic algorithms and evolutionary programming systems not only provide powerful and adaptive methods of generating and tuning fuzzy systems (finding the best cluster centers and exploring high-dimensional data through techniques such as genetically evolved regression analysis) but form the foundation for a new generation of robust, flexible, and easy-to-use optimization models.

This book addresses these issues on several fronts. First, it provides an overall *framework* for understanding the methods, technologies, and approaches used to explore data, build models from collections of underlying data, tune models, and design systems that incorporate both fuzzy and genetic properties. In this respect, the book gives the designer and modeler some guidelines for evaluating the trade-offs among various types of models and model architectures. Second, it provides the *techniques and technologies* necessary to construct robust, stable, and maintainable models by combining several advanced forms of knowledge discovery with machine learning techniques. Third, it provides a *roadmap* for model designers and developers in exploring data, selecting model system measures, organizing adaptive feedback loops, selecting a model configuration, implementing a working and workable model, and validating a final model.

The book's modeling methodologies are based on my experiences in building and implementing models over the past thirty years for a wide spectrum of clients in the public and private sectors. It incorporates those techniques and methods that have proven successful but also highlights approaches that have proven less successful. Because the methods are derived from established computer science and computational intelligence techniques, as well as more general "heuristics" in the analysis of processes and the representation of knowledge, the book is intended to serve as a handbook for working analysts who need to build and deliver working models in the commercial and public policy environments.

Objectives and Audience

This book presents a philosophical (and epistemological) discussion of the roles fuzzy logic and genetic algorithms play in knowledge discovery, system design, and business process modeling. In this regard, the book has several broad objectives.

- To provide a reasonable and understandable foundation in the nature of fuzzy logic and fuzzy systems. Although some attention is paid to control theory, the principal orientation is on the use of fuzzy systems in the area of information engineering and analysis as well as the construction of intelligent systems.

- To introduce the foundations for three important applications of fuzzy systems: the use of fuzzy qualifiers in database queries (fuzzy SQL), the introduction of fuzzy measures in cluster analysis, and the discovery and quantification of fuzzy *if-then* rules from data.

- To provide a clear and extensive foundation in the nature of genetic algorithms and evolutionary programming (with emphasis on genetic algorithms).

- To illustrate (through applications and modeling support features) how evolutionary strategies can be used to develop advanced optimization systems as well as provide fuzzy model architecture tuning and data exploration facilities.

Hence, this book, as the title suggests, is a guide to the concepts, basic algorithms, and principal features of machine intelligence capabilities that to a greater or lesser extent are based on biological models. Genetic and evolutionary systems are the obvious biological models. However, as a logic of continuous phenomena that directly handles ambiguity, uncertainty, and extensibility, fuzzy logic also has a strong relationship to ideas underlying biological systems.

Organization of the Book

Part I connects the themes in the book with various types of models and the nature of business and public policy modeling, and surveys various approaches to heuristic, analytical, mathematical, and statistical modeling. Part I also provides a foundation in the ideas underlying effective model building, data exploration, and data mining (or knowledge discovery). In particular, this first part couples the central ideas of intelligent knowledge discovery, rule-based expert systems, and data exploration with concepts related to self-monitoring adaptive feedback models. These models are often a fusion of subject-matter expert knowledge and knowledge derived from deep analysis of behavior patterns found in data.

Part II covers methods and techniques based on fuzzy logic. It introduces the concepts underlying fuzzy logic (fuzzy sets, membership functions, fuzzy operators, and so on) and then develops the foundations of fuzzy information decision and expert systems. From there Part II moves to an examination of the application of fuzzy logic to database queries, methods in fuzzy clustering, and the core algorithms for fuzzy rule induction.

Part III introduces and covers the methods and techniques of genetic algorithms and evolutionary programming. These genetic or evolutionary strategies form the core machine intelligence components of adaptive and self-tuning and provide the technologies necessary to build optimization, configuration, scheduling, and robust predictive models. Part III highlights the concepts of genetic algorithms by examining a multi-objective and multi-constraint crew scheduling system. This section concludes by exploring genetic methods of tuning fuzzy models.

Algorithm Definitions and Examples

Throughout the book, Java, C/C++, and (infrequently) Visual Basic code is used to illustrate how algorithms work, as well as flow of control associated with them. In several instances, however, algorithms and methods are illustrated though a form of "pseudocode" instead of actual computer code. This has several advantages, including the following.

- *Equal opportunity:* The mechanics of an algorithm are conveyed independently of a reader's knowledge of a particular computer programming language.

- *Clarity:* The algorithm description can avoid the complexities and obscurities of a programming language. The syntax of many programming languages often obscures the representation of data and the flow of control in the algorithm.

- *Consistency:* A pseudocode approach provides a consistent way of explaining the mechanics and the underlying principles of the algorithm.

The complete library for the algorithms and programs contained in this book, including source code, is located on the *www.scianta.com* web site.

As a book on designing and building models using knowledge discovery and machine learning techniques, a certain amount of mathematical notation is unavoidable. Too many authors allow collections of mathematical equations to stand on their own — as if the mathematics provided all of the necessary explanation. This is seldom the case. Particular care has been taken to ensure that all mathematical equations are explained in easy-to-understand language. An attempt has been made to eliminate evaluation ambiguities from equations by explicitly using parentheses to specify the order of evaluation. Mathematical notation is avoided altogether where a more philosophical, technical, or mechanical discussion of the process can be developed.

Acknowledgments

I would like to thank the following individuals for their help, support, criticism, and exchange of ideas.

My thank you to Jerry Bennett, Research Analyst, Applied Research, USAA, San Antonio, Texas; William (Bill) Combs, Computing Systems Architect, The Boeing Company, Seattle, Washington; Bill Siler, Scientist, Kemp-Carroway Heart Institute, Birmingham, Alabama; and Terry Hengl, Publisher, and Robin Okun, Vice President of Marketing, *PC/AI Magazine*, Phoenix, Arizona. I am particularly grateful to Terry and Robin for permission to use parts of articles I wrote for their magazine exploring some of the issues also raised in this book. I would also like to thank Michael and Nadja O'Hagan, Fuzzy Logic Inc., La Jolla, California; Will Dwinnell, Artificial Intelligence Consultant, Valley Forge, Pennsylvania; Paul Bergman, President, Foresight Logic, Saint Paul, Minnesota; Mary Dimmock, Pfizer Chemical, Groton, Connecticut; Art DeTore, Vice President, Parker Healthcare, Fort Wayne, Indiana; and Ed DeRouin, President, Peer Sciences, Altamonte Springs, Florida.

Jonathan G. Campbell, School of Computer Science, The Queen's University of Belfast, guided me through the decipherment of the fuzzy c-means algorithm, spent time patiently explaining its mechanics, re-documented his Java code in fine detail, and provided a copy of his excellent fuzzy c-means program for this book. I thank him.

I am also indebted to Professor Vladimir Cherkassky of the Department of Electrical and Computer Engineering, University of Minnesota, and coauthor with Filip Mulier of *Learning from Data* (John Wiley and Sons, 1998). Professor Cherkassky provided a copy of Yong-Jun Lee's doctoral thesis, "An Automated Knowledge Extraction System," as well as critical insights into the fuzzy adaptive clustering technique.

And a special acknowledgment must be made to the late Fred Hegge, Senior Scientist, Army Medical Materiel Command, Fort Detrick, Maryland.

Introduction

The Modern Connected World

Business process modeling is often a no-win situation. Developing reliable business forecasting models requires a successful collaboration between line management and knowledge engineers. And even where the fusion of working knowledge and abstract representation is successful, its result is too often thwarted by the unpredictable dynamics of the real world: corporate objectives change, companies are bought and sold, and new products are introduced (or existing products retired). To compound matters, corporate decision makers and model builders are also faced with the unprecedented uncertainties and pressures of the rapidly changing nature of electronic commerce. In fact, as Figure I.1 illustrates, the high rate of change in global economies will continue to exert pressures on the stability and viability of even well-established corporations.

Our entire world has become connected through a freely available and highly diverse information network, revolutionizing the way we communicate, conduct business, interact with organizations and public agencies, entertain ourselves, and perform scientific and business research. At the same time, the network suffers from increasing amounts of noise, bandwidth saturation, and criminal activity.

The Advent of Intelligent Models

As a result of these uncertainties, business-forecasting models have fallen out of favor in recent years. Instead, business planners tend to concentrate on the short-term analytical approach to business forecasting. In particular, intelligent models — known in the 1970s as decision support systems and later as expert systems (although they use different technologies) — have been replaced by the ubiquitous spreadsheet. Yet spreadsheets are no substitute for knowledge-based models in such critical areas as risk assessment, econometric modeling, new product positioning, customer profiling, cross marketing, sales forecasting, and impact analysis. In this

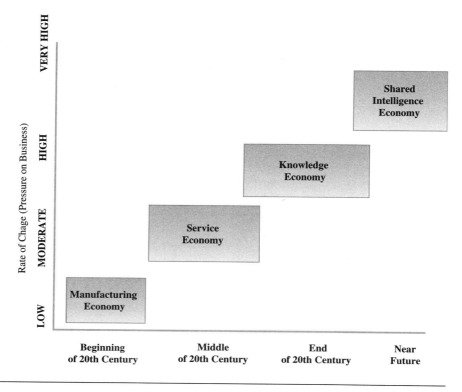

Figure I.1 Rates and types of changes in the global economy.

book we will examine new types of intelligent models that incorporate fuzzy measures as well as evolutionary or genetic techniques. These technologies provide ways to make your models more responsive to changes in demographics and the economy.

A less obvious solution to the problem of change and uncertainty is simply to incorporate these factors into the model itself. Naturally, this means going beyond a statistical analysis of the data or the inclusion of certainty factors or forms of Bayesian probabilities. We must create our models so that they automatically change their internal behavior structure to accommodate changes in the outside world. One approach to this is the adaptive model — a model that alters its rules based on changes in the outside world. A powerful and robust way of building an adaptive model involves the combination of three broad technologies: fuzzy logic, knowledge discovery, and genetic algorithms. Fuzzy logic provides a method for capturing the semantics or meaning of the data through a collection of fuzzy sets associated with each variable. Knowledge discovery (or data mining) uses these fuzzy sets to generate an initial model of *if-then* rules.

A genetic algorithm creates and tests many candidate models by changing the model parameters (such as the number of variables or the fuzzy sets underlying the variables) until it finds the configuration that performs the best.

Fuzzy Logic and Genetic Algorithms

This book examines the use of fuzzy logic and genetic algorithms in data exploration and model building. These two technologies provide a rich and robust platform of tools and methods that allow analysts and model builders to discover patterns buried deep in large repositories of data. They also allow us to construct rule-based models that quantify patterns and combine them, if necessary, with subject matter expert knowledge. In particular, the focus is on methods of exploring public and private (local or distributed) databases as well as the use of these technologies to design, develop, test, validate, and deploy business models.

Data exploration, often overlooked in the knowledge discovery (data mining) process, is a crucial component of business systems analysis, public policy development, and the design and development of intelligent models. This book examines two major data exploration facilities: the use of fuzzy logic in database queries (fuzzy SQL) and the use of fuzzy logic and genetic algorithms in fuzzy clustering. Fuzzy SQL provides a powerful method of using semantics to query a database and return records that match the intention of the query. Fuzzy clustering is a deep and robust method of discovering patterns in a multidimensional collection of data. As a form of unsupervised data mining, clusters can discover unlooked-for patterns and express these as collections of fuzzy rules.

The book's core model building capabilities are centered on two complementary technologies: a comprehensive fuzzy rule induction methodology (which can automatically build fuzzy knowledge bases from large collections of data) and a model-tuning facility built with a genetic algorithm that optimizes the fuzzy model's architecture. Coupled with a detailed discussion of multi-objective, multi-constraint genetic algorithms, the concepts of rule discovery and configuration optimization are combined with a general discussion of how evolutionary strategies can support more advanced intelligent modeling requirements.

This book is neither a mathematical discussion of fuzzy and genetic theory nor a detailed analysis of algorithms. It is intended, as the title implies, to be a broad exploration of critical concepts, a look at the principal algorithms, and a discussion of roadmap issues that will provide the foundation for the integration of fuzzy and evolutionary strategies into the creation of models and advanced applications in the public and private sectors.

Part I
Concepts and Issues

Contents

Chapter 1
Foundations and Ideas

In this introductory chapter we lay some of the foundations for the use of fuzzy-based data exploration techniques (in particular, rule-based data mining) in public and private sector organizations. We start by examining the modern distributed computing resource architecture of e-business, as well as traditional brick-and-mortar enterprises. We also look at the evolution of centralized data warehouses and data marts in business, industry, and government agencies. From this perspective we review the ways in which knowledge discovery techniques can be used to fuse behaviors from multiple sources into a set of effective models. We conclude with a brief example of a customer segmentation model.

Data mining (i.e., knowledge discovery) provides a structured methodology for discovering and quantifying patterns hidden in large quantities of historical and operational data. These patterns, in the form of predictive and classification models, play a critical role in supporting an organization's operational, tactical, and strategic decisions. As a consequence of the role these models play in providing deep insights into often ill-defined behaviors, data mining is becoming an integral part of an organization's business intelligence program. In addition, business intelligence will permeate the way an e-business of the future will conduct itself and protect itself from increasingly unpredictable economic, demographic, and technological change.[1] Responding to change before changes can adversely affect business becomes increasingly more difficult as the next generation of distributed business systems replaces relatively centralized computing facilities.

---

[1] The term *business intelligence* here refers to both the activities of private sector companies and the mission support activities of public sector entities (local, state, and federal government agencies and the military).

3

1.1 **Enterprise Applications and Analysis Models**

Modern businesses are increasingly moving into electronic commerce by establishing a presence on the World Wide Web (the Internet). And through the use of private networks and internal corporate networks (intranets), they are applying powerful modeling techniques to such activities as customer relations and supply chain management. Thus, through this on-line presence (their e-commerce portal) they not only conduct business-to-consumer (B2C) but an ever increasing amount of business-to-business (B2B) activities. Figure 1.1 shows a simplified structure of a modern corporation whose sales channels are divided between traditional brick-and-mortar retail outlets and an e-business web portal.

Modern corporations and government agencies rely on their increasingly distributed computer infrastructures — application, web, and database servers, as well as routers, load balancers, and firewalls — to support a broad and often unpredictable scope of clients and applications.

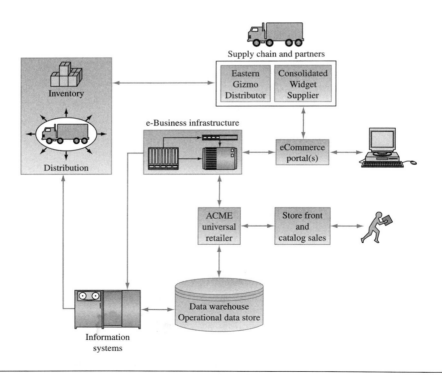

Figure 1.1 The modern web-enabled corporation.

In the modern interconnected world, the infrastructure is the backbone of the organization's mission capabilities; that is, the enterprise's local and distributed infrastructure is intimately and ineluctably tied to business strategy decisions. Further, the quality of these decisions is based on a reliable and sound application of business intelligence.

The organization of an enterprise's application framework extends across a wide array of data repositories, application servers, and web servers.

These application services and models are connected, as Figure 1.2 illustrates, through the machinery of distributed architectures. This distributed architecture consists of several parts,

- the HTTP (HyperText Transfer Protocol[2]),

- server pages[3] — such as ASP (Application Server Pages) and JSP (Java Server Pages) that deliver visual structure to the client as well as accept and display information,

- and the transaction message handlers (as well as general message services such as JMS — the Java Messaging System[4]) that move packets of data around the network.

Business to Business (B2B) opportunities in the Internet world establish lines of communication between business peers on the Web. Capitalizing on the opportunities in this world means leveraging knowledge and marketplace intelligence at ever accelerating rates. This has driven corporations into a race to build and use advanced computational models derived from sophisticated data mining and machine learning capabilities. In this scenario, businesses encapsulate organizational intelligence from transaction streams associated with the e-business interface and the brick-and-mortar sales interface (the combined points-of-sale interface) thus integrating all aspects of their business into a coherent and effective model.

---

[2] HTTP is the primary protocol used to move hypertext information over the Internet and other networks that use the Internet data protocols. HTTP uses an HTTP client on one end and an HTTP server on the other end.

[3] ASP allows the dynamic creation and management of pages containing either server-side or client-side scripts. ASP scripts can support complex functions such as database access, the generation and personalization of web pages, and a broad spectrum of interactive services. In many ways, ASP scripts are similar to CGI (common gateway interface) programs.

[4] Java Message Service is a J2EE interface, implemented for many Java container objects, that provides point-to-point message management, queuing, and publish-subscribe services.

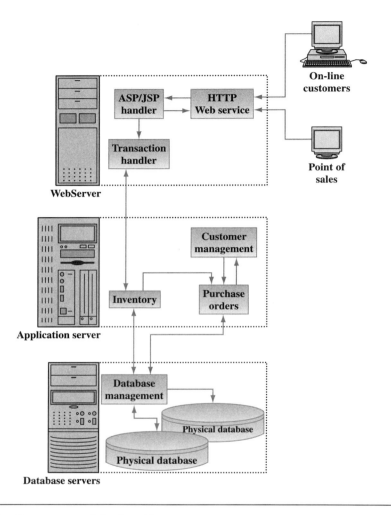

Figure 1.2 Organization of distributed business systems.

As Figure 1.3 illustrates, both strategic and line-of-business (LOB) models have a tight connection with an organization's computer resources. In most enterprises these models work together in a feedback loop that measures the impact of decisions at many levels of the organization.

Strategic models are created by integrating information from the organization's various lines of business (or agency bureaus) with information about incoming performance along the supply chain from raw materials

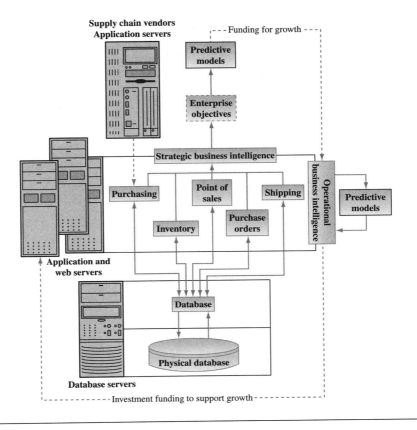

Figure 1.3   Modeling strategic and operational (LOB) processes.

and service vendors of. A strategic model, tied to the enterprise's mission and vision, both measures how well the organization is meeting its overall objectives (usually related to bottom-line profits) and predicts the organization's near-term future behavior for these objectives. Income or after-tax cash flow funds the various lines of business, which in turn generally have their own predictive models. Growth predictions (or agency requirements for managing expanded oversight and regulatory demands) fuel requirements for investment funds to support and sustain growth.

Building these decision models involves a fusion of subject matter expertise and models drawn from historical and operational repositories. These historical models often take the form of free-form database searches using a database query language and of rule-based models derived from patterns buried deep in the data itself.

The application of data mining in distributed systems is often facilitated by two related but often conflicting trends. The first trend is the consolidation of corporate information into a centrally managed and centrally controlled set of databases known collectively as the Data Warehouse. The second trend is the consolidation of line of business, geographically related, or functionally related business information into locally managed and locally controlled databases. These local repositories are known as Data Marts. In many organizations a loosely connected set of data marts, sharing data over a private or public network, form the organization's data warehouse. The ideas and implications associated the distributed nature of data warehouses and data marts are discussed in the next section.

1.2 **Distributed and Centralized Repositories**

Small and large corporations, the military, and public and governmental agencies throughout the world have begun to recognize that their vast stores of historical and active data represent a critical resource. These resources constitute the intellectual property of the organization, including its underlying proprietary knowledge, and potentially represent an explicit picture of its business process models. In addition to their archeological and often political significance as a record of business practices both past and present, these active and archival databases contain implicit relationships between crucial elements in the organization. As an example, Figure 1.4 illustrates some basic data relations in a retailing company.

For many organizations these relationships do not find expression as uniform business practices and well-ordered databases but as a potential in the broad and historically diverse set of data representing, for example, the natural connection between what the company sells and what customers actually purchase. And, of course, there are inherent relationships among such data collections, such as between sales and inventory, or among inventory, sales, and purchase orders. This diversity in data storage and ownership means that behavior patterns common to the organization's business practices or mission were both overlooked and not easily accessible for analysis. Further, even when traditional methods of statistical or systems analysis were applied to these data repositories many important and deep relationships went unobserved and undetected.

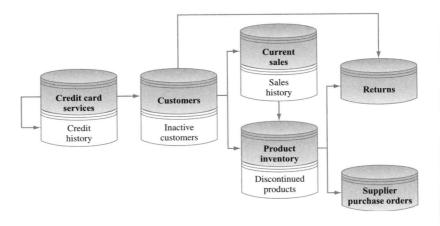

Figure 1.4   Retail data relationships.

The Rise of Data Warehouses

A recent response to the proliferation of corporate data across differing organizational database systems has been the idea of the *data warehouse*. In this emerging fusion of database and application control processes, corporate resources are unified under a single integrated structure. Figure 1.5 illustrates a simple data warehouse.

Just a few years ago, each corporate division or government agency created and administered its own databases. Discussions about database systems nearly always centered around the organization of data (whether tables were in third normal form, the best indexing scheme to facilitate rapid joins, the handling of volatile and time fluctuating data) rather than the uniform integrity and sharability of data and the use of corporate data resources to discover interesting trends and movements in the outside world. Today, these discussions almost always begin with the concept of a centralized data repository, the data warehouse.

Data warehouses are corporate- or agency-wide consolidations of an organization's operational data. They enforce common methods of key definition and representation, domain integrity checks, and data validity management. As Figure 1.1 pointed out, the warehouse makes an explicit commitment to the uniform management of diverse data elements, integrating principal information repositories to create a structure representing a single, well-behaved and well-defined interface for each type of user in each of the organization's business elements. It is this consistent and uniform approach to data management that delivers a wide

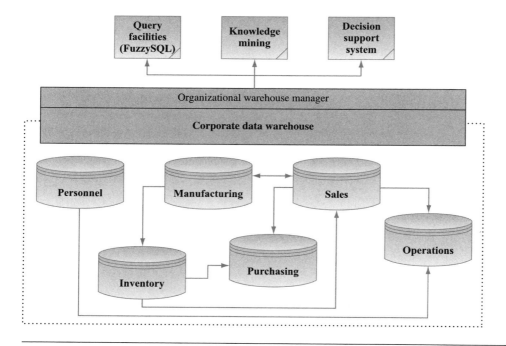

Figure 1.5 A simple data warehouse organization.

array of benefits to the organization. One of the collateral benefits of a data warehouse is the opportunity it affords to perform wide-ranging queries on the organization's fundamental data. Another benefit, awareness of which is only now emerging among data warehouse designers and managers, is the richness such a consolidated warehouse offers for the discovery of new and profitable pieces of information. Much (if not most) of this new information, in the form of unsuspected relationships between and among clusters of data, is hidden deep within the data warehouse.

Yet this consolidation of corporate resources into a central data warehouse need not imply that the warehouse is a monolithic entity, physically located and physically administered by a central information technology (IT) staff. The use of outsourcing, the development of private virtual networks (PVNs), and the proliferation of highly distributed server centers throughout corporations have turned the idea of a centralized data warehouse into the idea of a vigorous and logically homogeneous data management environment. In many organizations, the data warehouse has been profoundly influenced by the emerging age of distributed knowledge.

1.3   **The Age of Distributed Knowledge**

To almost no one's surprise the Internet has transformed our perspective on the nature and the availability of knowledge. Perhaps nowhere has this change been more keenly felt than in the corridors of business. Modern "chief technology" and "chief information" officers are struggling to fuse seemingly diametrically opposed data management objectives: reliability, availability, and integrity. At issue is the control of a corporation's intellectual property, which, as we move well into the next millennium, threatens to become the *sine qua non* of an organization's robustness. And, as Figure 1.6 illustrates, corporate knowledge assets are no longer isolated within the glass walls of the computer room.

Regardless of an IT manager's focus on a centralized data warehouse, corporate knowledge is distributed, often in an apparently random manner, throughout the organization. Internet, intranet, and local networks

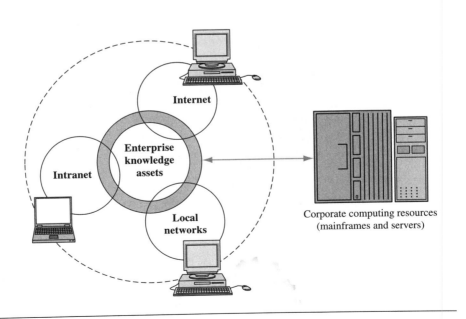

Figure 1.6   Corporate knowledge assets.

provide users with nearly immediate access to on-line client databases, human resource repositories, and departmental or division-level financials. An ever-increasing spectrum of users has access to corporate web sites. Understanding, maintaining, and managing this sea of data often tax the capabilities (and sometimes the vision) of the corporate data processing division. Yet, a failure to account for and integrate a corporation's knowledge assets will become a critical competitive and survival issue in the very near future.

Already corporate information officers have learned that their future is intimately tied to their past in that formal data modeling, data mining, and knowledge discovery processes have become critical components in such traditional business activities as risk assessment, customer profitability analysis, budgeting, and new product positioning. These formal methodologies, aimed at creating and maintaining a competitive edge, rely on the security and integrity of information. As we discussed previously, a consideration of these objectives has seen the rapid rise of the centralized data warehouse. But, as corporations and government agencies steadily move toward a consolidation of their data assets in data warehouse and data mart architectures the simple availability of vast amounts of readily accessible data coupled with ever-faster gigahertz desktop computers will drive an accelerated push toward deeper and broader forms of analysis. Conventional off-line data mining using historical data will give way to high-speed on-line analytical processing (OLAP) engines that dynamically integrate history with the on-line data store (ODS).

Perhaps a larger problem facing management is the synthesis of information into an adaptable knowledge base. Using this knowledge base, an organization can construct and connect an entire suite of cooperative and synergistic business process models. These models share information and support their conclusions through an accumulation of evidence only possible when they have access to the company's complete information framework. How to build these models and what technology should be used are common themes in distributed data warehouse projects. Throughout this book we look at an approach that combines several computational intelligence techniques. Fundamentally, after examining fuzzy database queries and fuzzy cluster analysis we look at the use of fuzzy rule induction in the building of business process models.

1.4   **Information and Knowledge Discovery**

The assemblage of techniques used to discover these deep and nearly invisible relationships is called data mining (or knowledge discovery).

As a consequence of this technique's ability to detect hidden variables and hidden dependencies in often vast collections of data, organizations of all sizes and missions are attempting to find "nuggets of gold"; that is, undiscovered relationships in data that will boost profitability, improve corporate productivity, and give the organization an edge in today's highly competitive environment. Some brief examples of how knowledge discovery is being used include,

- Marketing departments want to target sales in the most cost-effective manner to the most receptive prospects and current clients. Marketing managers need to open new markets and discover new audiences for their available products (or find a focused niche that can be rapidly exploited by new products or the realignment of a current product).

- Corporate information officers and strategic planners need to evaluate the risks of initiating capital-intensive projects based, if possible, on the success or failure of similar projects.

- Banks and other financial institutions want to structure new services and price current services based on customer profitability and customer growth potential. Banks need to understand how customers use such services as automated teller machines, credit cards, and refinancing services.

- Mortgage loan officers and other credit-issuing officials need deep knowledge about the credit worthiness of customers, their potential for defaults, and their potential as customers for new loans and related services.

- A large number of diverse organizations want to isolate anomalous behaviors buried deep in large amounts of operating data. The Treasury Department needs to recognize suspicious patterns in vast amounts of international fund-transfer records. The Internal Revenue Service needs to find unusual patterns in corporate tax returns and operating reports. Credit card companies are looking for sudden changes in customer spending habits. Insurance companies and managed health care organizations want to detect unusual patterns in doctor claims.

- Retailers and suppliers need fundamental information about the deep relationships that drive sales, control inventory levels, and cause shortages or surpluses. They want to separate seasonal changes in purchasing habits from actual shifts in such habits and preferences.

- Investment houses need to assess the issues of safety and suitability for new investors or balance the distribution or concentration of stocks or bonds in the portfolios of clients at various income levels.

- Engineering staffs need to determine the probable durability of new products or the long-term mean time between failure (MTBF) and mean time to repair (MTTR) for various classes of equipment.

- Help desks and customer service departments need information on the most likely centers of client problems, the predicted level of customer satisfaction given a set of solutions, and the likely direction of new problems.

Data mining has wide-ranging applications across many industries, spanning diverse applications in urban planning, transportation, petrochemicals, pharmaceuticals, manufacturing, managed health care, medical informatics, communications, and military operations planning. More and more, organizations are turning to their own data as a way of answering questions such as "How can we improve business performance?," "Where are we vulnerable to competitive attacks?," "How can we identify new markets for existing products?," and "Where should we position ourselves for the next century?"

The Knowledge Discovery Process

Through knowledge discovery (omit qualification), large collections of corporate historical and active data are cleaned, organized, statistically analyzed, and then explored in order to reveal any deep and potentially profitable relationships. Figure 1.7 illustrates this process.

Ideally, as indicated in Figure 1.7, a data mining process produces a *working model* of underlying data relationships. More often than not, however, the current generation of tools simply produces a report identifying any discovered dependencies among data elements (the difference between reporting and modeling, as will be noted later, is an extremely important factor in the knowledge discovery process).

A Synthesis of Techniques and Technologies

Data mining is not a unified, single approach, although it has a single aim. It involves a broad family of advanced technologies bridging the gulf between conventional statistics and nonparametric analysis and the frontiers of artificial intelligence (neural networks, fuzzy logic, and rule-based expert systems). The aim of a knowledge discovery process is twofold: identify collections of *dependencies* in data and fix a degree of *confidence* in each discovered relationship. This can be expressed as the simple

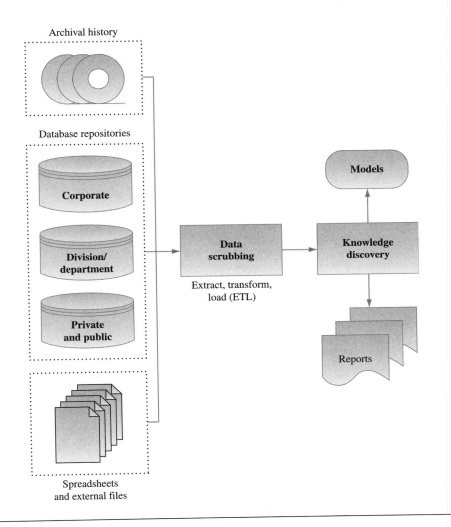

Figure 1.7 The data mining process.

ordered relationship

$$R_D \leftarrow \left[X_i^n \otimes Y_j^n \otimes \dots \right] \cdot C_n, \qquad (1.1)$$

where R_D is the dependency, X and Y form a set of related variables, and C_n is the confidence in the accuracy or strength of this relationship. This degree of confidence forms the basis of the believability metric associated with the discovered system. Relationships supported by sparse, corrupt, or unreliable data are ranked with less confidence than relationships based on a higher preponderance of evidence. Most data mining tools provide a filtering mechanism so that relationships with a confidence below some threshold are automatically discarded (or stored in a special audit file).

Two Types of Knowledge Discoveries

Knowledge discovery comes in two basic flavors: supervised and unsupervised (often called, respectively, directed and undirected). Both have their specific uses and both provide methods for isolating system behaviors in large database repositories. Although they have fundamentally different approaches to data mining, these methods share many of the same computational elements.

Supervised Knowledge Discovery

Supervised knowledge discovery (data mining), as the name implies, is controlled by the knowledge engineer and system designer. This technique uses an objective function (the dependent variable) and a set of data elements, the independent variables. Supervised database exploration attempts to identify causal relationships between independent and dependent variables, isolate the degree of correlation for each set of variables, and construct a model (or a report) showing the web of dependencies.

Supervised data mining tends to be highly scalable (that is, it can handle large amounts of data in time frames that do not increase unreasonably), generally fast, and converges toward a set of solutions.

This type of knowledge discovery is used when a definite goal is available and the user is seeking to uncover how changes in the data state influence the goal. The following are two examples of actual supervised data mining projects.

- A re-insurer offers disability insurance for medical professionals (such as pediatric surgeons). One provision of the insurance is an "own occupation" clause that pays if the individual is unable to continue in his or her own occupation. The insurer is suffering large, long-term losses due to an unexpectedly high number of medical professionals making "own occupation" claims but continuing to work in related medical fields. They used a supervised data mining search of the combined policy holder, claims, and medical history databases to find a clear relationship between "own occupation" claims and policyholder characteristics.

- The Chief Information Officer of a large bank needed a way to control cost overruns on a rising number of high-technology projects in the information systems group. Using a large database of failed or inadequately delivered projects, the bank ranked each project with a value of from 0 to 1 according to its perceived value (0 as a failed project with no value to 1 as a completely successful project). They also created fields to indicate the type of project, its perceived level of complexity, and its degree of dependence on advanced technology. A supervised data mining analysis discovered a clear relationship between low user satisfaction (as well as project failure) and a set of important project characteristics (surprisingly, the initial budget for the project rather than the final cost was an important indicator of long-term project success).

Unsupervised Knowledge Discovery

Unsupervised knowledge discovery starts out with a *tabula rasa*, a clean slate. It has no predefined objective function. In unsupervised mode, the knowledge discovery process selects one of several approaches to domain simplification, usually automatic cluster detection or dependency graphs. In either case, the unsupervised approach makes no distinction between dependent and independent variables. Rather, the process looks for collections of elements in the database that share similar properties. These similarities form clusters in the data, and collections of overlapping clusters reveal patterns among the clusters.

Unsupervised data mining often raises several issues of scalability (if some form of parallel evaluation is not used) and is generally slow, but it can converge toward multiple sets of solution states. This type of deep knowledge discovery is used when a specific goal is not available or when the user is attempting to uncover latent or hidden relationships in data. The following are two examples of actual unsupervised data mining projects.

- A large international retailer was seeking to increase its domestic sales and expand into new markets. Three possible expansion routes had been identified, but management could not reach a consensus on which to pursue. Each expansion option entailed the risk of many millions of dollars, a marketing commitment over several years (thus significantly increasing the opportunity cost risk), and exposure to new competitive pressures. A committee of executives from personnel, marketing, purchasing, store operations, and information systems initiated an unsupervised data exploration of the company's combined sales, inventory, client, credit, and store performance databases. From this analysis they generated two functional models: one relating sales and costs to demographics and the other relating store operations to consumer purchasing habits. Using these models, a successful and cost-effective movement into the second expansion route was executed.

- Managed health care accounts for 13% of the total U.S. gross national product. Estimates of abuse and fraud in managed health care run as high as 10 to 12% of this total, or approximately $600 billion annually. Several years ago a collection of insurance companies focused on provider- or doctor-initiated fraud. They wanted a way to find anomalous behaviors in doctors' claims. This suggested a nonparametric approach to anomaly detection; that is, behavior patterns would be considered unusual only in relation to their peers (doctors in the same geographic region, of the same specialty, and associated with the same size of organization).

  A deep unsupervised data mining project examined a very large database of claims and doctor profiles looking for clusters of similarity in billing practices, patient characteristics, and work habits. By iterating through the clusters, patterns emerged that identified relationships between anomalous payment, client visitation, billing structure, and periodic treatment patterns. A final set of models combined evidence from many clusters to provide a high level of specificity in detecting and quantifying fraudulent and other forms of anomalous behaviors.

By itself, cluster detection and generation are not solutions to the data mining process. Once a population of clusters is identified, rule-generation facilities are used to interpret the meaning of each cluster and produce the final model. In advanced unsupervised data mining systems, genetic algorithms explore many collections of clusters and their associated rules in parallel.

1.5 Data Mining and Business Models

At the heart of any data mining exercise is an occasionally unspoken objective. The user wants to develop a model of a particular business process. These are called, in fact, business process models. A *model*, as illustrated schematically in Figure 1.8, is a representation of some coherent, interdependent system of processes. These processes affect each other in a

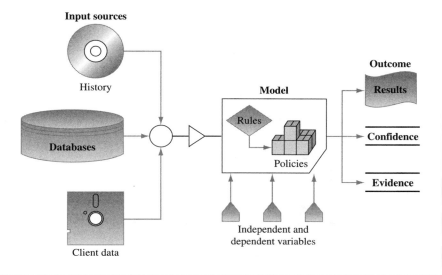

Figure 1.8   The idea of a model.

predictable way, and, thus, given a set of input values, we can predict the likely set of outputs.

A valid model connects a set of input values (the independent variables) to a set of output values (the dependent variables) through some type of functional relationship. Mathematically we can represent this as

$$V_d \leftarrow f\left(v_i^1, v_i^2, \ldots, v_i^n\right), \tag{1.2}$$

where V_d is the output dependent variable, often called the solution variable, and v_i is the input independent variable.

Difficulties in Building Business Models

Of course, real-world process models are not nearly as clean and straightforward as this functional relationship might suggest. In fact, for many problems the model can only approximate a true function. This is due to several important and difficult-to-handle factors.

Data Availability and Noise

Business processes are often ill defined and cluttered with "noise"; that is, the underlying processes contain a great deal of extraneous and even random information. In addition, quite often the values for many important process components are either missing, sparse, or unreliable. For models developed through a data mining process — wherein the intelligence is extracted principally through data relationships — the lack of clean, reliable, and complete data is often fatal.

Imprecision and Vagueness in Model Parameters

The permissible range of variables is not delineated by crisp or precise boundaries nor are the variables connected through crisply defined dependencies. That is, as one example, a relationship $Z = f(X$ and $Y)$ is not captured by a simple arithmetic expression (including ordinary and partial differential equations) but by a function; that is, it is in most cases "fuzzy." Thus, we might have a relationship such as the following.

> If **X** is somewhat less than **Y**
> then **Z** is slightly increased
>
> If **X** is expensive and **Y** is high
> then **Z** is about **R**
>
> When $\Delta(X,Y)$ is changing rapidly
> **Z** quickly approaches zero

Here, the qualifying coefficients such as "somewhat less," "slightly," "expensive," and "high" are parameters of a fuzzy relationship.

Nonlinear and Chaotic Relationships

Most business processes are deceptively complex. They are somewhat chaotic and highly nonlinear. The characteristics of nonlinearity and chaos mean that (1) the process is very sensitive to initial conditions and (2) that small perturbations to the system or small inputs do not necessarily result in proportionally small outputs. Nonlinear equations such as the logistic map

$$x_{n+1} = Ax_n(1 - x_n) \tag{1.3}$$

have regions of stability and instability separated by sudden bifurcation points. In business models, this same type of nonlinear behavior is often associated with complex lead- and lag-time relationships. As a simple example, consider a predictor of profits in one time period based on sales and costs in related periods.

If *costs(t − N) − profits(t)* is much less than *sales(t + N)*,
then *profits(t + N)* are about *discounts*sales(t − N)*.

When many such rules are combined in a single business policy, the resulting system becomes highly nonlinear. And it is this intrinsic nonlinearity that makes the evolution of business models so difficult.

Adaptive Feedback Processes

In the real world of business, commerce, and governmental decision making, the state of a system is often dependent on previous states of the system. That is, as illustrated in Figure 1.9, the output of the model is fed back into the model as one of its input parameters.

In fact, this feedback can permanently alter the way the model executes. Adaptive feedback means that the rules governing the behavior of a model are refined based on the changing state of the outside world (such as refinement of process characteristics based on an increase in available historical data).

It is precisely these difficulties that knowledge discovery tools and techniques attempt to overcome. They do this through a fusion of advanced nonparametric parameter or coefficient estimating and several

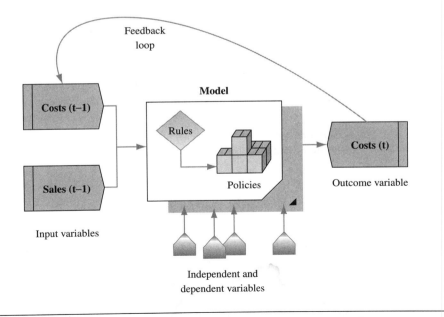

Figure 1.9   An adaptive feedback model.

types of artificial intelligence technologies. The degree to which they are successful in capturing the nature of deep relationships depends on how well they produce a believable and usable model. The criterion that a data mining tool must generate a working model separates two important and elegant classes of these tools. We will return to this issue in a discussion of rule-based models.

The Importance of Models Versus Reports

Many data mining tools produce a static snapshot of their uncovered relationships. This is not a model, but rather a report. The distinction is often missed by users of knowledge discovery tools without a background in dynamic systems. The difference is both fundamental and extremely important. As an example, given an $N \times 2$ matrix of numbers (large number of rows, two columns), we can use a statistical analysis program to discover that some numbers in column 1 are related to some numbers in column 2. A cluster analysis might produce a relationship such as that shown in the following table.

Cluster1		
A[I, 1]	**A[I, 2]**	**Corr**
[103,217]	[40,60]	.78

This relationship says: When A[I,1] 103 and A[I,1] 217, then A[I,2] is in range of [40,60] with a confidence of .78 degree. On the other hand, a dynamic system model with the ability to represent imprecise or vague concepts might generate a rule that says

> If A[I,1] is in the vicinity of 160,
>   then A[I,2] is about 50,

where *vicinity of 160* is a broad trapezoidal fuzzy set[5] and *about 50* is a bell-shaped fuzzy set.

A dynamic system is a set of rules. These rules, in the form of if *<condition>* then *<action>*, are evaluated by a special rule processing system called an inference engine. The inference engine decides which rules should be executed, orders the rules in the proper sequence, supplies data to the variables used by the rules, and then executes each rule in

---

[5] A fuzzy set is a way of representing vague and imprecise knowledge through the concept of a partial membership in the set or sets associated with a concept.

turn. When all the rules have been executed, the inference engine hands over the results to the application program that invoked the inference engine.

1.6 **Fuzzy Systems for Business Process Models**

A more focused and structured approach to model building in the age of distributed knowledge, fuzzy systems provide the means of combining, weighing, and using multiple competing experts. Often these experts are not people but other knowledge sources (such as other business models and expert systems). For example, Figure 1.10 (somewhat simplified) shows how several models work cooperatively in a distributed environment.

In a distributed environment, multiple experts compete for attention, either as peers in the decision process or as components of a larger

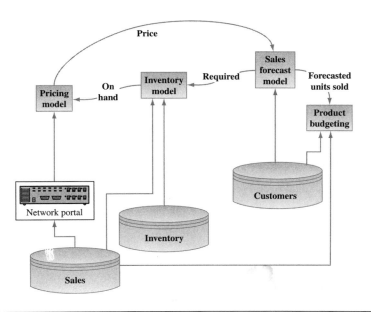

Figure 1.10 Multiple business process models.

decision making model. The ability of fuzzy models to easily incorporate evidence from several expert sources (as well as assign degrees of credibility to each source) makes them an ideal vehicle for building shared decision models in the distributed data warehouse and data mart environment. As an example, Figure 1.11 shows a product pricing model and its various distributed sources of information.

In Figure 1.11, the bold parts of the business rules represent fuzzy sets. These fuzzy sets are combined under the methods of fuzzy composition. Combining rules in this way accumulates evidence for the final product pricing position. Because fuzzy models are adept at handling evidence from many sources, they provide a flexible and powerful method of modeling distributed processes. These are typically the types of processes we find at the data warehouse and data mart level in Internet-centered organizations.

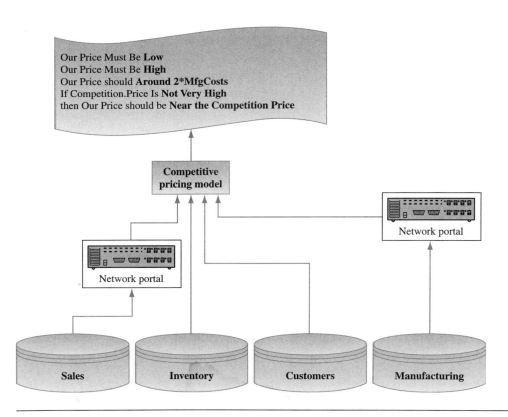

Figure 1.11 A product pricing model.

1.7 **Evolving Distributed Fuzzy Models**

Because fuzzy sets can represent approximate patterns, fuzzy models are especially easy to evolve using knowledge discovery techniques. Rule indication — the isolation and extraction of *if-then* rules from large databases — provides a way of creating a prototypical fuzzy model from patterns occurring naturally in data. Figure 1.12 illustrates how this step is used to combine knowledge from several distributed data sources.

By incorporating a rule induction step in your business models, you can maintain currency with the external world. As the long-term behavior of your customers changes, the model can adapt to those changes by discovering new rules reflecting a shift in purchasing habits (as one example). Rule induction, of course, should not be viewed as a complete model building technique. Rather, it can be used to "prime the pump" when you have many experts contributing knowledge to a set of models.

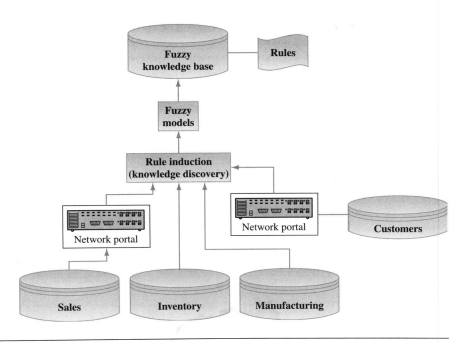

Figure 1.12 Building a fuzzy model with rule induction.

1.8 **A Sample Case: Evolving a Model for Customer Segmentation**

More and more companies today, small and large, are turning to the World Wide Web (WWW, also called the Web or the Net) as a vehicle to advertise their company's services and products, provide on-line catalogs or demonstration software, handle technical support, and even sell their products directly to the end user. In the demographics of primary interest to today's corporations (technically sophisticated, upper-income families), high-speed computers are becoming increasingly common. Most of these families have large disposable incomes and are not adverse to purchasing a wide spectrum of premium goods and services.

However, the Web is saturated with casual users. As a result, isolating potential customers from a vast, roiling sea of casual browsers has become increasingly difficult. Corporate sites are often visited thousands of times every day. A corporation has only a small window of opportunity to attract a visitor and make him or her a customer. Companies have reacted to this situation in a variety of ways. Some have used passive techniques to capture information about any visitor that shows interest in the page content. Others have gone to either a closed or open subscription service, providing access to their pages to a select cadre of potential clients. This last approach is used by corporations in such diverse industries as banking, insurance, investment, retail, and management consulting.

Even with a tighter focus on potential customers afforded by subscription services, the Internet is a fast-paced environment requiring advanced

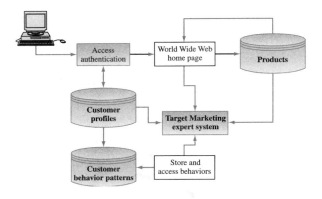

Figure 1.13 A target marketing system.

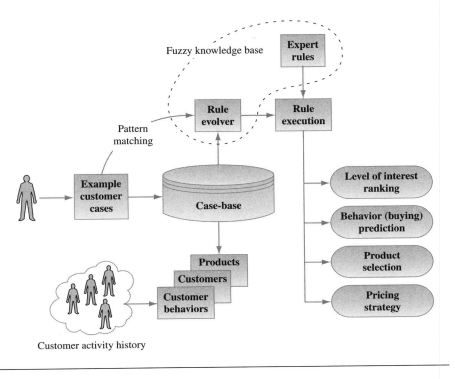

Figure 1.14   A case-based reasoning system.

technological approaches to keeping and expanding a customer base. One emerging approach to solidifying and growing customers is *target marketing*. For corporations that maintain customer profiles and purchasing (as well as general interest) behaviors, a knowledge discovery approach can often find relationships between product characteristics and clients. This allows companies to offer clients and prospects new services, display new products, and tailor their marketing approach on a customer-by-customer basis. Figure 1.13 schematically illustrates how a target marketing system is connected directly to a corporation's Web home page.

A target marketing expert system is built by the knowledge discovery and data mining process. It is often embedded in either a traditional expert system environment or in a case-based reasoning (CBR) system. Figure 1.14 illustrates how a CBR system uses past cases to predict a possible outcome.

In this environment, a customer and his or her purchasing habits constitute a "case," and data mining is used to discover the rules that can

TABLE 1.1 Customer Activity Case Base

Age	Gender	Site Visitation Counts				Product Statistics	
		This Week	This Month	Past 6 Months	Total	Products Visited	Products Bought
33	M	16	172	1281		19	2
58	M	44	304	3913		53	0
17	F	73	508	747		21	9
32	M	166	485	2036		59	0
35	F	179	202	409		6	4

match a new customer to products or services based on their similarity to existing customers and their preferences. The underlying "case base" need not be any special database. In fact, the case base can be a spreadsheet or simple binary file containing customer profiles and their browsing and purchasing histories. Table 1.1 illustrates a possible structure for the underlying customer profiles.

Of course this example is somewhat abbreviated. The visitation statistics might include such values as length of stay, number of pages visited, time of day, average time per page, and so forth. The product statistics would also include product identifier (perhaps the SKU (Stock Keeping Unit) used in retailing to identify the lowest, unique level of product inventory), product class, retail price, actual price, and quantity purchased.[6] Such a case base could include summary records (as implied by Table 1.1) or individual transaction records. With this type of information, a rule induction system can generate simple high-level rules that relate visitation frequency to purchasing propensities, such as the following.

```
If age is young
    And gender is male
    And (productclass is XYZ
            And site.visitcount is high)
    Then
        ProductsBought is elevated;
```

More complex rules of this nature might be generated. Such rules can also indicate, for example, preferences for particular products, purchasing behaviors at particular times of the day (perhaps discriminated by age or

---

[6] From a customer relationship and sales analysis perspective it might also be interesting to capture the transaction response times for the web server for each customer — thus detecting patterns that relate machine performance with customer buying behaviors.

gender), purchasing associated with discounted products, and so on. The important aspect of such an approach to customer segmentation and cross marketing is the fact that the rules are deduced from (discovered in) the underlying transaction data. As purchasing habits, new web structures, new product lines, and other internal and external market pressures arise, the system will automatically discover a new set of rules.

1.9 Review

Data exploration and modeling are critical components of operational, tactical, and strategic planning. However, in this age of distributed computing, data, and knowledge, building models solely from subject matter experts and a conceptual understanding of the problem is a long, protracted, and error-prone process. Coupling knowledge discovery with advanced forms of adaptive fuzzy models can produce highly robust systems that can detect and repair their own logic. After reading this chapter you should have an appreciation for the following.

- The nature of modern information architectures
- How data and knowledge are distributed over networks
- The difficulties inherent in building models of typical business systems
- The role knowledge discovery plays in building models
- The differences between supervised and unsupervised data mining
- How fuzzy systems can contribute to building robust, sustainable models
- How fuzzy models can be evolved from databases and other sources

Finding patterns in data (data exploration), quantifying these patterns into a predictive system (model building), and dynamically reorganizing a model to optimize its performance (evolutionary strategies) are the foundations of building modern information systems and client applications. Understanding the relationships among these concepts is crucial to maintaining a competitive marketing lead, assessing the effectiveness and consequence of public policy decision, and maintaining enterprise viability in a turbulent global economy. Following on this necessity, the next chapter surveys various types of models and how they are related to the types of decisions and the types of data in the problem space.

Chapter 2
Principal Model Types

This section provides the foundations (as well as the background) we need to discuss the concepts and features of predictive models. In examining the ways in which organizations approach the model building process, a wide variety of techniques emerges. These techniques often center on the types of models we need and how the model addresses such issues as the nature of the data, the reasoning processes that manipulate the data, and the types of outcomes the model can produce. The following takes a "high-altitude" look at the basics of creating and using a model.

Mathematical models — traditionally differential or difference equations — are notoriously difficult to build, tend to be very brittle, and are by their nature extremely difficult to extend and maintain. For these reasons, model builders have recently, within the past 15 to 20 years, turned to more flexible methods based on various forms of machine learning. Some of these approaches incorporate expert knowledge, others learn behaviors directly from archives of historical data, and some combine the two approaches. Although by no means exclusive, the most commonly used methods are as follows.

- *Expert systems:* A knowledge base of *if-then* rules defining solutions to problems in a specific and highly restricted domain. The rules forming a conventional expert system are derived from one or more subject matter experts (SMEs).

- *Statistical learning theory:* A collection of techniques that quantify and learn the periodic (seasonal and cyclical) behavior of data over time. Many statistical learning approaches employ forms of Bayes' Theorem, which estimates values based the amount of cumulative evidence.

- *Neural networks:* A nonlinear classification system of interconnected nodes that can learn the underlying behavior patterns in a collection of data using a set of examples.

- *Decision trees and classifiers:* A set of techniques for learning how to effectively classify patterns. Decision trees produce hierarchical maps between data attributes and can be used to produce a set of *if-then* rules.

- *Trend analysis:* A set of curve-fitting methods that can discover and quantify both linear and nonlinear trend lines through multidimensional sets of data. Trend lines can detect and predict the underlying periodicity or seasonal curves for time-varying data.

Systems and knowledge engineers use the term *model* in a variety of contexts, but nearly all of these imply some form of digital implementation of a well-defined process. However, the world of models and model building encompasses a wide variety of representations. Although we are primarily concerned with system models, the evolution of such models often crosses over into or encompasses other modeling organizations. Figure 2.1 shows the basic model types and some of their possible interconnections.

Naturally, neither the model taxonomies nor the model boundaries are absolutes. As the dashed lines in Figure 2.1 indicate, one model may be the prelude to another (we often develop a narrative model before expanding our ideas into a mathematical or system heuristic model). Further, the classification of a model into one class or another is not always possible,

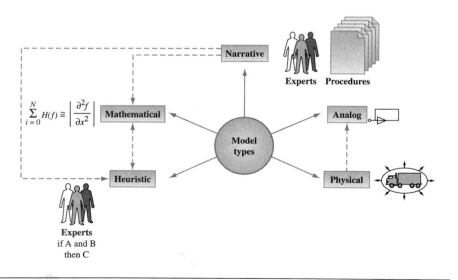

Figure 2.1 Types of models.

TABLE 2.1   Model Categories (Taxonomies)

Nature of Model	Organization and Use
Narrative	These models often consist of experts collaborating on a formal representation of some highly focused system. Examples of this include the Delphi method and many aspects of market research. In such models, a collection of questionnaires is repeatedly analyzed among the experts to typically predict such critical issues as vulnerabilities, market trends, long-range sales and margins, and penetration strategies for new lines of business.
Physical	These models are constructed to test or evaluate some essentially physical system. Examples of physical models include precision aircraft models for use in wind tunnels, architectural renderings of buildings and bridges, and the molecular construction kits used in organic chemistry and genetics to represent such things as benzene rings and the helical DNA molecule.
Analog (Simile)	These models combine the properties of one system to describe the behavior of another system using different physical forms. Thus, they are *similes* (i.e., one system functions much like any other system). Analog models work because there is a similarity or parallelism between the underlying forces that drive both models. Until the recent accessibility of the personal computer, electrical and mechanical analog systems were routinely used to model complex networks such as process plants and highway traffic flows.
Mathematical	Mathematical models (including statistical models) came into their own with the common availability of digital computers (through time-sharing in the early days and now routinely on desktop and laptop personal computers). A mathematical model consists of equations, often with interdependencies. The ubiquitous spreadsheet is a prime example of a mathematical model. Control engineering systems and embedded controllers are also examples of mathematical models. Many of the models used in knowledge discovery and data mining are also mathematical models. These include neural networks and other forms of classification schemes, such as decision trees (e.g., ID3 and C4.5), classification and regression trees (e.g., CART) and chi-squared automatic induction (CHAID) algorithms.
Heuristic	The recent rise in machine intelligence and expert system technologies has introduced another type of model into the mix: the *heuristic model*. Such a model is often called an *if-then-else* production system, which often forms the core knowledge repository of today's decision support and expert systems. These models depend solely on the high-speed, high-level computational capabilities of the computer. Heuristic models embody "rules of thumb" and other business processes. We often refer to them as policy-based models. Heuristic representations constitute the vast majority of modern business process models (BPMs).

in that the boundaries are very permeable. Table 2.1 summarizes how these models differ and how they are used.

The last two taxonomic classes — mathematical and heuristic — form the focus of nearly all business prediction models. These are roughly classed as symbolic models and generally incorporate algebraic and intellectual relationships. In the modern sense of the term *model*, we generally combine the two taxonomies into a single or hybrid class: the *knowledge-base model*.

2.1 Model and Event State Categorization

There is a more fundamental classification of models based on the way model states are generated and how model variables are handled. Table 2.2 outlines the partitioning of such classification, which divides models into discrete or continuous and into deterministic or stochastic.

Technically, the classification of models as discrete or continuous refers to the model's composite variable organization, but in actual fact and practice the term is used to describe the model's treatment of time. Many models have clear and precise demarcations of time that break up the system into regular intervals (such as many queuing applications, production or project schedules, traffic analysis models, portfolio safety and suitability models, and so on). Other models have a horizon that varies smoothly across time. These continuous models are rare in the business world, although they do occur in nonlinear random walk models that attempt to follow the chaotic trends of the stock market. In any event, of course, few continuous models are actually implemented continuously but use a form of periodic or random data sampling.

The model state categorization — a fundamentally important perspective on how the model is constructed — reflects the ways in which the underlying model relationships are or can be described. Outcomes in a deterministic model can be predicted completely if the independent variables (input values) and the initial state of the model are known. This means that a given input always produces a given output. The outcome for a stochastic system is not similarly defined.

TABLE 2.2 Model Classification by Internal Structure

Model State	Event State — Discrete	Event State — Continuous
Deterministic	Spreadsheets Econometric Budget Inventory control	Dynamic flow Process control Differential equations
Stochastic	Quality measurement Queuing models Market share Price positioning	Monte Carlo Econometric projections Game-theoretic models

Stochastic models introduce a degree of randomness or chance into a possible set of outcomes. This randomness is intrinsic to the behavior of the model and couples the values of the independent variables (which are randomly derived) to the values of the outcome or dependent variables (which are the result of processing these random values).

2.2 Model Type and Outcome Categorization

From a knowledge and system engineer's perspective, the most critical model classification isolates the type of outcome. There are two broad types: *predictive* and *classification*. Like taxonomic partitioning, these types are not "pure" (homogeneous), and models often involve both. Table 2.3 outlines model families sorted into clusters according to underlying model taxonomy and outcome type.

A predictive model generates a new outcome (the value of the dependent variable) based on the previous state of independent variables. Regression analysis, as an example, is a predictive time-series model. Given a least squares linear interpretation of data points $x_1, x_2, x_3, \ldots, x_n$, the regression model predicts the value of point x_{n+1} (and a vector of subsequent points with varying degrees of accuracy). On the other hand, classification models analyze the properties of a data point and assign it to a class or category. Cluster analysis is a classification model. Neural networks are also predominantly classifiers (they activate an outcome neuron based on the activation of the input neurons). Such taxonomies, however, are hardly rigid. A rule-based predictive model can, under some circumstances, be viewed as a classifier. And many classification models, especially those based on neural networks and decision tree algorithms,

TABLE 2.3 Model Classification by Taxonomy and Outcome

Model Type		Outcome	
		Predictive	Classifier
Knowledge-based		Expert system Fuzzy system Evolutionary program	Neural network Expert system Genetic algorithm
Mathematical		Regression analysis Statistical learning Correlation Radial basis functions Adaptive learning	Cluster analysis Classification and regression trees (CART) Self-organizing maps

can generate rules that produce a model prediction. After all, a neural network that learns to classify credit applicants into *Good*, *Review*, and *Reject* is making a prediction about the probable future fate of a loan.

2.3 **Review**

From an understanding of distributed intelligence and data mining in Chapter 1, this brief chapter provides a review of the various forms a model can take. Model building is more than applying statistics, creating rules, or generating a decision tree. Model building involves understanding the nature of the problem and finding the system representation that best reflects the expectations of the consumer, the capabilities of the systems engineer, and the availability of supporting data. From this chapter you should now understand the following.

- The various types of models and their uses
- The meaning of discrete and continuous variables
- The nature of deterministic and stochastic models
- How predictive and classifier models work
- The role knowledge-based systems play in modern models

A model represents the important aspects of some complex system. Our ability to understand the nature of models and how they relate to our analysis objectives is a critical prerequisite in gaining a deeper understanding of how systems that are tightly connected and highly distributed interact. Moving from the concepts of modeling and the nature of models, the next chapter surveys the types of technologies and techniques used to actually build computer models.

Chapter 3
Approaches to Model Building

As we saw earlier, discovery is not a single discipline but involves a combination of many techniques and technologies. Some of these techniques are used in combination with others as support or filtering services, whereas others constitute the major components of the data mining service. We now review some of the major methods of data mining and knowledge discovery.

This section is not intended as an exhaustive or even partially complete description of the various model building techniques (and this is especially true of the section on statistics). The primer is intended simply as an overview of each methodology, including brief observations of strengths and weaknesses. Comments about the relative merits of a particular approach are meant as general observations. Particular software implementations of the method or different approaches using alternate but related techniques could change one or more strengths or weakness.

3.1 Ordinary Statistics

This is generally the best starting point for any data mining project and often satisfies the needs of many organizations whose goal is simply to understand the mechanics of obvious data relationships. For statistical data mining projects, a complete statistical analysis of existing data repositories provides a keen understanding of how the data are clustered, their degree of variance, and the tightness of existing two-dimensional and three-dimensional relationships (generally expressed through scatter graphs and other forms of curve fitting).

For a population of data, the statistician must determine the data's principal statistical properties. These properties include, at a minimum, the mean or average value, the mode (the most frequently occurring value), the median (the middle value when all the observations are sorted into ascending or descending order), and the standard deviation (the amount of variance around the mean, that is, a measure of whether the distribution forms a wide bell curve around the average or a narrow bell curve around the average). The mean and the standard deviation, as two of the principal population descriptors, are known are the first and second statistical moments.

A thorough statistical analysis of large databases can often uncover many unexpected and interesting relationships. In addition to the ordinary descriptive statistics discussed in the previous paragraph, a more extensive statistical analysis attempts to find a wide range of subtle relationships between variables in the data. Some of the advanced statistical techniques used in an extensive analysis (but not an exhaustive or even an extensive list) include an analysis of variance (which finds difference in the means of one or more data collections), correlation analysis (which finds the degree to which changes in one variable are reflected by or related to changes in another variable), and linear regression (which finds the trend line between several variables and, in so doing, provides a mechanism for predicting the future values of related variables). Carefully studying the outcome from an advanced statistical analysis provides the data mining engineer with a deep appreciation for the fundamental dependencies locked in the data.

For more advanced data mining efforts, especially those using neural networks and fuzzy systems (see discussion following), the third and fourth statistical moments should also be calculated (the kurtosis and skew, respectively, of the distribution). Kurtosis is a measure of the flatness or peakness of the distribution, while skew measures the degree to which data are shifted to the right or the left of the mean and thus distorts the symmetric bell-shaped form of a normal distribution. Many of these explorations into the realm of population distributions lead the knowledge engineer into the supporting domain of nonparametric statistics. The strengths and weaknesses of ordinary statistics are outlined in Table 3.1.

3.2 **Nonparametric Statistics**

Very often statistical data mining is concerned with finding the overlap between data points in two populations (such as current clients and

TABLE 3.1   Strengths/Weaknesses of Ordinary Statistics

Strengths	■ Proven mathematical methods
	■ Many easy-to-use tools available
	■ Large number of skilled statisticians to handle experimental design and interpret results
	■ Designed for work with large data populations
	■ Isolates important and critical population parameters
	■ Can find causal relationships among large numbers of variables
Weaknesses	■ User must know what tests to apply and how to interpret the results; that is, what to look for
	■ Sensitive to population distribution assumptions and the actual population distribution
	■ Hypothesis formulation can be difficult and susceptible to Type I and Type II errors
	■ Results very sensitive to data bias
	■ Outliers can cause problems
	■ Statistical correlation does not necessarily mean causation

potential customers). Standard statistical measures such as an analysis of variance assume that the parent populations have a normal (Gaussian) distribution. In practice, knowledge engineers seldom know the underlying distributions in historical data. Further, collections of historical data are seldom normally distributed. When population distributions are not Gaussian or have significant skews, nonparametric tests give the data mining engineer a powerful set of tools for exploring the relationships inherent in multiple populations. Although some assumptions about the parent distribution are involved in nonparametric statistics, these assumptions are generally fewer in number, have a weaker impact on the validity of the correlation analysis, and are easier to satisfy with existing data than the more rigorous requirements of parametric correlations. In this regard, nonparametric tests are frequently called distribution-free tests. In any case, the range of statistical tests in nonparametric analysis is more limited than the broad class of tests in ordinary statistics and deals mostly with the distribution of nominal and ordinal data, often examining the depth of an interval displacement (plus or minus) from an arbitrarily chosen pivot point in the data. The strengths and weaknesses of nonparametric statistics are outlined in Table 3.2.

TABLE 3.2 Strengths/Weaknesses of Nonparametric Statistics

Strengths	■ Advanced and proven mathematical methods
	■ Techniques for finding parameters that describe an unknown population
	■ Useful in discovering the actual distribution in preparation for a more detailed analysis by ordinary, parametric statistics
	■ Ideal for looking at anomalies and differences in central measures of the population that have some underlying order or ranking
Weaknesses	■ Limited range of analytical tools.
	■ Not often included in statistical software products.
	■ Technique primarily familiar to advanced statistical users. This means that skilled statistical support for nonparametric analysis may be in short supply.
	■ Appropriate mainly for nominal (numbers that stand for the items themselves) and ordinal data. Nominal numbers stand for the items themselves, whereas ordinals, in ordinary usage, are 1st, 2nd, 3rd, and so on as opposed to 1, 2, 3, and so on (cardinal numbers). Ordinal numbers are properties of well-ordered sets.
	■ Difficult to structure hypothesis tests that can be easily verified.

3.3 Linear Regression in Statistical Models

Data mining engineers and model builders are concerned with issues involved in prediction. In a statistical model, the problem of predicting an outcome is based on the correlation between two or more variables, and consequently correlation and prediction are closely allied topics. Correlation is measured in a scale from -1 to $+1$.

Correlation and Prediction

If the correlation between two variables X and Y is zero, we can assume that they have a random relationship to each other. That is, a knowledge of X tells us nothing about Y and a knowledge of Y tells us nothing about X (therefore, predicting X from Y or Y from X we can do no better than a random guess). Figure 3.1 shows a scatter chart of a random relationship between X and Y.

A nonzero correlation between X and Y implies that if we know something about X we can know something about Y (and vice versa). A measure moving toward $+1$ indicates a positive correlation, which means that as

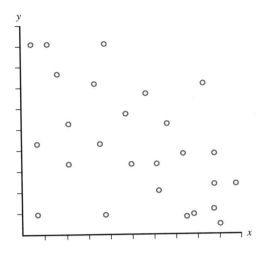

Figure 3.1   Random behavior (corr = 0).

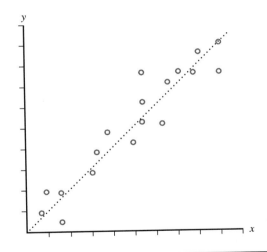

Figure 3.2   Positive correlation (corr = .82).

X moves up Y moves up. Figure 3.2 illustrates a positive relationship between X and Y.

A measure moving toward −1 indicates an inverse correlation, which means that as X moves up Y moves down. Figure 3.3 illustrates an inverse relationship between X and Y.

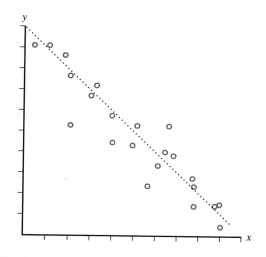

Figure 3.3 Inverse correlation (corr = −.78).

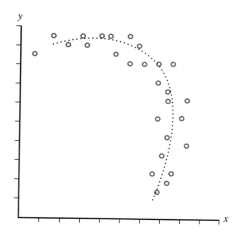

Figure 3.4 Nonlinear correlation.

The greater the absolute value of the correlation, the more accurate is the prediction of one variable from the other. If the correlation between X and Y is either −1 or +1, perfect prediction is possible. However, a near-zero correlation between X and Y does not necessarily mean that the two variables are uncorrelated. It is possible, as shown in Figure 3.4, that X and Y share a nonlinear relationship.

It is generally not possible to draw a straight line (that is, to super-impose a linear relationship) on a nonlinear function. In these cases the data analyst must use additional tools, such as polynomial least squares regression.

The Regression Equation

From the database of observations, a data mining engineer can determine the degree of correlation between two variables X and Y and then use linear regression techniques to find the equation that best fits the trend of the relationship. A linear regression produces an equation of the form

$$Y_i = bX_i + a,$$

where a is a constant and b is the slope of the line. Linear regression equations are powerful tools in building models from data for which dependencies can be precisely determined (or closely approximated). Linear regression can be used for some nonlinear data sets by converting the parameters to a logarithmic scale. Linear equations are often used in time-series data to predict $Y(t)$ given $X(t)$. The strengths and weaknesses of linear regression are outlined in Table 3.3.

TABLE 3.3 Strengths/Weaknesses of Linear Regression

Strengths	<ul><li>Proven mathematical technique</li><li>Easy to use, understand, and deploy</li><li>Creates a working mathematical model of the underlying system</li><li>Easy to adjust through data fitting</li><li>Good predictive strengths given highly correlated data</li></ul>
Weaknesses	<ul><li>Limited to linear models</li><li>Often difficult to use for more than two variables</li><li>Very sensitive to degree of correlation between variables</li><li>Necessary to convert nonlinear distributions to a linear representation (such as taking the logarithm of each data point)</li><li>Sensitive to outlier clustering</li><li>A fairly simplistic method of curve fitting and often fails to find the true underlying trend line for data with even moderate degrees of non-linearity (such as seasonal data)</li><li>Cannot easily fit seasonal data (see first weakness point)</li></ul>

3.4   **Nonlinear Growth Curve Fitting**

As business analysts, engineers, scientists, and social behaviorists soon discover, few real-world behavior patters follow linear trends. When forecasting changes in systems that have initial conditions containing fundamentally random elements, that exhibit characteristics of long-term population variability, or that have reinforced feedback properties, linear regression will fail to provide an accurate model of the system's behavior. In these cases, a more robust and accurate model of the data can be discovered by fitting the attributes to one or more growth curve templates. The data mining process attempts to find the coefficient parameters that best describe the data space. As Figure 3.5 illustrates, growth curves are highly nonlinear.

There are several types of nonlinear growth curves. Here we consider two of the most popular curves and their underlying dynamics.

The Logistic or Pearl Curve

The *logistic* (or *Pearl*) *curve* (named after the American demographer Raymond Pearl) is a symmetric S-curve (also called a sigmoid curve). Its equation is

$$y = \frac{L}{1 + ae^{-bx}},\qquad(3.1)$$

where L is the upper limit to y's growth, e is the base of the natural logarithms, and x is the independent variable (often expressed as t, the time horizon). The coefficients a and b are estimated from the data by converting the expression to its linear form and fitting the transformed data points, as follows.

$$y^{\circ} = \ln\left[\frac{y}{L-y}\right] = -\ln a + bx \qquad(3.2)$$

Once the coefficient estimation is complete (either by linear regression or back propagation), the values are fed back into the Pearl equation to make short-term horizon predictions. Because the coefficients of the Pearl growth curve can be adjusted independently (a changes the location and b changes the shape), the Pearl equation provides an ideal growth formula for data mining explorations controlled by genetic algorithms.

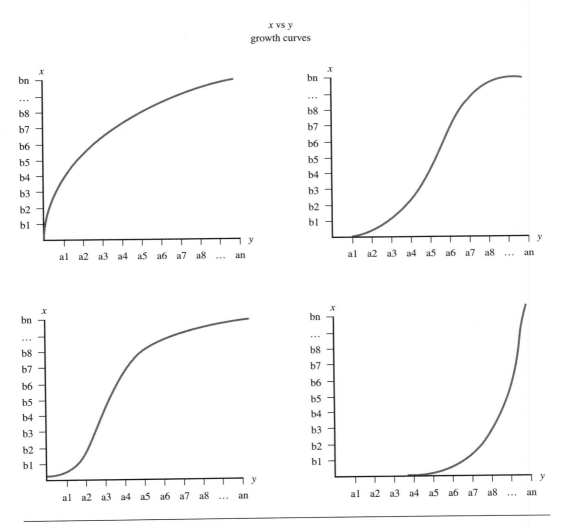

Figure 3.5   Sample growth curves.

The Gompertz Curve

The *Gompertz curve*, named after the British actuary and mathematician Benjamin Gompertz, is a nonsymmetric growth curve with an adjustable inflexion point. The equation for this curve is

$$y = Le^{-ae^{-bx}}$$ (3.3)

Like the Pearl curve, L is the upper limit of the dependent variable's domain, e is the base of the natural logarithms, and x is the independent variable (also usually expressed as t, the current time period). We can estimate the parameters a and b by transforming the expression into its linear representation:

$$y^\circ = \ln\left[\ln\left(\frac{L}{y}\right)\right] = \ln a - bx \tag{3.4}$$

The underlying behavior dynamics of the two curves are very different. The Pearl curve takes into account not only the upper limit (saturation) of the growth (distance yet to grow) but the fact that previous growth accelerates future growth (distance already covered). The Gompertz curve, on the other hand, considers growth as simply a function of the saturation point (the distance remaining until saturation). There are a number of other growth curves available, such as the Easingwood-Mahajan-Muller diffusion model and the Fisher-Pry semi-log growth curve. The strengths and weaknesses of the compertz curve are outlined in Table 3.4.

TABLE 3.4   Strengths/Weaknesses of Non-linear Growth Curves

Strengths	■ Models highly nonlinear patterns
	■ Good predictive capabilities
	■ Fairly easy to use
	■ Easy to understand and deploy
	■ Creates a working mathematical model of the underlying system of variables
	■ Easy to adjust through data fitting
	■ Works well with adaptive feedback models
Weaknesses	■ Limited to nonlinear growth models.
	■ Difficult to use for more than two variables (dependent variable and the time period variable).
	■ Very sensitive to degree of correlation between variables.
	■ Parameter estimation is sometimes difficult. Necessary to convert nonlinear distributions to a linear representation (such as taking the natural logarithm of each data point).
	■ Sensitive to outlier clustering.
	■ Complex method of curve fitting.
	■ Selecting proper curve formula can be very difficult unless fitting is done through techniques such as genetic or evolutionary programming.

3.5 **Cluster Analysis**

Cluster analysis attempts to isolate regions of similarity within a database and find the relationships between multiple clusters. Large commercial and governmental databases contain huge quantities of data. Data mining explorers discover that such large repositories are not lacking in features, patterns, and relationships but are instead saturated with patterns. There are just too many. Directed data mining techniques, pursuing a specific objective function, often find nothing but high levels of noise. It is here that cluster analysis, in the form of automatic cluster detection (ACD), provides a truly unsupervised approach to finding centers of related functionality in data. Figure 3.6 illustrates a cluster as a collection of data with related properties.

The differences among members of a cluster, in terms of their absolute difference from the cluster's calculated center or centroid, defines a metric of compactness and homogeneity. In a large database, of course, many overlapping clusters exist. Figure 3.7 illustrates how the data space for the customer database is partitioned into many clusters with ill-defined boundaries.

Techniques for forming clusters are varied. In conventional (crisp) cluster detection, attributes are collected and sorted to give the initial cluster seeds. The association and diffusion of elements in a cluster are

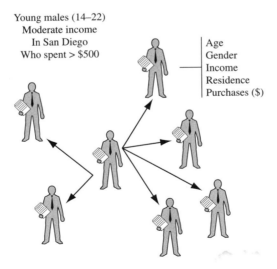

Young males (14–22)
Moderate income
In San Diego
Who spent > $500

Age
Gender
Income
Residence
Purchases ($)

Figure 3.6 A cluster of young purchasers.

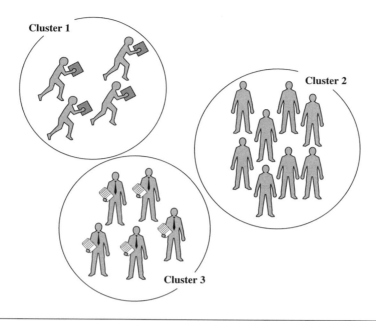

Figure 3.7 Multiple customer clusters in a database.

determined through a k-nearest-neighbor (KNN) approach (calculating the distance from a hypothetical center of mass to the candidate cluster member). An element is assigned to one and only one cluster. Fuzzy clustering (in particular, the fuzzy c-means and adaptive fuzzy clustering approaches described in Chapter 7) also measures the distance from a center of mass to an element, but allows an element to belong to more than one cluster (an element in multiple clusters has a different degree of membership in each cluster).

Automatic cluster detection thus forms the basis for almost all unsupervised data mining techniques. From the population of clusters, higher-level analytical and synthesis techniques are used to evolve a set of production rules. The strengths and weaknesses of cluster analysis are outlined in Table 3.5.

3.6 **Decision Trees and Classifiers**

Perhaps the most common method of data analysis and data mining (excluding statistics) is decision tree induction. A decision tree is a graph

TABLE 3.5   Strengths/Weaknesses of Cluster Analysis

Strengths	<ul><li>An unsupervised knowledge discovery technique forming the core engine in most data mining tools.</li><li>Several tools on the market for standalone cluster analysis. Easy to implement using standard statistical toolkits.</li><li>Relatively easy to find trained knowledge engineers and methods analysts to design and implement cluster analysis.</li><li>Works well with a wide spectrum of data types (numeric, categorical, and even textual data).</li><li>Measures the degree of cluster membership (allows for filtering of generated rules).</li><li>Robust methodology that can be easily tuned for various types of analysis.</li></ul>
Weaknesses	<ul><li>Clustering is not a standalone data mining technique but must be combined with other technologies to generate the final results (such as rules)</li><li>Clustering is very sensitive to the choice of similarity functions, distance metrics, and variable weights</li><li>Often very sensitive to the initial number of clusters and the initial (seed) values of the clusters</li><li>Undirected cluster formation can produce centers of randomness (i.e., the cluster may be an artifact of some other, perhaps as yet undiscovered, data behavior)</li></ul>

of the dependency relationships in clusters of data (and thus is generally subsumed by the category of classical cluster analysis).

There are a wide variety of decision tree algorithms (and associated software products) that work on both numeric and nonnumeric data attributes. Principal approaches to classification and categorization include the following.

- *Decision trees (ID3 and C4.5):* The C4.5 classifier is J. Ross Quinlan's most recent version of the original ID3 algorithm (first released in 1986).

- *Classification and regression trees (CART);* Initially developed by Brieman and Associates (1984) this algorithm is a very popular classification scheme. CART is a supervised classifier that builds a binary tree using a single independent variable.

- *Chi-squared automatic induction (CHAID) algorithms:* Developed by J. A. Hartigan (1975), this algorithm automatically isolates statistical correlations between variables. Continuous variables in CHAID must take on the form of intervals and in many ways are similar to ordinal fuzzy set names.

ID3-like algorithms use an increase or decrease in information gain to find the attribute that best partitions a set of data at the highest level. The algorithm then applies this same technique to partition the next level of attributes. This partitioning continues until a complete tree structure is created. The partitioning can be based on properties of the attribute (such as height, eye color, body temperature, and so on) or arithmetic and Boolean relationships. The partitioning or classification is maintained in the form of a graph. Figure 3.8 illustrates a small decision tree segment.

One path along this decision tree reads like a conventional expert system rule:

> **if** item price is less than fifty,
> **then** inventory action is stock as a regular item.

Edges in decision trees can also contain the strength of the relationship, the number of instances that confirm the relationship, and whether this is a one-to-one or one-to-many dependency.

Markov chains are extensions to the decision tree architecture where the edge contains the conjoint (or, occasionally, the cumulative) probability that the model will transition from one node in the tree to the next. In this case, a Markov chain maintains the law of motion for the system in terms of its limiting probabilities. Data mining tools construct Markov chains by observing the number of states that transition from one node to the next. This frequency distribution of edges gives an approximate probability for that node-to-node movement. The strengths and weaknesses of decision trees and classifiers are outlined in Table 3.6.

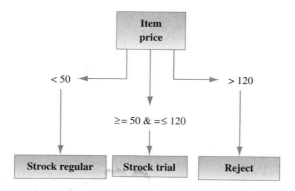

Figure 3.8 A small decision tree (generated by C4.5).

TABLE 3.6   Strengths/Weaknesses of Decision Trees and Classifiers

Strengths	■ Creates a set of classification rules
	■ Good for multidimensional data
	■ Easy-to-visualize dependency relationships
	■ Several tools available for decision trees (and case-based reasoning)
	■ Low computational requirements
	■ Organization sensitive to information gain (i.e., the amount of knowledge exposed by the tree)
	■ Usually capable of handling both continuous and categorical data
	■ Probabilities on Markov chain can highlight important relationships and depress rules created by spurious outliers
	■ Nearly always identify which variables make a significant contribution to the model
Weaknesses	■ Subject to "run away" errors when the number of classes grows too large
	■ Difficult to handle time-series data, especially models involving lead and lag relationships
	■ Many decision tree systems can only partition into true or false nodes
	■ Computationally expensive to train a large decision tree
	■ Partitioning is rectangular (N × M), which is not always consistent with actual data
	■ Trees can grow very large
	■ Rules are not generally associated with a working inference engine

3.7   **Neural Networks**

A neural network is a pattern classifier that behaves, in some ways, like the human mind. It consists of artificial neurons connected by edges, arrayed in a set of layers. The number of layers and the neurons per layer determine the power of the classifier and the number of fine grain patterns that can be recognized. Each edge connecting a node (a neuron) has a weight. It is the values of these weights, adjusted for each learned pattern, that induce the recognition process in a neural network. Figure 3.9 illustrates how a neural network is organized and how input patterns are classified (in this example a Yes/No classifier is shown, but the classifier can be almost any arbitrary pattern).

Neural networks can be taught to recognize specific patterns or they can be allowed to discover and arbitrarily learn patterns in large databases.

Because neural networks recognize patterns (and these can be patterns in data as well as visual images, handwriting, or metal fatigue faults), they

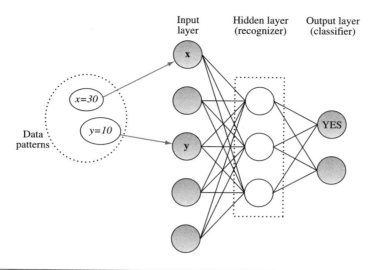

Figure 3.9 Neural network.

are well suited as data mining tools. In addition, neural networks are able to easily represent highly nonlinear and chaotic data, thus providing a platform well suited to many business process models. Unfortunately, neural networks are not able to model time-series data very well or data that is non-monotonically changing (e.g., data that have a wavelike pattern).

Neural networks have become the tool of choice in many large-scale data mining projects for several reasons. First, they are easy to use. A neural net system is essentially a "black box," meaning that the user supplies the data and the network learns the patterns. Second, there are many neural network tools and toolkits available on the market. Third, there is an abundance of highly skilled knowledge engineers who can design and implement a neural-network-based data mining system. The strengths and weaknesses of neural networks are outlined in Table 3.7.

3.8 Fuzzy SQL Systems

The introduction of semantic database query systems provides the knowledge mining engineer with a formidable and powerful data analysis and classification tool (see Chapter 6 for a discussion and examples of fuzzy queries). It is this latter ability to rank and classify sets of data based on the semantics of imprecision that makes the fuzzy query system an ideal

TABLE 3.7 Strengths/Weaknesses of Neural Networks

Strengths	■ Based on solid mathematics of learning in connectionist machines
	■ Well suited to modeling nonlinear and continuous data
	■ Easy to use (many software tools available)
	■ Many highly skilled neural network knowledge engineers available to design and implement system
	■ Able to work in both supervised and unsupervised modes
	■ Good data mining approach for large, unstructured databases
	■ Good choice when underlying reasons and explanations are not required
Weaknesses	■ Inputs must be well understood and often "normalized" to fall within a specific small range of values
	■ Outputs are continuous; categorical data can be difficult to generate or interpret
	■ Is a "black box," meaning it cannot explain its actions and user cannot examine the "rules"
	■ Requires expertise in neural network design to configure system for proper number of inputs, correct number of hidden layers, and suitable number of output classifiers
	■ Requires some skill in deciding on a proper training algorithm for many neural network configurations
	■ Can be computationally intensive in training mode
	■ Very difficult to handle nonnumeric data
	■ Requires large amounts of training data
	■ Network can be over-fit and over-trained (it simply "memorizes" the input and output)
	■ Produces a static model that must be retrained when new data are acquired (knowledge engineers cannot add rules or change the internal logic of a neural network)

"first approximate" tool in data mining. Conventional database queries select records using precisely defined arithmetic and logical expressions that resolve to a crisp yes or no answer. The following is an example.

```
Select *
From ieh01.projects
Where budget > 1000
    And duration > 90
    And (spent/budget)*100 in range[40,60];
```

On the other hand, a semantic query using fuzzy logic casts this same type of query into a request for records that match the intention of the user.

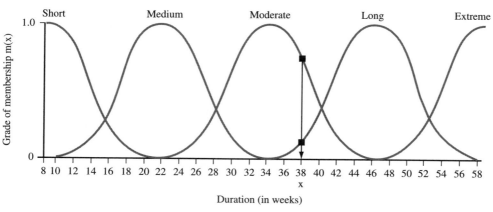

Figure 3.10 Fuzzy sets associated with project duration.

In a fuzzy query, the database variables (fields) are broken down into collections of overlapping fuzzy sets. This is illustrated in Figure 3.10 for the *duration* field of the project table.

The overlap of fuzzy sets shown in Figure 3.10 means that a variable's value (such as the position marked **x**) can simultaneously exist in more than one fuzzy set, usually with differing degrees of membership. These underlying fuzzy sets can then be used to select records from the database. As an example, the previous query can be recast as follows.

```
Select *
From ieh01.projects
Where budget is high
    And duration is long
    And (spent/budget)*100 is around 50%;
```

The fuzzy query *where* statement represents a template describing the cognitive model underlying the database query. In this case, the user's search template will match project records with some degree of high, some degree of long, and some degree of being about 50%. This captures, to a greater extent, the meaning of the query rather than simply its mechanics. A fuzzy query can also use hedges (such as *about 50%* or *near MfgCosts*) to dynamically create fuzzy sets from database table content, thus reducing the need to decompose all columns into fuzzy sets.

A fuzzy query returns not only the selected records but a compatibility index indicating how well individual records matched the template.

TABLE 3.8   Strengths/Weaknesses of Fuzzy SQL Systems

Strengths	■ Based on solid theory of fuzzy sets and approximate reasoning (fuzzy logic)
	■ Very easy-to-use and easy-to-understand method for exploring the nature of data
	■ Works on any conventional database system that has an ODBC driver as well as spreadsheets and comma-delimited files
	■ Semantics tailored to specific cognitive model (e.g., "young" in marketing is likely not the same as "young" in the credit department)
	■ Retrieves records based on "what I mean" not simply "what the arithmetic says"
	■ Results are ranked according to their compatibility (user can examine the best cases first)
Weaknesses	■ Not easy to use on very large databases (due to a lack of fuzzy index support) or across multiple tables (due to lack of fuzzy join)
	■ Requires an understanding of fuzzy logic and (to a lesser degree) fuzzy set theory
	■ Few tools to support fuzzy queries
	■ Few knowledge engineers trained in fuzzy logic (and those that do have some fuzzy logic experience generally have little if any experience with database systems and business problems)
	■ Cannot discover deep relationships
	■ Subject to proper definition of fuzzy sets and modifiers
	■ Relies on the knowledge of the query user
	■ Applicable to numeric data only
	■ Difficult to conceptualize complex query statements

The higher the compatibility index, the more closely the selected record matches the intent of the query. There are many ways to compute this compatibility (fuzzy minimum, weighted average, weighted product). Generally, a fuzzy query chooses many more records from the database than a conventional query. It is this ability to drill into large databases on a semantic rather than a crisp Boolean basis that makes fuzzy query a powerful first-step data mining tool. The strengths and weaknesses of fuzzy SQL systems are outlined in Table 3.8.

3.9   **Rule Induction and Dynamic Fuzzy Models**

All but three of the previous examples (linear regression, nonlinear growth curves, and neural networks) produce a static report as the

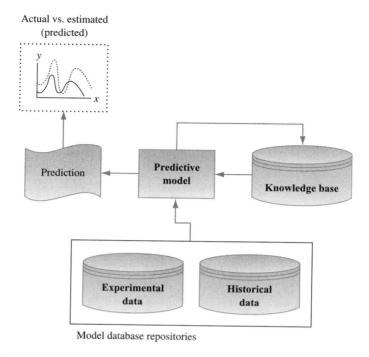

Figure 3.11 A dynamic rule-based model.

outcome of their data mining process. Bringing advanced computational intelligence techniques — such as genetic algorithms, fuzzy logic, and parameter estimation through back propagation — to bear on knowledge discovery process gives the knowledge miner a richer and much more powerful set of exploratory tools. These tools, in fact, allow the creation of adaptive feedback and a highly nonlinear rule-based systems. The rule induction process evolves a dynamic model of the underlying system through a set of *if-then-else* rules. Figure 3.11 illustrates how this dynamic model is structured.

This approach is a powerful method of data mining and knowledge discovery. Evolving or generating a dynamic rule-based model can be done in at least two ways: through the use of cluster analysis (see Chapter 7) or through the use of an *if-then* pattern discovery algorithm (see Chapter 8). The more important features of evolving a dynamic rule-based model include the following,

■ The automatic decomposition of variables into fuzzy sets (relieving the designer of this preliminary and time-consuming task)

- The automatic detection of fuzzy cluster centers (easily finding groups of records that share common and often imprecisely bounded properties)
- The use of genetic algorithms to regenerate models, reconfigure existing models, and explore large data spaces (see Chapter 11)

With a rule-based system the knowledge mining engineer can examine the actual relationships, run and simulate the behavior of the system, ask the system to explain its reasoning, and modify the evolved system to include additional rules or change the nature of one or more evolved rules. Because evolved dynamic models are regenerated from data, they are ideally suited to adaptive feedback systems and processes that are sensitive to rapid changes in the external world. Figure 3.12 shows a "high-altitude" schematic of the fuzzy rule evolution process.

Rules are statements of cause and effect. Fuzzy rules are statements of relationships between degrees of memberships and allow a much more powerful form of inference than ordinary crisp rules. They are cast in the form of *if-then-else* statements. The following is an example.

> **if** CompetitionPrice is high
> **then** OurPrice should be low

This statement says that "when the competition price has some degree of membership in the fuzzy set *high*, then our price should have a corresponding degree of membership in the fuzzy set *low*." This relationship looks something like the transfer function shown in Figure 3.13.

As Figure 3.13 indicates, the fuzzy sets *high* and *low* need not be congruent or conformal, and thus we can introduce as a natural part of the model highly nonlinear behaviors in even the simplest rules. In actual practice, of course, fuzzy models process many rules in parallel, combining the evidence from each rule (at the rule's contribution weight) into a composite assessment of the final solution value.

Supervised Model Generation

There are two types of fuzzy model generations, each of which is associated with a different type of data mining or knowledge discovery paradigm. The first, illustrated in Figure 3.14, is *supervised* data mining. In this methodology, the knowledge engineer or systems analyst specifies a dependent variable and a set of possible (or probable) independent variables. The data mining facility attempts to discover the relationships between the dependent and one or more of the independent variables.

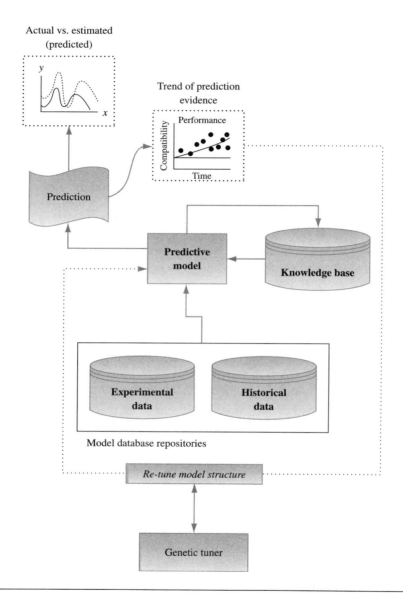

Figure 3.12 A dynamic fuzzy system model.

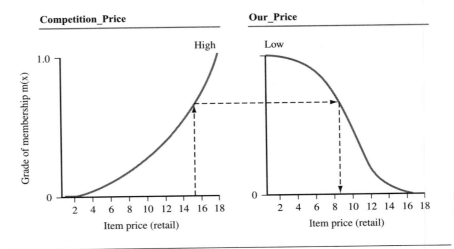

Figure 3.13   The monotonic truth function for *high* and *low*.

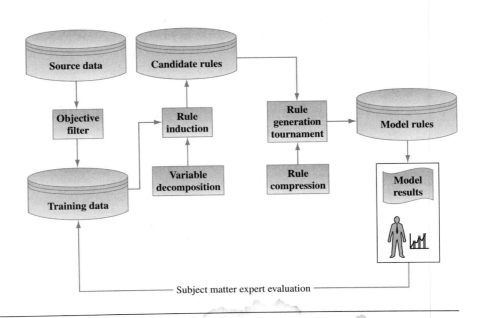

Figure 3.14   Supervised data mining.

Based on the Wang-Mendel rule of induction algorithm, this technique automatically decomposes variables into overlapping fuzzy sets (the decomposition is based on the type of variable), fits the data to the fuzzy sets, and generates a collection of candidate rules. Combining user belief estimates, noise filtering, and rule effectiveness weights, a tournament is conducted to select the best rules. These are compressed or combined with other rules to generate the final model.

Unsupervised Model Generation

The second approach to fuzzy model generation is unsupervised data mining. In this approach we employ two different types of unsupervised data mining technologies. The first, called cluster analysis, automatically organizes n-dimensional space into collections of elements with similar characteristics or properties. These collections, called clusters, have centers measured according to a fuzzy relationship function so that membership in the cluster is expressed as a fuzzy Euclidean distance. These clusters can also overlap, so that elements can sometimes belong to two or more clusters with different strengths. The second technology is called a genetic algorithm. This form of computational intelligence generates multiple simultaneous models and examines how well the cluster relationships map to some objective function. Genetic algorithms can arbitrarily select clusters along different axes in the n-dimensional space and examine their effectiveness in predicting model robustness. Figure 3.15 illustrates schematically how this model evolution technique works.

A genetic algorithm is a nonlinear optimization technique. It works from a population of candidate models. The model attributes are both randomly selected and randomly changed through a process of model "mating" and "mutation." The genetic algorithm also generates a fuzzy model. However, the rules are automatically executed by the genetic algorithm to measure the distance or difference between model prediction and the validation values (the actual value). Models with improved prediction capabilities are saved in the population, whereas models with inferior prediction capabilities are eventually eliminated. In this way, after a large number of parallel iterations a final best-fit model is produced.

Because the unsupervised data mining approach examines all possible cluster relations across the complete n-dimensional space, it can find even very deep relationships in the data. Furthermore, fuzzy clusters, because they measure cluster elements using partial memberships and can handle elements lying in overlapping clusters, often discover relationships that are transparent or invisible to conventional cluster analysis. By combining fuzzy clustering with powerful genetic algorithms, the unsupervised data mining process can examine large, very complex data spaces. The fuzzy

TABLE 3.9   Strengths/Weaknesses of Unsupervised Model Generation

Strengths	<ul><li>Based on mathematics of fuzzy sets and approximate reasoning (fuzzy logic), genetic algorithms, machine learning, and automatic parameterization (neural network back propagation)</li><li>Generates a fuzzy rule-based model executed to observe and analyze the underlying system behavior</li><li>Handles large databases with missing and noisy data</li><li>Weights evidence for rules so that outliers, sparse data, or unreliable data will not contribute to significant rule set</li><li>Uses a fuzzy mountain clustering technique to automatically find centers of knowledge</li><li>Easily handles nonlinear models</li><li>Models time-series with lead-lag relationships</li><li>Models adaptive feedback systems</li><li>Deep, elastic rule discovery process</li><li>Supervised or unsupervised modes (works with or without an explicit objective function)</li><li>System can explain its reasoning</li><li>User rules can be added and weights on existing rules changed (through a calibration feedback loop)</li><li>Implements Combs method for rule reduction to minimize size of model</li></ul>
Weaknesses	<ul><li>Significant computational demands during model evolution.</li><li>Requires knowledge of fuzzy logic, fuzzy set theory, and approximate reasoning to understand how model is created and works.</li><li>Few tools to support fuzzy system models.</li><li>Output rules must be compatible with and interconnected to the fuzzy modeling software.</li><li>Few knowledge engineers trained in fuzzy logic (and those that do have some fuzzy logic experience generally have little if any experience with database systems and business problems).</li><li>Rule generation mechanics require tuning such factors as the slot competition algorithm, compression techniques, belief functions, noise filtering, and empty rule actions.</li><li>Can produce a very large number of rules.</li><li>Objective functions (for supervised data mining) can be difficult to identify.</li><li>Default fuzzy decomposition of variables may not reflect actual semantics of the data. Knowledge engineer may need to handcraft critical fuzzy sets.</li><li>Often requires more than normal pre-processing of data.</li></ul>

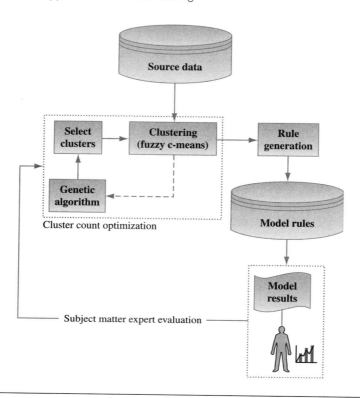

Figure 3.15 Unsupervised data mining.

model produced by this type of analysis tends to be more robust, in that the fuzzy rules are generated from cluster centroids rather than from a more simple (but nevertheless effective) tournament based on data fitting. The strengths and weaknesses of unsupervised model generation are outlined in Table 3.9.

3.10 **Review**

This chapter has provided a brief and "high-altitude" survey of various model building approaches and technologies. Although this book is primarily concerned with exploring data through intelligent technologies and building models from fuzzy rule discovery, an understanding of other modeling techniques as well as their strengths and limitations is a necessary foundation for any attempt at building effective, robust, and maintainable models. From this chapter you should come away with an understanding of the following.

- Basic statistical approaches to modeling structured numeric data
- Mathematical, clustering, and categorization methods of modeling-related data patterns
- The use and limitations of regression analysis in discovering and interpreting trends
- The nature of knowledge-based approaches to models, such as neural networks and fuzzy systems
- How to approach the modeling of general nonlinear growth (time-series) systems
- How fuzzy logic is used to explore databases and other data repositories
- The nature of rule induction (data mining) in the evolution of dynamic fuzzy models

A more comprehensive and exhaustive analysis of modeling techniques and technologies is outside the scope of this book. However, this chapter provides a relatively broad framework, covering ordinary statistical, mathematical, pattern discovery, and knowledge-based approaches to building models.

Further Reading

Data Mining

- Berry, M., and G. Linoff. *Data Mining Techniques for Marketing, Sales, and Customer Support*. New York: John Wiley and Sons, 1997.

- Cabena, P., P. Hadjinian, R. Stadler, J. Verhees, A. Zanasi. *Discovering Data Mining from Concept to Implementation*. Upper Saddle River, NJ: Prentice-Hall/PTR, 1997.

- Groth, R. *Data Mining: A Hands-On Approach for Business Professionals*. Upper Saddle River, NJ: Prentice-Hall/PTR, 1997.

- Kennedy, R. L., Y. Lee, B. Van Roy, C. D. Reed, R. Lippman. *Solving Data Mining Problems Through Pattern Recognition*. Upper Saddle River, NJ: Prentice-Hall/PTR, 1998.

- Weiss, S., and N. Indurkhya. *Predictive Data Mining*. San Francisco: Morgan Kaufmann, 1998.

Model Building

■ Cellier, F. *Continuous System Modeling*. New York: Springer-Verlag, 1991.

■ Cherkassky, V., and F. Mulier. *Learning from Data: Concepts, Theory, and Methods*. New York: John Wiley and Sons, 1998.

■ Fogel, D. *Evolutionary Computation: Toward a New Philosophy of Machine Intelligence*. Piscataway, NJ: IEEE Press, 1995.

■ Goldberg, D. *Genetic Algorithms in Search, Optimization, and Machine Learning*. Reading, MA: Addison-Wesley, 1989.

■ Liebowitz, J. (ed.). *Expert Systems for Business and Management*. Englewood Cliffs, NJ: Prentice-Hall, 1990.

■ Masters, T. *Practical Neural Network Recipes in C++*. San Diego, CA: Academic Press, 1993.

■ Martin, J., and J. Odell. *Object-oriented Methods: Pragmatic Considerations*. Upper Saddle River, NJ: Prentice-Hall/PTR, 1996.

■ Michalewicz, Z. *Genetic Algorithms + Data Structures = Evolution Programs*. New York: Springer-Verlag, 1994.

■ Pao, Y-H. *Adaptive Pattern Recognition and Neural Networks*. Reading, MA: Addison-Wesley, 1989.

■ Taylor, D. *Business Engineering with Object Technology*. New York: John Wiley and Sons, 1995.

■ Wasserman, P. D. *Neural Computing: Theory and Practice*. New York: Van Nostrand Reinhold, 1989.

■ Watkins, P., and L. Eliot. *Expert Systems in Business and Finance*. New York: John Wiley and Sons, 1993.

■ Weinberg, G. *An Introduction to General Systems Thinking*. New York: John Wiley and Sons, 1975.

Part II
Fuzzy Systems

Contents

Chapter 4
Fundamental Concepts of Fuzzy Logic

Fuzzy logic is a form or system of logic. Like Boolean logic, it is based on set theory. The sets in fuzzy logic, however, have degrees of membership. This slight change in the definition of a set has significant and far-reaching implications for knowledge representation and chains of reasoning. This chapter examines the differences between Boolean and fuzzy logic sets, explores the various operators that can be applied to both sets (and how such operators differ) and discusses operations that only make sense for fuzzy sets (such as hedges and alpha cut thresholds). Understanding the nature of fuzzy sets and fuzzy logic is crucial in understanding not only the clustering and rule induction techniques in Part I of the book but in understanding many of the advanced genetic modeling techniques in Part III.

From a modeling perspective, fuzzy logic is a logic of continuous variables. Its complement, Boolean logic, is a logic of discrete variables. With fuzzy logic we can represent such elastic and imprecise concepts as high risk, a long duration, a tall person, and a large transaction volume. We can also evaluate critical process factors in a model. Is X increasing rapidly? Is A close to B? Is N very much greater than M? In all of these cases fuzzy logic provides a way of finding the degree to which an object is representative of a concept or the degree to which a state is representative of a process. These degrees play a subtle but critical role in the evaluation of fuzzy models and fuzzy systems. They represent not only the degree of membership in a concept (that is, a set) but such important modeling concepts as supporting evidence, numeric elasticity, and semantic ambiguity.

It is the ability to represent intrinsic ambiguity that gives fuzzy logic some of its most impressive capabilities — allowing a single data point to belong simultaneously (with differing degrees of membership) to multiple, sometimes semantically conflicting, concepts (multiple sets). Such a small relaxation in the rules of Boolean logic has far-reaching and powerful consequences for models that incorporate fuzzy logic. Before moving on to the nature of how fuzzy systems model uncertainty and ambiguity, we need to lay a foundation in the nature of fuzzy sets, fuzzy set operations, and fuzzy implication methods. We start with the lexicon of fuzzy logic and then move on to the difference between Boolean and fuzzy sets.

4.1 The Vocabulary of Fuzzy Logic

Fuzzy logic suffers from a rich vocabulary of unfamiliar terms and reluctance among its researchers and developers to adhere to a standard vocabulary. It also suffers from an overuse of obscure mathematical symbolism in place of simple and explanatory narrative (but that is another issue). The literature of fuzzy logic and fuzzy systems is filled with a nomenclature derived from its own private world of continuous logic. We find ourselves speaking about fuzzification and defuzzification, hedges, membership functions, and linguistic variables. Before moving on to a more comprehensive and detailed exploration of fuzzy logic, fuzzy systems, and how they work, we need to understand the principal nomenclatures and how they are related to the elements of fuzzy systems.

Although not a complete dictionary of terms associated with fuzzy logic, a preview of the basic vocabulary at the beginning of this chapter will make reading and understanding the material in the chapters of Part II much easier. It is not always possible, while maintaining an uncluttered and coherent discussion of fuzzy systems, to ensure that every term is introduced before it is used. Many of these terms, of course, will be discussed in greater depth later in this and subsequent chapters.

Alpha Cut Threshold

An *alpha cut threshold* truncates the membership function of a fuzzy set or the truth value of a fuzzy rule's predicate at a specific truth value. Any value that falls below the alpha cut threshold is equivalent to zero. Alpha cuts come in two forms: strong (the comparison is less than) and weak (the comparison is less than or equal).

Boolean Logic

Boolean logic is a logic of crisp sets. A crisp set has two truth values: 1 and 0. Propositions in Boolean logic are either true or false, and membership in Boolean sets is either fully inclusive or fully exclusive. Boolean logic was initially formalized by George Boole (1815–1864). In 1854, he published *An Investigation into the Laws of Thought, on Which Are Founded the Mathematical Theories of Logic and Probabilities*, which unified the mathematical concepts of algebra and logic.

Crisp Set

Boolean sets are often called *crisp sets* as a way of distinctly differentiating them from fuzzy sets, as well as a way of indicating the sharpness or crispness of their membership function.

Domain

Often confused with the term *universe of discourse*, the *domain* of a fuzzy set is the explicit range of values over which the fuzzy set's membership function is defined. For vocabulary fuzzy sets (e.g., the term set of a variable), the domain is generally the same as the *support set*.

Expectancy

The width of a fuzzy number, usually measured from the center of the fuzzy set, is called the *expectancy* (a measure of the number's elasticity). The larger the expectancy the more imprecision is built into the fuzzy number. However, we should not confuse imprecision with a lack of accuracy. In many fuzzy models, relaxing the precision of a number increases the model's fault tolerance and reduces its brittleness, thereby making the model more precise over a wider range of values.

Fuzzy Logic

Fuzzy logic is a logic of fuzzy sets. A fuzzy set has, potentially, an infinite range of truth values between one (1) and zero (0). Propositions in fuzzy logic have a degree of truth, and membership in fuzzy sets can be fully inclusive, fully exclusive, or some degree in between. Fuzzy logic was initially formalized by Lotfi Zadeh (1921–) in his seminal 1965 paper "Fuzzy Sets" (see "Further Reading") followed in 1973 with "Outline of a New Approach to the Analysis of Complex Systems and Decision Process" (see "Further Reading").

Fuzzy Number

A bell-shaped, triangular-shaped, or trapezoidal-shaped fuzzy set represents a central value and is, in essence, a *fuzzy number*. Fuzzy numbers give fuzzy models a great deal of robustness and flexibility. The width of a fuzzy number is a measure of its overall expectancy (the degree to which it corresponds to a crisp number).

Fuzzy Quantifier

Fuzzy sets that are not numbers are *fuzzy quantifiers*. These sets generally have linear or sigmoid shapes. Concepts such as *Tall*, *Fast*, *Heavy*, and *Large* are examples of fuzzy quantifiers.

Fuzzy Set

A *fuzzy set* is distinct from a crisp or Boolean set in that it allows its elements to have a degree of membership. The core of a fuzzy set is its membership function: a surface or line that defines the relationship between a value in the set's domain and its degree of membership. The relationship (Expression 4.1) is functional because it returns a single degree of membership for any value in the domain.

$$t = f(s, x) \qquad\qquad (4.1)$$

Here,

- t is a truth membership value (degree of membership in fuzzy set)
- s is the fuzzy set
- x is a value from the underlying domain (universe of discourse)

Fuzzy sets provide a means of defining a series of overlapping concepts for a model variable, thus permitting rules to address the state of a model in terms of these fuzzy set names. Such names are called linguistic variables. They allow fuzzy sets to represent the underlying semantics of a variable (that is, the concept represented by a variable).

Hedge

Hedges act like adjectives or adverbs in the English language. They modify the shape of the fuzzy set's underlying membership function to or dilute the membership relationships, and they convert scalars (crisp numbers) into fuzzy sets through a process called approximation. They can be used in rules to modify the evaluation of both the premise and the consequent. The following is an example.

> **if** a is *very* Z,
>   **then** b is *somewhat* Y

Here, *very* and *somewhat* are intensifier and dilution hedges.

Linguistic Variable

A fuzzy set that forms part of the term set for a variable and is used in fuzzy rules as part of a fuzzy relation is called a *linguistic variable*. For example, in the rule **if** *height is Tall* **then** *weight is Heavy* both *Tall* and *Heavy* are linguistic variables representing one of the possible partitions of height and weight. Fuzzy sets used in this way are called linguistic variables because they are used in place of numbers and allow rules to be cast in form of linguistic statements (such as *height is Tall*).

Membership Function

The core of a fuzzy set is the *membership function*. See "Fuzzy Set" for a more complete description.

Overlap

Because fuzzy sets represent degrees of membership, values from the complete universe of discourse for a variable can have memberships in more than one fuzzy set. For example, consider the variable height with a term set of *Short*, *Medium*, and *Tall*. An individual's height can be, to some degree, both *Short* and *Medium*. This is because the *Short* and *Medium* fuzzy sets overlap (as the values for height increase, they become less *Short* and more *Medium*, but the transition is gradual, not abrupt).

Support Set

The region of the membership function in which the truth values are greater than zero is called the *support set*. The support set plays an important part in the evaluation of a fuzzy model because only within the support set region can a set actually contribute to the outcome of a model.

Term Set

The collection of fuzzy sets that define the semantics of a variable is called the variable's *term set*. Each variable used in a fuzzy rule must have a term set. The individual fuzzy sets in a term set are the linguistic variables associated with the variable. Thus, *Tall* in the rule **if** height is Tall **then** weight is Heavy is part of the term set for the variable height and *Heavy* is part of the term set for the variable *weight*.

Universe of Discourse

The complete range of values over which a variable can assume values is called the *universe of discourse* (UoD). Although this term is often applied to the range of values in a fuzzy set, the proper term for the fuzzy set is its *domain*. The Universe of discourse for a variable is decomposed into a collection of fuzzy sets (the term set), each set of which has a domain that overlays part of the universe of discourse.

4.2 Boolean (Crisp) Sets: The Law of Bivalence

A set is a collection of objects grouped because they share a common property. In crisp (or Boolean) logic, an object is either a member of a set or it is not. For a crisp set A, the membership or characteristic function, $\mu_A(x)$, shown in Expression 4.2, is defined in exactly these terms.

$$\mu_A(x) = \begin{cases} 1 & x \in A \\ 0 & x \notin A \end{cases} \qquad (4.2)$$

This is known as *the law of bivalence*, which forms the fundamental property of Boolean logic. The principle (or law) of bivalence is such an intrinsic part of Boolean logic that it is simply taken for granted. In fact, if we assume that bivalence is an axiom of Boolean logic, the associated laws of the *excluded middle* and *noncontradiction* (discussed in material to follow) can be proved as theorems.

Implicitly, the collection of elements in A is drawn from A's underlying domain or universe of discourse[1] (U), simply referred to as *UoD* in both Boolean and fuzzy sets. Thus, when we refer to a set (e.g., A)

---

[1] In a general modeling sense, however, *a boolean* domain defines a more extensive and more model-context-sensitive constraint on the set membership. As an example, the set of Customers with Poor Credit might have as its domain an SQL query against a database table of

and its characteristic function there is an implied qualification, illustrated in Expression 4.3, that the elements are selected from the corresponding UoD.

$$A \leftarrow \{(x_i, \mu_A(x_i)|x_i \in U)\} \qquad (4.3)$$

As the name implies, the UoD is the range or set of values under discussion when we are examining a set. In almost all cases the UoD will be the set of allowed values in the set, but is often drawn from a much larger (often infinite) set of values. Generally, for both crisp and fuzzy sets the UoD will be drawn from the larger universe, R (the monotonic line of positive and negative real numbers).

Most of us are familiar with Boolean sets from high school algebra, in which they are represented as Venn (or Euler) diagrams. These sets have well-defined characteristics (the set of all even numbers, the set of every odd number greater than 10, the Fibonacci numbers, and, less mathematically, the set of male history teachers, the set of yellow Chevrolets in the parking lot, and so forth). Sets are defined by their characteristic or specification function. This specification can be a list or any logical expression. For example, consider the Boolean set of *Tall* people (by this we mean any person over six feet in height). Given a height (x), Expression 4.4 shows the membership function for *Tall* people.

$$\mu_{Tall}(x) = \begin{cases} 1 & x > 6 \\ 0 & x \leq 6 \end{cases} \qquad (4.4)$$

When we constrain *Tall* so that its UoD is between 4 and 7 feet (in the future we will simply represent this as $T^U = \{4, 7\}$), Figure 4.1 shows the degree of membership profile for the set.

There are only two possible membership states in *Tall*: either a height is considered *Tall* or it is not. The bold line in Figure 4.1 represents the set membership for each height along the horizontal axis (the domain of the set). At a fraction of an inch above 6 feet the membership jumps from false (or 0) to true (or 1).

Boolean Set Operators

A complete discussion of Boolean logic is outside the scope of this book. However, a short review of the basic set of operations is necessary in order

---

poor risk clients. Thus the Universe of Discourse does not map to real numbers nor does it map to a comprehensible time-invariant set.

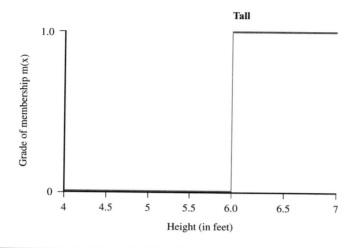

Figure 4.1 The Boolean *Tall* set.

AND				OR				XOR				NOT		
	0	1			0	1			0	1				
0	0	0		0	0	1		0	0	1		0	1	
1	0	1		1	1	1		1	1	0		1	0	

Figure 4.2 Truth tables for *And, Or, Exclusive-Or,* and *Not.*

to understand the differences in set algebra operations when we begin our discussion of fuzzy sets. As Figure 4.2 illustrates, there are four principal operations that can be performed on Boolean sets.

The *And* (or intersection) operator applied to set A and B returns a set containing all elements common to both sets. The *Or* (or union) operator when applied to sets A and B returns a set containing all elements that appear in ether set. Although not usually considered a basic logical operator, the *Exclusive-Or* when applied to sets A and B returns all elements that appear in either of the two sets but not in both. The *Not* operator is applied to a single set and reverses the membership value (that is, it returns the complement of the set).

The Laws of Excluded Middle and Noncontradiction

Although the rules underlying crisp logic were formulated in the mid-nineteenth century by George Boole, the ideas underlying Boolean logic can be traced back at least as far as Aristotle.

When Aristotle finished explaining how the physical world behaved, he turned to a deeper matter (in his mind, at least), explaining how we know what we know. Aristotle set about formulating the rules for separating truth from falsehood. The result of this effort was his six treatises on logic, collectively known as *The Organon*, or *The Tool*. It was Aristotle's insight into reasoning that led him to formulate a way of maintaining the "chain of custody" of truth through successive steps. These syllogisms, as they are known, have allowed generations of freshmen logic students to wrestle with deep propositions such as the following.

> All men are mortal
> Socrates is a man
> Socrates is mortal

The first part of the syllogism lays down a general proposition; in this case, that all men are mortal (all men will eventually die). The next two lines form an *if-then* chain of reasoning. The logic says, *if* Socrates is a man, *then* (or "therefore") Socrates is mortal. These *if-then* statements form not only an implicit part of the way we as humans reason about contingent events but, as we shall see later, lie at the core of modern rule-based machine reasoning systems.

Like today's Boolean logic, these syllogisms (as well as the rest of Aristotle's logic) depended on an ability to classify or categorize elements into distinct sets. It allows for no ambiguity in the classification. Aristotle took the idea of ambiguity to its natural consequences: the relationship between an object's membership in a set (A) and its membership in the complement of that set ($\sim A$). Aristotle came to the conclusion — the same conclusion reached by George Boole and still an integral part of Boolean logic — that an object cannot be in both A and $\sim A$. In somewhat formal terms, this is expressed as

$$\mu_{A \cap \sim A}(x) = \{\emptyset\}, \tag{4.5}$$

meaning that the intersection of a set with its complement (A and $\sim A$) is an empty set. This is the *law of noncontradiction*, which states that for any Boolean proposition (P *AND* $\sim P$) is false. From this we can also see that combining a set and its complement must return the entire population of possible elements (the UoD). This is represented as

$$\mu_{A \cup \sim A}(x) = \left\{ A^{U} \right\}, \tag{4.6}$$

meaning that the union of a set with its complement (X or $\sim X$) is the universe of elements that can be selected for either set. This is the *law of the excluded middle*, which states that for any Boolean proposition (P OR $\sim P$) is true.

4.3 **Fuzzy Sets**

In 1965, professor Lotfi Zadeh (Electrical Engineering and Electronics Research Laboratory, University of California, Berkeley) published his seminal paper on the idea of fuzzy sets (see "Further Reading"), thus establishing the foundation of a comprehensive and mathematically sound logic of imprecisely or ambiguously defined sets. This has come to be known as fuzzy logic, first given full treatment in Zadeh's 1973 paper "Outline of a New Approach to the Analysis of Complex Systems and Decision Process" (see "Further Reading").

The Anatomy of a Fuzzy Set

The core idea of fuzzy logic rests with the concept of a fuzzy set. These sets are not *fuzzy* in the conventional English-language sense of the word: blurred, hazy, out of focus, or indistinct. Rather, they are fuzzy in the way they treat their set boundaries. Fuzzy sets have a semipermeable membrane. In a fuzzy set, an element can be in three states: not a member of the set, a full member of the set, or a partial member of the set. Set membership is thus represented as a continuous range of values in the interval [0, 1] with [0] indicating no set membership, [1] indicating complete set membership, and values in the range [>0, <1] indicating a partial degree of membership.

Fuzzy logic is a superset of Boolean logic. Consequently, fuzzy sets are, in many respects, supersets of Boolean sets. A fuzzy set incorporates as part of its structure the intrinsic degrees of membership associated with each element. Figure 4.3 illustrates schematically the general components of a fuzzy set.

A fuzzy set has three principal components: a degree of membership measure along the vertical (Y) axis, the possible domain values for the set along the horizontal (X) axis, and the set membership function (a continuous curve that connects a domain value to its degree of membership in

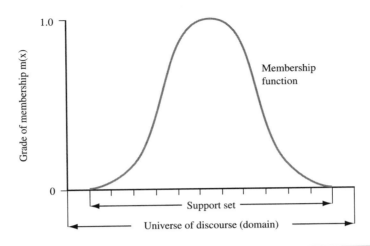

Figure 4.3 General components of a fuzzy set.

the set). The connecting curve is the crucial part of the fuzzy set. It defines the set membership relations. In addition to an underlying domain or universe of discourse, a fuzzy set also has a support set. This is the region of the domain at which the membership values are greater than zero.

The Taxonomy of Fuzzy Sets

Comparing the crisp set *Tall* (see Figure 4.1) with its fuzzy counterpart will illustrate these differences and expose the structure of a basic fuzzy set. Figure 4.4 shows one possible fuzzy set representation for the concept *Tall*.

The *Tall* fuzzy set defines how heights are related to the concept of *Tall*. All heights below 4.5 feet have zero membership values (and are outside the support set). From 4.5 to 6 feet, the degree of membership in the fuzzy set *Tall* gradually increases. At 6 feet it reaches [1.0] (all heights above 6 feet are fully members of the set). Alternatively, we can view the membership value as the degree of compatibility between the value of height and the concept *Tall*. As heights increase they become more and more compatible with the idea of *Tall*. At 6 feet and above all values of *Height* are completely compatible with the idea of *Tall*.

Fuzzy Quantifiers

The fuzzy set *Tall* represents a class of fuzzy sets known as quantifiers. These are sets whose structure is not built around a central value (see

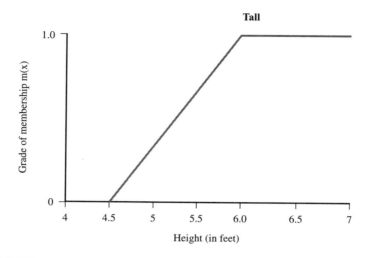

Figure 4.4 The fuzzy set *Tall* (for men).

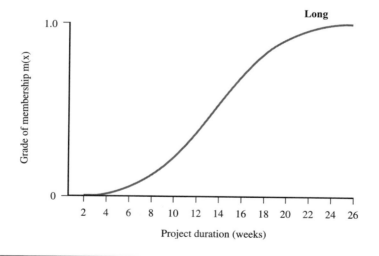

Figure 4.5 Fuzzy set for a *Long* project.

the section "Fuzzy Numbers"). A quantifier represents an open concept and is quite common in fuzzy expert systems. Although the membership function for the *Tall* fuzzy set (Figure 4.5) was a straight line, implying a linear relationship, quantifier sets more commonly use sigmoid (left- and

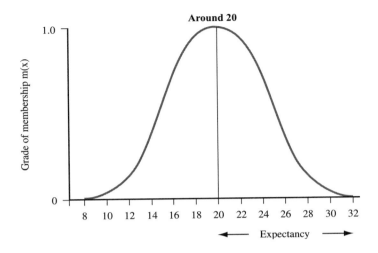

Figure 4.6 The fuzzy number *About 20*.

right-facing S-shaped) curves. Sigmoid curves, with inflection points and attenuated surfaces, can model a wide variety of growth curves (such as logistics, Gompertz, and Pearl curves). Figure 4.5 illustrates the fuzzy set for a *Long* project (with the project duration measured in weeks).

The *Long* fuzzy set uses a growth curve. The left-facing S-curve is called a *decay curve*. By adjusting the inflection point on an S-curve, as well as the degree of skew in the upper and lower curve segments, decay and growth curves can represent many highly nonlinear concepts. This ability is very important in types of fuzzy models that are sensitive to small changes in the underlying data (such as risk assessment and sustainability models).

Fuzzy Numbers

A much larger class of fuzzy sets represents approximate numbers of one type or another. Some of these fuzzy sets are explicitly "fuzzified" numbers, whereas others simply represent fuzzy numeric intervals over the domain of a particular variable (see the section "Fuzzy Term Sets"). Fuzzy numbers can take many shapes: bell curves, triangles, and trapezoids. Within each of these shapes the actual meaning of the fuzzy set depends on the width or spread of the set itself. Figure 4.6 illustrates a typical bell-shaped fuzzy number. This is a numeric quantity, *About 20*.

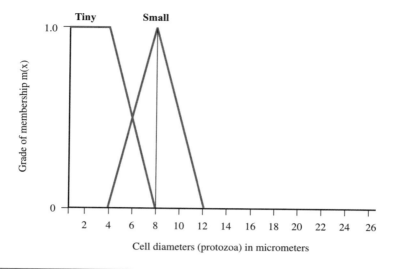

Figure 4.7 The fuzzy number *Small*.

The fuzzy set *About 20* shows two principal attributes of fuzzy numbers: a central value and a degree of spread[2] around the value. This degree of spread is called the expectancy (*e*) of the fuzzy number and is an important property. When $e = 0$, the fuzzy number is a single point and corresponds to a normal scalar value (called a singleton). As the expectancy increases, the number becomes fuzzier. This fuzziness is directly connected to the robustness or brittleness of a fuzzy model as well as to the separation of related concepts in the model. And, because expectancy increases confusion over the exact value of a fuzzy number, a wide expectancy also increases information entropy.

Another very common fuzzy number shape is the triangle. Due primarily to the low computational cost of creating and interrogating triangular fuzzy sets they are used extensively in control applications. In general, a triangular fuzzy number is more brittle and therefore less robust than a bell-shaped fuzzy number. Figure 4.7 illustrates a triangular fuzzy set for the concept *Small* and shows that fuzzy numbers are often used to represent the underlying numbers in terms of a particular concept. In this instance, the cell diameter of a protozoa is taken to be *Small* (to some degree) when it lies between 4 and 12 micrometers.

---

[2] *Degree of spread* is not to be confused with *degree of membership*. *Degree of spread* is here used in the ordinary sense of the term: a location on a scale of intensity, or an amount or quality.

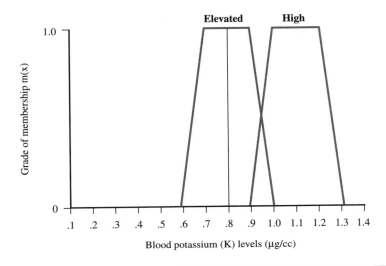

Figure 4.8 The fuzzy numbers for *Elevated* and *High*.

The fuzzy number *Small* in Figure 4.7 is also bounded by another fuzzy number, *Tiny*. Although this might appear to be a linear fuzzy quantifier, it is actually a representative of the third type of fuzzy number, the trapezoid. A trapezoidal representation is slightly but crucially different from the bell and triangle numbers. Figure 4.8 shows two overlapping fuzzy numbers represented as trapezoids.

The semantics of a trapezoidal number are slightly different from the bell and triangular numbers because the set does not pivot, so to speak, around a single, central number. Although we can continue to treat a trapezoid as a special case of the triangular fuzzy set (with a plateau width of zero), some model builders consider the trapezoid as a categorical or class fuzzy set — interpreting the plateau as a class of numbers equivalent to the fuzzy set concept. In this case, for example, *Elevated* is a class of values near {0.6 to 1.0}. Just how *near* is determined by the width of the trapezoid's expectancy spread (which is measured from the edge, not the center, of the plateau).

The existence of a plateau means that a set of values in the fuzzy set has maximum membership values in the set. In both the bell and the triangular sets only a single value is completely compatible with the set concept. On either side of this single number, the fuzzy membership values can (and usually do) drop off rather rapidly. By introducing plateaus into the fuzzy number, we establish a class of values that in a fuzzy model tends to create local areas of concentration.

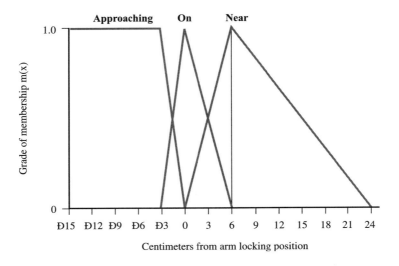

Figure 4.9 Asymmetric fuzzy numbers.

Asymmetric Fuzzy Numbers

Unlike crisp numbers that have a precise value, fuzzy numbers have a certain amount of ambiguity or spread around them. This spread or expectancy is actually measured in two directions, to the left and the right of the central value (or, for a trapezoid, the edges of the plateau of values). Having two measures of fuzziness allows fuzzy numbers to have asymmetric shapes. A fuzzy number can have both a kurtosis and a skew (although these are not computed or measured as the equivalent concepts in statistics). Figure 4.9 illustrates several asymmetric fuzzy numbers in a robotic arm controller.

Nonsymmetric fuzzy sets are frequently encountered in control systems (such as the robotic arm controller) but they also play important roles in both the development of complex nonlinear expert systems as well as in the automatic, genetic tuning of rule-based fuzzy systems (see Chapter 11 for an in-depth exploration of genetic tuning).

Psychometric Fuzzy Sets

In the previous fuzzy set examples the underlying domains were drawn from a measurement associated with the property of data. *Tall* is a concept overlaid on the measured values of *Height*. *Long* is a concept overlaid on the measured values of *project duration*. Many models, however,

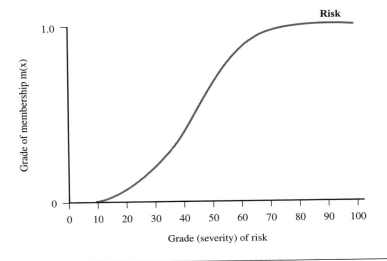

Figure 4.10 The psychometric *Risk* fuzzy set.

use or produce fuzzy sets that correspond to concepts unsupported by any measured data. Such fuzzy sets often represent subjective mappings between a concept and its intensity or degree of realization. Hence, these fuzzy sets use a psychometric scaling for their domain. Psychometric (or nonmeasured) fuzzy sets include a broad range of concepts, such as *Risk*, *Aptitude*, *Aggression*, *Sustainability*, *Indicated*, *Acceptable*, and *Compatible*. Figure 4.10 shows a fuzzy set representation for *Risk*.

The underlying domain must correspond to the granularity of the model. The wider the domain, the larger the degree of evident separation (a matter of resolution or discrimination) between the relative domain points. In the *Risk* example (Figure 4.9), a small movement along the membership function around the slope at the $m[.5]$ region would be difficult to detect if the domain were [0, 10], would be moderately easy to see with range [0, 100], and would produce a large displacement with range [0, 1000]. At the same time, the range of the psychometric scale must be associated with the model's objectives in resolving small or large changes along the horizontal axis.

Collections of Fuzzy Sets (Term Sets)

In fuzzy systems, the underlying numeric (and often categorical and enumeration) variables are broken down into a collection of fuzzy sets. These fuzzy sets ordinarily define the underlying semantics of the variable and

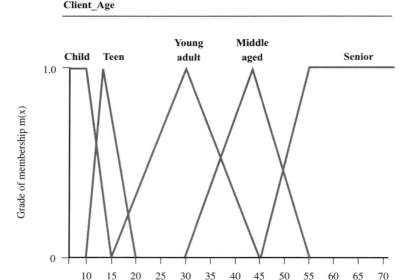

Figure 4.11 The linguistic variables for *Client_Age*.

are the names by which fuzzy rule-based systems refer to the variable itself. Because it is through the underlying fuzzy sets that fuzzy models reference their variables, these sets are often called *linguistic variables*. As an example, Figure 4.11 shows the variable *Client_Age* with its set of underlying fuzzy sets.

Each underlying fuzzy set defines a portion of the variable's domain. But this portion is not uniquely defined. Fuzzy sets overlap as a natural consequence of their elastic boundaries. Such an overlap not only implements a realistic and functional semantic mechanism for defining the nature of a variable when it assumes various data values but provides a smooth and coherent transition from one state to another.

This transition from one semantic state to another can be seen, for example, for the *YoungAdult* and *MiddleAged* fuzzy sets (Figure 4.11). As we move to the right from 30 years old (the point of maximum grade of membership in *YoungAdult*), the degree of membership in *YoungAdult* falls off and the degree of membership in *MiddleAged* begins to increase. Between 30 and 45 years old an individual is, to some degree, both a young adult and middle aged. When they are close to 30, their membership in the middle-aged concept is very small, and when then they are close to

45 their membership in the young adult concept is very small (and goes to zero at both of these end points). As we move further to the right, the individual's compatibility with the idea of middle aged begins to fall off and they become more and more representative of a senior citizen.

Hedges: Fuzzy Set Transformers

In keeping with their use as semantic descriptors, fuzzy sets can be modified through a family of adjectives known as hedges. A hedge acts on a fuzzy set in the same way an adjective acts on a noun (or other adjective) in English, by amplifying or otherwise modifying the noun's meaning. Hedges are used to:

- Turn crisp values into fuzzy numbers
- Increase or decrease the expectancy of a fuzzy number
- Intensify or dilute the membership function of a fuzzy set
- Change the shape of a fuzzy set through contrasts and restrictions

Hedges are used in fuzzy models, especially rule-based models, to dynamically create new fuzzy sets and change the meaning of linguistic variables. In this way, new fuzzy sets can be dynamically created and existing fuzzy sets can be temporarily modified in ways that give the underlying linguistic variable a different meaning or intention. A hedge changes the shape of a fuzzy set in a predictable way according to six broad classes of actions.

- *Approximation:* Increases or decreases the expectancy of a fuzzy number. When applied to a scalar, an increasing approximation hedge converts the number into a fuzzy number.[3] Approximation hedges include *about, around, near, close to,* and *in vicinity of.*
- *Contrast:* In a method similar to approximation, increases or decreases the membership function's central measure of membership by focusing in the area around the 50% membership space. Examples of contrast hedges include *almost, definitely, positively, generally,* and *usually.*
- *Dilution:* Softens the membership function over the fuzzy set. Dilution weakens the membership constraints on the fuzzy set so that a

---

[3] An ordinary (crisp) number can be viewed as a fuzzy set with an expectancy value of zero. An approximation hedge simply increases this expectancy value.

point on the domain is truer than it would be for the undiluted set. Dilution hedges include *quite*, *rather*, *slightly*, and *somewhat*.

- *Intensification:* Hardens the membership function over the fuzzy set. Intensification strengthens the membership constraints on the fuzzy set so that a point on the domain is less true than it would be for the unintensified set. Intensification hedges include *very* and *extremely*.

- *Negation:* Reverses the truth membership of the fuzzy set. *Not* is the primary hedge for producing the complement of a fuzzy set.

- *Restriction:* Restricts the membership function relative to the shape of the underlying fuzzy set. Restriction hedges include *above*, *below*, *more than*, and *less than*.

For example, Figure 4.12 illustrates the application of the *about, somewhat*, and *very* hedges to a model's unit manufacturing costs (*MfgCost*). The *about* hedge turns the scalar manufacturing costs into a fuzzy number. The *very* intensification hedge reduces the expectancy of the resulting fuzzy number, whereas the *somewhat* dilution hedge increases the expectancy.

As Figure 4.12 also illustrates, hedges are applied according to the ordinary rules of English grammar (from the inside out). The expression *somewhat around MfgCost* is evaluated by first applying (*around*

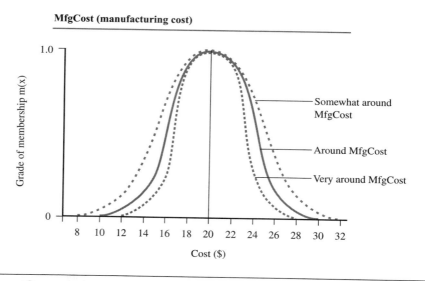

Figure 4.12 Hedges applied to *MfgCost*.

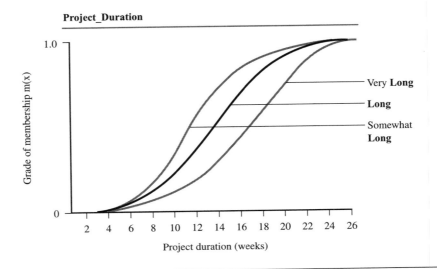

Figure 4.13   Hedges applied to the *Long* fuzzy set.

MfgCosts) to create a fuzzy number (*M*), then by applying *somewhat*(*M*) to produce the final results.

Whereas approximation hedges are limited to bell and triangular fuzzy numbers, most of the other hedge classes can also be applied to fuzzy qualifiers. For example, Figure 4.13 shows the fuzzy sets produced by applying *somewhat* and *very* to the *Long* project duration fuzzy set.

Most hedges involve complex algorithmic processing of the membership function. The basic intensification and dilution hedges, however, simply modify each point on the fuzzy set by applying a power function. Expression 4.7 shows the power function for the intensification hedge.

$$\mu_{intensify(A)}(x_i) = \mu_A^n(x_i) \qquad (4.7)$$

The *very* hedge has $n = 2$ and so simply squares the membership value; *slightly* has $n = 1.2$, and other intensification hedges have stronger or weaker exponents on the membership function. Expression 4.8 shows the power function for the *dilution* hedge.

$$\mu_{dilute(A)}(x_i) = \mu_A^{1/n}(x_i) \qquad (4.8)$$

The *somewhat* edge has $n = 2$ and so simply takes the square root of the membership values. Other forms of the dilution hedge class supply different exponent values and hence take different roots. Power hedges must be used with some care, however, in that the dilution or intensification hedge with larger exponents causes very large and semantically difficult changes to the membership function.

It is well to remember that the philosophy and the mechanics underlying hedges are heuristic in nature. Although we can justify some of the transformations as the products of an intuitive feel for the final results, there is no supporting mathematical or logical apparatus that evolves a hedge operation from fundamental axioms and theorems in fuzzy set theory (see "Further Reading," De Cock).

In rule-based fuzzy systems, the use of hedges provides a valuable and powerful method of performing transformations on a basic vocabulary of linguistic variables. This allows a single fuzzy set (such as *Tall*) to be used in different but related contexts as demanded by the semantics of the model at that time and place (thus, we can speak about *very Tall* without having to create ahead of time a separate fuzzy set that represents the hedged shape of *very Tall*).

Further, the approximation hedges — whether applied explicitly or implicitly — allow fuzzy models to treat all numeric values as fuzzy numbers, thus reducing complexity and allowing a uniform approach to knowledge acquisition and management.

Alpha Cut Thresholds

An alpha cut threshold for fuzzy set A (or A^α) defines a minimum truth membership level for a fuzzy set. All membership values below the alpha cut are considered equivalent to zero. In most cases, the alpha cut is *zero* ($\alpha = 0$). As the alpha cut threshold is increased, the overall support set is reduced. Figure 4.14 shows the shape of the *Long* fuzzy set when the alpha threshold is set to [.35].

Alpha cuts play a crucial role in many fuzzy models by removing unnecessary noise and specifying a degree of strength — often a level of evidence — necessary in the model to effect a correct outcome. Thresholds must be used with care, however, in that very high alpha cuts can have serious deleterious effects on a model's performance. Further, for a collection of overlapping fuzzy sets an alpha cut higher than the crossover point in the overlap will create voids in the UoD — creating areas that are not covered by the support region of any fuzzy set.

Fuzzy Set Operators

Fuzzy logic supports a family of set operators analogous to those available in Boolean logic. Unlike Boolean logic, however, the universe of possible

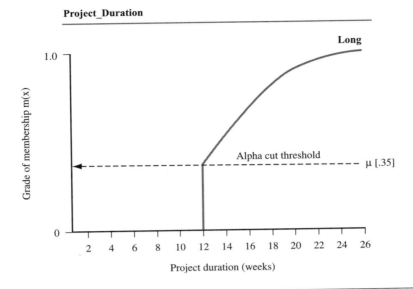

Figure 4.14 Alpha cut threshold applied to fuzzy set *Long*.

TABLE 4.1 The Meanings of Fuzzy Operators

Fuzzy Operator	Definition
And	$\mu_T(x_i) = \min(\mu_A(x_i), \mu_B(x_i))$
Or	$\mu_T(x_i) = \max(\mu_A(x_i), \mu_B(x_i))$
Not	$\mu_T(x_i) = 1 - \mu_A(x_i)$

truth values is nearly infinite. And an infinite spectrum of truth values means that we cannot construct simple 2×2 truth tables. Although there are many types of fuzzy set operators, a basic functional set corresponding to *union*, *intersection*, and *complement* are defined as specified in Table 4.1.

It is clear that the fuzzy set operators parallel their Boolean logic counterparts. We can use the *Client_Age* variable (see Figure 4.11) to examine how these methods apply logical operators to fuzzy sets.

The Fuzzy *And* Operator

Figure 4.15 illustrates the fuzzy region produced by the proposition *YoungAdult And MiddleAged*. This is the region were an age is a member of (compatible with) both the *young adult* and *middle-aged* concepts.

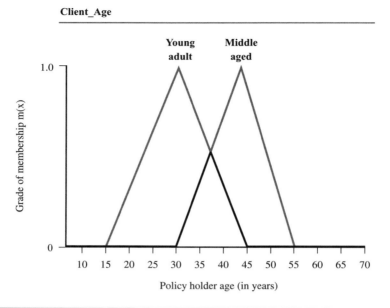

Figure 4.15 The fuzzy *And* operator.

In Figure 4.15, the bold line traces the resulting truth function. The area falls into the triangular region that forms the intersection of both adjoining fuzzy sets.[4]

The Fuzzy *Or* Operator

Figure 4.16 illustrates the fuzzy region produced by the proposition *YoungAdult Or MiddleAged.* This is the region in which an age is a member of (compatible with) either the *young adult* or *middle-aged* concepts.

In Figure 4.16, the bold line traces the resulting truth function. The area, represented by the twin peaks, spans the width of both fuzzy sets.

The Fuzzy *Not* Operator

Figure 4.17 illustrates the fuzzy region produced by the proposition *Not MiddleAged.* This is the region in the linguistics variables supporting *Client_Age* that forms the complement of the *middle-aged* concept.

---

[4] For this reason, the family of fuzzy conjunctive (or intersection) operators is known collectively as a T-norm.

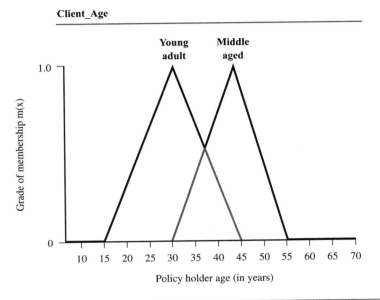

Figure 4.16 The fuzzy *Or* operator.

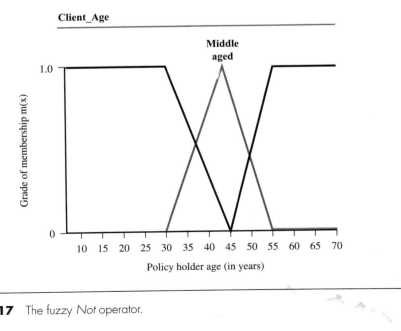

Figure 4.17 The fuzzy *Not* operator.

Notice in Figure 4.17 that a fuzzy *Not* (the negation) does not form a rectangular region from 30 to 55 but is an inverted triangle representing the degree to which each domain value is not a member of the *MiddleAged* fuzzy set.

Consequences of the Negation Operator

As we previously noted, fuzzy set membership curves represent semipermeable boundaries. This means that two or more fuzzy sets often share the same elements — each set having a particular degree of membership for the shared elements. The simplest perspective on this is evident in Figure 4.18 when we look at the fuzzy sets for *Short* and *Tall*.

These two sets are *complements* of each other; that is, *Short* is the negation of the membership function for *Tall*. As you can see, the two sets completely overlap so that each element (*Height* value) has a degree of membership in *Tall* and a degree of membership in *Short*. This agrees with the ambiguity normally found in nature. As an individual's height increases we move down the *Short* membership curve and up the *Tall* membership curve. At any point along the height axis, a value has a partial degree of membership in *Short* and a partial degree of membership in *Tall*.

Complementary fuzzy sets, and by extension fuzzy logic, break Aristotle's law of the excluded middle and noncontradiction. The break is

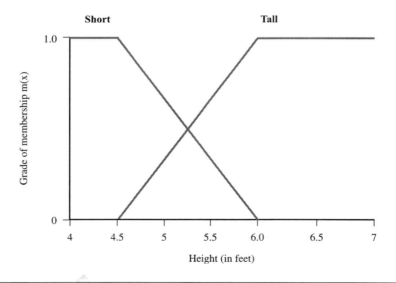

Figure 4.18 *Tall* and *Short* fuzzy sets.

due to the way a complement is constructed in fuzzy logic using the negation operator (see Table 4.1). A complement measures the degree of distance between complete membership (having a truth value of [1]) and the complement set's corresponding membership.

Therefore, when $A[x]$ has a membership of $\mu[.8]$, the complement, $\sim A[x]$, has a membership of $\mu[.2]$. We interpret this to mean that x is strongly a member of fuzzy set A and weakly a member of fuzzy set $\sim A$. In such a case we are — in violation of Aristotle's law and the prevailing law of bivalence in Boolean logic — affirming that x is a member of both sets. We can easily see this in Figure 4.18, across the region in which *Tall* and *Short* overlap. Of course, fuzzy logic and Aristotelian or Boolean logic converge at the extreme edges of the fuzzy set. If $A[x]$ has a membership of [1], then $\sim A[x]$ has a membership of zero.

These are the basic fuzzy set operators. However, they are not the only possible logical operators. A very wide range of additional union, intersection, and negation operators have been defined by several researchers. Further, a class of operators developed by Yager and O'Hagan have adjustable parameters that increase their *Or*-ness as well as their *And*-ness.[5]

4.4   **Review**

This chapter introduces and explores the nature of fuzzy sets. Understanding the nature of fuzzy sets and the principles of fuzzy logic is necessary in order to fully appreciate the fuzzy system techniques discussed in this part of the book. You should now be familiar with the following.

- The difference between Boolean and fuzzy sets
- The results of comparable operations on Boolean and fuzzy sets
- The organization and structure of a fuzzy set
- The various types of fuzzy sets (quantifiers and numbers)
- How variables are broken down into fuzzy sets
- The meaning of overlap in a collection of fuzzy sets
- The use of hedges and alpha cut thresholds

---

[5] Although not explored in this book, the adjustable properties of compensatory operators are ideal for the genetic tuning of fuzzy rule-based models and fuzzy clustering. For comprehensive details on compensatory operators, see Cox in the "Further Reading" section.

Fuzzy sets are only the building blocks of complex analytical systems, such as rule-based expert systems, clustering, and fuzzy database queries. To gain an appreciation of how fuzzy sets are used to build complex models, make policy decisions, and represent knowledge, we need to examine the general principles underlying fuzzy systems. The next chapter introduces these principles through the ideas behind rule-based fuzzy models.

Further Reading

■ Cox, E. *The Fuzzy Systems Handbook* (2d ed.). New York: Academic Press, 1999.

■ De Cock, M. "Representing the Adverb Very in Fuzzy Set Theory," *Proceedings of the ESSLLI Student Session*, Chapter 19, 1999.

■ Lotfi, Z. "Fuzzy Sets," in *Information and Control*, vol. 8, New York: Academic Press, pp. 338–353, 1965.

■ Lotfi, Z. "Outline of a New Approach to the Analysis of Complex Systems and Decision Process," in *IEEE Transactions on Systems, Man, and Cybernetics, SMC-3* pp. 28–44, 1973.

Chapter 5
Fundamental Concepts of Fuzzy Systems

This chapter examines the nature of fuzzy logic as a method of making implications with approximate or vague concepts and continues through the development of approximate reasoning techniques used in fuzzy expert and decision support systems. The nature of fuzzy implication methods is contrasted with probabilities, showing how the two approaches model different aspects of uncertainty. In the final sections of the chapter we look at fuzzy rule-based decision systems and see how they are intimately connected to the process of knowledge discovery and rule induction. This tutorial on fuzzy logic and fuzzy systems provides the foundation needed to understand how knowledge discovery mechanisms such as clustering and rule induction generate operational models.

As we noted in the previous chapter, fuzzy logic is a system of logic. It is not a high-level mechanism such as a neural network or genetic algorithm. Until fuzzy logic is combined with some reasoning framework, such as rule-based expert systems or decision trees, it is simply a way of representing and manipulating data. Fuzzy systems incorporate fuzzy logic into their reasoning mechanism to gain a decided advantage over the crispness of Boolean logic for a wide range of problems. Thus, rule-based expert systems or control systems cast their rules using fuzzy sets and fuzzy operators. Clustering algorithms can use fuzzy set membership as part of their feature partitioning. A neural network might use fuzzy logic as part of its representation strategy or as part of its outcome space. A genetic algorithm can use fuzzy numbers in its genome representation, or fuzzy logic as a part of its "goodness of fit" evaluation. In each of these cases the use of fuzzy logic provides a high degree of flexibility and robustness in the underlying model. As a comprehensive example that introduces a wide spectrum of fuzzy knowledge representation and reasoning features, this chapter examines the nature of fuzzy rule-based models.

5.1 **The Vocabulary of Fuzzy Systems**

Fuzzy systems also have a rich vocabulary of unfamiliar terms. The vocabulary is occasionally difficult to understand because, in addition to terms unique to fuzzy systems, it combines terms from conventional system theory as well as expert and decision support systems and often uses them in a completely different way. Thus, on top of the vocabulary of fuzzy logic, we now need to understand such concepts as aggregation, defuzzification, and correlation as they apply to fuzzy system.

Once more, this is not a complete dictionary of all the terms in fuzzy systems. A preview, however, of the fundamental vocabulary terms at the beginning of this chapter will make reading and understanding the material much easier. It is not always possible, while maintaining an uncluttered and coherent discussion of fuzzy systems, to insure that every term is introduced before it is used. Many of these terms, of course, will be discussed in greater depth later in this and subsequent chapters.

Aggregation

The process of combining the outcome fuzzy sets in a rule is called *aggregation*. As an example, when two rules such as

> *if x is Y then z is R*
> *if w is A then z is T*

are executed, the fuzzy sets R and T are aggregated to produce the current representation for the outcome variable z (which is also represented as an under-generation fuzzy set). Aggregation is done by either adding the fuzzy set membership functions together or by taking the maximum value across their combined membership functions.

Alpha Cut Threshold

An *alpha cut threshold* truncates the membership function of a fuzzy set or the truth value of a fuzzy rule's predicate at a specific truth value. Any value that falls below the alpha cut threshold is equivalent to zero. Alpha cuts come in two forms: *Strong* (the comparison is less than) and *Weak* (the comparison is less than or equal).

Approximate (or Fuzzy) Reasoning

The general term for a rule-based reasoning process incorporating fuzzy sets, hedges, fuzzy operators, and a set of decomposition rules is called *approximate reasoning*.

Conditional Fuzzy Rule

A conditional rule is executed only when the premise (or predicate) of the rule is true. Thus, in a rule such as **if** *a is Z* **then** *b is Y*, the outcome expression *b is Y* is only evaluated when the premise (or predicate) *a is Z* is true. See also "Unconditional Fuzzy Rule."

Consequent Fuzzy Set

A fuzzy set that appears on the right-hand side of an outcome expression and is aggregated with the outcome fuzzy set is called the *consequent fuzzy set*. In the rule **if** *a is Z* **then** *b is Y*, *Y* is the consequent fuzzy set. The consequent fuzzy set is usually one of the fuzzy sets in the term set associated with the outcome variable (that is, *Y* is one of the fuzzy sets associated with *b*).

Correlation

The process of adjusting the height of the consequent fuzzy set based on the truth of the rule's premise is called *correlation*. Thus, in the rule **if** *a is Z* **then** *b is Y*, the height of the consequent fuzzy set *Y* (which directly affects its contribution to the outcome variable *b*) is reduced by the amount of truth in the fuzzy proposition *a is Z*. Consequent fuzzy sets are adjusted in two ways: by truncating the fuzzy set at the truth of the premise or by scaling the fuzzy set using the truth of the premise. Correlation is one of the primary mechanisms for adjusting the outcome of a fuzzy knowledge base using the amount of evidence in the rules.

Defuzzification

The process of converting the under-generation outcome fuzzy set to a single representative value is called *defuzzification*. For example, when a collection of fuzzy rules such as

if x is Y then z is R
if w is A then z is T

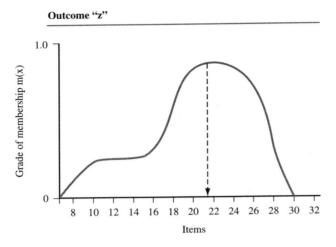

Figure 5.1   Defuzzifying an outcome fuzzy set.

are executed, the outcome variable z must be defuzzified in order to resolve a single crisp value for the variable. There are many ways of defuzzifying an outcome fuzzy set. The most common approach, illustrated in Figure 5.1, is by using the center of gravity (or centroid) of the outcome set.

The center of gravity is actually the weighted average value of the membership function. Note that not all fuzzy models use defuzzification to find the value of an outcome fuzzy set. In many models, the outcome fuzzy set is used as the input to another model (the outcome of one model that determines the estimated disposable income for a class of buyers might be input to another model that handles cross marketing and special-offer sales to customers based on their spending habits and probable income).

Fuzzy Associative Memory (FAM)

A FAM is a fuzzy knowledge base (KB). It is a compact way of representing fuzzy rules used primarily in control applications (but it also has its uses in fuzzy information modeling as a way of representing rules discovered during the rule induction process). A FAM can be visualized as an N-dimensional "cube." Each edge represents the fuzzy sets associated with a particular independent variable. The region formed by the intersection of each fuzzy set on each edge is the fuzzy set that contributes to the outcome or dependent variable. Fuzzy associative memory representations are not only very compact, they also provide a very high speed way of executing rules that do not involve hedges, subscripts, and expressions.

Fuzzification

The process of finding the membership value of a scalar (a number) in a fuzzy set is called *fuzzification*. Fuzzy rule-based models work by fuzzifying the input values. In the rule **if** *a is Z* **then** *b is Y*, the membership of *a* in *Z* is found and this truth is used as part of the premise evaluation.

Knowledge Base

A collection of fuzzy rules representing a single model is called a *knowledge base* (or simply a KB). A fuzzy knowledge base consists of both conditional and unconditional rules. All rules are run effectively in parallel to create the final under-generation fuzzy set associated with each outcome variable.

Outcome Fuzzy Set and Variable

Each solution (or dependent) variable associated with a fuzzy model is also an outcome variable for one or more rules in the model's knowledge base. Every outcome variable has an associated outcome fuzzy set that is created through the aggregation of consequent fuzzy sets for each rule that contributes to the outcome variable. In the rule **if** *a is Z* **then** *b is Y*, *b* is the outcome variable and is an outcome fuzzy set. When all the rules that contribute to *b* have been executed, the underlying (or under-generation) fuzzy set for *b* is defuzzified, and the resulting value assigned to the variable *b*.

Rule

A *rule* specifies a fuzzy relationship. There are two types of rules: conditional and unconditional. A conditional rule is executed only when the premise (or predicate) of the rule is true. Thus, in a rule such as **if** *a is Z* **then** *b is Y*, the outcome expression *b is Y* is only evaluated when the premise (or predicate) *a is Z* is true. An unconditional rule is always executed. Unconditional rules, such as *c is X*, state an underlying fuzzy relationship and are always executed before any conditional rules are executed.

Unconditional Fuzzy Rule

An unconditional rule is always executed. Unconditional rules, such as *c is X*, state an underlying fuzzy relationship and are always executed before any fuzzy conditional rules. A model with unconditional fuzzy rules provides a supporting framework that can supply an answer when none of the conditional rules is executed.

Under-generation Fuzzy Set

Each outcome variable in a fuzzy rule-based model has an associated fuzzy set of the same name. This fuzzy set is initially empty but is built by each rule that contributes to the value of the outcome variable. As a result, the outcome fuzzy set is "under generation" during the execution of the fuzzy rules. The effect of this under-generation process is to simulate the workings of parallel rule execution: an outcome variable in a fuzzy model does not have a value until all rules have been executed and their consequent fuzzy set added to the outcome variable's fuzzy set.

5.2 Fuzzy Rule-based Systems: An Overview

A fuzzy rule-based system is, in a general sense, a fuzzy expert system. The expertise can be derived from subject matter experts or extracted from data through a rule induction process. The rules represent nonprocedural statements of knowledge in the form of *if-then* sentences. These rules reference a collection of local variables that in turn references a collection of fuzzy sets that define control regions over the variable's domain. The architecture of a rule-based system is relatively uncomplicated. Figure 5.2 provides a general perspective on the principal components.

All elements of the system's knowledge are stored in a central repository (the KB). The actual reasoning process of the system is handled by an inference engine. The processes underlying a rule-based fuzzy system are, roughly, as follows.

- The inference engine collects and executes rules.
- Rules evaluate problem states and, as a group, set the value for one or more outcome variables.
- To evaluate states and set outcome variables, rules reference variables and their associated fuzzy sets.

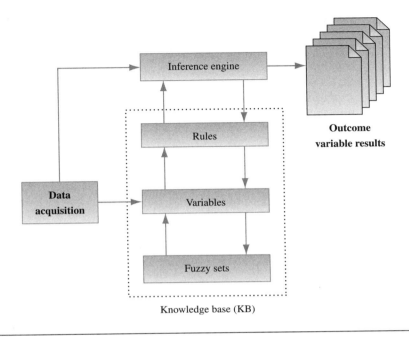

Figure 5.2   The principal components of a fuzzy rule-based system.

- Variables contain the current set of problem-specific data. These data are acquired in one of two ways — regularly and automatically from a collection of external sensors or from a data acquisition process invoked by the inference engine (such as starting a separate backward chaining inference process to find the value of a variable that appears in the outcome of some other rules).

- When all rules have been executed, the inference engine makes the values of the outcome variable available to the application that invoked the inference engine.

If the inference engine is part of a continuously running system, the knowledge base is returned to its initial state, a new set of data values is acquired, and the reasoning process is started again.

We will return to a more detailed discussion of a knowledge base later. Now we need to explore the nature of rules and how variables are organized into a collection of fuzzy sets. This exploration prepares the way for a more extensive discussion of fuzzy reasoning: how rules are used to solve a particular problem.

Fuzzy Rules

A fuzzy rule-based reasoning system uses a collection of rules to accumulate evidence and generate the proper shape of a fuzzy set associated with a solution variable. Rules take knowledge, usually from subject matter experts (SMEs) and express this knowledge in the form of conditional and unconditional rules. These rules and their associated variable definitions are stored in a KB. The KB is then used by the machine reasoning system (called an inference engine) to compute the final value for one or more outcome variables.

Conditional Rules

Nearly all rules in a conventional fuzzy KB are conditional. Conditional rules are in the form of *if-then* and, without exploring the complete semantics of the possible rule language, have the general form

if *premise* **then** *outcome.*

Where:

premise   (also called the predicate or antecedent) is one or more fuzzy propositions connected by the *And* or *Or* operator. A fuzzy proposition is a relationship between a variable and a fuzzy quantity. The following is an example.

If **a is Y and b is X** then c is Z

The rule premise is the expression shown in bold. The fuzzy quantity can be a fuzzy number or one of its underlying fuzzy sets (such as *project_length is Long*, where *project_length* is a variable in the model and *Long* is one of the fuzzy sets associated with this variable).

outcome   is a fuzzy proposition that assigns a fuzzy value to a solution variable. The following is an example.

If a is Y and b is X then **c is Z**

The rule outcome is the expression shown in bold. The outcome contains an outcome or *solution* variable (in this case, *c*) and a *consequent* fuzzy set. Every outcome variable in a fuzzy model is represented by an "under-generation" fuzzy set created and maintained automatically by the reasoning mechanism. This outcome fuzzy set contains the aggregation of all rules that update the associated outcome variable.

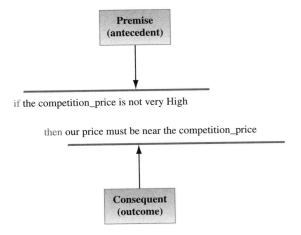

if the competition_price is not very High

then our price must be near the competition_price

Figure 5.3   Parts of a fuzzy rule.

Conditional rules contribute to a solution for a particular variable by reshaping the consequent fuzzy set and then combining it with the outcome variable's under-generation fuzzy set. Thus, the final outcome reflects the amount of evidence (the amount of truth) in each of the supporting conditional rules.

A rule is called conditional when its execution is predicated on the truth value of its premise. For a fuzzy rule to be executed, the premise must be true.[1] Conditional fuzzy rules can often be quite complex, involving intersection and union operations as well as dynamically created fuzzy sets (such as fuzzy numbers created by approximation hedges). Figure 5.3 illustrates, using a rule from a product pricing model, the major structural parts of a conditional rule.

If we examine the lexical organization of a conditional fuzzy rule a bit closer, many features of its fuzzy logic support become apparent. Figure 5.4 steps down one more layer and highlights the various technical components of the rule.

As complicated as this rule appears it is still a simple version of the posit *if a is Y then c is Z*. The antecedent expression *not very High* produces a fuzzy set (*Y*) and the outcome expression *near the competition_price* produces a fuzzy number centered around the current

---

[1] Actually, a fuzzy rule can also have its own truth threshold (similar to the alpha cut threshold on a fuzzy set). In order for a rule to execute, the degree of truth in the premise must be equal to or greater than this rule truth threshold.

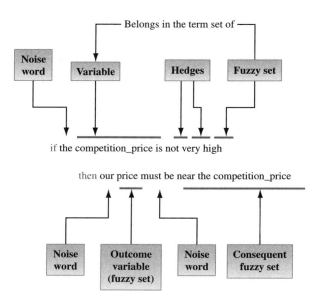

Figure 5.4 Detailed parts of a fuzzy rule.

value for the variable *competition_price* (*Z*). Thus, the rule is basically **if** *competition_price* is Y **then** *price* is Z.

Unconditional Rules

An unconditional fuzzy rule establishes the default support space for an outcome variable. The rule is cast in the form of the outcome proposition *outcome*, with the same syntax as the *outcome* statement in a conditional rule.

An unconditional rule, as the name implies, is always executed (and all unconditional rules for a specified outcome variable are executed before any of the conditional rules for the same outcome variable). Generally, an unconditional rule contributes to the solution only if none of the conditional rules fires or none of the conditional rules has a premise truth greater than the maximum truth of any unconditional rule.

5.3 Variable Decomposition into Fuzzy Sets

In the previous section on the fundamentals of fuzzy logic, the ways in which variables are decomposed into fuzzy sets were briefly discussed.

We now take up this issue in more detail, exploring how fuzzy systems can segment variables into various types of fuzzy sets and how these fuzzy sets, known as linguistic variables, are used as part of the basic rule language. As we will see, there are three principal structural organizations, as follows.

- *Semantic decomposition*, in which the fuzzy sets represent true linguistic terms within the vocabulary framework of the model (terms such as *fast*, *high*, *elevated*, *expensive*, *moderate*, and so forth).
- *Control decomposition*, in which the fuzzy sets represent rates of change and degrees of movement and similar physical measurements often expressed at positive and negative displacements.
- *Data space partitioning*, in which the fuzzy sets represent arbitrary or statistically derived overlapping interval slices in the variable's domain.

Each type of variable decomposition or partitioning is associated with a particular type of model and, although not mutually exclusive, they are seldom found together in a single model. Thus, as we will see, how a variable is decomposed depends to a great extent on the actual purpose of the model.

Before examining variable decomposition, it is important to understand an important fact about fuzzy systems: there are no universal fuzzy sets. All fuzzy sets are context dependent. Thus, the concept *Long*, for example, is different for different concepts (a long project, a long river, a long coast line, and so on). Even the same fuzzy concept can have different representations. The idea of what constitutes a long project may differ within an organization from department to department and will certainly differ between small, large, and very large enterprises and federal government agencies. Thus, for semantic and control decompositions, one of the chief responsibilities of a knowledge engineer is eliciting domain and semantic information from SMEs in order to precisely define the underlying fuzzy sets for each variable.

Semantic-based Fuzzy Sets

Nearly all fuzzy expert and decision systems use semantic fuzzy sets. These fuzzy sets establish the working vocabulary of the model. As we will see, fuzzy rules establish relationships by mapping a variable to one or more of its underlying fuzzy sets. These underlying fuzzy sets, the linguistic

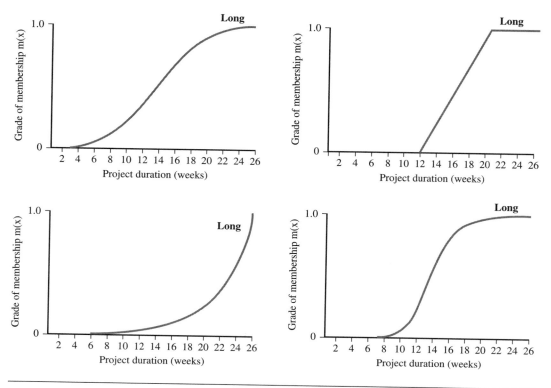

Figure 5.5 Possible shapes for *Long* project.

variables, constitute the vocabulary for the rule language. The semantics are reflected in the shape of the membership curve. Thus, the concept of a *Long* project might have different membership curves depending on the culture of the organization or how the set is used in a particular model. Figure 5.5 illustrates several possible (but hardly exhaustive) fuzzy sets for the idea of a *Long* project.

The differences in the possible shapes for the *Long* fuzzy set reflect the model builder's expectation of how a user of the model will ultimately view the concept of *Long*. This is expressed both in the choice of the membership function shape and in the range of the underlying domain. In all of the *Long* fuzzy sets shown in Figure 5.5 a project is unambiguously long after 26 weeks and generally considered fairly long after 18 to 20 weeks (although the exact rate of change over the membership function is different).

The choice of a fuzzy set membership function is not, however, arbitrary. In a broad sense, fuzzy sets reflect the semantics of a particular concept. The mapping between the domain and the grade of membership must roughly coincide with the actual meaning of the overlying concept. Also, each fuzzy set used in a model has at least one point with a membership value of 0 and at least one point with a membership value of 1. These sets are called *normal fuzzy sets*.

In a fuzzy model, many of the independent and all of the dependent variables are decomposed into a collection of overlapping fuzzy sets. Each of the fuzzy sets has a label (or name). The collection of fuzzy sets associated with a variable is called the *term set*. Each fuzzy set in a term set is also known as a linguistic variable. In a fuzzy model, rules reference a variable through one or more linguistic variables rather than through specific data values. For example, Figure 5.6 shows the term set (or linguistic variables) associated with the variable *Client_Age*.

Each of the fuzzy sets associated with *Client_Age* assigns a name to a region of the underlying domain. These names are used in a rule as part of the mechanisms that establish a degree of membership relation between the current value of *Client_Age* and one or more of the fuzzy sets. Given a *Client_Age* of 52, therefore there are two non-zero linguistic variable regions: *MiddleAged(μ[.43])* and *Senior(μ[.57])*. These relations are used

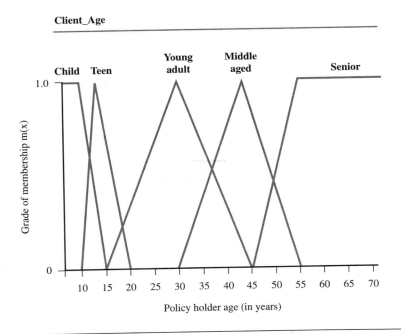

Figure 5.6   Term set for variable *Client_Age*.

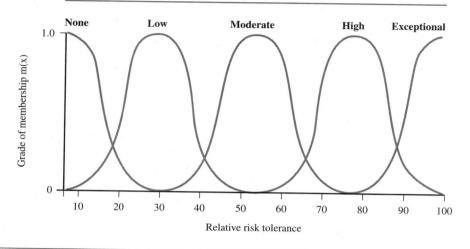

Figure 5.7 The risk tolerance term set.

in rules to determine the composite truth of the premise and to modify the outcome fuzzy region.

Suppose, for example, we have a model connecting age with risk tolerance. This might be expressed functionally as shown in Expression 5.1.

$$y_{risk} = f(x_{age}) \tag{5.1}$$

Risk tolerance is the dependent variable, and *age* is the independent variable. In a fuzzy model we need to create the *RiskTolerance* variable and define its underlying collection of fuzzy sets. Figure 5.7 shows one possible term set for the dependent variable.

These underlying linguistic variables provide the vocabulary for our rules. Through them we express the relationships between data and semantics. In the simplest form, a rule consists of a set of premise relationships and an outcome relationship. For example, consider the following code fragment.

```
If Client_Age is MiddleAged or ClientAge is Senior
    Then Risk_Tolerance is Low;
```

Fuzzy rules can also manipulate the underlying linguistic variables in ways that create new fuzzy regions and often subsume one or more term set members. The role of linguistic variable transformer is played by hedges.

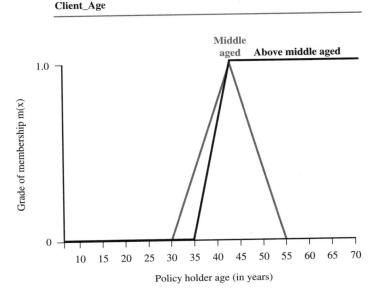

Figure 5.8 The *Above MiddleAged* fuzzy set.

For example, consider a rule that is similar in actual meaning and function as the previous rule,

```
If Client_Age is above MiddleAged
    Then Risk_Tolerance is Low;
```

The *above* hedge creates a new fuzzy set that overlays the *MiddleAged* term and absorbs the *Senior* term. Figure 5.8 illustrates how this hedge provides the rule language with the ability to manipulate the underlying terms of a variable.

Thus, semantic decomposition breaks down the domain of a variable into a collection of overlapping fuzzy sets that gives each region of the domain a specific name associated with some aspect of the model's functionality. These fuzzy sets are called linguistic variables because they allow linguistic rather than algebraic manipulation of the model's control space.

Control Fuzzy Sets

A fuzzy control system is, in effect, a fuzzy expert system. The fuzzy sets in a control system, however, usually take the form of variations in the

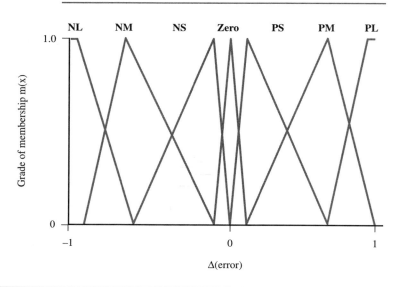

Figure 5.9 Term set for a *Change_In_Error* variable.

physical parameters and states of the plant (a "plant" is an engineering term defining the actual process being controlled). These sets reflect such elements as current flow, angular displacement, the rate of change in angular moment, the rate of change in measured error, and so forth. In the case of control systems, the fuzzy sets have less to do with the semantics of the model than with critical areas of control and degrees of granularity. For example, Figure 5.9 illustrates the underlying fuzzy sets for a *Change_In_Error* variable.

The *Change_In_Error* variable measures the difference in the error for successive executions of the controller. The normalized error falls in the domain [−1, 1]. There are seven fuzzy sets measuring this change: *Zero*, *PS* (a small positive change), *PM* (a medium positive change), *PL* (a large positive change), *NS* (a small negative change), *NM* (a medium negative change), and *NL* (a large negative change). Increasing the number of fuzzy sets increases the granularity of the variable and generally increases the precision of the controller. This increase, however, comes at a price because the number of rules in a system increases exponentially with the number of fuzzy sets associated with each of the control variables.

Like conventional expert systems, the shape and distribution of the fuzzy sets underlying control variables must correspond to the way in

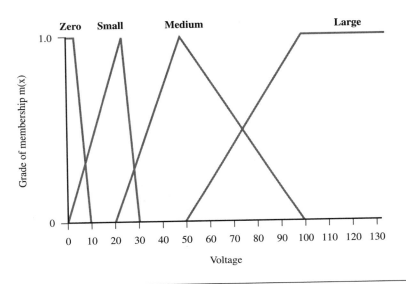

Figure 5.10   The term set for *Current_Flow*.

which control is expressed in the model. This level of control is expressed in the number of fuzzy sets and their degree of overlap. Figure 5.10 illustrates this idea through the *Current_Flow* variable.

The asymmetry of the *Current_Flow* term set represents the way the controller focuses on critical measures. The shape of the fuzzy sets and their overlap control the transition between one control state and the next. In this, fuzzy controllers and fuzzy expert systems with their semantic sets share a common architecture. In general, however, fuzzy controllers represent a much more restricted space in the universe of fuzzy systems. Fuzzy controllers typically use triangular fuzzy sets (due to their high-speed interpolation properties), do not employ hedges to transform their fuzzy sets, and do not use an alpha cut threshold to constrain the truth of fuzzy sets or rule predicate truth values.

Data-space-partitioning Fuzzy Sets

Fuzzy data mining, exploration, clustering, and ranking methods often decompose variables into either arbitrary or statistical fuzzy regions in

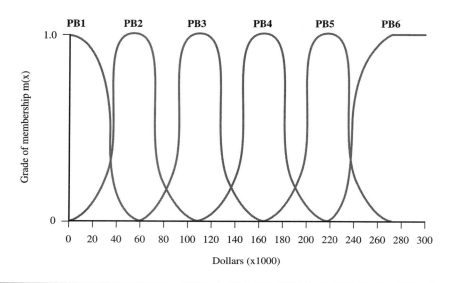

Figure 5.11 An arbitrary partitioning of the *Project_Budget* variable.

order to "slice" the data space into overlapping regions of similar elements. Where partitioning is based on arbitrary segmentation or statistics, the names associated with the underlying fuzzy sets are also arbitrary. These names simply reflect a fuzzy partitioning space. Figure 5.11 illustrates the arbitrary segmentation of the *Project_Budget* variable.

In the case of arbitrary partitioning, names are also assigned to the fuzzy region in a somewhat arbitrary manner, often by abbreviating the variable name and assigning a monotonic numbering sequence. Arbitrary partitioning often follows a naming convention similar to that of a control variable, (such as *Zero*, *P1*, *P2*, *P3*, and so forth) for the positive region of the domain.

Variables can also be partitioned according to their statistical properties. In this case, the segmentation is not completely arbitrary but is based on the statistical distribution properties of the variable. If we compute the average budget of all completed projects for the enterprise along with its standard deviation, Figure 5.12 shows one likely way of partitioning the *Project_Budget* variable.

A fuzzy region is centered on the mean of the project budget distribution. The width of the fuzzy region is usually some fractional multiple of the standard deviation. Partitioning is then accomplished by moving out

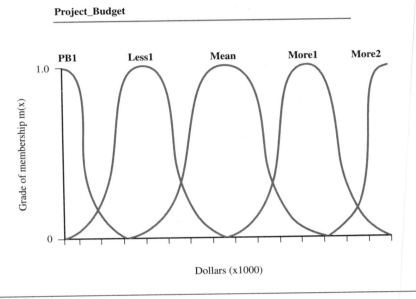

Figure 5.12 A statistical partitioning of the *Project_Budget* variable.

to the left and right of the mean fuzzy set. The width of these new fuzzy sets can also be some fraction or ratio-biased proportion of the standard deviation. More advanced statistical partitioning techniques also take into account the skew (symmetry) and kurtosis (flatness) of the distribution.

5.4 **A Fuzzy Knowledge Base: The Details**

As we noted in the introduction, a collection of variables, fuzzy sets, and fuzzy rules is called a knowledge base (or KB). The KB is a representation of a particular problem space. However, a KB is generally not a complete representation of a problem. Rather, a collection of KBs may cooperate to form a solution to complex problems. In this section we examine the organization of a KB in more detail, the nature of rule explosions in a KB, and the way in which fuzzy rules are executed in a fuzzy KB.

Knowledge Base Architectures

KBs are containers; they encapsulate the data definitions (variables) and solution heuristics (rules) necessary to solve a set of outcomes associated

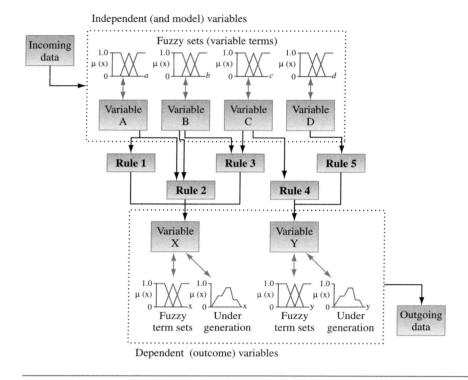

Figure 5.13 The internal organization of a KB.

with the problem. As Figure 5.13 illustrates, a KB contains all independent (basically, input) and dependent (basically, outcome) variables, as well as the rules that connect the inputs to the outcomes.

As a general principle, when a fuzzy KB contains only conditional rules the order of the rules in the KB is unimportant. This is because in a fuzzy model all rules for a particular outcome variable are effectively run in parallel. However, if the KB contains unconditional rules, these must appear and be executed before any of the conditional rules. The order in which the rules appear in the physical KB, however, are not the order in which they are executed. It is the inference engine that collects and orders the rules in the proper firing sequence. Listing 5.1 shows a typical fuzzy KB for a business application (in this case, the product pricing model we will shortly examine in much more detail).

This knowledge base creates a set of fuzzy sets. These will later be assigned to variables as their underlying term set. Each variable is then defined. The *price* variable is an outcome variable and is public

```
#
#------------------------------------------------------------
# This is the standard retail pricing model. It runs in a
# full fuzzy environment(parallel rule processing,
# evidence aggregation, and relaxation of Aristotle's
# excluded middle [non-contradiction] law).
#------------------------------------------------------------
#
kb pricingPolicy

fuzzyset high   shape(linearup)   range(0,48) surface(0,48);;
fuzzyset low    shape(lineardown) range(0,48) surface(0,48);;

variable public outcome   price
    datatype(double) range(0,48) fuzzysets(low,high);;
variable        mfgCosts
    datatype(double) range(0,48) getFrom(costs,MfgCost);;
variable        compPrice
    datatype(double) range(0,48) fuzzysets(low,high)
    getFrom(costs,CompCost);;
#
#------------------------------------------------------------
# These rules establish the new product pricing policy.
#------------------------------------------------------------
#
rule rule1 our price must be high;;
rule rule2 our price must be low;;
rule rule3 our price must be around 2*mfgCosts;;
rule rule4 if the compPrice is not very high
      then our price should be around the compPrice;;

end pricingPolicy;;
```

Listing 5.1   The product pricing KB.

(it can be accessed outside the KB). *MfgCosts* (manufacturing costs) and *compPrice* (competition price) are independent variables with associated specifications on how to retrieve their data values. Each variable is a double-precision floating point number.

Because rules connect the inputs and outputs (i.e., they transform the dimensionality of the input space into a new dimensional space representing the outcome space), the amount of detail invested in the term sets associated with each variable plays an important part in the precision of the model. This granularity also plays an important part in the complexity and corresponding execution speed of the rules. This brings us to another property of the KB: its degree of granularity and specificity. These properties are related to the number of rules needed in a KB to represent a particular problem space.

Rule Specificity and Growth Explosion

This problem space should be specific and reasonably bounded in order to build an efficient, robust, and focused KB system. This tends to be particularly true of fuzzy systems, in that the rules are effectively run in parallel and the number of rules increases very rapidly with the number of total fuzzy sets. In fact, to cover the data space for N independent variables the total rule count (R^c) is found by Expression 5.2.

$$R^c = \prod_{i=0}^{N} m_{v_i} \tag{5.2}$$

Here, m_{v_i} is the number of fuzzy sets for the i-th variable. The finer the level of fuzzy set granularity underlying each of the model variables, the larger the number of rules necessary to cover the decision space. We can see this more clearly with an extension of the risk tolerance model (see Expression 5.3) to include a client's annual income. In this case we want to model the functional relationship.

$$y_{risk} = f(x_{age}, z_{income}) \tag{5.3}$$

Here, risk tolerance is a function of the client age and income. As Figure 5.14 shows, the independent variable *Client_Income* is decomposed into a number of fuzzy sets defining a relationship between the client income and the model builder's perception of client wealth.

With the fuzzy sets associated with client age and client income defined, as well as our scaling for relative degree of risk, we can specify a rule-based fuzzy model that predicts a client's risk tolerance. *Client_Age* has five underlying fuzzy sets and *Client_Income* has six fuzzy sets. Applying Expression 5.4,

$$R^c = \prod_{i=0}^{N} m_{v_i} = 5 \times 6 = 30, \tag{5.4}$$

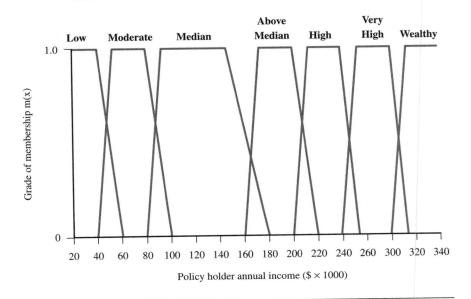

Figure 5.14 The term set for *Client_Income*.

we see that if all rules are expressed in the form

If *Client_Age* is **X** and *Client_Income* is **Y** then *RiskTolerance* is **Z**

a minimum of 30 rules is necessary to cover all fuzzy relationships in the model. This can also be visualized as an M × N table, called a fuzzy associative memory (FAM). Table 5.1 outlines the general organization of the FAM for the risk tolerance model with a few of the possible rules.

As a measure of the exponential increase in rules with the dimensionality of the data, this equation is more applicable to control systems. In business and technical models, the use of hedges, unconditional rule constraints, and default values often means that although the model builder might decompose a variable into a number of fuzzy sets only a subset of these linguistic variables is used in the rules.

Fuzzy Rule Execution

A KB is the representation of a problem. To derive a problem solution the rules in the KB must be executed. Fuzzy rules are, in effect, executed in parallel. This is due to the way the outcomes are constructed from

TABLE 5.1 The Risk Tolerance Fuzzy Associative Memory

		Child	Teen	Young Adult	Middle Aged	Senior
				Client_Age		
Client_Income	Low	None	Low	Moderate	Low	None
	Moderate	None	Moderate	Moderate	Low	None
	Median	Low	Moderate	Moderate	Low	None
	Above Median	Low	High	High	Moderate	Low
	High					
	Very High					
	Wealthy					

each contributing rule. Before all rules for a specific outcome have been executed, the outcome variable does not have a value. This means that the outcome variable of one fuzzy rule cannot appear in the premise of another rule in the same KB.[2] For example, the two rules shown in Figure 5.15 are not allowed.

The second rule cannot use *weight* in its premise because *weight*, as an outcome variable, is still undergoing generation. This is the result of the way in which evidence is collected and used in a fuzzy KB system. Figure 5.16 shows the overall way in which rules are collected and then executed to produce the outcomes for a KB.

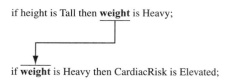

if height is Tall then **weight** is Heavy;

if **weight** is Heavy then CardiacRisk is Elevated;

Figure 5.15 Improperly specified rules in a KB.

---

[2] Unless, of course, a knowledge base is organized so that the dependencies between outcome variables that are used as dependent variables in other rules are identified and handled by grouping and evaluating rules in a specific order. This can be done by dividing the KB into a collection of connected Policies (or groups). In essence, however, we have simply created a collection of smaller knowledge bases — the same prohibition in outcome variable used exists in these smaller blocks.

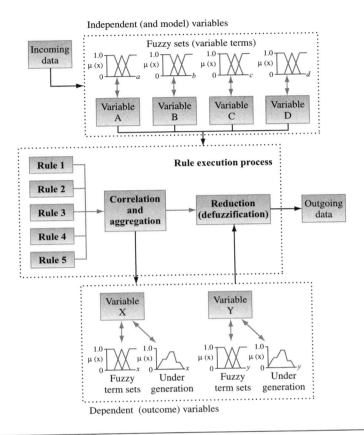

Figure 5.16   Rule execution in a KB.

As Figure 5.16 illustrates, the rules are essentially run in parallel. The consequent fuzzy sets are correlated with the truth of the rule premise, and then this correlated (shape-modified) fuzzy set is aggregated with the current under-generation set of the outcome variable. Finally, in most KB processes each under-generation set is reduced to a single representative value (a process known as *defuzzification*). The mechanism that connects to a knowledge base, runs the rules, and produces all outcomes is called the *inference engine*. The workings of the inference engine are the subject of the next section.

5.5   **The Fuzzy Inference Engine**

A fuzzy inference engine consists of four main components: *assessment*, *correlation*, *aggregation*, and *reduction* (or *defuzzification*). Together,

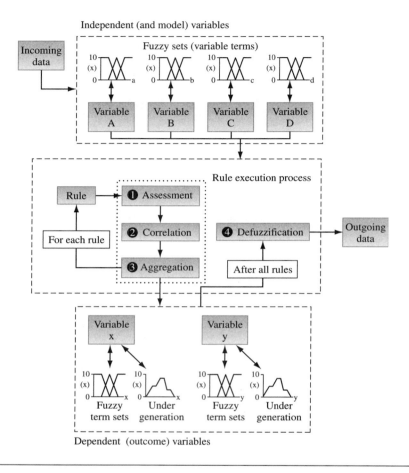

Figure 5.17 The fuzzy inference engine methods.

these facilities process all rules in the KB as if they were executed in parallel. Figure 5.17 depicts further details of KB processing to expose the inner workings of the inference engine.

❶ Assessment

Assessment is the process of gathering initial evidence and determining the truth of the rule antecedent. We assess the amount of evidence in a rule by combining the individual fuzzy propositions in the premise according to their connecting operators (*And* or *Or*). A fuzzy proposition such as *height is Tall* produces a degree of membership (DOM) measure. This is, of course, a measure of the amount of evidence that the value for *height* is considered *Tall*. When the rule premise contains multiple fuzzy propositions, they are combined with *And* and *Or* operators. An *And* takes the minimum of the degrees of membership from two propositions, whereas an *Or* takes the maximum of the degrees of membership. The final evaluation is a truth value measuring the degree of evidence for the rule's antecedent.

❷ **Correlation**

Correlation matches the truth of the premise to the truth of the consequent; that is, the truth of the current rule's consequent cannot be any greater than the implicit truth of the rule's premise. Correlation takes the form of either scaling or truncating the consequent using the premise's truth. As Expression 5.5 shows, scaling multiplies the consequent fuzzy set's membership function (*A*) by the premise's degree of evidence, or truth (*E*).

$$\mu_A[x_i] = \bigvee_{i=0}^{N} \mu_A[x_i] \times E_p \tag{5.5}$$

Truncation, on the other hand, reduces the height of the consequent fuzzy set (*A*) by the limit imposed through the premise's evidence (*E*). Expression 5.6 shows how this function is applied.

$$\mu_A[x_i] = \bigvee_{i=0}^{N} \min(\mu_A[x_i], E_p) \tag{5.6}$$

In all cases, the correlation is done by reducing the truth in the consequent based on the composite truth of the antecedent. This adjusts the consequent using the amount of evidence in the premise.

❸ **Aggregation**

Aggregation updates the current outcome fuzzy set using the correlated consequent fuzzy set. Each rule, in turn, updates the outcome fuzzy set with its own correlated fuzzy sets. There are two methods of aggregating fuzzy sets into the outcome fuzzy set: addition and maximization. Expression 5.7 shows the additive method. The outcome (*O*) and correlated consequent (*A*) fuzzy sets are added together.

$$\mu_O[x_i] = \bigvee_{i=0}^{N} \mu_O[x_i] + \mu_A[x_i] \tag{5.7}$$

The maximization approach, shown in Expression 5.8, in effect takes the union (logical-*Or*) of the outcome and correlated consequent fuzzy sets.

$$\mu_O[x_i] = \overset{N}{\underset{i=0}{\forall}} \max(\mu_O[x_i], \mu_A[x_i]) \tag{5.8}$$

Aggregation is the actual heart of the fuzzy inference engine. Through this process the evidence from each rule is collected and properly applied to the outcome variable. Because every rule in the KB must be run before all evidence is collected, the inference engine, in effect, runs all rules in parallel.

❹ Defuzzification

Defuzzification (the process of reduction) produces a single scalar result from the final outcome fuzzy set. There are many methods of defuzzification. The most common is the centroid (or center of gravity), which is essentially the weighted average of the outcome fuzzy set. Expression 5.9 shows how this is done.

$$x = \frac{\sum_{i=1}^{N} d_i \times \mu_{d_i}}{\sum_{i=1}^{N} \mu_{d_i}} \tag{5.9}$$

Further details on the application of the center-of-gravity method can be found in "The Inverted Pendulum Model" section.

5.6 Inference Engine Approaches

There are two major inference techniques in fuzzy modeling. The first, and perhaps the oldest, is the approach developed in the late 1970s called the Mamdani inference method. The second, developed in the late 1980s and early 1990s by Bart Kosko, is called the Standard Additive Model (SAM). Both of these methods will be illustrated in the section "Running a Fuzzy Model." However, the SAM has evolved as the conventional method of exploiting fuzzy rules. The SAM is part of a general proof that fuzzy systems are universal approximators; that is, they can approximate any continuous mathematical function to an arbitrary degree of precision.

The Mamdani Inference Method

Perhaps first formalized by Ebrahim Mamdani of King's College, London, in the early 1970s, the Mamdani method is one of the earliest working inference techniques. The fuzzy inferencing algorithm for applying this technique is relatively simple and straightforward, and looks as follows.

```
Start:
Set Outcome Fuzzy Set (F_o) to Empty³
For Each Rule
    Evaluate truth of the premise (E_p)
    Truncate consequent fuzzy set at E_p giving F_c
    If Outcome Fuzzy Set (F_o) is Empty
        Set F_o = F_c
    Else
        Set F_o = max(F_o,F_c)
End For Each
Set Outcome Value (V_o) = defuzzify(F_o)
Goto Start
```

The Mamdani method is often called the min-max inference technique. This name comes from the method of correlation and aggregation: the consequent fuzzy set is truncated (or *minimized*) to the truth of the premise, whereas the outcome fuzzy set is set to the *maximum* of the current outcome fuzzy set and the truncated consequent fuzzy set.

The Standard Additive Model

Professor Bart Kosko, in his influential and groundbreaking book *Neural Networks and Fuzzy Systems: A Dynamical Systems Approach to Machine Intelligence*, provides the mathematical foundations for the SAM. The fuzzy inferencing algorithm for applying this technique, as follows, is also relatively simple and straightforward.

```
Start:
Set Outcome Fuzzy Set (F_o) to Empty
For each Rule
    Evaluate truth of the premise (E_p)
    Scale consequent fuzzy set using E_p giving F_c
    Set F_o = Add(F_o,F_c)
End For each
If max(F_o) > 1
    Normalize(F_o)
Set Outcome Value (V_o) = defuzzify(F_o)
Goto Start
```

---

[3] An *empty* fuzzy set is one with all of its membership values set to zero (0).

This method differs from the Mamdani approach in a few critical areas. First, the consequent fuzzy set is scaled (using the truth of the premise) rather than truncated. Second, the outcome fuzzy set is constructed by adding the correlated consequent to the current outcome. Because the outcome fuzzy set is created by adding together the consequent fuzzy set, its membership values for a single domain value may exceed [1]. If you are using the center-of-gravity defuzzification, you do not need to normalize the outcome fuzzy set. Otherwise, you will have to normalize the outcome fuzzy set to ensure that the membership values are in the range [0, 1].

5.7 Running a Fuzzy Model

Fuzzy models take measurements of the outside world, fuse these with the current model state, and using a set of transformation rules produce an estimate of a new model state. Data values from each independent variable are used to find and execute multiple rules in the model. These rules combine possible states of the outcome (also called the dependent) variable based on the degree of truth or evidence in each rule's antecedent. When all rules have been fired, the final outcome fuzzy region is reduced, by a process called defuzzification, to a single value. The outcome value changes the state of the model or plant. Sensors record the new state and feed this data back into the fuzzy model. Figure 5.18 schematically illustrates the fuzzy modeling cycle.

This generalized fuzzy model process works for control models and for information decision models. Control models tend to be embedded in hardware and work very rapidly in real time, whereas information models generally work against corporate databases and spreadsheets and operate at a much slower rate.

Regardless of whether the model is used in control engineering or decision support, a fuzzy model works by collecting evidence for and against the outcome variable's solution state. Fuzzy models combine data with the semantics of the input and output variables to generate a new value for the output variable. How does this work?

In this section we will examine two fuzzy models in varying and increasing levels of detail. The first model is the inverted pendulum balancing controller (see "Fuzzy Associative Memories") This is a classical control engineering technique popularized by Dr. Bart Kosko, Dr. Fred Watkins, and many of the early companies who pioneered fuzzy control systems (such as Togai InfraLogic and Aptronix). The second is a new product pricing model employing many advanced features of fuzzy expert systems.

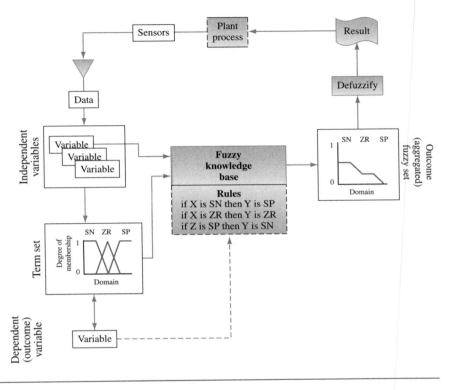

Figure 5.18 The generalized fuzzy model mechanism.

The Inverted Pendulum Model

Balancing an inverted pendulum is one of the typical exercises in control engineering. The inverted pendulum is an inflexible shaft with a weight at one end (the top) and a motor drive attached to the other (the bottom). The motor can impart an angular momentum to the pendulum, causing it to move to the left or to the right. Figure 5.19 illustrates the components of an inverted pendulum plant.

The fuzzy controller measures the pendulum's distance from the vertical — the angle theta (θ) — and the rate at which the pendulum is moving form the vertical [delta theta $(\Delta\theta)$]. From these two measurements one or more fuzzy *if-then* rules are fired in the FAM. The rules specify the amount and direction of angular momentum or motor force (Δm) that should be supplied by the motor to bring the pendulum back toward the vertical. Before we can actually write the rules for the inverted pendulum controller, however, we need to create a collection of fuzzy sets for each of the variables. Figure 5.20 shows these fuzzy sets.

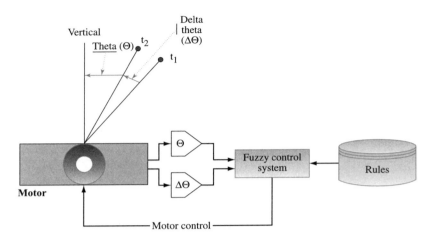

Figure 5.19 The inverted pendulum.

In a fuzzy model, rules are written in terms of each variable's fuzzy sets. These fuzzy sets define the semantics of the variable's UoD (its range of permissible values). Thus, the selection of fuzzy sets and their organization can have a profound effect on the nature and performance of the model.

A Review

Although the fuzzy sets in our inverted pendulum example have generally the same shape, number, and organization, this is neither required by the fuzzy model nor by the process of building production models. Figure 5.21 shows an alternative representation of the principal independent variables.

However, fuzzy shapes and structure cannot, generally, be arbitrarily selected. Rather, they must map to the underlying control states in the model itself. In control engineering problems, such as the inverted pendulum, the decomposition of the variables into fuzzy sets follows a somewhat semantic-free approach: the variables are broken down into labeled fuzzy regions corresponding, roughly, to degrees of change in the plant. The control engineer simply decides on the number of fuzzy sets, thus determining the number of possible rules and hence the level of granularity in the controller. For business and other information decision models, the fuzzy sets are more closely allied with the actual semantics of the variable. The shape, number, and overlap of the fuzzy sets correspond to real-world states of the model itself.

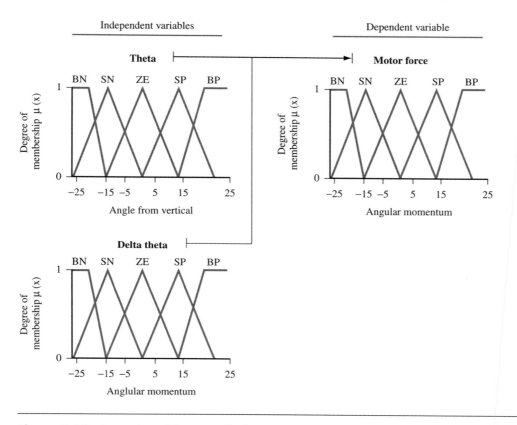

Figure 5.20 Inverted pendulum controller fuzzy sets.

To see how the motor force value is derived, we return to the FAM for the inverted pendulum. This matrix describes the rules for the controller. Fuzzy sets are activated by finding the terms that have non-zero membership values for the current independent variables. In our example, we assume the following plant values.

Theta (Θ)	10°
Delta Theta ($\Delta\Theta$)	0

As we can see from the fuzzy sets (Figure 5.20), these values overlap the zero (*ZE*) and small positive (*SP*) regions of theta and lie completely within the zero (*ZE*) region of delta theta. The highlighted region in Figure 5.22 shows which rules are candidates for firing.

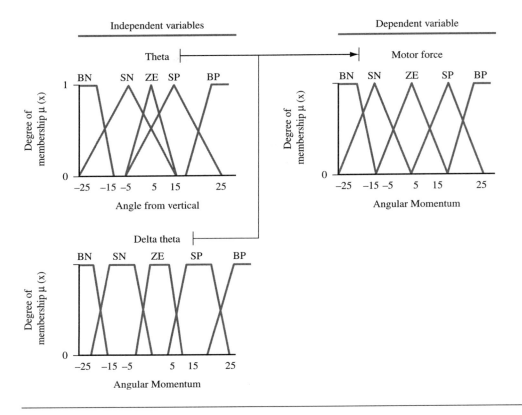

Figure 5.21 Alternative fuzzy set for the inverted pendulum FAM.

		Theta (θ)				
		BN	SN	**ZE**	**SP**	BP
	BN			BP		
Delta	SN		ZE	SP	ZE	
Theta	**ZE**	BP	SP	**ZE**	**SN**	BN
(Δθ)	SP		ZE	SN	ZE	
	BP			BN		

Figure 5.22 The inverted pendulum 5 × 5 FAM.

Examining the FAM shows that the following two rules will be selected for this set of values.

```
If Theta is SP and DeltaTheta is ZE then MotorForce is SN
If Theta is ZE and DeltaTheta is ZE then MotorForce is ZE
```

Theta's value [10°] a partial membership in two fuzzy sets: the zero (*ZE*) fuzzy set (with a membership of [.47]) and the small positive (*SP*), with a membership of [.68]. Delta theta's value [0] has a membership of [1.0] in only the zero (*ZE*) fuzzy set.

We now examine the way these rules are interpreted and the evidence used to scale the outcome variable's composite fuzzy set. This composite (or aggregated) outcome fuzzy set is then defuzzified to produce the new *MotorForce* value.

Rule 1

If Theta is SP and DeltaTheta is ZE then MotorForce is SN

Figure 5.23 shows the outcome fuzzy set after the first rule is executed.

The FAM combines the two antecedent propositions using the *And* operator, thus taking the minimum of the two truth values, per the following rule and rule membership table.

If (x) and (y) then (z)

Theta is **SP**	**DeltaTheta** is **ZE**	**MotorForce** is **SN**
[.68]	[1.0]	[.68]

Thus, the outcome fuzzy set small negative (*SN*) is truncated at the [.68] membership level and moved into the dependent variable's outcome fuzzy region.

Rule 2

If Theta is ZE and DeltaTheta is ZE then MotorForce is ZE

Figure 5.24 shows the outcome fuzzy set after the second rule is executed.

In this case, the zero (*ZE*) fuzzy set is truncated at the [.47] membership level and added to the outcome variable's fuzzy set region. Although we scale the fuzzy set using the minimum of the antecedent truth memberships, when we update the outcome fuzzy reason for conditional rules

if Theta is SP and DeltaTheta is ZE then MotorForce is SN

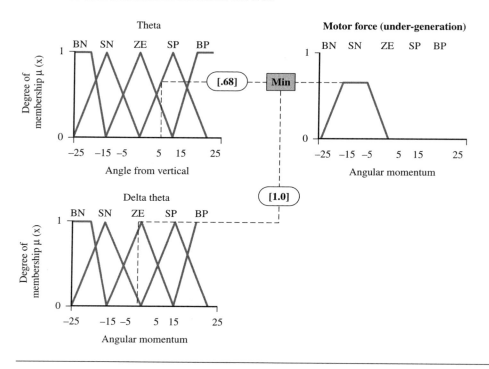

Figure 5.23 Firing the first FAM rule (inverted pendulum).

(rules in the form *if-then*) we take the maximum of the fuzzy member-ships (that is, we perform a union operation on the outcome fuzzy sets). Figure 5.25 shows the final outcome fuzzy region for the *MotorForce* variable after both rules have been fired.

At this point, we must find a value for *MotorForce* using this fuzzy region. The most common method of selecting a value is through the centroid — or center-of-gravity (COG) — technique. The COG is the point on the fuzzy set membership curve where the curve would be balanced. Mathematically, this is a weighted average of the domain values covered by the fuzzy region (weighted by the domain value's degree of membership in the fuzzy region). This is expressed as

$$x = \frac{\sum_{i=1}^{N} d_i \times \mu_{d_i}}{\sum_{i=1}^{N} \mu_{d_i}}, \qquad (5.10)$$

if Theta is SP and DeltaTheta is ZE then MotorForce is SN

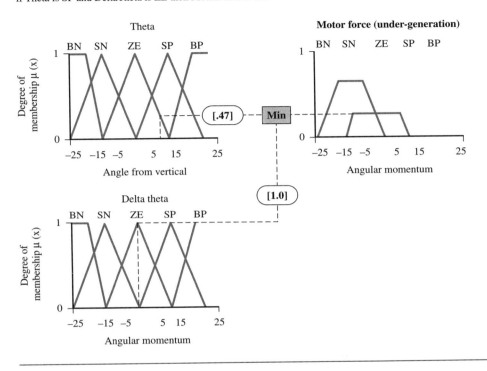

Figure 5.24 Firing the second FAM rule (inverted pendulum).

where d_i is a domain value and μ_{di} is the domain value's membership value. As Figure 5.26 illustrates, computing the COG of the output space effectively smooths the surface of the outcome fuzzy space before dropping a plum line to the horizontal axis to find the solution variable's value.

Defuzzifying the outcome fuzzy set generates a *MotorForce* (Δm) value of [−6.2]. This value, as the evidence suggests, is somewhere between the maximum of small negative and zero. This value is fed back into the motor controller, which adjusts the pendulum. New sensor readings are made and another *MotorForce* value computed (see Figure 5.19 for the general plant control cycle).

The inverted pendulum balancing controller is simply one class in a large family of commercial fuzzy logic engineering applications. In a production environment, fuzzy inference engines are incorporated in microprocessor chips, connected to sensors and actuators, and embedded in a wide range of machines. These fuzzy engines often cycle at high rates

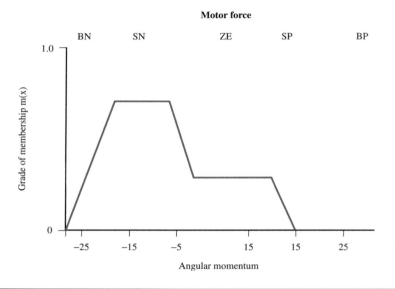

Figure 5.25 The *MotorForce* outcome fuzzy region.

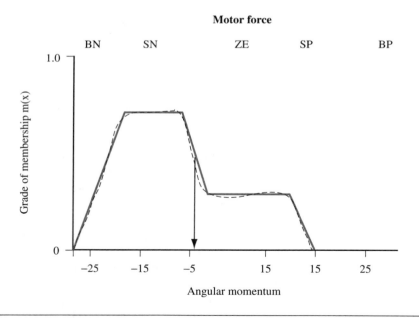

Figure 5.26 Defuzzifying the *MotorForce* fuzzy region.

of speed. It is the overall simplicity coupled with engineering robustness that gives fuzzy controllers such a wide range of applicability. Unfortunately, when we move from balancing pendulums, controlling antilock braking systems, and defrosting refrigerators to the everyday world of business and industrial problems the simplicity of the FAM becomes a severe handicap.

New Product Pricing Model

Let us suppose we are bringing a new product to market. What price should we charge for the product? This is a classical problem in multicriteria decision making. We now present an actual fuzzy model that sets the initial product price based on constraints imposed by an organization's sales, marketing, manufacturing, and financial divisions.[2] The model is deceptively simple and contains just four rules, as outlined in the following table.

Rule Number	Rule
R1	Our price must be *High*.
R2	Our price must be *Low*.
R3	Our price must be about 2*MfgCosts*.
R4	If the *competition_price* is not very *High* then our price must be near the *competition_price*.

The pricing model introduces another important feature of fuzzy models: the ability to bring together and fuse knowledge from multiple, often conflicting, experts. In the real world of information decision modeling, we seldom find a set of experts that are in general agreement. This fusion, illustrated in Figure 5.27, allows the knowledge engineer to write rules that often have contradictory objectives (such as rules 1 and 2).

Unlike the inverted pendulum model, the new product pricing model incorporates unconditional fuzzy rules, dynamically created fuzzy numbers, and the use of hedges to change the shape of existing fuzzy sets. These features and concepts are discussed as each rule is processed. We can also see that like nearly all real-world fuzzy systems in information decision making this model cannot be expressed as a FAM. As Figure 5.28

---

[2] The new product pricing model, along with C/C++ code that implements various forms of the model, is also discussed in my book *The Fuzzy Systems Handbook*, Second Edition (Academic Press Professional, 1999). The Visual Basic pricing model (*pricing.vbp*) and the fuzzy set image display program (*fzyimage.vbp*) are included with the software for this book.

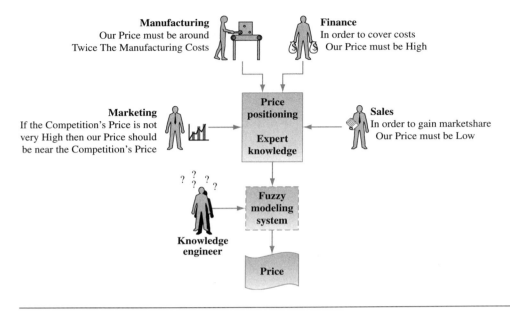

Figure 5.27 The pricing model multiple peer fusion.

illustrates, the model does follow, however, our general architecture for a fuzzy model.

There are only two vocabulary (or predefined) fuzzy sets for the pricing model, and these are associated with the outcome variable. These sets declare the semantics of what we mean by *High* and *Low* pricing. As it happens, the fuzzy sets are simply the complements of each other. Figure 5.29 shows the *Low* and *High* fuzzy sets for price.

The remainder of the fuzzy information in the model is dynamically created from the input parameters. In fact, the model only accepts two parameters: the manufacturing costs and the competition's price in the same market. As we will see, these facts will be converted to fuzzy sets using members of the approximation family of hedges.

A Review

Conditional Versus Unconditional Rules

Before we examine the pricing model, we will look at the way a fuzzy model treats conditional and unconditional rules. Unlike the processing of an unconditional statement in a conventional expert system, a fuzzy

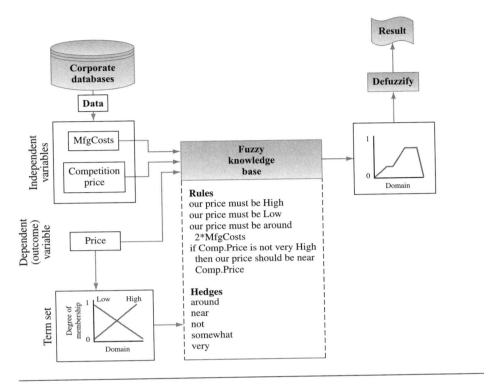

Figure 5.28 The product pricing model.

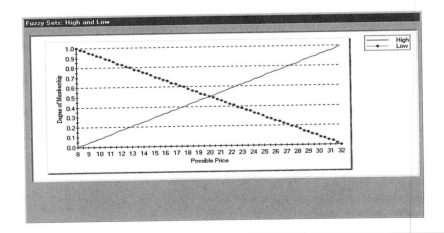

Figure 5.29 The *High* and *Low* fuzzy sets for price.

unconditional statement (which looks like an assignment statement) is treated in a completely different manner. A *conditional rule* takes the form

If *premise* **then** *outcome*.

This is the type of rule we use most often in fuzzy and conventional models. When a conditional fuzzy rule is executed, the premise is evaluated to determine its degree of truth. The degree of truth is used to truncate or scale the consequent fuzzy set before it is added to the outcome fuzzy regions. When the scaled fuzzy set is added to the outcome, it is done in one of two ways (depending on the inference method): in the SAM, the fuzzy set's membership values are added to the outcome; in the Mamdami model, the consequent and outcome regions are *Or*'d together by taking the maximum of the membership values along each point in the domain. An *unconditional* rule, on the other hand, takes the form

outcome.

These rules are statements of fuzzy relations using an unconditional proposition. In essence (but not in principle), an unconditional rule is only the consequent or outcome part of the more familiar conditional rule. Because an unconditional rule does not have a premise, its truth is always taken as [1.0]. Furthermore, unconditional rules are applied to the outcome by *And*ing the current outcome fuzzy region and the unconditional rule's fuzzy set. We perform an *And* operation by taking the minimum of the membership values along each point in the domain (unless the outcome is empty, in which case we simply copy the consequent fuzzy set into the outcome region).

Important: When you use unconditional rules, the fuzzy knowledge base is no longer a declarative rule set. This means that the order of rule execution is important and not determined by the inference engine. All unconditional rules must be executed before any of the conditional rules. The unconditional rules. The set of unconditional rules provides a default support set for the model if none of the conditionals fires (or if none of the conditionals has more truth than the combined surface formed by all conditionals). In control engineering applications, the entire control surface is overlaid with fuzzy sets. However, in business models the very complexity of the high-dimensional decision surface means that our rule set may not define a value decision space for a set of input parameters. The concept underlying the use of unconditional rules is explored more fully in the pricing model.

To run the new product pricing model, a very simple KB has been designed to hold the variable, fuzzy set, and rule definitions. The KB (*pricing.mkb*) contains the following statements.

```
var price      float 8 32
fzy High    1   8 32
fzy Low     2   8 32
var compprice  float 8 32
var mfgcosts   float 4 15
r001 price must be High;
r002 price must be Low;
r003 price must be around 2*mfgcosts;
r004 if compprice is not very High
then price must be near compprice;
```

Listing 5.2 The price KB.

To execute the model, you start the Pricing Visual Basic application (pricing.vbp). Running the model is a two-step operation. The first step, illustrated in Figure 5.30, involves loading and activating the KB (using the Compile command).

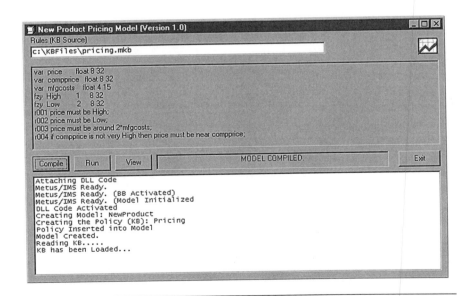

Figure 5.30 Starting the fuzzy pricing model.

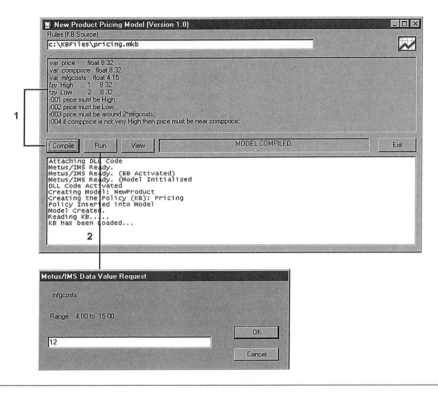

Figure 5.31 Prompting for model parameter values.

The actual pricing model is executed by clicking on the Run command. When the model is running, a backward chaining process is used to find the values for the manufacturing costs (*mfgcosts*) and the current competition price (*compprice*). Because no other rules supply a value for these model parameters, a prompt dialog is used to ask for the values. Figure 5.31 illustrates this process (showing one of the prompting dialogs).

Using the output from this model, we will now examine the way this fuzzy KB combines evidence to arrive at a suggested price for the product.

Rule 1

Rule 1 is as follows.

Our Price must be High

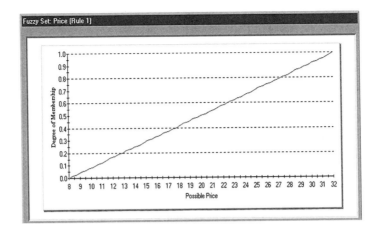

Figure 5.32 Firing the first pricing model rule.

This is an unconditional rule. Figure 5.32 shows the result of executing the first unconditional rule.

Because the outcome fuzzy region is empty, the *High* fuzzy set is simply copied into the outcome fuzzy set. This essentially "primes the pump" for the remainder of the unconditional. If we *And*ed the fuzzy set *High* with an empty fuzzy set (whose membership values are all zero), we would produce nothing but another empty fuzzy set.

Rule 2

Rule 2 is as follows.

Our Price must be Low

This is also an unconditional rule. Figure 5.33 shows the result of executing the second rule.

When the second rule is executed, a new outcome fuzzy region is built by taking the intersection of the *Low* fuzzy set and the current outcome region (in this case, the fuzzy set *High*). As Figure 5.34 shows, the left-hand segment of *Low* and the right-hand segment of *High* are truncated.

Thus, the outcome fuzzy region for *Price* is a triangular region formed by the intersection of *High* and *Low*. If these were the only two rules in the model, we could defuzzify the outcome and find an estimated price of $20.00.

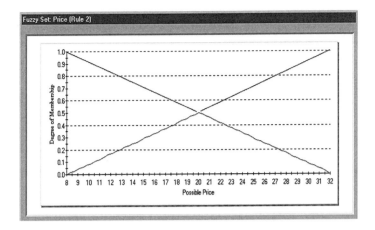

Figure 5.33   Firing the second pricing model rule.

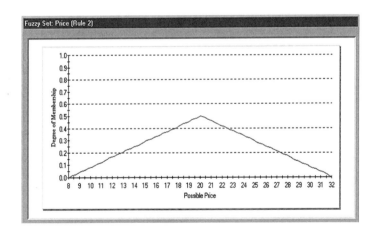

Figure 5.34   The constrained outcome space.

Rule 3

Rule 3 is as follows.

Our Price must be about 2*MfgCosts

This is another unconditional rule. In applying rule 3 to the outcome, a two-step process is required. First, we need to take the manufacturing

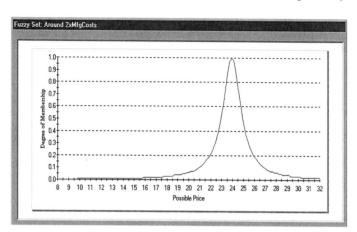

Figure 5.35 The fuzzy number *About 2*MfgCosts*.

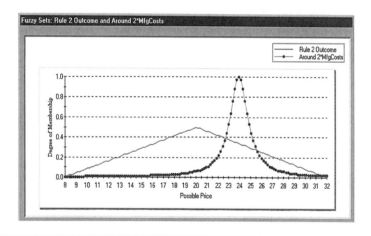

Figure 5.36 Price outcome with fuzzy number overlaid.

costs and create a fuzzy set (a fuzzy number) that represents twice this cost. This dynamically created fuzzy set is then applied to the outcome region. Figure 5.35 shows the result of creating the fuzzy set *about 2*MfgCosts* when the manufacturing cost is $11.

As Figure 5.36 illustrates, the dynamically created fuzzy number representing twice the manufacturing cost is added to the outcome solution area. The preliminary figure shows the placement of the bell-shaped fuzzy number along with the rules that contributed to each part of the outcome.

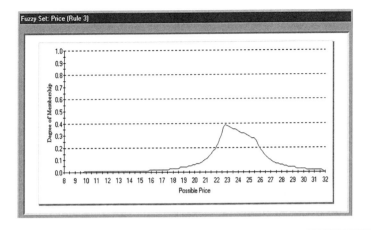

Figure 5.37   Firing the third rule.

Rule 3 is unconditional, and thus the new fuzzy number is applied to the outcome fuzzy set by taking the minimum of the membership values along the possible range of values. Figure 5.37 shows the final outcome region after executing rule 3.

The initial three unconditional rules in the pricing model define a default region for the price outcome value. If none of the conditional rules executes (or executes very weakly), the final price position will be determined by defuzzifying this region. We now turn to the execution of the model's conditional rule.

Rule 4

Rule 4 is as follows.

> If the competition_price is not very High
> then our Price must be near the competition_price

A conditional fuzzy rule should already be familiar to you from the inverted pendulum example, although in the pricing model the form is quite a bit more complex. The first step in executing the rule is evaluating the rule's premise condition. We need to determine the degree to which the model variable, *competition_price*, is not very *High*. Figure 5.38 shows schematically how this is done.

As Figure 5.38 shows, hedges are applied in a specific order. The hedge *very* (an intensifier) is applied to the fuzzy set *High*, producing

R4 if the competition_price is **not very High**
then our price must be near competition_price

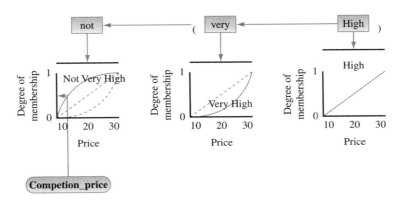

Figure 5.38 Evaluating the premise of rule 4.

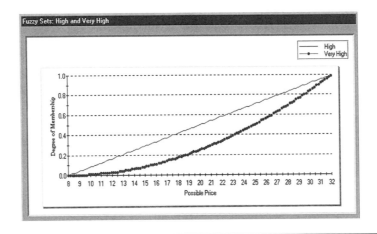

Figure 5.39 The fuzzy sets *High* and *Very High*.

a new fuzzy set *Very High*. Figure 5.39 shows how these fuzzy sets are generated.

The hedge *not* (the complement operator) is then applied to the *Very High* fuzzy set, producing the fuzzy set *Not Very High*. Figure 5.40 shows how these fuzzy sets are generated.

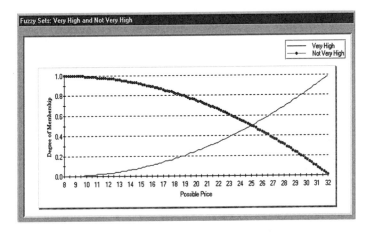

Figure 5.40 The fuzzy sets *Very High* and *Not Very High*.

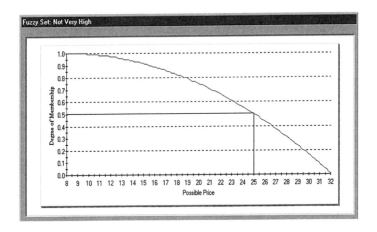

Figure 5.41 Finding the degree of membership in *Not Very High*.

The value of *competition_price* is then found in the *Not Very High* fuzzy set (Figure 5.41), and its degree of membership is determined.[4] This degree of membership, [0.504], is the truth value for the rule's premise.

---

[4] Notice that hedges are applied to fuzzy sets according to rules much like rules of interpreting modifiers in operation in the English language. Each hedge operation produces a new fuzzy set. Thus, *not very high* and *very not high* are two distinct and completely different fuzzy sets.

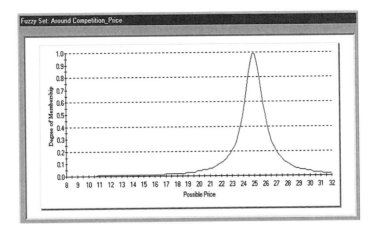

Figure 5.42   *About* the competition price.

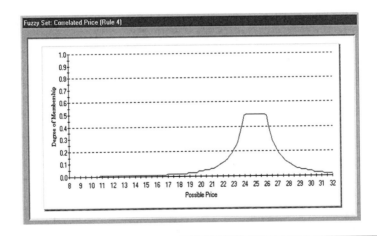

Figure 5.43   The correlated (minimum) competition price.

With the rule premise's truth in hand, the consequent action is evaluated and applied to the outcome fuzzy set. The first step applies the approximation hedge *about* to the current competition price variable. Figure 5.42 shows this bell-shaped fuzzy number.

After the consequent fuzzy set has been formed, it must be correlated with the truth of the premise. Applying the maximum (or truncation) method of correlation reduces the height of the *About Competition_Price* fuzzy set to the maximum of the bell-shaped fuzzy number. Figure 5.43 shows the result of this correlation.

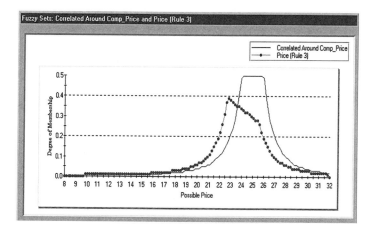

Figure 5.44   Outcome price overlaid with competition price.

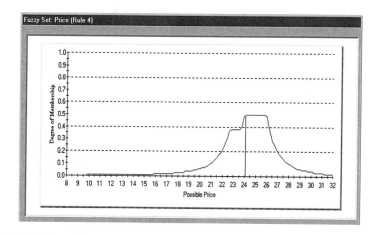

Figure 5.45   Final outcome fuzzy set for price.

Once correlation has been performed, the modified consequent fuzzy set is added to the current outcome fuzzy set. Figure 5.44 shows in finer detail how the adjusted consequent fuzzy set is overlaid with the current fuzzy set to represent the predicted (or possible) price.

The fourth rule is completely executed when the outcome fuzzy set is updated with the correlated *About Competition_Price* value. The resulting outcome fuzzy set, shown in Figure 5.45, is used to actually derive the predicted product pricing position through the process of defuzzification.

We are using the centroid — or center-of-gravity (COG) — defuzzification to find the predicted product price. This involves finding the balance point on the membership curve and dropping a "plumb line" to a value on the fuzzy set's domain. The vertical line under the outcome fuzzy set in Figure 5.45 is the point of defuzzification. When applied to the outcome fuzzy set, the model returns a price of $24.13, with a degree of evidence (the compatibility index) of [0.5039].

5.8   **Review**

Fuzzy systems replace the crispness of Boolean logic with the elasticity of fuzzy logic. In this chapter we examined the principles underlying fuzzy rule-based models to show how the use of fuzzy logic provides a more flexible, more robust, and less brittle approach to knowledge management. We also compared two types of fuzzy systems: a control system for balancing an inverted pendulum and a business system for new product pricing. You should now be familiar with the following.

- The syntax and meaning of fuzzy rules
- The organization and purpose of a fuzzy knowledge base
- The problem with exponentially increasing rules
- How a fuzzy inference engine executes rules
- How evidence is combined to produce an outcome
- The techniques for reduction (or defuzzification)

Understanding how fuzzy sets are used in production fuzzy systems is a crucial step in appreciating the ways fuzzy elements are used in a wide range of related techniques and methodologies. In the next several chapters we will look at fuzzy logic measures, as well as at fuzzy system components embedded in database queries, clustering, and the discovery of fuzzy rules in large and small databases. The ability to dynamically discover and measure the effectiveness of discovered rules is an important component of machine learning and adaptive systems. In the next chapter we begin this journey by turning our attention to the use of the Structured Query Language (SQL) as a vehicle for the semantic interrogation of data as well as for finding and quantifying patterns.

■ ■ ■

Chapter 6
Fuzzy SQL and Intelligent Queries

Nearly all model development (as well as data mining) projects begin with an exploration of the underlying data space. With the exception of statistical analysis, the most common tool for data exploration is the Structured Query Language (SQL) facilities associated with nearly all modern relational databases. In this chapter, we examine ways of improving SQL requests using fuzzy forms of the where *and* having *statements. By applying fuzzy logic and approximate reasoning to the evaluation of record selection and clustering, we significantly improve the robustness and utility of database query operations. In this chapter, we will be primarily concerned with the* where *statement and its various forms. We will also be examining the way database columns are decomposed into fuzzy sets.*

In the rush to apply advanced computational intelligence, clustering, and factoring techniques to large databases, knowledge and data mining engineers often bypass an important analytical tool: the SQL processor associated with the database. SQL gives business analysts, knowledge engineers, and others a powerful method for seeking out and exploiting patterns in data. Although SQL does not necessarily discover patterns in the same sense as rule induction or multidimensional clustering, as a tool to augment the analyst's exploration of data it has the ability to see through database noise and expose relationships that are not readily visible. With general ideas in hand about how the data should be organized and what information or patterns are expected in the data, analysts can manipulate data to verify that the data has these patterns and structure. The ability to connect tables, filter records, and combine columns enables the exploration of probable patterns in data. Thus, SQL is a tool for combining a cognitive model with the actual data model. In a data mining, knowledge discovery, and even ordinary business process, modeling this is a very important capability and lies at the heart of any knowledge acquisition project.

6.1 The Vocabulary of Relational Databases and Queries

A complete discussion of relational database systems and the calculus of relational queries is beyond the scope or intent of this chapter. Modern relational databases are, in principal, simply a collection of rectangular tables connected by the data they share. In that the fuzzy SQL approach is designed to access and retrieve data from these tables, a basic understanding of the principal nomenclatures used in relational databases is important. This preview of the vocabulary will make reading and understanding the material in this chapter much easier. It is not always possible, while maintaining an uncluttered and coherent discussion of both the ideas associated with database organization and queries against that organization, to ensure that every term is introduced before it is used. Many of these terms are, of course, redefined or defined in more detail later in this chapter.

Column

Each row in a table consists of one or more columns of data. A *column* represents a unique class or category of data and has a unique name within the table. A column also has a date type (numeric, string, Boolean, and so on) and a domain (a restriction on the allowable value for the column, which, in many but not all cases is implicit in the data type). In the same way that rows are more or less the same as records in a file system, columns are similar to fields in a record.

Composite Key

Every column in a relation is identified by its primary identifier. This can be a single value or a set of values. When the primary key consists of multiple values it is called a *composite key*. Table 6.1, for example, illustrates the composite key for a project precedence relationship table.

Each precedence relationship is defined by two values: a base (*From*) project identifier and a successor (*To*) project identifier. The table also contains the type of relationship (in this case, a finish-to-start connection) and any lead or lag value that offsets the precedence relationship. Figure 6.1 shows the critical path precedence network defined by the composite keys in this table.

TABLE 6.1   Project Precedence Table

From-Project	To-Project	Type	Lead-Lag
A	B	FS	0
A	C	FS	0
B	D	FS	0
C	D	FS	0
D	E	FS	0

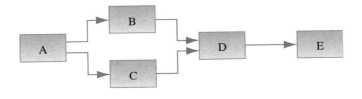

Figure 6.1   The precedence network from the composite keys.

A composite key uniquely identifies a single row in the table. Composite keys can consist of any number of columns, but the complete set of columns must be specified to access the corresponding row.

Crisp Number

A *crisp number* is an ordinary number that has a single value (see the fuzzy logic vocabulary in Chapter 4 for a discussion of crispness and expectancy).

Domain

A column's *domain* is its universe of allowable values. Unless otherwise specified, it is usually associated with the column's underlying data type (numeric columns are limited to numbers, string columns can contain text, Boolean columns contain true or false values, and so forth). A column can also have an extended domain. When used in this sense, a domain is an explicit constraint on a column's value and takes the form of a lookup table, an *if-then-else* rule, or an arithmetic or logical expression.

Foreign Key

A column in one table that contains data values from the primary key of another table is a *foreign key*. Table 6.2, for example, shows a projects table. The table has a primary key (the project identifier) and two foreign keys.

The Department column contains values from the primary identifier of the departments table (see Table 6.3). The ProjectMgr column contains values from the primary identifier of the employees table (see Table 6.4).

TABLE 6.2 Projects Table

Project Id	Status	Duration	Department	ProjectMgr
P1	Active	190	MKTG	1077
P2	Active	30	IT	1633
P3	Pending	65	IT	1601
P3	Complete	205	ENGR	5809
Primary Key			**Foreign Key**	**Foreign Key**

TABLE 6.3 Departments Table

Department	DeptMgr	Site
ENGR	8932	East
IT	7734	East
MKTG	3077	West
Primary Key	**Foreign Key**	

TABLE 6.4 Employees Table

Employee Id	Last Name	Salary
1077	Jones	32000
1633	Miller	43000
1601	Smith	25400
8932	Sommers	67050
Primary Key		

The DeptMgr column in the departments table is also a foreign key because it contains employee ID values from the Employees table. The connections made through foreign keys are one of the principal ways relationships are established through the database. Foreign keys are also important domain management mechanisms in the database (so that, as an example, you cannot enter a department name in the projects table that does not also exist in the departments table).

Fuzzy Number

A number whose value is "smeared" out over an underlying range of values is called a *fuzzy number*. Fuzzy numbers are generally bell curves, but can be triangles and trapezoids. A fuzzy number can be part of the variable's term set or it can be created by the application of an approximation hedge.

Index

Columns containing non-key data can be indexed for high-performance retrieval and joins. An *index* is a multi-way tree that organizes the column's data in a manner that allows individual data items or collections of rows with the same data item to be found and retrieved very quickly. In many database systems, foreign keys are automatically indexed. For example, consider the Status column in the projects table (see Table 6.2). If there are thousands of projects in the table, finding all active projects would require searching the entire table, comparing the content of the Status column with the string *Complete*. An index extracts each unique value from the column, as well the set of all rows that have that value. Thus, finding all complete projects by indexing the Status column is extremely fast.

Join

The process of connecting two (or more) tables based on common data is called a *join*. Joins are the primary mechanism in a relational database for realizing structure in the data. This structure can be quite deep. A simple example of a join, using the projects and departments tables (see Tables 6.2 and 6.3), would be to answer a query such as "What projects are being run out of the East site?" In this case, the projects and departments tables are joined using the Department column in the projects table and the Department column in the departments table. The conventional SQL query to perform the join and then select those projects in the East site looks as follows.

```
Select ProjectId, Site
From Projects,Departments
Where Projects.department = Departments.Department
      And Departments.Site = "East";
```

There are many types of joins. A join on the same data is called an equi-join (an equal join). Relational query languages also support more advanced types of joins, such as unions, outer joins, and inner joins — used to connect and then create new tables based on the presence or absence of data values.

Normal Form

The process of organizing data in a relation to remove redundancies and eliminate update or deletion anomalies is called normalization. There are three principal levels of normalization.[1] The first level is concerned with the basics of how rows and columns appear in a relation. The last two are basically concerned with eliminating redundancies and ensuring that all columns are dependent on the primary key set. In *first normal form* (1NF), every row contains the same columns and every row and column intersection contains a single value (that is, a column cannot be an array or some other multivalued form). In *second normal form* (2NF) and *third normal form* (3NF), all columns that are not fully dependent on the primary key are removed and placed in their own relation.

Predicate

A *predicate* is a fuzzy or crisp expression in the *where* (or *having*) statement that is evaluated to produce a truth value. Predicates determine which rows in a table participate in a query. A query often contains many predicates, as the following is an example.

```
Select projects
Where project_length is Long
   And project_budget is High
   And project_priority is Low;
```

---

[1] Technically, there are five levels of normalization. However, in practice, placing a table in third normal form is generally sufficient.

This is a query with three predicates in the *where* statement. The predicates evaluate fuzzy relationships involving the project length (duration), budget, and priority.

Primary Identifier (or Primary Key)

Each row in a table must be identified by a unique key. This is the *primary identifier*. The identifier can consist of one or more contiguous columns (if it consists of more than one column, it is a composite key). In the projects table (Table 6.2), the project ID is the primary identifier. No other row in the table can have the same value in this column. Note that although usually considered a poor design it is possible for a table to have more than one unique key (a project might also have a unique budget reference number, for example), in which case the other unique identifiers are called candidate keys.

Query Compatibility Index (QCIX)

The degree of compatibility with the semantic intent of a fuzzy SQL query is called the *query compatibility index (QCIX)*. Each returned row from a query is assigned its own QCIX value. The fuzzy SQL query manager automatically ranks the returned row set in descending order by the QCIX. The QCIX reflects, in essence, the distance between the complete realization of the query and the degree of semantic membership in the returned row.

Relation (Table)

Data in the relational database is maintained in tabular form. When organized according to a set of precise rules, the tabular data is called a *relation* (or *relation table*). In general use, however, the relations are simply called tables. Each table consists of a fixed number of columns and a varying number of rows. Tables are connected through the join process, and these connections establish the rich variety of relationships in the relational model.

Row

Each table consists of one or more rows of data. A *row* consists of one or more columns, and each row contains the same number of columns. A row is more or less equivalent to a record in a file system. (See "Column" for additional information.)

Secondary Identifier (or Key)

Any indexed column is known as a *secondary identifier*. Secondary identifiers play an important role in data modeling, query, and organization.

6.2   Basic Relational Database Concepts

In the 1970s the concept of a relational database emerged as the standard way of representing large quantities of complex information. Unlike the previous generation of database systems, the relational model did not rely on embedded pointers, links, and other internal structural edifices to maintain relationships between data elements. Instead of links and pointers, a relational database creates its relationships through a shared set of common data elements (that is, the data itself) carefully structured (in a process called normalization) throughout the database.

The basic building block of a relational database is the table: a fixed set of columns and a varying number of rows. Each row and column intersection contains a single data element. Figure 6.2 shows how these tables are organized in a database.

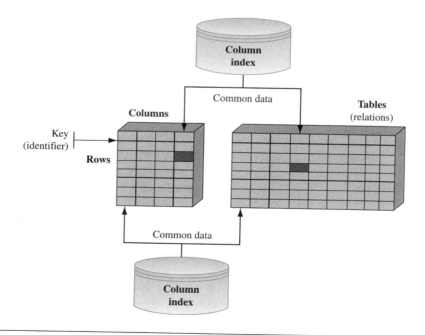

Figure 6.2   Relational database tables.

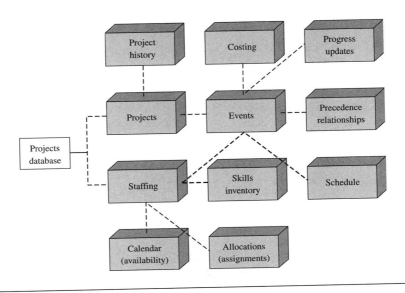

Figure 6.3   The projects database structure.

Tables are connected through a process is called a join. Rows are selected based on the content of their columns. To provide high-speed joins, primary and secondary keys are indexed. This allows sets of records containing a specific value to be retrieved without reading the entire table. We can see how a relational database is organized by examining a corporate information technology division's projects database. Figure 6.3 shows the schematic representation of the various tables in the database.

Focusing on a small segment of the database gives us some insight into the fine-grain details of the database organization at the table level. The project table contains information about each active project. The staffing table contains information about each employee. Figure 6.4 shows the structure of the database.

Each table is uniquely indexed on a primary key, *ProjectId* and *EmployeeId*, respectively. This unique index ensures that no duplicate records are entered in the table. In addition to the table's primary key, a table can contain several secondary keys. A secondary key (which refers to the primary key of another table) is called a foreign key. The project table maintains an index of project managers, and the staffing table maintains an index of departments associated with each resource.

The database relationships are expressed in the data. The relationships are actually realized through the join operation. For example, suppose we

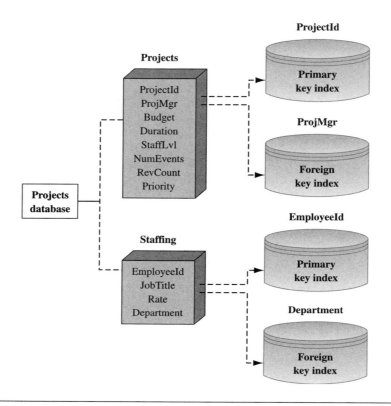

Figure 6.4   The projects and staffing table structure.

want to find projects with budgets in excess of $80,000 that are managed by project managers in the Engineering department. Figure 6.5 illustrates the schematics of the underlying join.

A join between the projects and the staffing tables connects the proper staffing record with each project manager, ensuring that we have the ability to find only those project managers in the Engineering department. The result of a join is a new, physical table (using a temporary relation). Forming a new table from a join, a process known as closure, ensures that these new tables can be used like any other table in additional joins (some of which are performed automatically by the database query manager and may be invisible to the client). In fact, it is the task of a relational database's query language to manage the implicit relationships among database tables.

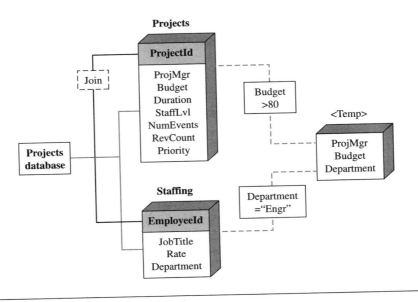

Figure 6.5   Explicit joins between project and staffing.

6.3   **Structured Query Language Fundamentals**

SQL evolved from the work of Edgar Codd and Chris Date as a standard and uniform method of creating, accessing, and manipulating relational databases. In SQL, the user tells the computer what columns they want, which tables are involved, how the tables should be joined, and which rows from the tables will participate in the query. The query language also provides a clear method of performing joins among all specified tables. SQL is a *relational calculus* approach to database access and information management: it selects and organizes sets of records through a high-level language that tells the system *what* records to select, not *how* to select records. In this way it becomes a tool for expressing the desired result of a database retrieval instead of the mechanics necessary to achieve this result. Expressing the mechanics of a query is a *relational algebra* process. For example, the following is an example of a relational algebra query against project and staffing tables.

```
define TotCost as double;
define ThisResCost as double;
open table projects, table staffing;
TotCost=0;
```

```
for each project find projects.dept = "ENGR";
    connect staffing via projects.projmgr=staffing.employeeid;
    If connect.status==0 do;
        If projects,budget > 40 then
            compute ThisResCost=projects.duration*staffing.rate;
            TotCost=TotCost+ThisResCost;
        end if;
    end if;
end for;
```

Most of the older database query languages took this approach. They required their client to open tables, set up working variables, and explicitly navigate through the database (such as following links between hierarchical relationships). SQL, the outgrowth of the initial SEQUEL language of IBM's System R database project, removed the client from the mechanical view. This freed the user to focus on data management and data analysis issues. As Figure 6.6 schematically illustrates, SQL incorporates a variety of data management features.

The *where* statement performs a dual role of specifying how tables should be joined and which rows from a table should be selected. Thus, it filters and connects multiple tables in the database. For example, the following SQL request shows a join and a filter.

```
select projectid,projects.duration*staffing.rate
from projects,staffimg
where projects.projmgr = staffing.employee
    And projects.budget > 4000.00;
```

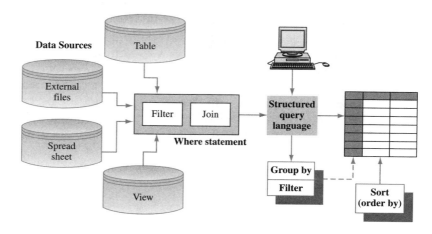

Figure 6.6 SQL data management features.

This request connects each project manager to his or her staffing (personnel) table entry so that the total management costs for each project with a budget in excess of $4000 can be calculated (compare this to the previous relational algebra request, which does the same thing).

On the other hand, the *group by* statement collects sets of records according to one or more related columns. The associated *having* statement functions like a filter on the group, indicating which records should participate in the group. The following example illustrates the use of a *group by* and *having* statement.

```
select projmgr
from projects
group by projectid Having count(*) > 1
```

This query selects all project managers who manage more than one project. The *having* statement provides a way of applying a filter to an entire collection of records.

An important characteristic of a relational query language is the idea of closure. This means that the result of a query is a new table, not simply a collection of rows. Using SQL we can connect any number of database tables to produce a result. How the tables are connected and which rows are selected are determined by the arithmetic, logical, and string comparisons found in the *where* statement. As criteria become more and more complex, the set of records selected by the *where* statement becomes more and more brittle.

Thus, as a component of any data mining engineer's toolkit SQL has several significant limitations. In this chapter, we address one of its principal analytical shortcomings: its lack of discrimination among database records. The precise nature of an SQL request's selection and grouping of predicates, as we will see, lies at the heart of this shortcoming.

6.4 **Precision and Accuracy**

We live in a world obsessed and infused with precision. We wear wrist watches accurate to a hundredth of a second a year (often automatically coupled to the atomic clock at the National Institute of Standards and Technology (NIST). Ultra-high-density computer chips are made possible by nearly nanometer-level placement of circuits on a silicate substrate. Hunters, hikers, drivers, and, of course, the military use the Global Positioning System (GPS), which can locate individuals and troops within a meter or so anywhere on earth. As a demonstration of manipulating nanometer objects, IBM wrote its name with individual Xenon atoms. Intelligent missiles speed near ground level across a thousand miles of mountainous terrain to strike a single target in a crowded city. We can calculate irrational numbers, such as pi, to over a billion decimal places. Our space craft slingshot around the sun and rendezvous a year later with a distant planet on a time schedule that is exact to a few hundredths of a second. And changes in the economy are measured, and reported, down to a tenth of a percent.

These are our models of precision — models that provide the gauge for measuring other physical phenomena. We judge our weather forecasts, for example, as highly imprecise (and consequently less accurate) because they cannot predict the exact weather for this weekend. We believe statistical analysis is less precise than calculus. And we believe, above all other things, that numbers are more precise than words. In our modern analytical world, tempered by the rise of the scientific method, fields of study that cannot reduce their axiomatic truths to sets of equations are viewed with skepticism and placed outside the scope of the "hard" sciences. And this type of drive for precision has been carried forward to our tools for data analysis and knowledge discovery. It is, in fact, the often unstated assumption that precision is a necessary requirement of truth and rigor that has impeded the use of such technologies as fuzzy logic. In this chapter, we look at ways imprecision can be made to work for us in important and powerful ways when searching production databases. In fact, we will see that *a decrease in precision gives us an unexpected increase in accuracy*.

6.5   **Why We Search Databases**

It seems like a trivial question to ask why we search databases, yet it lies at the heart of our need for precision and accuracy (as well as how we measure both of these properties). The simple answer is: *To retrieve data we need to make a decision*. The "we" can be either a person sitting at a computer terminal or an application running on some computer. And this simple answer is important. It links the process of data retrieval with the cognitive process of decision making. In making a decision we want to have all the facts. And we want the facts to be as accurate as possible. In a perfect world, with perfect tools, we might expect complete access to the supporting facts. In fact, however, due to the ambiguous and imprecise nature of information actual "facts" are difficult to discover.

TABLE 6.5 The Project Table (Subset)

Project Id	Budget (×00)	Duration	StaffLvl
P01	55	108	29
P02	48	115	33
P03	57	90	10
P04	81	87	40
P05	78	92	16
P06	63	102	25
P07	91	125	41
P08	90	88	27
P09	65	117	37
P10	73	102	30
P11	93	93	45
P12	60	110	31
P13	59	121	37
P14	89	92	18
P15	51	101	23

Before we jump into the middle of how this dilemma can be resolved, we should examine a relatively simple example to understand how and why the problem exists in real databases and other information repositories. Let us consider a few of the columns in the projects table, as shown in Table 6.5. Suppose we need to find all projects with a high budget and a short duration. In a conventional query, we must decide on a clear set of boundaries defining what set of budgets are considered "high" and what set of durations are considered "short." In this case, we decide a budget over $80,000 is high and a duration less than 90 days is short. The SQL query is cast as follows.

```
Select ProjectNo, Budget, Duration
    From Projects
    Where Budget > 80 and Duration < 90;
```

The query selects the projects that have both a budget greater than $80,000 and a duration less than 90 days. Table 6.6 shows the result of this query.

The query meets the precise requirements of the selection criteria expressed in the *where* statement. As Figure 6.7 shows, the query delimits a decision space in the data.

TABLE 6.6 Selected Rows

Project Id	Budget (×00)	Duration	StaffLvl
P01	55	108	29
P02	48	115	33
P03	57	90	10
P04	81	87	40
P05	78	92	16
P06	63	102	25
P07	91	125	41
P08	90	88	27
P09	65	117	37
P10	73	102	30
P11	93	93	45
P12	60	110	31
P13	59	121	37
P14	89	92	18
P15	51	101	23

TABLE 6.7 Rows Matching Intent of Query

Project	Budget (x00)	Duration	StaffLvl	
P01	55	108	29	
P02	48	115	33	
P03	57	90	10	
P04	81	87	40	←
P05	78	92	16	←
P06	63	102	25	
P07	91	125	41	
P08	90	88	27	←
P09	65	117	37	
P10	73	102	30	
P11	93	93	45	←
P12	60	110	31	
P13	59	121	37	
P14	89	92	18	←
P15	51	101	23	

However, the query is not very accurate in terms of our intended objective. There are projects with budget and duration values that are conceptually close to our ideas of high and short but are not selected by the query. Table 6.7 illustrates some of these candidate rows.

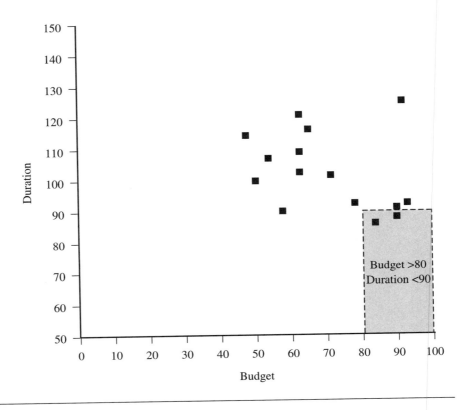

Figure 6.7   The Boolean *High Budget* and *Short Duration* space.

In a small database, such as our example, this is not a problem because we can visually see other candidate records. But in large production databases such a visual pattern recognition is not possible. Thus, how can we improve our ability to find the needed data? There are two ways: by expanding the scope of our selection criteria or by changing the way we perform our query against the database. We will look at each in turn.

6.6   Expanding the Query Scope

One intuitively obvious way of enriching the amount of data retrieved from the database is by expanding the scope of our query. This means changing the selection criteria so that they encompass more data. As an example, in our previous query we might extend the selection criteria as follows.

```
Select ProjectNo, Budget, Duration
From Projects
Where Budget > 75 and Duration < 100
```

This moves the budget limit down to projects with a budget greater than $75,000 and moves the duration threshold up to durations less than 100 days. Indeed, as Table 6.8 shows, we now pick up the rows shown in Table 6.7. This seems to solve the problem. We simply have to broaden the search criteria. As Figure 6.8 shows, this expansion neatly encloses several of the neighboring data points.

But extending the search space introduces several additional problems. First, we have diluted the meaning of the query in order to capture these adjacent records. Second, we have no way of telling which additional records are closely associated with the intent of our query and which are, essentially, "satellite" records. And third, of course, we now miss records that are near our new boundaries. Table 6.9 shows some candidate neighboring records (P07 and P10) that might be included in the new selection space.

TABLE 6.8   Rows Selected by Expanding Selection Criteria Scope

ProjectId	Budget (x00)	Duration	StaffLvl
P01	55	108	29
P02	48	115	33
P03	57	90	10
P04	81	87	40
P05	78	92	16
P06	63	102	25
P07	91	125	41
P08	90	88	27
P09	65	117	37
P10	73	102	30
P11	93	93	45
P12	60	110	31
P13	59	121	37
P14	89	92	18
P15	51	101	23

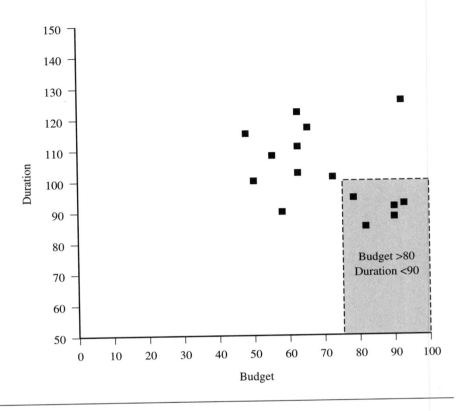

Figure 6.8 The extended Boolean decision space.

We now begin to see the futility of extending the scope of the selection criteria. More records from the database are selected, but we have completely lost the accuracy of our query. The pool of returned records includes both those that meet our criteria of high budget and short duration and many others selected simply to catch information along the "edge" of the decision space. In a simple two-predicate query against a small table of data, the intrinsic brittleness of Boolean selection criteria is not often apparent (in that we can visually see adjacent records and discern patterns). But against a large complex database, we lose this ability to see which records out of several hundred belong to the core set of desired records. For example, Table 6.10 outlines a projects table with some additional columns.

In assessing project risk or anticipating project bottlenecks, we want to find projects with "a high budget, short duration, moderate to large staffing, fair complexity (at least 45 events or tasks), previous revisions to

TABLE 6.9 Neighboring Records in the Extended Scope

Project Id	Budget (x00)	Duration	StaffLvl	
P01	55	108	29	
P02	48	115	33	
P03	57	90	10	
P04	81	87	40	
P05	78	92	16	
P06	63	102	25	
P07	91	125	41	←
P08	90	88	27	
P09	65	117	37	
P10	73	102	30	←
P11	93	93	45	
P12	60	110	31	
P13	59	121	37	
P14	89	92	18	
P15	51	101	23	

TABLE 6.10 Project Table with Additional Columns

Project	Budget (x00)	Duration	StaffLvl	Num Events	Rev Count	Priority
P01	55	108	29	14	0	3
P02	48	115	33	77	3	1
P03	57	90	10	22	0	1
P04	81	87	40	31	1	5
P05	78	92	16	49	5	0

the project plan, and high to moderate priority." Such a query might look as follows.

```
Select *
From Projects
Where Budget > 80
    and Duration < 90
    and Staff > 30
    and NumEvents > 45
    and RevCount > 2
    and Priority < 5
```

Applied against the project operational data store or (in a data mining exercise) against a database of historical projects, this query may retrieve many hundreds of records. Along each dimension of the *where* statement, there will be values that are close to the cutoff threshold. To ensure that we capture a robust set of records we might relax our selection criteria somewhat to capture a portion of these nearby records. However, given the set of selected records there is no effective way to tell which records are strongly compatible with the meaning of our query and which are only weakly compatible.

The question is, how do we go about making a database query that improves the accuracy of our results? The problem lies in how we express our query. Instead of simply changing the boundary conditions in the *where* statement, we need to change the way in which the *where* statement is evaluated. More to the point, the Boolean or crisp predicates are replaced with fuzzy predicates. Making this change has some far-reaching and important consequences. We now turn our attention to some fundamental principles of the relational database before addressing the issues associated with fusing fuzzy logic and the relational query language.

6.7 **Fuzzy Query Fundamentals**

A fuzzy SQL request introduces a new way of retrieving information from a relational database. Using this query facility, you tell the computer what you want based on concepts rather than numbers and text strings. These concepts are sometimes vague and often imprecise. For example, you can look for risky projects in the corporate project database using a query such as the following.

```
select *
from projects
   where projects.budget is High
      and projects.duration is Short
```

With fuzzy SQL, terms such as *High* replace the more conventional (and restrictive) method of specifying a range of budget values, such as the following.

```
project.budget >= 40 and project.budget =< 80
```

The same type of conceptually based query is used across a wide spectrum of public, corporate, governmental, and military databases. For example, a military query against division-level resources might take the following form.

```
select battalionid
from imemilorg.divmrrpt
where toe_staffing is complete
    and mr_availability is near toe.staffing
        and transport_redline is low
```

This query accesses the materiel readiness report to find battalions within a division for which TO&E (table of organization and equipment) staffing is complete, the morning report availability is close to the staffing level (nearly everyone is present), and the number of vehicles on redline (in for repair) is low.

The idea behind a fuzzy query process is simply this: you tell the computer what you want in terms that mean something to you. These terms, expressed as the names of fuzzy sets, define the semantics of a query rather than the mechanics of a query. By expressing your thoughts through semantics rather than arithmetic, Boolean, and comparison operators, you can find information that expresses the intent of your query. In a while we will see why this new way of qualifying records from a database is not only more natural but much more powerful and comprehensive. But first, we briefly review the idea of fuzzy sets in the context of query requests (the building blocks of fuzzy SQL) and see how they work and how they are used in a basic query process.

Understanding Fuzzy Query Predicates

Most of us are familiar with conventional logic. This is often called Boolean logic after George Boole, the nineteenth-century cleric and mathematician who formalized its rules of logic. The core of both Boolean and fuzzy logic is the idea of a set. A set is a collection of things, both real and imaginary. The big difference between the two is simply this: in Boolean logic a thing is either a member of a set or it is not a member of the set. In fuzzy logic, things can have a partial membership in a set. As we will shortly see, such partial memberships have far-reaching implications. A rather easy way to see the difference between Boolean sets (which we often call *crisp* sets) and fuzzy sets is by examining the concept of *Tall*. In conventional set membership, we must specify a boundary point: individuals with heights above the boundary are *Tall* and those below the boundary are *not Tall*.

Suppose we select 6 feet as the boundary. Expression 6.1 shows how the set is defined.

$$\mu_{Tall} = \{height \geq 6\} \qquad (6.1)$$

As a reminder, throughout the chapter we continue to use the Greek μ (mu) to indicate a set membership. Figure 6.9 shows what this set looks like in crisp form.

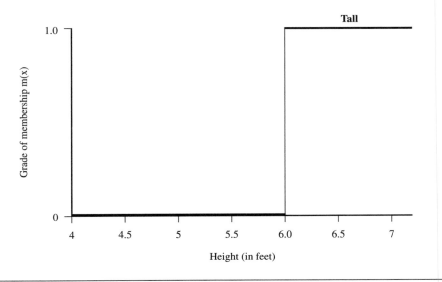

Figure 6.9   The crisp *Tall* definition.

We can see that the most obvious characteristic of the Boolean set is the sharp boundary between the items not in the set and those that are members of the set. Thus, someone five and one-half feet in height is not *Tall*, whereas someone six feet three inches is a member of *Tall*. This sharp boundary also introduces some artificial classification constraints on the logic that uses the set. These constraints are most pronounced in real-world applications in which the boundaries between states of some value are continuous. In the case of *Tall*, this means that someone five feet eleven and seven-eighths inches is not *Tall*. However, by adding one-eighth of an inch the set membership immediately shifts into the *Tall* set. From a database selection viewpoint, this can lead to some significant problems. Consider a (hypothetical) retailer's store database. Figure 6.10 schematically illustrates how this database might be organized.

The marketing department is using the information to find prospects for a sale of special items. They want to find *Tall*, *Heavy*, and *Middle-aged*

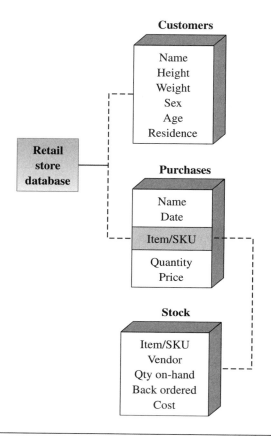

Customers

Name
Height
Weight
Sex
Age
Residence

Purchases

Name
Date
Item/SKU
Quantity
Price

Stock

Item/SKU
Vendor
Qty on-hand
Back ordered
Cost

Retail store database

Figure 6.10   The store database.

men who have bought expensive suits in the past few months (for a sale of large suits in a conservative cut). Table 6.11 shows part of the customers table in this database. If we use the Boolean definition of *Tall*, only individuals that are six feet in height or over are selected. The corresponding SQL query would look as follows.

```
select name
from ieh.customers
where customer.height >= 6;
```

Only two individuals are selected from the customers table. Table 6.12 shows these two individuals. A quick review of the Height column shows,

TABLE 6.11   The Customers Table (Partial)

Name	Height	Weight	Age
Jackson	5'3"	170	38
Sanders	6'2"	215	52
Miller	5'11"	157	25
Cassey	6'1"	188	40
O'Malley	5'5"	163	48
Freeman	5'10"	202	44

TABLE 6.12   Tall customers (Boolean Criteria)

Name	Height	Weight	Age	Tall
Jackson	5'3"	170	38	
Sanders	6'2"	215	52	←
Miller	5'11"	157	25	
Cassey	6'1"	188	40	←
O'Malley	5'5"	163	48	
Freeman	5'10"	202	44	

nevertheless, that some of these customers (such as Miller and Freeman) are very close to being categorized as *Tall*. But this is the penalty we pay for using crisp logic in our selection criteria. Naturally, we could change our definition of *Tall* by lowering the boundary between *Tall* and *not Tall*. In the case in which we have only a few outlier records (as in the previous example), this might be an acceptable approach, but as a general solution it will not work. Changing the boundary points on our query changes the meaning of the query and introduces records whose relationship to the idea behind our query is unknown (see the section "Expanding the Query Scope"). What we need is a better way of expressing the concept of *Tall*. This brings us to the idea of a fuzzy set.

A fuzzy set does not represent fuzzy data; it is simply a method of encoding and using knowledge that does not have clearly defined boundaries. Many of the phenomena we encounter every day fall into this class. *Tall* is one example. Other concepts — such as *heavy*, *high*, *low*, *fast*, *slow*, *full*, *empty*, *many*, *few*, *light*, and *dark* — are often associated with variables that have ill-defined boundaries. A fuzzy set maps a value in the data to its degree of membership in a set of ill-defined elements. To see this, let's look at a fuzzy set that might define the idea of *Tall*. Figure 6.11 shows this fuzzy set definition.

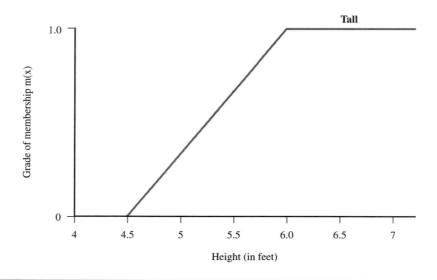

Figure 6.11 The fuzzy *Tall* definition.

Here we have a completely different type of representation for *Tall*. The line moving diagonally up and across the height values is the membership function for the fuzzy set. It associates a height value with a degree of membership. Figure 6.12 shows how the value of five feet has a membership of [*0.43*] in the fuzzy set *Tall*.

What does a number such as [*0.43*] mean? It means that a height of five feet is a moderate member of the fuzzy set *Tall*. We can look at membership values as a measure of compatibility or a measure of representation. They answer questions such as the following.

- How compatible is five feet with the concept *Tall?*
- To what degree is five feet representative of the concept *Tall?*

Thus, a fuzzy set takes a concept, such as *Tall*, and expresses it through a mapping of data to membership functions. The magnitude of the number reflects how well an item matches the semantics (or meaning) of the fuzzy set. Using this new tool, we can now find *Tall* customers with a slight change in our query statement.

```
select name
from ieh.customers
where customers.height is Tall;
```

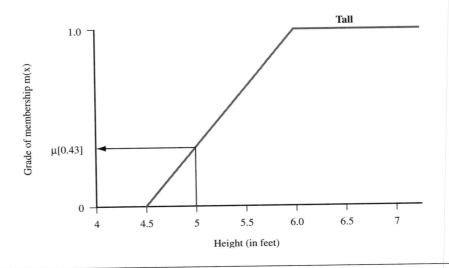

Figure 6.12   Fuzzy memberships.

TABLE 6.13   *Tall* Customers per QCIX

Name	Height	Weight	Age	μ (Tall)
Sanders	6'2"	215	52	.91
Cassey	6'1"	188	40	.90
Miller	5'11"	157	25	.87
Freeman	5'10"	202	34	.83
O'Malley	5'5"	163	48	.62
Jackson	5'3"	170	38	.53

Each value of *customers.height* is located in the fuzzy set *Tall*, and its degree of membership is returned. This type of query measures the degree to which each customer's height is a member of the *Tall* fuzzy set. This degree of membership, called the QCIX, is used to rank the selected records according to how well they agree with our request (we discuss this in more detail in the section "Measuring Query Compatibility"). Table 6.13 shows the result of this query.

The resulting table is sorted in descending order by the compatibility index, which in this case is the membership of *Height* in the fuzzy set *Tall*. Because our definition of *Tall* covers the entire possible domain of interested heights and is linear (a straight line), each record will be graded according to its membership. You can fine-tune the definition of *Tall* by

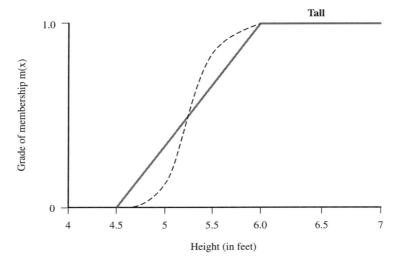

Figure 6.13 Redefining the *Tall* fuzzy set.

changing its range of values or the shape of its membership function. Figure 6.13 illustrates a possible reorganization of the set using an S-curve rather than a linear curve (the underlying linear curve is shown in the background).

In this version of *Tall* we have moved the curve to the right and changed it into an S-curve (also known as a growth curve). Membership values fall off rapidly below the "inflexion" point. Table 6.14 shows the result of the same fuzzy SQL query using the new fuzzy set. Note the change in membership values.

This new set of membership functions brings us to an important fact about fuzzy sets. They are *not* universal descriptors. They are dependent on your data and on your own, sometimes subjective, judgment about the

TABLE 6.14 Tall Customers per New Fuzzy Set

Name	Height	Weight	Age	μ(Tall)
Sanders	6'2"	215	52	.90
Cassey	6'1"	188	40	.88
Miller	5'11"	157	25	.79
Freeman	5'10"	202	34	.67
O'Malley	5'5"	163	48	.13
Jackson	5'3"	170	38	.00

way a concept is expressed in the data. The shape of a fuzzy set reflects the meaning of the concept. This is an important notion: fuzzy sets couple the semantics of your request to the actual mechanics of the request.

> **Semantic,** *si-man'tik, adj.* Relating to meaning, esp. of words – n. (usu. *pl.* treated as *sing.*) the science of the development of the meaning of words. Pertaining to the actual meaning of words. [Gr. σεμαντικοζ, significant].

As a consequence, we are able to state our queries in a form that means something to both us and the computer. But first we have to tell the computer what we mean by such terms as *Tall*. This meaning is expressed in terms of the fuzzy set membership functions. Changing the membership function changes what we mean when we issue a query. Figure 6.14 illustrates this by showing four different but plausible versions of the *Tall* fuzzy set.

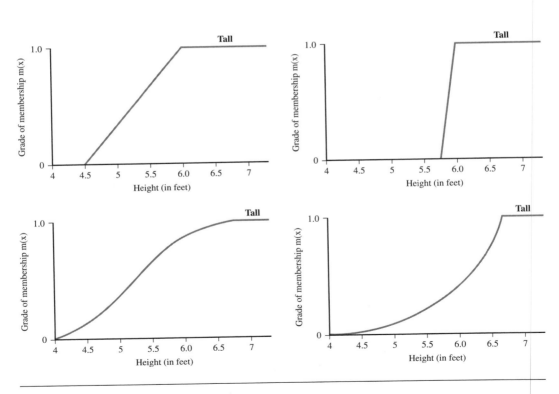

Figure 6.14 Different forms of the *Tall* fuzzy set.

When you design a fuzzy set in the fuzzy SQL system you must ask yourself how data values in the table (or spreadsheet) are related to your semantic concept. However, it is important to realize that this mapping need not be extremely exact. As the membership functions in Figure 6.11 illustrate, the general shape of the curve is sufficient to make the connection. The final fuzzy sets, naturally, may need to "tune" your function after selecting and examining sets of data.

Combining Fuzzy Sets

The real potential of fuzzy queries becomes apparent when we move from one fuzzy set to queries that combine many fuzzy sets. With multiple fuzzy sets we want to find candidates in the data that have, to some degree, characteristics of our combined concepts. Let's look at the query for *Tall* and *Heavy* men. In our crisp query we need to establish a boundary point for the definition of *Heavy*. Suppose we select 195 pounds. Then the SQL query is as follows.

```
select name
from ieh.customers
   where customers.height >= 6
      and customers.weight >= 195;
```

The result of this query is reflected in Table 6.15. Only a single customer is both *Tall* and *Heavy*.

But if we glance down the table, it appears that several of the customers might be potential candidates. They are excluded simply because of the sharp boundary points imposed by the crisp SQL query. We can do better by replacing the query with its corresponding fuzzy version, as follows.

```
select name
from ieh.customers
   where customers.height is Tall
      and customers.weight is Heavy;
```

The intent of this query is obvious: we want customers that are both *Tall* and *Heavy*. To resolve the query we need to tell the computer what constitutes a *Heavy* person. Figure 6.15 shows one possible way to represent this concept.

When we have a value from the customer's Weight column we can find that value's membership in the *Heavy* fuzzy set. Table 6.16 outlines the membership values for each of the weights in the table (ranked by their membership values). Our fuzzy query has identified three customers

TABLE 6.15 *Tall* and *Heavy* Customers (Crisp)

Name	Height	Weight	Age	(Tall and Heavy)
Jackson	5'3"	170	38	
Sanders	6'2"	215	52	←
Miller	5'11"	157	25	
Cassey	6'1"	188	40	
O'Malley	5'5"	163	48	
Freeman	5'10"	202	34	

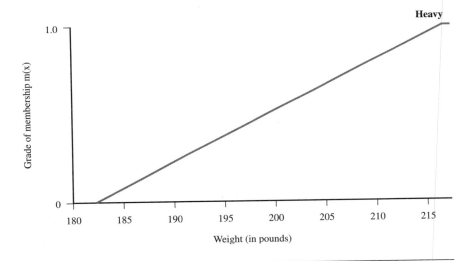

Figure 6.15 The *Heavy* fuzzy set.

TABLE 6.16 *Tall* and *Heavy* Customers

Name	Height	Weight	Age	μ(Heavy)	μ(Tall)
Sanders	6'2"	215	52	.9	.91
Freeman	5'10"	202	34	.55	.83
Cassey	6'1"	188	40	.25	.90
Miller	5'11"	157	25	.00	.87
O'Malley	5'5"	163	48	.00	.62
Jackson	5'3"	170	38	.00	.53

(Sanders, Freeman, and Cassey) who have memberships in both the *Tall* and *Heavy* fuzzy sets. These memberships express a degree of compatibility between the intent of the query and the actual results. In the next section we take up the issues associated with quantifying this compatibility.

6.8 Measuring Query Compatibility

We now need some way to combine the membership functions so that the total effect of the query can be expressed and ranked. The final result of evaluating a fuzzy *where* statement is the aggregation of each predicate's truth value. As we have seen, a typical SQL request specifies a set of columns from tables that meet a set of filtering and connection requirements.

```
select column₁, column₂, ..., columnₙ
from table
where predicate₁ AND predicate₂ ... AND predicateₙ
```

Each predicate (qualifier) in the form defined by Expression 6.2,

$$x \text{ is } [not] \ \overline{X}, \tag{6.2}$$

involves a mapping of a value in the column (x) into one of the fuzzy sets defined for that column. This mapping returns a value in the interval $[0,1]$, which is the degree of membership for that value in the fuzzy set. This degree of membership, as we discussed previously, indicates a degree of compatibility between the data value and the semantics imposed by the fuzzy set. Figure 6.16 shows the underlying truth-functional nature of a query predicate.

When a fuzzy query *where* statement contains multiple predicates, the aggregation or fusion of the predicates' truth values indicates a measurement of how well the query matched the intent of our query. This is called the CQIX, a major departure from the way conventional SQL queries treat retrieved data. *Each record (or row) retrieved from a relational database with a fuzzy SQL query has an associated compatibility index.* Records are returned in a descending-order ranking of the compatibility value (most compatible record first). This compatibility index is stored in a new column and can be used just like any of the other table columns. There are three broad methods of combining results to produce a compatibility ranking: minimum of memberships, weighted average of memberships, and weighted product of memberships.

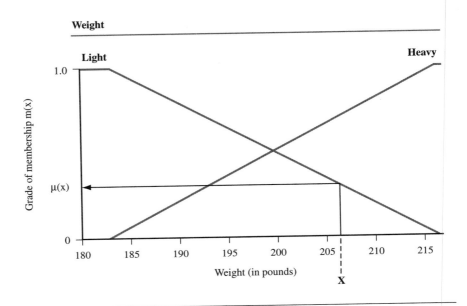

Figure 6.16   The truth-functional nature of a predicate.

Minimum-of-Memberships Compatibility

The simplest method of calculating the overall compatibility index for a query X_i takes the minimum of the predicate truth memberships (this assumes, of course, that the predicates are connected with an *And* operator). Expression 6.3 shows how this QCIX is computed for the complete query.

$$X_{qcix} = \overset{n}{\underset{i=1}{\vee}} \min(\mu_i(p_i)) \tag{6.3}$$

Here,

X_{qcix} is the query compatibility index for query X
n is the number of evaluated predicates in the query
$\mu_i()$ is a function that returns the minimum membership value
p_i is the *i*-th predicate in the query

The minimum approach functions like the traditional *And* operator. Each query predicate is treated as an expression that is dependent on the complete set of predicates. Table 6.17 illustrates how the minimum-of-memberships value works.

TABLE 6.17 Minimum of *Tall* and *Heavy* Customers

Name	Height	Weight	Age	μ(Heavy)	μ(Tall)	Minimum μ(Heavy, Tall)
Sanders	6'2"	215	52	.95	.91	.91
Freeman	5'10"	202	34	.55	.83	.55
Cassey	6'1"	188	40	.25	.90	.25
Miller	5'11"	157	25	.00	.87	.00
O'Malley	5'5"	163	48	.00	.62	.00
Jackson	5'3"	170	38	.00	.53	.00

As you can see, the minimum of the membership values constrains the solution to the weakest element in the data. This means that all *where* statement *And* conditions must be true (or have some degree of truth) before the entire SQL statement is true. Thus, minimum compatibility measurements are highly sensitive to a single zero membership predicate (this includes predicate memberships that are zero because the original membership value fell below the query's alpha cut threshold).

Weighted-Average-of-Memberships Compatibility

A more robust method of viewing the compatibility measurement for query X_i takes the weighted average of the predicate truth values. In this approach, each column is given a bias weight in the interval $[1,n]$, where n is a large number relative to all weights greater than 1. Expression 6.4 shows how the weighted average compatibility index is computed.

$$X_{qcix} = \frac{\sum_{i=1}^{n} (\mu_i(p_i)) \times w_i}{\sum_{i=1}^{n} w_i} \tag{6.4}$$

Here,

X_{qcix}	is the query compatibility index for query X
n	is the number of evaluated predicates in the query
$\mu_i()$	is a function that returns the minimum membership value
p_i	is the i-th predicate in the query
w_i	is the contribution weight associated with the i-th predicate

When the weights for columns are ignored (each column weight is one [1]), Expression 6.4 shows that the QCIX is computed as the ordinary

TABLE 6.18 Average of *Tall* and *Heavy* Customers

						Average
Name	Height	Weight	Age	μ(Heavy)	μ(Tall)	μ(Heavy, Tall)
Sanders	6'2"	215	52	.95	.91	.930
Freeman	5'10"	202	34	.55	.83	.690
Cassey	6'1"	188	40	.25	.90	.575
Miller	5'11"	157	25	.00	.87	.435
O'Malley	5'5"	163	48	.00	.62	.310
Jackson	5'3"	170	38	.00	.53	.265

average for the complete query. The average membership approach computes the mean of the entire memberships values. This is reflected in Table 6.18.

The averaging method balances the truth membership functions across each of the *where* statement predicates. Because it is an average, a low and high membership will produce a moderate truth value. However, as the last three rows in Table 6.18 illustrate, the average method often produces a significant truth result even when one of the selection criteria has a zero truth membership.

Weighted-Product-of-Membership Compatibility

A method that naturally biases the overall compatibility for query X_i toward the weakest truth memberships, but does not automatically settle on the single predicate with the minimum truth, takes the weighted product of the predicate truth values. In this approach, like the weighted average, each column is given a bias weight in the interval $[1,n]$, where n is a large number relative to all weights greater than 1. Expression 6.5 shows how the weighted average compatibility index is computed.

$$X_{qcix} = \prod_{i=1}^{n} \min(\mu_i(p_i)) \times w_i \qquad (6.5)$$

Here,

X_{qcix} is the query compatibility index for query X
n is the number of evaluated predicates in the query
$\mu_i()$ is a function that returns the minimum membership value
p_i is the i-th predicate in the query
w_i is the contribution weight associated with the i-th predicate

TABLE 6.19 Product of *Tall* and *Heavy* Customers

Name	Height	Weight	Age	μ(Heavy)	μ(Tall)	Product μ(Heavy, Tall)
Sanders	6'2"	215	52	.95	.91	.86
Freeman	5'10"	202	34	.55	.83	.46
Cassey	6'1"	188	40	.25	.90	.23
Miller	5'11"	157	25	.00	.87	.00
O'Malley	5'5"	163	48	.00	.62	.00
Jackson	5'3"	170	38	.00	.53	.00

When the weights for columns are ignored (each column weight is one [*1*]), Expression 6.4 shows that the QCIX is computed as the ordinary product for the complete query. The product membership approach computes the chained product of the entire membership values. This is reflected in Table 6.19.

The product, like the minimum method is sensitive to a predicate with zero truth membership. However, unlike the minimum method, which is totally biased toward the query predicate with the smallest degree of truth, the product method tends to move more slowly in the direction of the overall minimum (the interpretation of the membership products, of course, is a percentage of each other; thus, **prod**(*.25,.90*) is either 25% of 90 or 90% of 25).

6.9 Complex Query Compatibility Metrics

Understanding the dynamics of a fuzzy query is fairly easy once you see how the query manipulates the set of incoming truth memberships. Let's complete our example by extending the fuzzy query to include *Age*. In this case, the marketing group is looking for *Tall*, *Heavy*, and *Middle-aged* customers. Once more, the conventional SQL statement requires us to define what we mean by *Middle-aged*. Suppose we say that people between 35 and 45 are *Middle-aged*. The SQL query is then as follows.

```
select name
from ieh.customer
   where customer.height >= 6
      and customer.weight >= 195
      and (customer.age >=35 and customer.age =< 45);
```

TABLE 6.20   *Tall, Heavy,* and *Middle-aged* Customer (crisp)

Name	Height	Weight	Age	Tall, Heavy, and Middle-aged
Jackson	5'3"	170	38	
Sanders	6'2"	215	52	←
Miller	5'11"	157	25	
Cassey	6'1"	188	40	
O'Malley	5'5"	163	48	
Freeman	5'10"	202	34	

However, as Table 6.20 indicates, this criterion does not change the records retrieved from the database (because we only had one from the previous criterion). Thus, only Sanders is *Tall, Heavy,* and *Middle-aged.* Once more, examining the table we can see that there are customers who might be candidates if we can relax the crisp boundaries on our query. We can do better by replacing the query with its corresponding fuzzy version, as follows.

```
select name
from ieh.customer
    where customer.height is Tall
        and customer.weight is Heavy
        and customer.age is MiddleAged;
```

The intent of this query is also obvious: we want customers that are *Tall, Heavy,* and *Middle-aged.* To resolve the query we need to tell the application what constitutes a *Middle-aged* person. Unlike the *Tall* and *Heavy* fuzzy sets, *Middle-aged* represents a fuzzy number. Fuzzy numbers are bell- or triangular-shaped fuzzy sets. The *Middle-aged* fuzzy set is centered around 40, the essential point of middle age. Figure 6.17 shows one possible way to represent this concept.

Now when we have a value from the customer's age column we can find its membership in the *Middle-aged* fuzzy set. Table 6.21 shows the membership values for each of the weights in the table (ranked by their membership values). With this extension to our fuzzy query, we have found that all of our customers have some small degree of membership in the *Middle-aged* fuzzy set, although two of these (Sanders and Miller) have very small degrees of membership. We note that in this final slice through the table (see Table 6.22) Sanders has moved from its top position toward the bottom of the list (for selected records with minimum method compatibility indexes greater than zero).

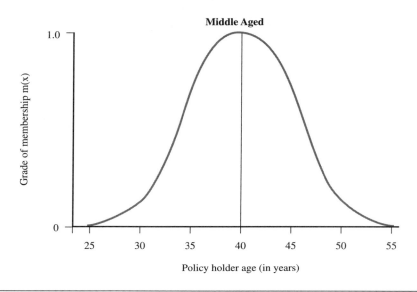

Customer_Age

Figure 6.17 *Middle-aged* fuzzy set.

TABLE 6.21 *Tall, Heavy,* and *Middle-aged* Customers

Name	Height	Weight	Age	μ(MA)	μ(Heavy)	μ(Tall)
Cassey	6'1"	188	40	**1.0**	**.25**	**.90**
Jackson	5'3"	170	38	**.97**	**.00**	**.53**
Freeman	5'10"	202	34	**.90**	**.55**	**.83**
O'Malley	5'5"	163	48	**.70**	**.00**	**.62**
Sanders	6'2"	215	52	**.12**	**.95**	**.91**
Miller	5'11"	157	25	**.10**	**.00**	**.87**

TABLE 6.22 *Tall, Heavy,* and *Middle-aged* Customers

Name	Height	Weight	Age	μ(MA)	μ(Heavy)	μ(Tall)	Min	Avg
Freeman	5'10"	202	34	**.90**	**.55**	**.83**	**.55**	**.760**
Cassey	6'1"	188	40	**1.0**	**.25**	**.90**	**.25**	**.716**
Sanders	6'2"	215	52	**.12**	**.95**	**.91**	**.12**	**.660**
Jackson	5'3"	170	38	**.97**	**.00**	**.53**	**.00**	**.500**
O'Malley	5'5"	163	48	**.70**	**.00**	**.62**	**.00**	**.440**
Miller	5'11"	157	25	**.10**	**.00**	**.87**	**.00**	**.323**

Thus, using a fuzzy query approach instead of a conventional SQL query we have found three customer candidates instead of one. Indeed, the fuzzy query selected customers that matched the intent of our query rather than the strict algebraic rules of the query. As we can see, as the number of column attributes increases the brittleness of conventional SQL queries also rapidly increases. The fuzzy query approach strikes a balance in the process by including records that to some degree meet the intent of our query. Selecting the minimum or average result analysis then allows us to choose records that have some truth in each of the selection criteria (minimum) or some overall truth in the complete query (average).

6.10   Compatibility Threshold Management

In practice, the retrieval of records through a fuzzy query can produce extensive lists ranked by ever-decreasing query compatibility index values. An analyst needs some mechanism for selecting just the first n records. Generally, we set the limit for n records by specifying the minimum acceptable compatibility index value. By indicating a QCIX threshold, only those records with a compatibility index value equal to or above the threshold will be actually returned by the query. For example, the query process returns all rows in Table 6.17 when the threshold is zero [0]. On the other hand, if we raise the minimum allowed QCIX to [0.2] only a subset of rows is returned. Table 6.23 shows the records from the minimum QCIX method.

On the other hand, as Table 6.24 shows, the same compatibility threshold returns *all* records when the average method is used.

The query threshold is a form of alpha cut threshold applied to the aggregate truth membership. A QCIX value below the threshold is treated as though its value were zero. By adjusting the QCIX threshold, an analyst can enforce either a weak or strong degree of compatibility between the selected data rows and the underlying query concept. If the QCIX threshold is low, compatibility is weakly enforced, whereas a high QCIX threshold enforces a strong degree of compatibility.

TABLE 6.23   Minimum QCIX Method Threshold Screening with QCIX Threshold 0.2

Name	Height	Weight	Age	μ(MA)	μ(Heavy)	μ(Tall)	Min
Freeman	5'10"	202	34	.90	.55	.83	.55
Cassey	6'1"	188	40	1.0	.25	.90	.25

TABLE 6.24 Average QCIX Method Threshold Screening with QCIX Threshold 0.2

Name	Height	Weight	Age	μ(MA)	μ(Heavy)	μ(Tall)	Avg
Freeman	5'10"	202	34	.90	.55	.83	.760
Cassey	6'1"	188	40	1.0	.25	.90	.716
Sanders	6'2"	215	52	.12	.95	.91	.660
Jackson	5'3"	170	38	.97	.00	.53	.500
O'Malley	5'5"	163	48	.70	.00	.62	.440
Miller	5'11"	157	25	.10	.00	.87	.323

6.11 Fuzzy SQL Process Flow

Having examined the way *where* predicates control which records participate in the query, this section summarizes the flow of control and action in the fuzzy SQL environment. From this we lead into an example of a query from the Fuzzy Data Explorer. The basic fuzzy query paradigm is amazingly simple, thus providing a powerful data exploration tool available to both information technology (IT) users and knowledge engineers. Figure 6.18 shows a flow schematic for the query process.

The fuzzy SQL process is essentially a protracted *do... while* loop. Each record is read from the data date (or spreadsheet or flat file). The values for the variable specified in the *where* statement are extracted $(x_1, x_2, x_3, \ldots x_n)$ and their memberships in the associated fuzzy sets determined. As shown in Expression 6.6, this generates a vector, V^m, of memberships.

$$V^m = (\mu_1(x_1), \mu_2(x_2), \ldots \mu_n(x_n)) \tag{6.6}$$

The QCIX processor also creates a default weight vector, as shown in Expression 6.7, containing the bias weights for each field.

$$V^w = (w_1(x_1), w_2(x_2), \ldots w_n(x_n)) \tag{6.7}$$

Thus, as Expression 6.8 illustrates, the effective compatibility index is found by multiplying the actual membership vector by the weight vector.

$$V^c = V^m \times V^w \tag{6.8}$$

Naturally, if column or field weights have not been specified the vector defaults to a series of ones [1] so that the result is simply the base membership values. These vectors constitute the basic building blocks for the

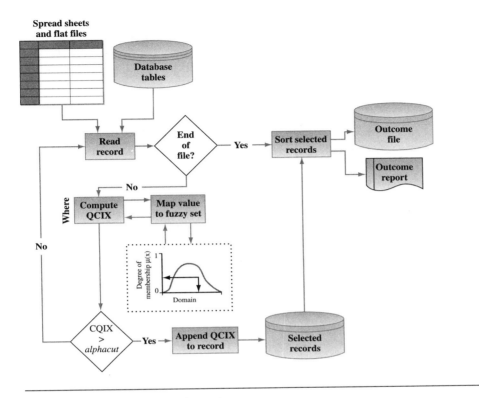

Figure 6.18 The fuzzy SQL flow schematic.

weighted average compatibility index. Expression 6.9 shows Expression 6.4 cast in terms of these vectors.

$$QCIX = \frac{\sum_{i=1}^{N} V_i^c}{\sum_{i=1}^{N} V_i^w} \tag{6.9}$$

Here,

$QCIX$ is the query compatibility index for query
N is the number of evaluated predicate vectors
V^c is the effective compatibility index (see Expression 6.8)
V^w is vector of weights

Once the QCIX is computed, it is compared against the minimum QCIX threshold. Only records with a QCIX equal to or greater than this minimum value are selected. The selected record's QCIX is added as a new column, and the record is written to the query-retained records file. When the end of the file is encountered, the retained records are sorted by their QCIX (for rows with the same QCIX value, the sort uses the primary identifier or the first column specified in the *select* statement as a discriminator).

Code Preview

Executing Fuzzy SQL (Visual Basic Code)

The previous schematic provided a general view of the fuzzy query's control architecture. How is this translated into a working software system? The complete Fuzzy SQL Visual Basic code (with supporting C/C++ utilities) is found on the companion CD-ROM. However, the following local subroutine is the actual code that implements a defined query.

```
Public Sub   mpRunQuery()
Dim sFzyId            As String
Dim i                 As Integer
Dim iCOffset          As Integer
Dim iStatus           As Integer
Dim iAndType          As Integer
Dim bMultiHedge       As Boolean
Dim bColHedge         As Boolean
Dim bUseWgts          As Boolean
Dim lRowNum           As Long
Dim lRowCnt           As Long
Dim lVecIdx           As Long
Dim dData             As Double
Dim fMem(1 To 64)     As Single
Dim fWgt(1 To 64)     As Single
Dim fCIX              As Single
Dim fCAlfa            As Single

giStatus = 0
```

We begin the procedure by retrieving two important parameters: the minimum QCIX threshold and the type of *And* operator. The minimum QCIX (also known as the alpha cut threshold) is stored in *fCAlfa*, and the *And* operator type is stored in *iAndType*. The procedure also looks to see if column or field weights are in use. If so, the Boolean variable *bUseWgts* is set to *True*.

```
fCAlfa = Val(FQMcixThreshold.Caption)

If FQMoptAMin.value = True Then
    iAndType = 1
End If
'
If FQMoptAAvg.value = True Then
    iAndType = 2
End If
'
If FQMoptAPro.value = True Then
    iAndType = 3
End If
'
bUseWgts = False
If FQMUseWgts.value = Checked Then
    bUseWgts = True
End If
```

This is the main query-processing loop. The procedure allocates a working array dimensioned to hold all possible rows and columns (note that we add one additional column to hold the QCIX for the record). For each row in the data table we process each *where* statement component (*iQryItems*).

```
ReDim gsQueryData(1 To glDataRows, 1 To iQryColCnt + 1)
lRowCnt = 0
For lRowNum = 1 To glDataRows
    For i = 1 To iQryItems
        iCOffset = iFzyColumn(i)
```

We also move the column data into *dData*, fetch the fuzzy set associated with this query item (*lpFDB* holds a pointer value to the fuzzy set), and find the membership of *dData* in the fuzzy set *lpFDB*. This is then stored in the vector of memberships [*fMem*(1 ... *n*)]. If column weights are used, we also compute the weights vector [*fWgt*(1 ... *n*)].

```
dData = CDbl(tgDataGrid(lRowNum, iCOffset))
lpFDB = mpGetFuzzySet(i, lRowNum, iStatus)
fMem(i) = FzyGetMembership(lpFDB, dData, lVecIdx, lStatus)
If bUseWgts Then
    fWgt(i) = fColWgts(iCOffset)
```

```
Else
   fWgt(i) = 0
End If
Next I
```

All columns have been evaluated and the *fMem( )* vector contains the membership values for each *dData* and *lpFDB* relationship. From this vector (and the weight vector, if needed), the current record's query compatibility index (*fCIX*) is computed by *mpCompIdx*.

```
fCIX = mpCompIdx(fMem(), fWgt(), iQryItems, iAndType, iStatus)
If iStatus > 0 Then
     Exit Sub
End If
```

If the current query compatibility index is greater than or equal to the cutoff threshold, we select this record. This means incrementing a record count, storing the *fCIX* as the first column in the outcome array, and moving the rest of the record's field into the remainder of the slots.

```
If fCIX >= fCAlfa Then
lRowCnt = lRowCnt + 1
gsQueryData(lRowCnt, 1) = fCIX
For i = 1 To iQryColCnt
   gsQueryData(lRowCnt, i + 1) = tgDataGrid(lRowNum,
      iQryOffsets(i))
Next i
End If
Next lRowNum
```

If no records were selected, we set the status code, display a message on the main fuzzy SQL query execution panel, and exit the procedure. Although a fuzzy query generally selects more records than a conventional crisp query, there are instances in which no records are selected. Essentially this means that none of the records had a query compatibility index above the threshold level (*fCAlfa*).

```
If lRowCnt = 0 Then
   giStatus = 101
   FQMrunMsg.Caption = "No Records Above CIX
      Threshold."
   Exit Sub
End If
```

Now the QuickSort routine is invoked to sort the stored records in descending or ascending order.

```
If FQMSortDes.value = True Then
    Call mpSortDESQuerydata(1, lRowCnt, iStatus)
Else
    Call mpSortASCQueryData(1, lRowCnt, iStatus)
End If
```

The query is now concluded by showing the selected records on the visual interface's spreadsheet (see Figure 6.27). The processing statistics are also displayed. A graph of the CQIX values is produced (this shows the degree to which the query sliced through the set of candidate records). Finally, the selected records are saved on the output file (see the *INTO* parameter, Figure 6.16).

```
Call mpUpdateQryGrid(FQMGrid, lRowCnt, iStatus)
FQMRead.Caption = Trim(Str(glDataRows))
FQMSelected.Caption = Trim(Str(lRowCnt))
FQMPercent.Caption = Format((lRowCnt / glDataRows) *
    100, "###.00")
Call mpGraphResults(lRowCnt)
Call mpWriteResults(lRowCnt, iStatus)
End Sub
```

6.12 Fuzzy SQL Example

The examples in this chapter are screen images from the Fuzzy Data Explorer (included with the book's software, see the *dataexplorer.vbp* Visual Basic project). This fuzzy data mining and knowledge discovery application contains an integrated fuzzy SQL component. The project and customers databases used in this chapter are also located in the application knowledge base directory (*dxbook/appkb*).

In this section, the initial project risk database is revisited. A fuzzy query is formulated to find projects with a high budget and a short duration. The actual mechanics of fuzzy set decomposition, *where* statement construction, and query execution are followed in a step-by-step process. The initial step in a fuzzy SQL request is, in most ways, similar to conventional SQL. The table sources are specified and the columns are identified. In this example, we are accessing a standard "flat file" of project data. The columns are simply separated by blanks. A file name associated with the outcome process is also entered if the analyst wants the selected column data, ranked by their compatibility index, saved to an external file. Figure 6.19 shows the main fuzzy SQL request definition dialog.

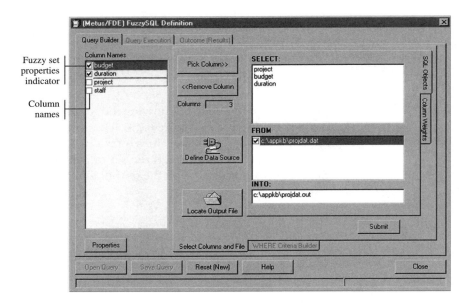

Figure 6.19 Fuzzy SQL definition request.

The first principal difference between traditional and fuzzy SQL queries is evident in the list of available column names appearing in the left-hand side of the main definition dialog. Every column used in a *where* statement must have at least one fuzzy set defined in its range of values. Fuzzy sets and additional data characteristics are defined by selecting the column name and clicking on the Properties command button. A column with existing fuzzy sets is indicated with a check mark next to its name.

Fuzzy Set Definitions

Figure 6.20 shows the definition of the *High* fuzzy set for the Budget column. This is an S-curve extending from 70 on the horizontal axis (where its membership is zero) to the right-hand edge of the variable's current domain (at a value of 93 on the horizontal axis).

Figure 6.21 shows the definition of the *Short* fuzzy set for the Duration column. This is a decay (or left-facing) S-curve extending from 87 (where its membership is one) down to the horizontal axis at 95 (where the fuzzy set membership value is 0).

It is worth repeating at this point that these fuzzy sets represent one possible series of definitions for the concepts of *High Budget* and *Short Duration*. Figure 6.22 shows one such alternate view of *Short Duration*.

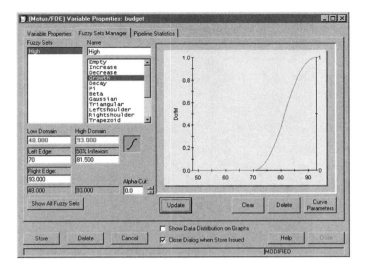

Figure 6.20   Defining *High* budget fuzzy set.

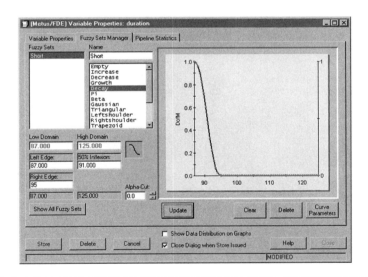

Figure 6.21   Defining *Short* duration fuzzy set.

The *Left Shoulder* membership function provides a more trapezoidal form to the definition of *Short* — a fact that could allow the decomposition of the Duration column into a collection of trapezoids. Figure 6.23 illustrates the definition of the *Medium* project duration in this fashion.

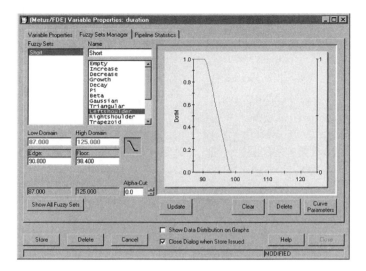

Figure 6.22 Defining *Short Duration* fuzzy set.

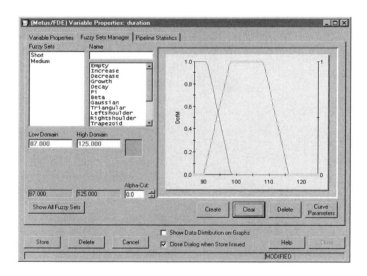

Figure 6.23 Defining *Short* and *Medium Duration* fuzzy sets.

The choice of sigmoid curves of trapezoids is not arbitrary. The fine-grain detail of the fuzzy membership function controls how truth membership is interpreted and returned to compatibility measurement functions. In all cases, however, the actual set membership functions reflect the semantics of the analyst's understanding of these concepts.

Forming Fuzzy *Where* Predicates

These fuzzy sets now form the vocabulary for the fuzzy query. They are used in the *where* predicates in place of exact values. This brings us to the next principal difference in a fuzzy SQL request: predicates are expressed in terms of fuzzy vocabularies. Figure 6.24 shows the definition of the fuzzy *where* predicate *Budget is High*.

The main graphical window, shown in the center of the dialog screen, shows all fuzzy sets defined for the column Budget, which in this case is the single fuzzy set *High*. However, any number of fuzzy sets, each representing some semantic mapping of a column's data space, can be defined. Figure 6.25 shows one such partitioning of the Budget column into the three fuzzy sets *Low, Moderate*, and *High*.

The decomposition of a column into multiple fuzzy sets provides a complete semantic description of the data space. These fuzzy sets are made visible during the *where* predicate statement definition. Figure 6.26 shows the predicate definition dialog for the Budget column when the *Low, Moderate*, and *High* sets are defined.

The selection criteria are completed with the specification of the *Duration is Short* predicate. Like the Budget column, the criteria for the Duration column are completed by selecting the appropriate fuzzy set. Figure 6.27 shows the definition of the fuzzy *where* predicate *Duration is Short*.

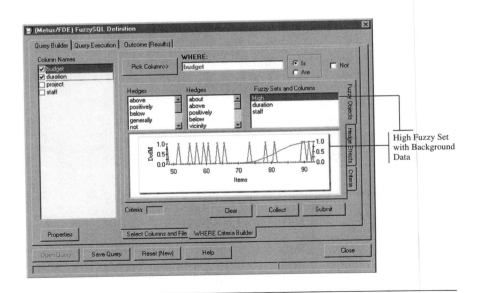

Figure 6.24 Specifying *Budget is High* predicate.

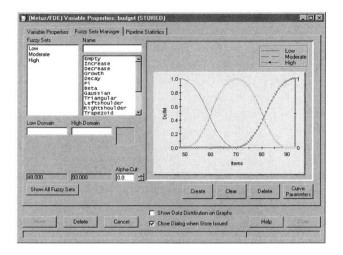

Figure 6.25 Budget with multiple fuzzy sets.

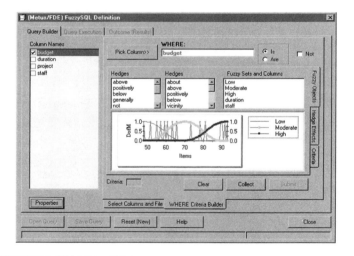

Figure 6.26 Budget column with multiple fuzzy sets.

After each *where* predicate expression is completed, the Collect command is clicked to save the expression. These expressions are automatically connected with the *And* operator. The complete *where* statement is saved using the Submit command. Figure 6.28 shows how the command buttons are used.

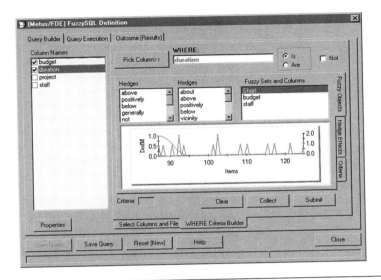

Figure 6.27   Budget column with multiple fuzzy sets.

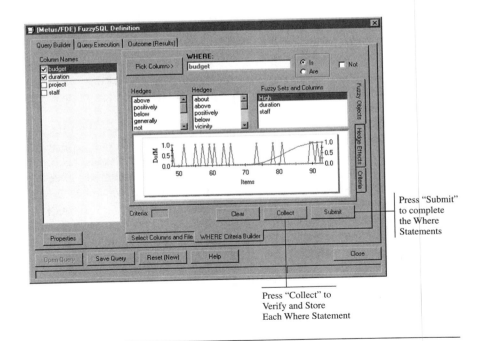

Press "Submit" to complete the Where Statements

Press "Collect" to Verify and Store Each Where Statement

Figure 6.28   Collecting and submitting *where* statements.

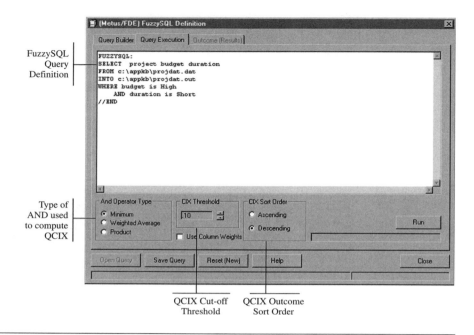

FuzzySQL
Query
Definition

Type of
AND used
to compute
QCIX

QCIX Cut-off
Threshold

QCIX Outcome
Sort Order

Figure 6.29 The fuzzy SQL request definition.

When the *where* filter has been constructed and submitted, the fuzzy SQL request is ready for execution. Clicking on the Submit command button switches to the Query Execution tab. Figure 6.29 shows the final SQL request and the surrounding controls.

Prior to executing the fuzzy SQL request, a number of controls can be changed, including the type of *And*, the cutoff threshold for the QCIX, and the order of presentation for the selected records. Clicking on the Weighted Average *And* type also automatically checks the Use Column Weights control (you can unclick this to ignore any column weights). Sort order is normally descending, showing the records with the highest QCIX values first. In some cases, an ascending sort is more useful. This sort would display the records with the smallest QCIX first.

6.13 **Evaluating Fuzzy SQL Outcomes**

Executing the fuzzy SQL statement causes the database access engine to loop through the database projects table, evaluating the *where* statement

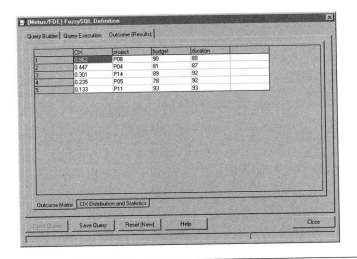

Figure 6.30   Fuzzy SQL outcome results.

```
CIX,      project,  budget,  duration
0.962,     P08,       90,       88
0.447,     P04,       81,       87
0.301,     P14,       89,       92
0.235,     P05,       78,       92
0.133,     P11,       93,       93
```

Listing 6.1   The Fuzzy SQL outcomes file.

for each record. The membership of each data element in the corresponding fuzzy set is determined, and these memberships are used to compute the final QCIX. Figure 6.30 shows the outcome results table.

In this query, the minimum QCIX threshold was set to [*.10*], and thus records with a compatibility value below this cutoff level are not shown and are not stored.

In addition to the visual display of records, the query facility saves the output in a data file (in this case, *projects.out*). The data file organization is comma-delimited with column names. Listing 6.1 shows the outcome records stored in the results file.

Saving the outcome in this format means that we can use the fuzzy query facilities to read and interrogate the outcome in the same manner as any other data file. As Figure 6.31 schematically illustrates, the outcome

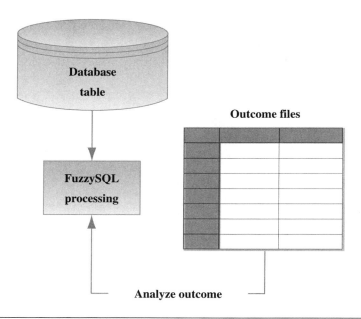

Figure 6.31   Interrogating the outcome file.

of the query is used by fuzzy SQL to evaluate the records that were selected by the base query.

By defining how we interpret the range of QCIX values, we can easily reread the outcome file and select records that meet our perception of what constitutes acceptable record sets. Figure 6.32 shows one possible collection of fuzzy sets defining the range of values for the compatibility index.

With these fuzzy set definitions in hand, the query language can select records from the outcome meeting our semantic expectations about the quality of their compatibility with our request. As one example, the following request selects records with *Acceptable* and *Good* compatibility index values.

```
select *
from projects.out
into myprojs.csv
where CIX is above Acceptable
```

Applying *above* hedge to the fuzzy set *Acceptable* creates a flattened S-curve spanning the plateau of the *Acceptable* fuzzy set's trapezoid and continuing to the end of the QCIX's range of values (thus covering the *Good*

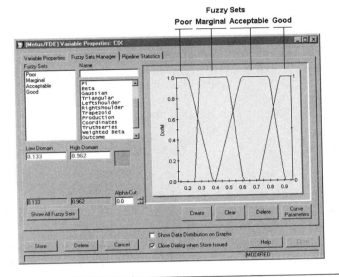

Figure 6.32 The compatibility index fuzzy sets.

fuzzy set). Figure 6.33 shows this hedged fuzzy region superimposed on the collection of base fuzzy sets.

Thus, we wind up with a file ranked by a compatibility index based on the compatibility index of the incoming file. For a small data file, such

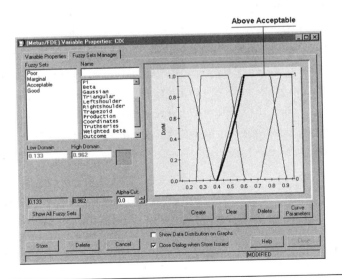

Figure 6.33 The *above Acceptable* fuzzy set.

as the projects table, this is not much of an advantage. However, for very large data files the ability to screen or filter the outcome of a query based on our perception of the QCIX ranking gives us a powerful way of handling data. A filtering based on the semantics of the QCIX becomes even more important when we consider that record selection is often performed using an application framework. Encoding our record filtering allows an automated way of coupling the fuzzy query with a post-selection filtering mechanism, both of which are predicated on the query compatibility concept.

6.14 **Review**

Fuzzy SQL forms one of the core data exploration tools needed by business analysts and knowledge engineers at the start of any knowledge discovery project. In addition to the general necessity of data profiling (developing a statistical knowledge of each variable's properties), fuzzy query capabilities give analysts and engineers a highly flexible and robust method of semantically scouring large databases for new relationships, as well as for studying the degree to which known behaviors and relationships exist and can be isolated. You should now be familiar with the following.

- The basic ideas of row and column data, and relational databases
- How data is retrieved through the *select* and *where* statements
- How fuzzy sets are used to describe the semantics of database columns
- How a degree of truth is calculated for each *where* statement predicate
- The various ways of computing a query compatibility index (QCIX)
- How the QCIX effectively ranks records by the query intent
- How fuzzy queries isolate and quantify patterns in data
- The way the fuzzy outcome of a query can be reevaluated

Fuzzy SQL is a powerful tool for data exploration and pattern discovery. However, it relies on the ingenuity and perceptions of the human analyst. In the next two chapters we begin an examination of pattern discovery techniques that find, extract, and quantify patterns directly from the data. The first method, fuzzy cluster detection, provides a visual tool for understanding how data elements are related across multiple dimensions and a simple technique for generating the associated classification rules. Following fuzzy clustering we explore a comprehensive and flexible method of discovering and extracting *if-then* fuzzy rules from large collections of data.

Further Reading

■ Bezdek, J. C. (ed.). *Analysis of Fuzzy Information, Volume II: Artificial Intelligence and Decision Systems*. Boca Raton, FL: CRC Press, 1987.

■ Dubois, D., H. Prade, and R. Yager (eds.). *Fuzzy Information Engineering*. New York: John Wiley and Sons, 1996.

■ Kerschberg, L. (ed.). *Expert Database Systems: Proceeding from the Second International Conference*. Redwood City, CA: The Benjamin/Cummings Publishing Company, 1989.

■ Li, D., and D. Liu. *A Fuzzy Prolog Database System*. New York: John Wiley and Sons, 1990.

■ Zadeh, L., and J. Kacprzyk (eds.). *Fuzzy Logic for the Management of Uncertainty*. New York: John Wiley and Sons, 1992.

■ ■ ■ ■   Chapter 7
Fuzzy Clustering

In this chapter we examine methods of analyzing data using fuzzy cluster-ing techniques. Fuzzy clustering provides a robust and resilient method of classifying collections of data elements by allowing the same data point to reside in multiple clusters with different degrees of membership. By way of comparison, we also look at a crisp clustering method, the k-means algorithm. The algorithms we use in this chapter are the fuzzy c-means (Duda and Hart, and Bezdek) and the fuzzy adaptive clustering algorithm (Young-Jun Lee, based on work by Krishnapuram and Keller).

Attempts to find meaning and patterns in chaotic or turbulent systems, whether natural or artificial, have been at the root of western analytical thought since the time of Aristotle. Modern scientific methods, supported by powerful mathematical and machine intelligence capabilities, have given business analysts, knowledge engineers, and systems architects a wide spectrum of tools for probing the unstructured and often chaotic nature of business data. Following a reductionist methodology (the core of modern scientific method, first developed by William of Okkham and Roger Bacon), knowledge engineers have turned to techniques that parti-tion data into related families. This simple act of partitioning reduces com-plexity and helps expose hidden order and deeply buried patterns in data.

Large databases in such commerce-driven industries as retailing, manu-facturing, insurance, banking, and investments contain a staggering amount of raw data. Knowledge engineers and systems analysts, faced with the prospect of maintaining a competitive edge in the world of e-commerce and rapidly changing delivery channels, must look to this data to find new customer relationships, possible newly emerging lines of business, and ways to cross sell existing products to new and existing customers. Yet trying to make sense out of this data (seeking patterns, for example) requires an analytical perspective not easily achieved through either statistical analysis or even multidimensional visualization alone. High-altitude views of the raw data space more often than not reveal largely noise. Close-in views are often overpowered by the sheer quantity of data.

7.1 **The Vocabulary of Fuzzy Clustering**

If you exclude mathematical equations, the vocabulary of fuzzy clustering is surprisingly sparse. In fact, much of the underlying terminology related to cluster configuration, membership, and overlap has already been covered in the chapters on fuzzy logic fundamentals. A review of some vocabulary terms used in fuzzy clustering, however, will make reading and understanding the material in this chapter somewhat easier. It is, however, not always possible, while maintaining an uncluttered and coherent discussion of the clustering process, to ensure that every term is introduced before it is used.

Centroid

The center of a cluster. A symmetric cluster can be visualized as an n-dimensional region balanced on its center of gravity. Hence, the center of a cluster is also called the *centroid* of the cluster.

Cluster (Clustering)

A cluster is a group of observations ("things") that have similar properties. The process of clustering involves finding sets of groups (clusters), each containing all observations that share a collection of specified properties (or attributes). When the clusters or categories are not predefined, clustering provides a form of unsupervised knowledge discovery in which deeply buried or distributed patterns emerge, revealing a variety of behavior patterns in the underlying data.

Cluster Seeds

Clustering often starts with an estimate of the cluster population (N clusters). These N cluster centers are then initially populated with random values drawn from the domain of each dimension in the cluster. The random values used to initialize the clusters are called the *cluster seeds*.

Entropy (or Noise)

Large collections of data are often filled with noise (obvious outliers, and missing, improperly transcribed, erroneous, and duplicate data). The noise acts like background scattering and can obscure the actual patterns buried in the data. *Entropy* is a measure of disorder in a system. The higher the entropy the greater the degree of disorder. One of the goals of a clustering technique is to identify noise and reduce its impact on clustering.

Euclidean Distance

The most commonly used measure of the distance from the current cluster center to a data point, called the *Euclidean distance*, is based on the Pythagorean theorem. For two points, *x* and *y*, in N-dimensional space, Expression 7.1 is the Euclidean distance.

$$d = \sqrt{\sum_{i=1}^{N} (x_i - y_i)^2}$$

(7.1)

Here,

d is the distance
N is the number of dimensions in the data
x_i is the *i*-th value x
y_i is the *i*-th value y

This is generally considered the ordinary (or conventional) distance between two points — one that could, theoretically, be measured by a straight edge. There are many other methods for measuring the distance between points in multidimensional space, but the Euclidean distance is the most commonly used.

Iteration

The process of adding a new point to a cluster and then recomputing the center is called *iteration*. This is the core mechanism in compiling a cluster.

Membership

In conventional clustering, a data point is a member of one and only one cluster. In fuzzy clustering, a data point can have a membership in multiple clusters (each to a different degree). *Membership* is a measure of how strongly a data point is a member of a particular cluster. This measure is important in the rule-generation process.

Stability

The idea of *stability* is a measure of the steady state of a cluster. As new data points are added to a cluster, the center is recalculated. The center moves as the weighted center of gravity changes. At some point, when enough points are added, the center no longer changes. At this point the cluster is stable.

7.2 Principles of Cluster Detection

Cluster analysis is a technique for breaking data down into related components in such a way that patterns and order become visible. In fact, cluster analysis has the virtue of strengthening the exposure of patterns and behaviors as more and more data becomes available. A cluster has a center of gravity, which is basically the weighted average of the cluster. Data points arrayed around the center have, in the fuzzy clustering approach, a degree of membership in each of the centers. By evaluating the strength of membership in clusters for sets of records, we can often discover new and interesting relationships in the data.

Clustering is an important approach to understanding business process models. By looking at the relationships between multiple attributes in the data (variables in the model) we expect to find indicators of the model performance. Isolating these indicators, such as market segmentation factors, provides valuable insights into the order hidden in the data. Figure 7.1, for example, shows a simplified retailing system and some of the common attributes associated with each component.

Our investigation of the retailing data might lead us to approach market segmentation by looking for discriminators among customers and purchases. We would like to know which customers are likely to purchase what quantities of products according to their pricing stratification. Figure 7.2 illustrates a hypothetical clustering of the data based on two attributes (income divided by age against amount spent and the price times quantity purchased).

In this example, two discrete and easily identifiable clusters emerge (such is of course not usually the case in the real world). Here, in examining the ratios two groups emerge. From this we might predict the purchasing habits of new clients, the product mix offered to current customers, or the profitability of potential clients. Clustering, then, is an attempt to gather points in the sample space that share similar attributes. This similarity can be explicit in the data or defined through some similarity or association function. In the end, we hope that clustering reveals

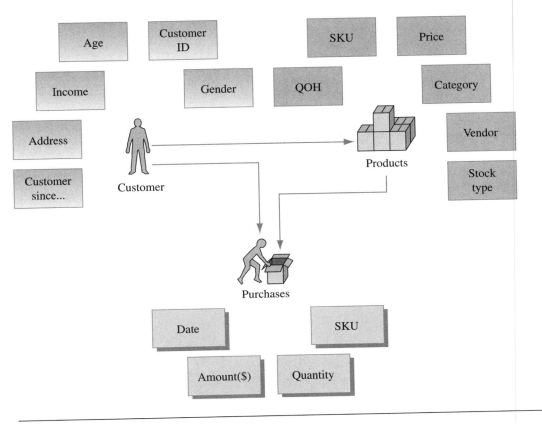

Figure 7.1 Patterns and relationships in a retailing system.

hidden patterns and hidden order in the data so that new insights into our business processes are gained.

7.3 **Some General Clustering Concepts**

As we will discuss shortly, clustering in actual data analysis often involves data with high dimensionality. In our example, we used two dimensional data groups (x_i, y_i), but normally our data contains many data elements $(a_i, b_i, c_i, \ldots, z_i)$ so that cluster analysis penetrates deeply into our data's sample space. Before moving on to the process of crisp (hard) and fuzzy clustering methods, we need to understand some principles common to

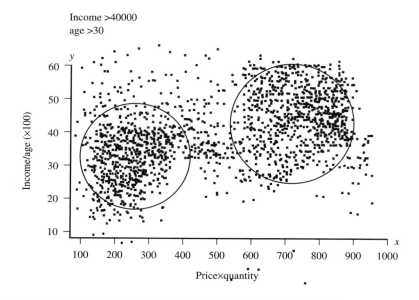

Income >40000
age >30

Figure 7.2   Clusters representing income versus spending habits.

both approaches. These include the issues of what is clustered in the sample space and how we go about assigning a data point to a particular cluster. The first issue involves understanding the attributes of clustering, and the second centers on using these attributes to measure distances in a sample space of arbitrary dimensionality.

Cluster Attributes

Clustering takes a vector of ordered values (columns in a database or spreadsheet, for example) and maps them into similar groups. Every point (x_i) in a cluster space consists of a multidimensional vector (X) containing the column or field values.[1] Expression 7.2 shows how this is constructed.

$$X_i(x_{1i}, x_{2i}, x_{3i}, \ldots, x_{ni}) \tag{7.2}$$

---

[1] In this chapter we generally use the term x_i to mean the complete data point, more formally represented by the n-tuple vector, X. Thus, x_i is the attribute vector $X(a_1, a_2, \ldots, a_n)$, each attribute (a_j) specifying a dimension in the sample space.

Attributes

	MPG	CYL	DISP	HP	WGT	ACCL	YR	ORG	Model
	18.0	8	307.0	130.0	3504.	12.0	70	1	"chevrolet chevelle malibu"
	15.0	8	350.0	165.0	3693.	11.5	70	1	"buick skylark 320"
	18.0	8	318.0	150.0	3436.	11.0	70	1	"plymouth satellite"
	16.0	8	304.0	150.0	3433.	12.0	70	1	"amc rebel sst"
	17.0	8	302.0	140.0	3449.	10.5	70	1	"ford torino"
	15.0	8	429.0	198.0	4341.	10.0	70	1	"ford galaxie 500"
Rows	14.0	8	454.0	220.0	4354.	9.0	70	1	"chevrolet impala"
	14.0	8	440.0	215.0	4312.	8.5	70	1	"plymouth fury iii"
	14.0	8	455.0	225.0	4425.	10.0	70	1	"pontiac catalina"
	15.0	8	390.0	190.0	3850.	8.5	70	1	"amc ambassador dpl"
	15.0	8	838.0	170.0	3563.	10.0	70	1	"dodge challenger se"
	14.0	8	340.0	160.0	3609.	8.0	70	1	"plymouth 'cuda 340"
	15.0	8	400.0	150.0	3761.	9.5	70	1	"chevrolet monte carlo"
	14.0	8	455.0	225.0	3086.	10.0	70	1	"buick estate wagon (sw)"
	24.0	4	113.0	95.00	2372.	15.0	70	3	"toyota corona mark ii"

Vector

Figure 7.3 Components of cluster data attributes.

Correspondingly, every cluster center (C_k) — which is also a point in the cluster space — has the same organization, as shown by Expression 7.3.

$$C_k(x_{1k}, x_{2k}, x_{3k}, \ldots, x_{nk}) \qquad (7.3)$$

In most cluster analyses, there may be hundreds or thousands (and sometimes millions) of points but only a few cluster centers. We can visualize the clustering operation as working on a relational database table. Figure 7.3 shows a table of automobile characteristics and their properties.

A vector is derived from a row in the table. The columns represent the vector attributes. Not all table columns, of course, will participate in the clustering operation. In the automobile database shown in Figure 7.3, if we want to apply a clustering algorithm to the cylinder (CYL), horsepower (HP), weight (WGT), and acceleration (ACCL) columns the input to the clustering process must be a set of vectors with just these attributes. It is these vectors that are used in the clustering algorithm.

Cluster Memberships

Membership in a cluster is determined by measuring the distance from a cluster center to a data point (see the previous section "Cluster Attributes"). Figure 7.4 shows the array of points around a cluster center with the distance metrics for several points.

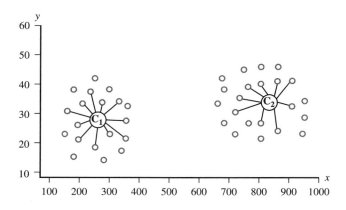

Figure 7.4 Data point distances within a cluster.

The overall process of clustering takes the distance between a point X_m and each of the clusters $C_{1...k}$ as the simple sum of the differences between X_m and C_i (any cluster center). If there are n attributes in each cluster vector, we can represent this process as Expression 7.4.

$$diff_{k \to C} = \sum_{i=1}^{n} (X(x_i) - C(x_i))^2 \qquad (7.4)$$

Here,

    diff   is the difference (distance) between a data point and a cluster center

    n   is the number of attributes in a cluster

    $X(x_i)$ is the i-th data point in vector X

    $C(x_i)$ is the i-th data point in a cluster center (centroid)

Here, the Euclidean distance between the point and a center is calculated. Other distance methods can be used, but the Euclidean calculation is fast and appears to work very well in a wide variety of real-world clustering applications.

More formally, perhaps, computing the distance between a point and the cluster center is done through a process called a sum of the squared difference. Expression 7.5 provides the mathematical summary of the approach.

$$d_k = \sum_{j=1}^{n} \left\| X_j^k - C_j^i \right\|^2 \qquad (7.5)$$

Here,

d_k is distance of the k-th data point (where a "data point" is an individual vector of attributes, thus k will vary from 1 to M, the number of vectors being clustered)

n is the number of attributes in a cluster

X_j^k is the j-th value of the k-th data point

C_j^i is the j-th value of the i-th cluster center

A distance from X_k is calculated for each of the cluster centers ($C_1 \dots i$) using the n attributes in each vector. To find the distance (d_k) from point X_k to the center C_i we sum the squared difference between the j-th attribute of X_k and the j-th attribute of the i-th cluster center. From this we can see that if the X_k lies on or close to the cluster center the value will be at or near zero. On the other hand, as the distance between X_k and C_i increases the distance measure also increases rapidly. Listing 7.1 shows the code for computing a Euclidean distance between a cluster center and a data point.

```
double PE FCEucDist(
double dData[],double dCenters[],int iCentCnt,int
*ipStatus)
/*-----------------------------------------------------*
| Calculate the standard Euclidean distance from the   |
| clusters to the data points. This is the sum of the  |
| squared distances.                                   |
*-----------------------------------------------------*/
{
int i;
double dSum;

*ipStatus=0;
dSum=0;
for(i=0;i<iCentCnt;i++)
   dSum+=pow(dData[i]-dCenters[i],2);
return(dSum);
}
```

Listing 7.1   A Euclidean distance metric.

The distance represents the sum of the squared difference between each attribute of the data point vector (X_i) and the corresponding attributes of the cluster center (C_j).

We can now see that Figure 7.5 is a simplification. In actual clustering analysis, each point is measured from all cluster centers. The data

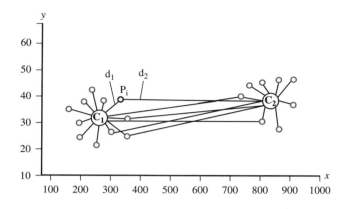

Figure 7.5 Points coupled to multiple centers.

points nearer one center than another move the point into that cluster. Figure 7.5 illustrates how a point $(X_i$ indicated by point P_i) has a distance measurement to center C_1 (the d_1 distance) and center C_2 (the d_2 distance).

Thus, the clustering technique computes a distance metric for each point to each cluster center. We then simply assign the point to the cluster center that has the smallest distance value (that is, of course, to the nearest cluster). This becomes the initial assignment of points to clusters. Figure 7.6 schematically illustrates how a cluster is identified by its center value.

Thus, in this example, the clusters are defined by two centers C_1 and C_2. Center C_1 is located at (30,250) and center C_2 is located at (38,875). Each point in the data is assigned a membership in one of these clusters. For crisp clustering, the membership is either [1] or [0] and a data point belongs unambiguously to one and only one cluster. For fuzzy clustering, the membership is in the interval [0,1] and a data point can belong to multiple clusters with varying degrees of membership.

Higher-dimensional Clustering

Although the majority of examples in this chapter deal with 2D clusters (for the sake of clarity and comprehension), real-world clusters are often spread out across many dimensions. Figure 7.7 illustrates a set of clusters arrayed in three dimensions.

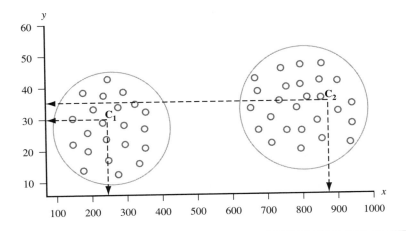

Figure 7.6   Clusters and cluster centers.

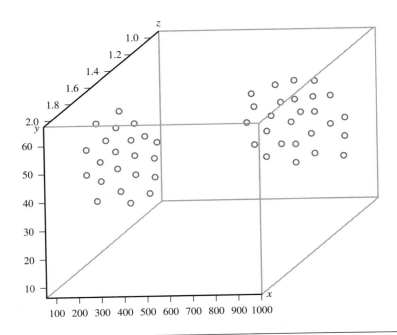

Figure 7.7   A 3D cluster space.

In the case of 3D clusters (as in Figure 7.7), each cluster center is defined by three values (the X, Y, and Z axes). Thus, for any n-dimensional cluster space the centers of the cluster (C_i) are defined by values along the axis of each dimension (d_k) as follows.

$$C_i(d_1, d_2, \ldots, d_n) \tag{7.6}$$

Both 2D and 3D clusters are generally easy to visualize, allowing us to check that our sense of an appropriate cluster center matches the center generated by the computer. Above three dimensions, however, this visualization is not usually possible. Although there are some mathematical techniques for evaluating the quality of a cluster set, we must quite often apply both a *reductionist* approach to cluster verification and some common sense. Reduction analysis simply consists of analyzing the clusters by slicing across two or three dimensions and evaluating the degree to which these clusters are reasonable.

7.4 Crisp Clustering Techniques

Traditional clustering techniques attempt to segment data by grouping related attributes in uniquely defined clusters. Each data point in the sample space is assigned to only one cluster. And, as long as the data can be partitioned in this manner, crisp clustering approaches, such as the k-means algorithm, will perform satisfactorily. In partitioning the data, it is important to remember that none of the data points is moved. Only the centers of the clusters are moved. Thus, clustering is an iterative process of finding better and better cluster centers (this is true for both crisp and fuzzy clustering).

The k-Means Clustering Algorithm

The k in the k-means algorithm stands for the number of cluster seeds initially provided to the algorithm (in the same way the c in the fuzzy c-means algorithm stands for the initial number of cluster centers). The crisp (or hard) k-means algorithm itself is fairly straightforward, involving the basic parameters outlined in Table 7.1.

The goal of the hard k-means algorithm is the assignment of each data point into one and only one cluster. The cluster centers are moved according to a nearness or similarity function defining the distance from a cluster center to the data point. There are two fundamental equations

TABLE 7.1   Basic Parameters of the k-means Algorithm

x_i	A vector of training data, where $i = 1, 2, \ldots, n$. These are the cluster attributes selected from source data elements (such as columns in a database table).
k	The number of fuzzy clusters specified as part of the algorithm.
c_j	The center (or centroid) of a crisp cluster ($j = 1, 2, \ldots, k$). This value is repeatedly calculated by the algorithm (see Expression 7.3).
S_j	A cluster in the sample space. This is a set of points associated with the cluster whose center is at c_j.
$\delta_{sj}()$	The characteristic function of set S_j. Note that the characteristic function of a set A is as follows.

$$\delta(\forall x_i \in A) = \begin{Bmatrix} 1 & x \in A \\ 0 & x \notin A \end{Bmatrix} \tag{7.7}$$

In other words, the function is one for all points of the set, but zero for points outside the set.

used to manage the partitioning of data points. Expression 7.8 establishes the set membership for clusters.

$$S_j^{(t)} = \left\{ x_i \,\middle|\, \left\| x_i - c_j^{(t)} \right\| < \left\| x_i - c_k^{(t)} \right\|, j \neq k \right\} \tag{7.8}$$

Here,

$S_j^{(t)}$ is the set membership in the j-th cluster center under development.

t is the current iteration cycle value. The value of t will vary from 1 to P, the maximum number of iterations used to define the final clusters.

x_i is the i-th data point.

c_j is the center of the j-th cluster.

c_k is the center of the k-th cluster.

That is, in iteration time (t) a point x_i belongs to cluster S_j if its distance to the center of cluster S_j (indicated by c_j) is smaller than the distance to the k-th cluster center (for S_k). We skip over the current cluster center (we do not compare the distance to ourselves!). The distance ($\| \cdot \|$) is generally calculated using a Euclidean metric, but this could, of course, be calculated via any standard distance method.

The cluster centers are initially seeded, usually with a random configuration drawn from the domains (ranges) of the attributes (for other approaches, see the section "Initial Clusters and Cluster Seeds").

The centers are then updated during each cycle (t) using Expression 7.9.

$$c_j^{(t+1)} = \frac{\sum_{i=1}^{n} x_i \delta_{S_j^t}(x_i)}{\sum_{i=1}^{n} \delta_{S_j^t}(x_i)} \tag{7.9}$$

Here,

$c_j^{(t+1)}$ is the set membership in the j-th cluster center under development.

t is the current iteration cycle value. The value of t will vary from 1 to P, the maximum number of iterations used to define the final clusters.

x_i is the i-th data point.

$\delta()$ is the characteristic or set membership determination function.

$S_j^{(t)}$ is the set membership function form (see Expression 7.8).

This is a form of a weighted average, and thus we are calculating the centroid of the j-th cluster center. The characteristic function will return either [1] or [0], indicating whether or not the point x_i is in the particular cluster (S_j). Thus, we effectively have a bit vector (across the complete sample space) constructed for each cluster center indicating whether a data point x_i is a member of that cluster. We add all cluster members where the bit at location x_i is [1] and divide by the sum of the [1] bits. This is shown in Expression 7.10.

$$c_j^{(t+1)} = \frac{\sum_{i=1}^{n} x_i (\delta_{S_j^t}(x_i) = 1)}{\sum_{i=1}^{n} (\delta_{S_j^t}(x_i) = 1)} = \frac{\sum_i x_i}{\sum_i 1} \tag{7.10}$$

Here,

$c_j^{(t+1)}$ is the set membership in the j-th cluster center under development.

t is the current iteration cycle value. The value of t will vary from 1 to P, the maximum number of iterations used to define the final clusters.

x_i is the i-th data point.

$\delta()$ is the characteristic or set membership determination function.

$S_j^{(t)}$ is the set membership function form (see Expression 7.8).

Note that a data point must belong to at least one cluster; otherwise, we will have a division by zero. From these expressions we formulate a somewhat formal definition of the k-means algorithm.

Initialize k=Number of Clusters,
Initialize c_j (cluster centers)
Set cycle variable t=1
Repeat:
For $i = 1$ to n: Distribute sample points (x_i) into the K clusters
For $j = 1$ to k: Resolve $S_j^{(t)}$ for x_i applying (7.8)
For $j = 1$ to k: Compute new cluster centers $c_j^{(t+1)}$ applying (7.9)
t = t+1
Until c_j estimates stabilize

The algorithm itself is fairly simple: cluster centers are randomly initialized
and we assign data points (x_i) into clusters $(S_j; j = 1$ to $k)$ by resolving
Expression 7.8. This beginning state is illustrated in Figure 7.8. The dashed
line represents the initial assignment of points into cluster centers C_1
and C_2.

When all data points have been assigned to clusters, new cluster centers (centroids) are calculated using Expression 7.10. As we can see in
Figure 7.9, the cluster center calculation causes the previous centroid
location to move toward the center of the cluster sets. This also changes
the partitioning of the sample space.

The process of calculating cluster memberships and recalculating cluster centers continues until the cluster centers no longer change from one
cycle to the next (or the change is so small that it falls below some threshold value). Thus, as Figure 7.10 illustrates, the shift in the cluster centers
becomes smaller and smaller until it settles on the final value.

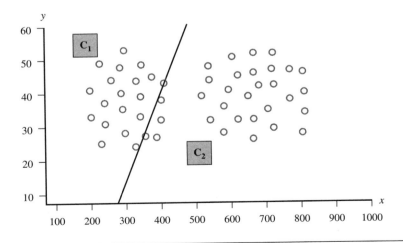

Figure 7.8 Initial k-means partitions.

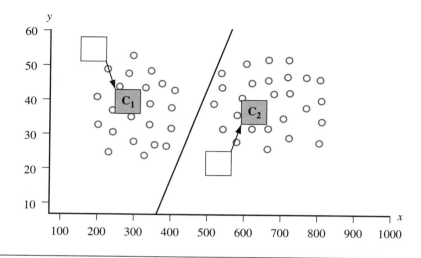

Figure 7.9 Cluster centers repositioned after iteration.

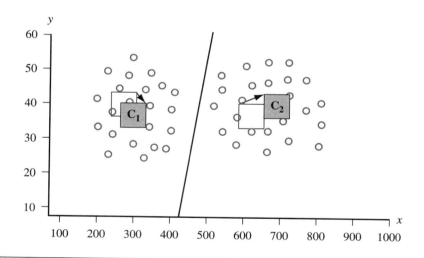

Figure 7.10 Final cluster centers after end of iterations.

The k-means algorithm belongs to a family of crisp (or hard) clustering techniques that uniquely partitions the sample data points into disjoint clusters. The Euclidean distance metric measures how far away a point is from a cluster center, and thus points that share common attributes will naturally cohere into the same cluster. All is well and good if the clusters are distinctly arranged in the *n*-dimensional sample space. In practice (that is, in reality), however, cluster perimeters are often quite ambiguous. Data points in the sample space share attributes from one or more clusters and should thus be placed in more than one cluster (albeit with a degree of membership in one cluster that is higher or lower than the degree of membership in another). This brings us to the focus of the chapter: fuzzy clustering and classification.

7.5 Fuzzy Clustering Concepts

A cluster brings together instances in the data that share a common set of attributes. For each of these clusters a central value representative of the cluster's principal value is calculated. This is the center of gravity (or centroid) of the cluster. An array of these centroids for a collection of data elements from a database provides the cluster centers, thus telling us which set of rows in the database are closely related.

In the simplest manifestation, clusters are groups of related data elements. These groups are defined through a set of attributes. For example, Figure 7.11 illustrates a clustering of data points for the attributes (X, Y).

In this example, there are two well-defined clusters. We can visually pick out the clusters and there are no significant outliers (points well outside either cluster) or points that might belong ambiguously to one or

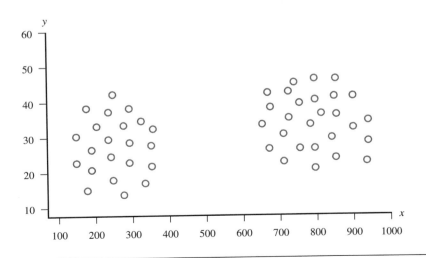

Figure 7.11 Sample clusters.

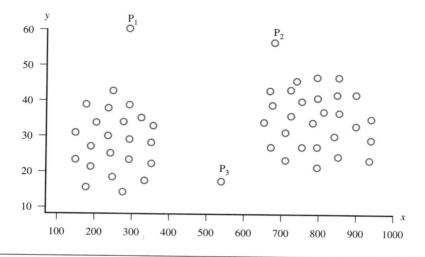

Figure 7.12 Clusters with outlier points.

more clusters. The goal of cluster analysis is the recognition and quantification of these groupings. This quantification involves two processes: identifying the membership of a data point in some group and locating the center of the cluster (the *centroid*). Establishing cluster centers is an iterative process (described in detail later in the chapter).

Even in situations in which clearly defined clusters exist, the data is seldom neatly packaged in well-defined groups. As Figure 7.12 shows, there will often be points (such as P_1, P_2, and P_3) lying well outside the perimeter of any cluster.

These apparently extraneous data points, clearly belonging to neither of the clusters, are called *outliers*. Many crisp clustering techniques have difficulties handling extreme outliers, whereas fuzzy clustering algorithms tend to give them either very small or a higher than warranted membership degree in surrounding clusters (this latter effect is common in the fuzzy c-means algorithm, which we will discuss in some detail).

Real-world data is almost never arranged in such clear-cut groups as we see in Figure 7.11. Instead, clusters have ill-defined boundaries that smear into the data space, often overlapping the perimeters of surrounding groups. If we move our two clusters toward each other, Figure 7.13 illustrates this problem.

The gray area in Figure 7.12 shows the set of points that could conceivably belong to either of the two clusters. In conventional crisp techniques (such as the standard k-means clustering approach), the methodology is forced to make a difficult decision about which cluster "owns" a point.

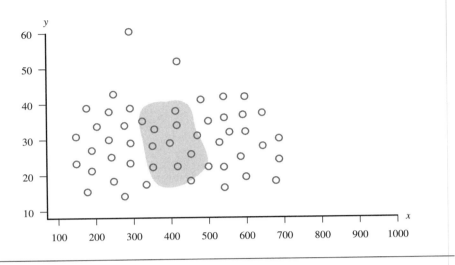

Figure 7.13   Ambiguous data points in two clusters.

In a fuzzy clustering approach, however, points are given partial degrees of membership in multiple nearby clusters. Figure 7.14 shows how a set of points, in the overlap area of the two cluster perimeters,[2] are partly in one set and partly in another.

Running a fuzzy clustering process on these data points using the fuzzy c-means algorithm, we can see the cluster centers as they are actually produced, as well as the membership values for each of the points. Figure 7.15 is a screen image from the Fuzzy Data Explorer showing the cluster centers and the points.

There are two cluster centers (C_1 and C_2) indicated by the squares in Figure 7.15. Table 7.2 outlines the calculated cluster centers at specific points.

A central theme in fuzzy clustering is the often nonunique partitioning of the data in a collection of clusters. Data points, specified as loci in the multidimensional decision space, are assigned membership values for each of the clusters. In some cases, this membership may be zero, but often the membership shows the degree to which the data point is considered representative of the cluster. Figure 7.16 shows the membership assignments for some data points in the overlap between two clusters (see also Figure 7.14).

---

[2] These and all subsequent cluster perimeters are rough outlines of approximately where the edge of the cluster should lie. They are not intended as exact representations of the cluster area.

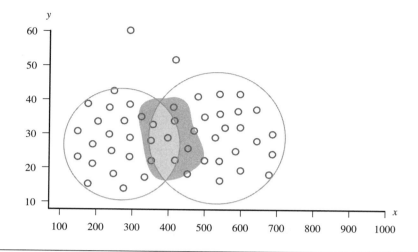

Figure 7.14   Common points in two neighboring clusters.

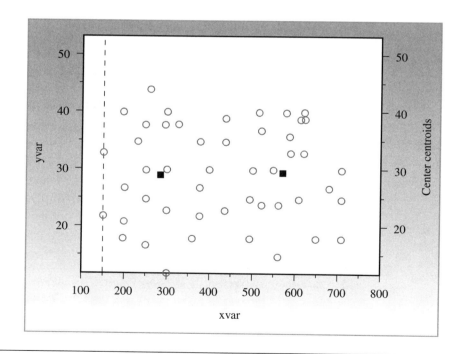

Figure 7.15   Output from fuzzy clustering.

TABLE 7.2 Fuzzy c-means Cluster Centers

Center	YVAR	XVAR
C_1	28.988	286.610
C_2	29.592	571.226

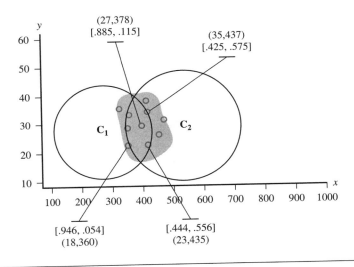

Figure 7.16 Points with partial degrees of membership.

As Figure 7.16 illustrates, a fuzzy clustering provides a flexible and robust method of assigning data points into clusters. Each data point will have an associated degree of membership for each cluster center in the range *[0,1]*, indicating the strength of its placement in that cluster. This becomes particularly important for those data points on the border between clusters. We can imagine the diameter of a cluster space as the base of a bell-shaped fuzzy set. The membership curve defines the degree to which a point is in the cluster. Figure 7.17 illustrates this relationship.

Thus, at the center of the cluster we are also at the apex of the member-of-cluster fuzzy set, with data points in the region having a membership at or near *[1.0]*. As you move left or right away from the center, the degree of membership for data points drops toward zero (the tails of the curve never reach zero but become increasingly small). The tails of the fuzzy regions for neighboring clusters overlap so that data points can be in several clusters simultaneously, affording us an opportunity to observe the actual relationship between data elements. Thus, unlike ordinary crisp cluster

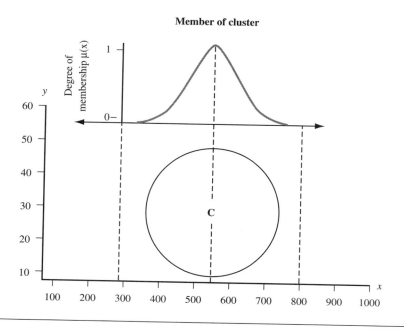

Figure 7.17 Fuzzy cluster membership mapping.

techniques we are not forced to make arbitrary classification decisions along cluster boundaries. The softness of the fuzzy clustering technique gives us a more realistic approach to data analysis.

7.6 **Fuzzy c-Means Clustering**

The most well-known fuzzy clustering algorithm is fuzzy c-means, a modification by Jim Bezdek (see "Further Reading," Bezdek) of an original crisp clustering methodology. This initial approach, the hard ISODATA algorithm, employed a center of means technique, but provided a hard (or crisp) partitioning of elements into the clusters. Bezdek introduced the idea of a *fuzzification* parameter (*m*) in the range [*1, n*], which determines the degree of fuzziness in the clusters. When $m = 1$,[3] the effect is a crisp clustering of points, but when $m > 1$ the degree of fuzziness

---

[3] As you will see when the equations for the fuzzy c-means are discussed, you cannot actually set $m = 1$ because this would result in division by zero. We only mean that when *m* is very near *[1]* the clustering provides an almost completely crisp partitioning of the data points.

among points in the decision space increases. The fuzzy c-means algo-rithm itself is fairly straightforward and involves the basic parameters outlined in Table 7.3. Essentially, the parameter m controls the perme-ability of the cluster horizon, which can be viewed as an n-dimensional cloud moving out from a cluster center. Figure 7.18 illustrates clustering when $m = 1$.

When $m = 1$, the clouds do not overlap, but as you increase the value of m (say, $m = 1.25$) the clouds begin to overlap and share many of the

TABLE 7.3 Basic Parameters of the Fuzzy c-means Algorithm

x	A vector of training data, where $i = 1, 2, \ldots, n$. These are the cluster attributes selected from the source data elements (such as columns in a database table).
d_{ij}	The distance of the i-th data point from the j-th cluster center. Although we use the Euclidean distance, the choice of other distance metrics can be easily incorporated into the fuzzy c-means algorithm.
p	The number of fuzzy clusters specified as part of the algorithm.
m	A fuzzification parameter in the range [>1, $<w$], indicating the width of the n-dimensional cluster perimeter. The larger the number the more fuzzy the point assignments into each cluster. Normally m is the range [$1.25, 2$] inclusive.
c_j	The center (or centroid) of a fuzzy cluster ($j = 1, 2, \ldots, p$). This value is repeatedly calculated by the algorithm (see Expression 7.12).
$\mu_j(x_i)$	A fuzzy membership qualification indicating the membership of sample x_i to the j-th cluster.

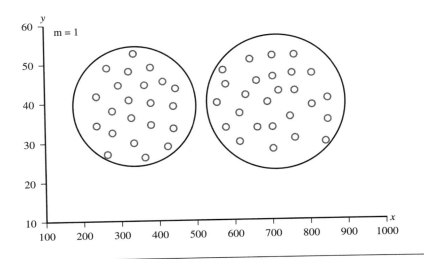

Figure 7.18 Crisp cluster partitioning.

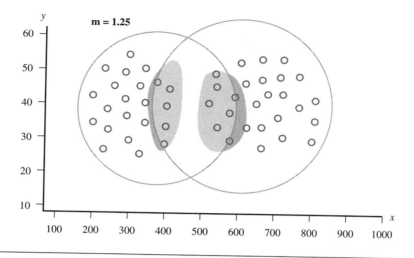

Figure 7.19 Overlapping clusters.

same points. Figure 7.19 illustrates a rough approximation of how two clusters overlap when the fuzzification parameter is increased.

The fuzzy c-means algorithm uses a fixed number of cluster centers, indicated by the parameter (p). The algorithm, however, does not determine the number of clusters; this parameter (p), as well as the fuzzification parameter (m), must be supplied as an external constraint on the algorithm behavior. Before discussing the actual behavior of fuzzy c-means, we need to examine the algorithm itself and review some of its strengths and limitations.

The Fuzzy c-Means Algorithm

Fuzzy c-means clustering involves two processes: the calculation of cluster centers and the assignment of points to these centers using a form of Euclidean distance. This process is repeated until the cluster centers have stabilized. Fuzzy c-means imposes a direct constraint on the fuzzy membership function associated with each point, as follows.

$$\sum_{j=1}^{p} \mu_j(x_i) = 1; \qquad i = 1, 2, 3, \ldots, k \tag{7.11}$$

Here,

p is the number of specified clusters
k is the number of data points

x_i is the i-th data point

$\mu_j()$ is a function that returns the membership of x_i in the j-th cluster

That is, the total cluster memberships for a point in the sample or decision space must add to [1]. As we will see later, this restriction introduces a major weakness into the algorithm when handling outliers or remote clusters.

The goal of the fuzzy c-means algorithm is the assignment of data points into clusters with varying degrees of membership. This membership reflects the degree to which the point is more representative of one cluster than another (or all the others). In effect, we are attempting to minimize a standard loss function, expressed simply as

$$l = \sum_{k=1}^{p} \sum_{i=1}^{n} \left[\mu_k(x_i)\right]^m \|x_i - c_k\|^2 , \tag{7.12}$$

where:

l is the minimized loss value

p is the number of specified clusters

n is the number of data points

$\mu_k()$ is (as in Expression 7.11) a function that returns the membership of x_i in the k-th cluster

x_i is the i-th data point

m is the fuzzification parameter

c_k is the center of the k-th cluster

From this we can derive the two fundamental equations necessary to implement the fuzzy c-means clustering algorithm. Expression 7.13 is used to calculate a new cluster center value.

$$c_j = \frac{\sum_i \left[\mu_j(x_i)\right]^m x_i}{\sum_i \left[\mu_j(x_i)\right]^m} \tag{7.13}$$

Here,

c_j is the center of the j-th cluster

$\mu_j()$ is (as in Expression 7.12) a function that returns the membership of x_i in the j-th cluster

x_i is the i-th data point

m is the fuzzification parameter

You will note that this is simply a special form of weighted average. We modify the degree of fuzziness in x_i's current membership and multiply this by x_i. We then divide by the sum of the fuzzified membership. You will note that we have encountered these operations before. Modifying the degree of fuzziness is equivalent to applying a form of intensification hedge to the current membership (see Chapter 4). Computing the centroid (or center) of the cluster has the same expression as defuzzification (see Chapter 4, section "The Fuzzy Inference Engine").

Code Preview

Updating the Cluster Centers (C/C++ Code)

Each time we compute membership values for the points, the centroids (cluster centers) must be recomputed. The algorithm is fairly straightforward. In order to use this procedure on the first iteration, the memberships for the rows must be initialized (usually to some random value). The following code shows the procedure for updating the cluster centroids.

```
void mpUpdateCentroids(int iRows,long
lCentersCnt,long lVarCount,int *ipStatus)
/*-------------------------------------------------*
| Once we have measured all the membership values   |
| (based on the data element's distance from each   |
| center), we have to go back and recalculate the   |
| cluster centers.                                   |
*-------------------------------------------------*/
{
int i,j,k,ic;
double dMemTot[FCCENTMAX],
    dMem [RDVARMAX],
    dX [RDVARMAX];
```

This code initializes the current cluster centers (centroids) for each vector (row) to zero. We also set the total membership for the cluster to zero.

```
for(ic=0;ic<lCentersCnt;ic++)
{
for(j=0;j<lVarCount;j++)
    XFCCtl.dpXFCCenters[ic][j]=0;
```

```
dMemTot[ic]=0.0;
 }
```

For each vector (row), we extract the data values and the current degree of membership in each of the clusters. From this we sum the memberships and calculate the proportional degree of the data space extent based on the membership. This is the nominator (upper part, for the algebraically challenged) of the center of gravity calculation.

```
for(i=0;i<iRows;i++)
{
for(j=0;j<lVarCount;j++)
    dX[j]=XFCCtl.dpXFCData[i][j];
for(j=0;j<lCentersCnt;j++)
    dMem[j]=XFCCtl.dpXFCDom[i][j];

for(ic=0;ic<lCentersCnt;ic++)
    {
    dMemTot[ic]+=dMem[ic];
    for(k=0;k<lVarCount;k++)
        XFCCtl.dpXFCCenters[ic][k]+=dX[k]*dMem[ic];
    }
}
```

To complete the centroid calculation, the nominator of each center is divided by the sum of the memberships. (For further details, see Expression 2.18).

```
for(ic=0;ic<lCentersCnt;ic++)
for(k=0;k<lVarCount;k++)
    XFCCtl.dpXFCCenters[ic][k]/=dMemTot[ic];
return;
 }
```

The second step, determining the cluster membership for a sample point, is only slightly more complicated. We first need to know the distance from a point x_i to each of the cluster centers $c_{1...j}$. This is done, as illustrated in Expression 7.14, by taking the Euclidean distance between the point and the cluster center.

$$d_{ji} = \left\| x_i - c_j \right\|^2 \tag{7.14}$$

Here,

d_{ji} is the distance of xi from the center of cluster cj
x_i is the i-th data point
c_j is the j-th cluster

(For additional details on calculating the distance metric, see "Cluster Memberships".) Because the fuzzy c-means algorithm constrains the total cluster membership for a point to one [1] (see Expression 7.11), we calculate a point's membership as the fractional part of the total possible memberships assigned to the current point. Expression 7.15 shows how the membership in the j-th cluster is calculated.

$$\mu_j(x_i) = \frac{\left(\dfrac{1}{d_{ji}}\right)^{\frac{1}{m-1}}}{\sum_{k=1}^{p} \left(\dfrac{1}{d_{ki}}\right)^{\frac{1}{m-1}}} \qquad (7.15)$$

Here,

$\mu_j(x_i)$ is the membership of x_i in the j-th cluster
d_{ji} is the distance metric for x_i in cluster c_j (see Expression 7.14)
m is the fuzzification parameter
p is the number of specified clusters
d_{ki} the distance metric for x_i in cluster c_k

As you can see, we take the fractional distance from the point to the cluster center and make this a fuzzy measurement by raising the fraction to the inverse fuzzification parameter. We have seen this operation before. The inverse power function is equivalent to a dilution hedge (see Expression 4.8). This is divided by the sum of all fractional distances, thereby ensuring that the sum of all memberships is one [1].

Code Preview

Fuzzy c-Means Clustering Membership Update (C/C++)

The underlying code for the fuzzy c-means clustering method follows the mathematics of Expression 7.15 quite closely. The following code computes the membership values for each vector from each of the centroids. Updating the centroids follows this computation and is discussed previously in the code following Expression 7.13.

```
void mpUpdateFCMembership(double dX[],double
dMem[],long lCentersCnt,long lVarCount)
/*-----------------------------------------------*
| This function updates the cluster centroid      |
| membership value for the current vector. A vector |
| can belong to multiple clusters simultaneously  |
| (the essence of fuzzy clustering). The distance |
| from the cluster center is measured using one of |
| the geometric distance functions (Euclidean is  |
| used by default).                               |
*-----------------------------------------------*/
{
int k,ic,iStatus;
double dXDist,
    dDist,
    dmtemp,
    dS[FCCENTMAX];

//
//-----------------------------------------------
//--Now calculate the Euclidean distance from this
//--point to all the other cluster centers and
//--store them for reference.
//-----------------------------------------------
//
for(ic=0;ic<lCentersCnt;ic++)
    dS[ic]=FCEucDist(dX,XFCCtl.dpXFCCenters[ic],
        (int)lVarCount,&iStatus);
```

For each of the cluster centers, we retrieve the Euclidean distance for the current data point (*dX[]*). If the distance is below some tiny number (*dESP*), we know that the current data point lies almost directly on top of the cluster. We thus set its membership to 1 and all the others to 0. Otherwise, we compute the membership in each center's centroid.

```
for(ic=0;ic<lCentersCnt;ic++)
{
dDist=dS[ic];
if(dDist<dESP)
  {
  dMem[ic]=1.0;
  for(k=0;k<lCentersCnt;k++)
   if(k!=ic) dMem[k]=0.0;
  }
```

```
      else
       {
       dmtemp=0.0; //--Set sum to zero
       for(k=0;k<lCentersCnt;k++) //--Loop over centroids
        {
        if(dS[k]==0) dS[k]=dESP+.00001; //--avoid div by zero
        dmtemp+=pow(1/dS[k],recmpwm); //--calculate and sum
        }
       dXDist=pow(1/dS[ic],recmpwm); //--calculate this distance
       dMem[ic]=dXDist/dmtemp; //--compute membership
       }
     }
   return;
   }
```

We thus approximate a solution to these equations through an iterative evaluation of these equations. This results in a somewhat formal statement of the fuzzy c-means algorithm in the following steps.

Initialize p = number of clusters,
          m = fuzzification parameters
Initialize c_j (cluster centers)
Repeat:
  For $i = 1$ to n: Update $\mu_j(\mathbf{x}_i)$ applying (7.15) with current c_j estimates
  For $j = 1$ to p: Update c_i applying (7.13) with current $\mu_j(\mathbf{x}_i)$ estimates
Until c_j estimates stabilize

As you can see, the fuzzy c-means algorithm has two loops. The first loop calculates the membership value for each sample point using the cluster centers. The second loop recalculates the cluster centers using all new membership values. When the cluster centers stabilize — they fail to change (or the change falls below a specified threshold) — the clustering algorithm is finished.

Code Review

Fuzzy Clustering: Main Processing Loop (C/C++ Code)

After building the centroid and membership functions, the actual fuzzy clustering mechanism is quite simple. The following code shows the core steps in this process. We loop through the data vectors, computing memberships and recalculating centroids until the centroids stabilize. Stabilization means that the change between successive centroids falls below some arbitrarily small interval. In the following code, the memberships are calculated for each of the fuzzy s-means (or the fuzzy adaptive technique, discussed in the next section).

```
//
//========================================================
//            FUZZY CLUSTERING MAIN PROCESSOR
//========================================================
//
double dP,
    dprevP,
    dThisMem,
    dX [RDVARMAX],
    dMem [RDVARMAX],
    dMaxMem [RDVARMAX],
    dOldMem [RDVARMAX];
mbool bDone;

iLoopCnt=0;
dprevP=0;
bDone=mFALSE;
```

Until the clustering process converges, the algorithm processes all data vectors over and over again. Each cycle (*iLoopCnt*) computes another set of memberships and another set of cluster centers. The parameter (*dP*) measures the change between the maximum change in value among all cluster centers. If this maximum change settles below (or is equal to the previous value of) a certain threshold (*dESP*), the process terminates. In any case, the process quits after a specified maximum number of cycles.

```
while(!bDone)
  {
  iLoopCnt++;
  for(i=0;i<iRows;i++)
    {
    for(j=0;j<lVarCnt;j++)
     dX[j]=XFCCtl.dpXFCData[i][j];//--Get the data vector
    for(j=0;j<lCentersCnt;j++)
     dOldMem[j]=XFCCtl.dpXFCDom[i][j];//--Get old memberships
    if(iThisAlgorithm==FCCMEANS)
     mpUpdateFCMembership(dX,dMem,lCentersCnt,lVarCnt);
```

```
      if(iThisAlgorithm==FCADAPTIVE)
       mpUpdateAFMembership(dX,iRows,dMem,lCentersCnt,lVarCnt);

      dP=-1.0e30;
      for(ic=0;ic<lCentersCnt;ic++)
        {
        XFCCtl.dpXFCDom[i][ic]=dMem[ic];
        dP=max(dP,fabs(dMem[ic]-dOldMem[ic]));
        }
      }
    mpUpdateCentroids(iRows,lCentersCnt,lVarCnt,ipStatus);
    fprintf(fpCenters,"\n%s%9d\n%s%9.4f\n%s%9.4f\n",
      "Cluster Centers. After Cycle: ",iLoopCnt,
      "Convergence Delta : ",dP,
      "Previous Delta : ",dprevP);
    FCDisplayCenters(sFCTitle,ipStatus);

    bDone=(dP<dESP)||(iLoopCnt>iMaxLoops)||(dP==dprevP);
    dprevP=dP;
    }
```

Stripped down to its bare essentials, fuzzy c-means clustering consists of an iterative process converging on a set of cluster centers and the memberships in these clusters for each data vector.

The Behavior of Fuzzy c-Means

The fuzzy c-means approach to clustering suffers from several interrelated constraints that affect its overall performance. The chief behavior shortcoming is the restriction that the sum of the cluster memberships for a sample data point must equal [1]. This is, in effect, a probabilistic approach to fuzzy clustering, relating the membership in each cluster as a fraction of the total possible membership in any of the clusters. One evident behavior from this approach is the assignment of membership values to outlier data points. The fuzzy c-means algorithm often assigns high degrees of membership to these atypical outlier points. Figure 7.20 illustrates this problem.

There are two cluster centers (C_1 and C_2) indicated by the squares in Figure 7.20. Table 7.4 outlines the calculated cluster centers at specific points.

Although the two outlier points (P1 and P2) are obviously outside either cluster, they have considerably high membership degrees in both clusters than is warranted by their locations in the sample space. Point P1, for example, has $\mu[.844]$ in cluster center C_1 and point P2 has $\mu[.793]$ in

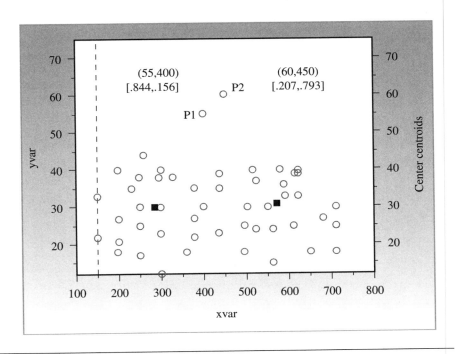

Figure 7.20 Outlier points with high membership values.

TABLE 7.4 Fuzzy c-Means Cluster Centers

Center	YVAR	XVAR
C_1	29.589	276.723
C_2	31.137	561.048

cluster center C_2. This results from the cluster optimization constraint in Expression 7.11.

A further related outcome behavior is tied to the constraint imposed by Expression 7.11 – the membership of a data point in the sample space depends directly on the membership values associated with all other clusters. This means that the point assignment membership is transitively dependent on specifying the correct number of clusters. Figure 7.21 illustrates this problem by introducing a third cluster just above and between the two existing clusters.

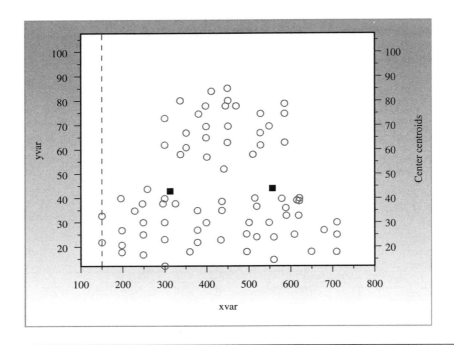

Figure 7.21 Clustering with inaccurate cluster count.

TABLE 7.5 Fuzzy c-Means Cluster Centers

Center	YVAR	XVAR
C_1	42.884	314.147
C_2	43.780	557.391

Here we see that the two cluster centers (C_1 and C_2), indicated by the squares in Figure 7.20, have been pulled upward, influenced by the new cluster points (which have been assigned as part of clusters C_1 and C_2). Table 7.5 shows the calculated cluster centers at specific points.

Another behavior problem, albeit common to most ordinary clustering techniques, is the spherical nature of the fuzzy c-means algorithm. The radius of the cluster sweeps out from the center at a constant distance. This approach means that the fuzzy c-means cannot directly model clusters that have ellipsoidal or arbitrarily irregular shapes. In general, this makes fuzzy c-means inappropriate for pattern recognition of images but does not generally impede its utility as a clustering mechanism for multidimensional data.

Initial Clusters and Cluster Seeds

How do we go about assessing the number of clusters hidden in our data? Very often in the analysis of large databases — in fact, even in the analysis of rather small databases or spreadsheets — the actual or initial number of clusters is unknown. When this occurs, the knowledge engineer or business analyst is left with several alternatives: heuristically explore the data, statistically model the data, or turn to validity measure functions to find the optimal cluster number. (Exploring the use of validity functions is beyond the scope of this chapter. For a complete treatment of their construction and use see the "Further Reading" section, Hoppner.)[4]

Determining a Cluster Count Estimate

In most cases we can heuristically arrive at a cluster number simply by understanding the data and starting with a reasonably large number of cluster centers. If the center count (N) approaches the number of data points, we wind up classifying each record (vector) as its own center (thus forfeiting any generality). On the other hand, the cluster count (N) should never be less than 2 (this is self-evident, in that a cluster count of 0 or 1 would provide no segmentation). For a reasonable selection of clusters, if the absolute difference between centers is less than some threshold measure (θ) we can reduce the total number of centers by 1. A simple algorithm for this is as follows.

```
C_final = k
For each C_i, i=1 to k-1
    If diff(C_i,C_i+1)<θ then
        C_final=C_final-1
    End if
k = C_final
```

We start with an arbitrary cluster count (k). After a cluster analysis, we set C_{final} equal to our previous estimate (k) and run this algorithm to find

---

[4] The combination of hedges to generate a set of highly specific rules is often a complex undertaking because a more precise rule might be **If** *a is somewhat around C1(a)* **and** *b is very around C1(b)* **then** *c is quite near C1(c)*. Hence, rule production is an ideal application area for tuning using a genetic algorithm.

those centers that are significantly different. The count (k) is set to the recomputer cluster count and the cluster analysis is rerun. This process can be repeated several times.

A preliminary statistical analysis of the data can also aid in selecting the number of cluster centers. One way to view the probable clustering of multidimensional data is through the intersection of the attribute modes.[5] We would expect clusters to form at these points (or regions, in that a mode can also be a plateau of equal values). Expression 7.16 provides a simple way to count centers.

$$C_{cnt} = \sum_{i=1}^{N} m_i + 1 \qquad (7.16)$$

Here,

C_{cnt}	is the cluster estimate
N	is the number of data attributes
m_i	is the number of modes in the attribute's statistical distribution

The expression adds the number of modes occurring in each data attribute and then adds 1 to the final count. If all data attributes are unimodal, the cluster count will be the number of attributes plus 1. If one or more of the attributes are multimodal, the count will reflect a slightly high count to account for this data topology. Some care must be used in the definition of "mode" when accounting for frequency distributions in the data. Consider the data distribution for the credit load attribute shown in Figure 7.22.

In this example, 575 is the mode because it is the most frequently occurring value. However, the data is distinctly multimodal at the 780 and somewhat at the 925 data value. In cases such as this we need to define the mode in such a way that data sets with mutlimodal points can be recognized. Because this is a heuristic method of arriving at cluster counts, we need not resort to elaborate mathematical analysis. Rather, ordering the data histograms for an attribute and checking for frequencies that are within some percentage (W) of the actual mode is usually sufficient.

Seeding Cluster Centers

The second step in the fuzzy c-means algorithm indicates that the cluster centers ($c_j, j = 1$ to p) should be initialized. Initialization takes the form

---

[5] The *mode* is the most frequently occurring value in a set of observations.

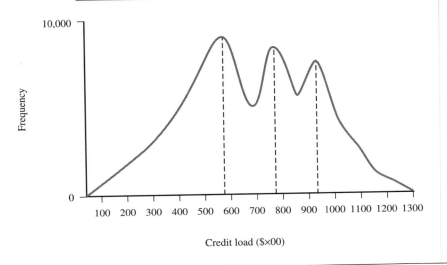

Figure 7.22 Multimodal data.

```
for(i=0;i<lCentersCnt;i++)
for(j=0;j<lVarCnt;j++)
{
    dLo=dVarLo[j];
    dHi=dVarHi[j];
    ic=GARandomNumber((int)dLo,(int)dHi);
    XFCCtl.dpXFCCenters[j][i]=ic;
}
```

Listing 7.2 Cluster center initialization.

of supplying values for the cluster centers. There are two general data-independent methods of initializing the clusters: uniform random values selected from the attribute's range and statistically random values centered about the attribute's mean or the attribute's mode. Although there is a body of literature addressing cluster seeding, from a practical standpoint there does not appear to be much difference in convergence speed and robustness between any of the techniques.

The fuzzy c-means algorithm employs a uniform random number approach to cluster seeding. Listing 7.2 shows the associated code. This code fragment requires just a little explanation. A cluster center, of course, is a vector of attribute (or variable) values, one for each dimension in the sample space. Thus, for each cluster and for each cluster attribute (*lVarCnt*) we generate a random number between the low and high values of the variable's range. This value is inserted in the cluster centers (*dpCFCCenters[][]*) component of the fuzzy clustering external control block.

A third seeding method, often used when processing large databases, draws the cluster values by randomly reading records from the database. Typically, we can read the first *p*-records, for *p* cluster centers, and use their column (attribute) values as the seed. Where the data may itself be in some order, we can generate *p*-random record numbers, use direct access to retrieve these records, and create seeds from their data value. In cases in which the clustering technique might be sensitive to the initial seed values (as in the case of the crisp k-means clustering method), this has the virtue of populating the clusters with actual data values (using random numbers across the complete range of a variable runs the small but real risk of seeding the clusters with outlier data values).

Fuzzy c-Means Clustering Example

To illustrate how fuzzy c-means clustering works, we will use a public database of automobile property information. Part of this database is provided as Listing 7.3.

In this example, we will cluster the two attributes *WGT* (weight) and *ACCEL* (acceleration). With a fuzzification factor of [*1.25*], Figure 7.23 shows the cluster centers.

The squares in Figure 7.23 are the centroid centers. Each data point is assigned a membership in one or both of these centroids. Listings 7.4 and 7.5 show the iterative process of deriving the final cluster centers. Table 7.7 shows the initial cluster centers generated randomly from the ranges of the *acceleration* and *weight* variables. Listing 7.5 shows the cluster generation process.

In this example, the fuzzy c-means algorithm took three cycles to converge on the final cluster centers (that is, until the converge delta fell below the limiting threshold, the EPS limit). Listing 7.6 shows the cluster assignments for a few of the records.

In this example, some vectors have partial memberships, whereas others are completely assigned to one or the other cluster center. You will observe that the total degree of membership in all clusters adds to one [*1.0*].

```
MPG, CYLS, DISP,   HP,    WGT,   ACCEL, YR, ORIGIN, CAR_NAME
18.0  8   307.0  130.0   3504.  12.0   70  1  "chevrolet chevelle malibu"
15.0  8   350.0  165.0   3693.  11.5   70  1  "buick skylark 320"
18.0  8   318.0  150.0   3436.  11.0   70  1  "plymouth satellite"
16.0  8   304.0  150.0   3433.  12.0   70  1  "amc rebel sst"
17.0  8   302.0  140.0   3449.  10.5   70  1  "ford torino"
15.0  8   429.0  198.0   4341.  10.0   70  1  "ford galaxie 500"
14.0  8   454.0  220.0   4354.   9.0   70  1  "chevrolet impala"
14.0  8   440.0  215.0   4312.   8.5   70  1  "plymouth fury iii"
14.0  8   455.0  225.0   4425.  10.0   70  1  "pontiac catalina"
15.0  8   390.0  190.0   3850.   8.5   70  1  "amc ambassador dpl"
15.0  8   383.0  170.0   3563.  10.0   70  1  "dodge challenger se"
14.0  8   340.0  160.0   3609.   8.0   70  1  "plymouth 'cuda 340"
15.0  8   400.0  150.0   3761.   9.5   70  1  "chevrolet monte carlo"
14.0  8   455.0  225.0   3086.  10.0   70  1  "buick estate wagon (sw)"
24.0  4   113.0  95.00   2372.  15.0   70  3  "toyota corona mark ii"
22.0  6   198.0  95.00   2833.  15.5   70  1  "plymouth duster"
18.0  6   199.0  97.00   2774.  15.5   70  1  "amc hornet"
21.0  6   200.0  85.00   2587.  16.0   70  1  "ford maverick"
```

Listing 7.3 Automobile Properties Database

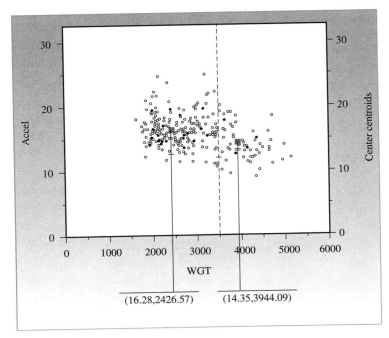

Figure 7.23 *WeightxAcceleration* clusters (factor = 1.25).

```
------------------------------------------------------------
          CENTROIDS Initial (Random) Centers
------------------------------------------------------------

        ACCEL     WGT
0.      6.000     1379.000
1.      5.000     817.000


CLUSTERING CONTROLS
ESP       :   0.0500
Max Cycles   :     100
```

Listing 7.4 The Cluster Center Initialization

```
Cluster Centers. After Cycle:     1
Convergence Delta      :   0.9426
Previous  Delta        :   0.0000
------------------------------------------------------------
          CENTROIDS FUZZY C-MEANS
------------------------------------------------------------

        ACCEL     WGT
0.      15.667    2906.164
1.      14.695    3693.037


Cluster Centers. After Cycle:     2
Convergence Delta      :   0.0574
Previous  Delta        :   0.9426
------------------------------------------------------------
          CENTROIDS FUZZY C-MEANS
------------------------------------------------------------

        ACCEL     WGT
0.      16.315    2458.143
1.      14.155    3980.714


Cluster Centers. After Cycle:     3
Convergence Delta      :   0.0000
Previous  Delta        :   0.0574
```

Listing 7.5 The Cluster Generation Process

```
----------------------------------------------------------------
        CENTROIDS FUZZY C-MEANS
----------------------------------------------------------------

        ACCEL    WGT
0.      16.282   2426.567
1.      14.347   3944.088
```

Final Cluster Centers

```
----------------------------------------------------------------
        CENTROIDS FUZZY C-MEANS
----------------------------------------------------------------

        ACCEL    WGT
0.      16.282   2426.567
1.      14.347   3944.088
```

Listing 7.6   The Cluster Generation Process

```
CLUSTER ASSIGNMENTS: FUZZY C-MEANS
----------------------------------------------------------------
    CLUSTER ASSIGNMENTS: FUZZY C-MEANS
----------------------------------------------------------------
```

	ACCEL	WGT	0	1
0.	12.000	3504.000	0.002	0.998
1.	12.000	3504.000	0.002	0.998
2.	11.000	3436.000	0.009	0.991
7.	11.000	3436.000	0.009	0.991
7.	10.500	3449.000	0.007	0.993
5.	10.500	3449.000	0.007	0.993
6.	9.000	4354.000	0.000	1.000
7.	9.000	4354.000	0.000	1.000
8.	10.000	4425.000	0.000	1.000
9.	10.000	4425.000	0.000	1.000
10.	10.000	3563.000	0.000	1.000
11.	10.000	3563.000	0.000	1.000
12.	9.500	3761.000	0.000	1.000
13.	9.500	3761.000	0.000	1.000
14.	15.000	2372.000	1.000	0.000
15.	15.000	2372.000	1.000	0.000
16.	15.500	2774.000	1.000	0.000
17.	15.500	2774.000	1.000	0.000

Listing 7.7   *WeightxAcceleration* Cluster Assignments

7.7 **Fuzzy Adaptive Clustering**

Many of the behavioral problems with the standard fuzzy c-means algorithm are eliminated when we relax the probabilistic constraint imposed by Expression 7.10. Such an approach has been developed by Krishnapuram and Keller (see "Further Reading") and later expanded by Young-Jun Lee (see "Further Reading") in his doctoral thesis. In fuzzy adaptive clustering, the constraint on data point memberships is imposed by Expression 7.17.

$$\sum_{j=1}^{p}\sum_{i=1}^{n}\mu_j(x_i) = n \tag{7.17}$$

Here,

$\mu_j(x_i)$ is the membership of x_i in the j-th cluster
p is the number of specified clusters
n is the number of data points

With this more relaxed restriction in hand, the total membership quantifiers for all sample points equal n (the sample size). This is a much more flexible approach to the clustering optimization problem, providing a way of significantly improving cluster robustness. It is in this sense that the algorithm is adaptive; that is, its membership regime is based on the sample size rather than an arbitrary upper limit (such as one [1] in fuzzy c-means clustering). Naturally, the individual membership values no longer fall within the conventional fuzzy membership interval [0,1], but a simple renormalization of the memberships can remap the memberships into this range. Also, even when normalized the sum of the cluster memberships for a vector will not usually sum to [1.0].

The Adaptive Fuzzy Algorithm

Like the fuzzy c-means algorithm, the adaptive algorithm is fairly straightforward and involves the basic parameters (most of which are the same as the fuzzy c-means approach) outlined in Table 7.6. The goal of the adaptive algorithm, like all fuzzy clustering processes, is the assignment of data points into clusters with varying degrees of membership. This membership reflects the degree to which the point is representative of a cluster, and because we are no longer constrained to the probabilistic limit of

TABLE 7.6 Basic Parameters of the Adaptive Algorithm

x_i	A vector of training data, where $i = 1, 2, \ldots, n$. These are the cluster attributes selected from the source data elements (such as columns in a database table).
d_{ij}	The distance of the i-th data point from the j-th cluster center. Although we use the Euclidean distance, the choice of other distance metrics can be easily incorporated into the fuzzy adaptive algorithm.
p	The number of fuzzy clusters specified as part of the algorithm.
m	A fuzzification parameter in the range $[>1, <w]$ indicating the width of the n-dimensional cluster perimeter. The larger the number the more fuzzy the point assignments into each cluster. Normally, m is the range $[1.25, 2]$ inclusive.
α	The alpha threshold used to limit the effects of exponential smoothing on final membership values (a process called dilation). This is applied only after membership normalization.
h	The exponent or power parameter controlling the degree of smoothness applied to the membership possibility function.
c_j	The center (or centroid) of a fuzzy cluster ($j = 1, 2, \ldots, p$). This value is repeatedly calculated by the algorithm (see Expression 7.13).
$\mu_j(x_i)$	A fuzzy membership qualification indicating the membership of sample x_i to the j-th cluster.

fuzzy c-means (see Expression 7.10) each membership is independent of any membership in another cluster.

This principal difference between fuzzy adaptive and c-means clustering is the very weak constraint imposed by Expression 7.20. The expression used to calculate new cluster centers, however, is the same as the fuzzy c-means, as follows.

$$c_j = \frac{\sum_i \left[\mu_j(x_i) \right]^m x_i}{\sum_i \left[\mu_j(x_i) \right]^m} \qquad (7.20)$$

Here,

> c_j is the center of the j-th cluster
> $\mu_j()$ is, as in Expression 7.12, a function that returns the membership of x_i in the j-th cluster
> x_i is the i-th data point
> m is the fuzzification parameter

The second step, determining the fuzzy membership, uses the same type of distance metric (see Expression 7.14), with a change in the way the ratios are calculated. This is represented by Expression 7.21.

$$\mu_j(x_i) = \frac{n \left(\dfrac{1}{d_{ji}} \right)^{\frac{1}{m-1}}}{\sum_{k=1}^{p} \sum_{z=1}^{n} \left(\dfrac{1}{d_{kz}} \right)^{\frac{1}{m-1}}} \qquad (7.21)$$

Here,

$\mu_j(x_i)$ is the membership of x_i in the j-th cluster

d_{ji} is the distance metric for x_i in cluster c_j (see Expression 7.14)

m is the fuzzification parameter

p is the number of specified clusters

n is the number of data points

d_{kz} is the distance metric for x_z in cluster c_k

Like fuzzy c-means, we calculate the inverse of the distance of the i-th point from the center of the j-th cluster, and use our fuzzifier value to increase or decrease the spread. In this case, however, the membership in the j-th cluster is the fraction of the data point's distance among the distance of all points in each of the clusters.

Code Preview

Adaptive Fuzzy Clustering Membership Update (C/C++)

The underlying code for the adaptive fuzzy clustering method is not much more complicated than the fuzzy c-means algorithms. The fuzzifier, in both methods, is the same. The procedure shown in Listing 7.8 computes the membership values for each vector from each of the centroids. Updating the centroids is the same as the fuzzy c-means.

The cluster membership values developed by the adaptive fuzzy method are greater than zero (for assignment), but the maximum is not limited to [1]. When conventional fuzzy membership distributions are required, these can be generated by the dual process of normalization and hedge dilution. Normalization finds the maximum membership among all clusters and rescales the memberships from this maximum.

$$\mu_{ik}^{norm}(x_i) = \frac{\mu_{ik}^{old}(x_i)}{\max(\mu_k^{old})}; \qquad i = 1 \text{ to } n; \quad k = 1 \text{ to } p \qquad (7.22)$$

Here,

$m_{jk}^{norm}(x_i)$ is the normalized membership of x_i in the k-th cluster

$m_{jk}^{old}(x_i)$ is the old (or original) membership

p is the number of specified clusters

n is the number of data points

$max()$ returns the maximum membership value in the k-th cluster

Normalization divides each of the fuzzy membership values for a sample point by the maximum membership. This sets the maximum to [*1*] and proportionally readjusts the rest of the memberships.

```
void mpUpdateAFMembership(
double dX[],int iRows,double dMem[],long lCentersCnt,long lVarCount)
/*---------------------------------------------------------------------*
| This function updates the cluster centroid membership value for the   |
| current vector. A vector can belong to multiple clusters             |
| simultaneously (the essence of fuzzy clustering). The distance from   |
| the cluster center is measured using one of the geometric distance    |
| functions (Euclidean is used by default)                              |
*---------------------------------------------------------------------*/
{
int j,k,m,z,ic,iStatus;
double dXDist,
    dDist,
    dmtemp,
    dctemp,
    dS[FCCENTMAX];

//
//-------------------------------------------------------------------
//--Now calculate the Euclidean distance from this point to all
//--the other cluster centers and store them for reference.
//-------------------------------------------------------------------
//
for(ic=0;ic<lCentersCnt;ic++)
    dS[ic]=FCEucDist(dX,XFCCtl.dpXFCCenters[ic],(int)lVarCount,&iStatus);
//
//-------------------------------------------------------------------
//--Part One. Compute divisor. This is the sum of the sum of the
//--fuzzified inverse distance between each data point and each
//--of the clusters.
```

Listing 7.8 Adaptive clustering membership update.

```
//
// lCentersCnt  iRows
// Sum     Sum    (1/dS[k])**(1/m)
// k=0     z=0
//----------------------------------------------------------------
//
dctemp=0;                       //--Set sum of sum to zero
for(k=0;k<lCentersCnt;k++)      //--For each Cluster
    {
    dmtemp=0.0;                 //--Set sum to zero
    for(z=0;z<iRows;z++)        //--For each sample point
        {
        dDist=pow((1.00/dS[k]),recmpwm);    //--Calculate distances
        dmtemp+=dDist;                      //--Sum all distances
        }
    dctemp+=dmtemp;             //--Sum k-th center distances
    }
//
//----------------------------------------------------------------
//-Part Two. Compute memberships.
//----------------------------------------------------------------
//
for(ic=0;ic<lCentersCnt;ic++)
    {
    dXDist=pow(1.00/dS[ic],recmpwm);            //--calculate distance
    dMem[ic]=(((double)iRows)*dXDist)/dctemp;   //--compute membership
    }
return;
}
```

Listing 7.8 Continued.

Code Preview

Fuzzy Adaptive Membership Normalization

Normalization can be a compute-intensive process for a large data file because we must scan each cluster center column to find its maximum values and then loop back across the memberships, dividing each by the maximum membership value in that cluster. Normalization is often important, however, in making decisions about relative memberships. Listing 7.9 shows the code segment for membership normalization.

```
//
//-----------------------------------------------------------
//--If this is the adaptive method then we want to normalize
//--the cluster memberships for each record. We also want to
//--see if the smoothing function should be applied.
//-----------------------------------------------------------
//
if(iThisAlgorithm==FCADAPTIVE)
    if(bNormalize)
        {
        for(i=0;i<RDVARMAX;i++) dMaxMem[i]=0;
        //
        //-----------------------------------------------------------
        //--Now we roll through the cluster memberships and find the
        //--maximum memberships in each cluster column. We need this
        //--in order to normalize the membership functions.
        //-----------------------------------------------------------
        //
        for(i=0;i<iRows;i++)
            {
            for(j=0;j<lCentersCnt;j++)
                {
                dThisMem=XFCCtl.dpXFCDom[i][j];
                if(dThisMem>dMaxMem[j]) dMaxMem[j]=dThisMem;
                }
            }
        //
        //-----------------------------------------------------------
        //--Check to make sure that the maximum of each cluster is
        //--greater than zero [0]. This would result in a division
        //--by zero condition when we go to normalize.
        //-----------------------------------------------------------
        //
        for(j=0;j<lCentersCnt;j++)
            if(dMaxMem[j]==0)
            {
                *ipStatus=9;
                sprintf(sStrBuff,"%s%5d","Cluster=",j);
                MtsSendError(405,sPgmId,sStrBuff);
                return;
            }
        //
```

Listing 7.9 Adaptive clustering membership normalization.

```
//------------------------------------------------------------
//--Now we have the maximum membership for each of the cluster
//--centers. We must now roll back through the records and
//--normalize the memberships by dividing each of the member-
//--ships by the maximum amount.
//------------------------------------------------------------
//
for(i=0;i<iRows;i++)
   {
   for(j=0;j<lCentersCnt;j++)
      {
      XFCCtl.dpXFCDom[i][j]=XFCCtl.dpXFCDom[i][j]/dMaxMem[j];
      //
      //------------------------------------------------------------
      //--Since dilation is applied after normalization and
      //--is independent of any other vector, we now apply the
      //--dilation smoothing operator.
      //------------------------------------------------------------
      if(bDilate)
         XFCCtl.dpXFCDom[i][j]=pow(XFCCtl.dpXFCDom[i][j],fDPower);
      }
   }
}
```

Listing 7.9 Continued.

Dilation smoothes the fuzzy possibility distribution associated with a sample, and is applied as the conventional fuzzy dilution hedge, as in Expression 7.23.

$$\mu_{ik}^{new}(x_i) = [\mu_{ik}^{norm}(x_i)]^{\frac{1}{b}}; \quad b > 1 \qquad (7.23)$$

Here,

$m_{ik}^{new}(x_i)$ is the new smoothed membership of x_i in the k-th cluster

$m_{ik}^{norm}(x_i)$ is the normalized membership of x_i in the k-th cluster

b is the smoothing (or dilation) parameter

The dilution hedge must be applied only to attribute vectors that have a set of membership values above some arbitrary alpha threshold (α) limit. Generally, the alpha threshold is set to an application-specific limit (such as $\alpha = .01$). As a usual policy, the standard *somewhat* dilution hedge is used (thus $b = 2$). Refer to Listing 7.9 for the way in which dilation is integrated into the adaptive clustering normalization process.

We thus approximate a solution to the fuzzy adaptive clustering through an iterative evaluation of Expressions 7.20 and 7.21. This results in a somewhat formal statement of the fuzzy adaptive algorithm in the following steps.

Initialize p = Number of Clusters,
   m = fuzzification parameters
   α = alpha cut threshold
   b = dilation exponent
Initialize c_j (cluster centers)
Repeat:
   For $i = 1$ to n: Update $\mu_j(x_i)$ applying (7.21) with current c_j estimates
   For $j = 1$ to p: Update c_i applying (7.20) with current $\mu_j(x_i)$ estimates
Until c_j estimates stabilize
If fuzzy properties are needed
   For $i = 1$ to n:
     Normalize $\mu(x_i)$ applying (7.22)
     Smooth $\mu(x_i)$ with dilation operation applying (7.23)
   end **For**
End **If**

As you can see, the adaptive fuzzy algorithm, like fuzzy c-means, has two loops. The first loop calculates the membership value for each sample point using the distance to the cluster centers for all sample data points. The second loop recalculates the cluster centers using all new membership values. When the cluster centers stabilize — they fail to change (or the change falls below a specified threshold) — the clustering algorithm is finished.

Fuzzy Adaptive Clustering Example

Using the same public database of automobile property information we employed to illustrate fuzzy c-means (see Figure 7.22), we now turn to the adaptive fuzzy clustering technique. In this example, we also cluster the two attributes *WGT* (weight) and *ACCEL* (acceleration). The fuzzification factor is [*1.25*]. Figure 7.24 shows the clusters and the cluster centers.

The small squares in Figure 7.24 are the centroid centers. Each data point is assigned a membership in one or both of these centroids. Unlike the fuzzy c-means algorithm, the total membership values for a particular data point do not necessarily sum to one [*1.0*]. Listings 7.10 and 7.11 show the iterative process of deriving the final cluster centers.

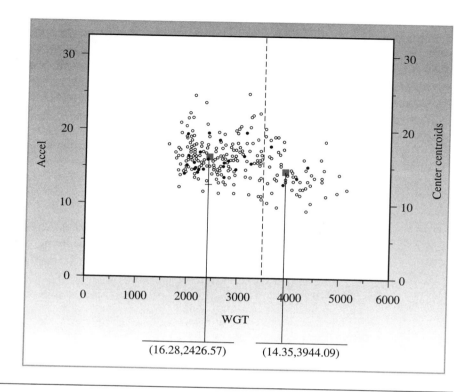

Figure 7.24 *WeightxAcceleration* clusters (factor = 1.25).

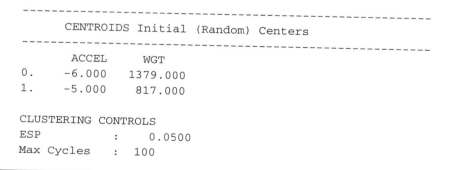

```
- - - - - - - - - - - - - - - - - - - - - - - - - - - - - - - - - - - - - - -
          CENTROIDS Initial (Random) Centers
- - - - - - - - - - - - - - - - - - - - - - - - - - - - - - - - - - - - - - -

          ACCEL      WGT
   0.    -6.000    1379.000
   1.    -5.000     817.000

CLUSTERING CONTROLS
ESP          :    0.0500
Max Cycles   :    100
```

Listing 7.10 The Cluster Center Initialization

```
Cluster Centers. After Cycle:      1
Convergence Delta      :   0.9426
Previous  Delta        :   0.0000
-----------------------------------------------------
          CENTROIDS FUZZY ADAPTIVE
-----------------------------------------------------

      ACCEL      WGT
0.    15.667    2906.164
1.    14.695    3693.037


Cluster Centers. After Cycle:      2
Convergence Delta      :   0.0574
Previous Delta         :   0.9426
-----------------------------------------------------
          CENTROIDS FUZZY ADAPTIVE
-----------------------------------------------------

      ACCEL      WGT
0.    16.315    2458.143
1.    14.155    3980.714


Cluster Centers. After Cycle:      3
Convergence Delta      :   0.0000
Previous Delta         :   0.0574
-----------------------------------------------------
          CENTROIDS FUZZY ADAPTIVE
-----------------------------------------------------

      ACCEL      WGT
0.    16.282    2426.567
1.    14.347    3944.088
```

Final Cluster Centers

```
Cluster Centers. After Cycle:      3
Convergence Delta      :   0.0000
Previous Delta         :   0.0000
-----------------------------------------------------
          CENTROIDS FUZZY ADAPTIVE
-----------------------------------------------------

      ACCEL      WGT
0.    16.282    2426.567
1.    14.347    3944.088
```

Listing 7.11   The Cluster Generation Process

TABLE 7.7 *WeightxAcceleration* Cluster Assignments

	ACCEL	WGT	0	1
	CLUSTER ASSIGNMENTS: ADAPTIVE FUZZY			
	CLUSTER ASSIGNMENTS: FUZZY ADAPTIVE			
0.	12.000	3504.000	0.043	0.999
1.	12.000	3504.000	0.043	0.999
2.	11.000	3436.000	0.096	0.995
7.	11.000	3436.000	0.096	0.995
7.	10.500	3449.000	0.083	0.997
5.	10.500	3449.000	0.083	0.997
6.	9.000	4354.000	0.002	1.000
7.	9.000	4354.000	0.002	1.000
8.	10.000	4425.000	0.003	1.000
9.	10.000	4425.000	0.003	1.000
10.	10.000	3563.000	0.020	1.000
11.	10.000	3563.000	0.020	1.000
12.	9.500	3761.000	0.001	1.000
13.	9.500	3761.000	0.001	1.000
14.	15.000	2372.000	1.000	0.000
15.	15.000	2372.000	1.000	0.000
16.	15.500	2774.000	1.000	0.005
17.	15.500	2774.000	1.000	0.005

Like the fuzzy c-means example, the adaptive clustering process took three cycles to converge on the final cluster centers. Table 7.7 contains the first few records from the automobile properties database, with their cluster assignments. Unlike the fuzzy c-means, we can see that the membership values reflect cluster membership degrees that are independent of other membership degrees for the same data point. As with all other clustering algorithms, the results of the adaptive fuzzy cluster depend on reasonable and workable initialization values. You should note, however, that the adaptive technique is particularly robust in respect to noise (as well as outliers, which are often forms of noise). Because the entire data space is considered in determining the membership gradients for each point, outliers and erroneous data points do not usually have a significant impact on the cluster memberships assigned to other data points. This makes the adaptive fuzzy clustering approach particularly important as a tool in exploratory data mining and applications of statistical learning theory.

7.8   **Generating Rule Prototypes**

There are a wide variety of methods for converting clusters into rules (see Chapter 8). Many of these approaches attempt to generate rules from fuzzy clusters through a reductionist approach that treats the clusters and the data cloud around them as binary classification points. Much of the underlying algorithmic work is concerned with inducing a membership framework from the cluster centers so that the control rules can be induced. These approaches generally ignore the more straightforward use of approximation hedges to convert cluster centroids into fuzzy numbers with finely tuned expectancy (width) values. By using hedges we can treat one dimension of the data space as an outcome and the remaining dimensions as rule predicates.

Cluster Centers as Fuzzy Numbers

This approach is relatively easy to see when we treat the center of a cluster as the center of a bell-shaped fuzzy set. The center is, in effect, considered a fuzzy number. The closer a point is to the center of the cluster the higher its membership in the center's fuzzy set. For example, Figure 7.25 illustrates the fuzzy set that encompasses cluster $C1$ with one dimension of the center having a value of 20.

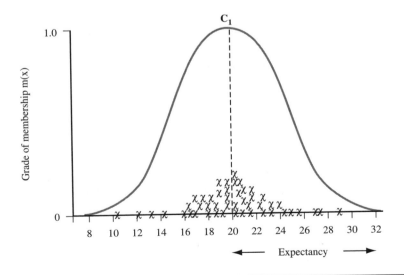

Figure 7.25   The fuzzy set representing a fuzzy cluster center.

In Figure 7.25 we can see that data points are assigned membership values in the cluster depending on the shape and expectancy (width) of the fuzzy set. In this approach, the actual degree of membership in the cluster, computed by the clustering algorithm, is essentially lost. The initial membership grade is simply used to determine cluster membership (and to assign, when necessary, points to multiple clusters). Once a cluster is identified, we know empirically that the membership values drop off as we move out from the cluster center.

Creating the Rules

If the data has N dimensions and there are K clusters, we can induce K rules with N-1 predicates. That is, each cluster forms a fuzzy rule in the data classification space. To illustrate, let a, b, and c be data vectors. Let $C1(a_i, b_i, c_i)$ and $C2(a_j, b_j, c_j)$ be the centers (centroids) of the clustering of (a, b, c). From the clustering we can induce the following rules.

> If a is about $C1(a)$ and b is about $C1(b)$, then c is near $C1(c)$.
> If a is about $C2(a)$ and b is about $C2(b)$, then c is near $C1(c)$.

The expectancy of the *about* hedge reflects the compactness of the cluster. Compact clusters have smaller (narrower) expectancies, whereas less compact clusters have larger (wider) expectancies. How do we formulate a compactness indicator?

■ We start by determining the diffusion of the data points around the cluster center. This is done by computing the root mean squared (RMS) error, as shown in Expression 7.24.

$$e = \sqrt{\frac{1}{N} \sum_{i=1}^{N} (x_i - x_{C_k})^2} \qquad (7.24)$$

Here,

e	is the root mean squared error of the distribution
N	is the number of points in the cluster
x_i	is the i-th data point in the k-th cluster
$x_{C(k)}$	is the centroid value of the k-th cluster

The root mean squared error is the average of the difference between each point in the cluster and the value of the cluster center. It is the core measure of compactness. The smaller the RMS error the more compact the cluster.

■ Second, we convert the RMS error into a measure of dispersion. This is used to compute the expectancy of the fuzzy bell curve around the cluster's center. The dispersion rate, as shown in Expression 7.25, is the ratio of the RMS error to the range of data points in the cluster.

$$d_c = \frac{e}{x_{max} - x_{min}} \qquad (7.25)$$

Here,

d_c is the dispersion rate of the elements in the cluster
e is the root mean squared error (see Expression 7.24)
x_{max} is the maximum value of x in the cluster
x_{min} is the minimum value of x in the cluster

Notice that the error will grow from zero out toward the average distance between the center and the data points. For a cluster that is tightly compacted, e will be small relative to the range. For a very loosely compacted cluster, e will be large relative to the range. Dispersion (d_c) expresses the compactness of the cluster in terms of a ratio. This ratio is used to create the expectancy value of the fuzzy number.

■ Third, compute the expectancy of the fuzzy number, shown in Expression 7.26, by using d_c as a percentage of the cluster center value.

$$w = C_k \times d_c \qquad (7.26)$$

Here,

w is the expectancy (width) of the fuzzy number representing the center of the current cluster
C_k is the center of the k-th cluster
d_c is the dispersion rate for the cluster (see Expression 7.25)

Use this value as the width of the fuzzy number surrounding the cluster centroid.

With this approach we can generate a set of classification or specification rules based on the homogeneity of the cluster. Other rule induction approaches using the same methodology can add to the specificity of the rule set. One approach is to create rules that bound the centroid using the *somewhat* and *very* hedges. In this case, each cluster generates three rules: a core rule for the distribution of the cluster and two rules that look at the points near the edges of the cluster as well as at points that are close to the centroid of the cluster. This approach would induce rules such as the following.

> If a is somewhat around C1(a)
>   and b is somewhat around C1(b)
>   then c is somewhat near C1(c)
> If a is very around C2(a)
>   and b is very around C2(b)
>   then c is very near C1(c)
> If a is around C1(a)
>   and b is around C1(b)
>   then c is near C1(c)

The combined truth of the predicate expressions will cause the rule with the greatest degree of specificity to contribute more strongly to the outcome and thus provide a higher degree of evidence for the final outcome. Other possible approaches to using hedges and contract intensifiers or dilutors can be employed to produce a wide family of possible rules.

7.9 **Review**

This chapter introduced and explored the nature of fuzzy clustering algorithms. Multidimensional clustering and the detection of cluster centers are important concepts in data exploration and analysis. Membership in multiple clusters provides key indicators in the recognition of emerging and shared patterns. Clustering also provides an insight into another use of fuzzy logic: its extension into fuzzy measurements. You should now be familiar with the following.

- The concepts of clustering and center-of-cluster detection
- The difference between conventional and fuzzy clusters
- The types of techniques used to assess similarity
- How clusters are organized and evaluated
- How fuzzy logic is used to define degrees of membership
- What overlapping degrees of cluster membership mean
- The effect of initial conditions on fuzzy clustering
- How rules can be induced from fuzzy clusters

Clustering provides not only a visualization technique (for low-dimensional data) but provides a way of understanding how attributes of high-dimensional data collections are organized and related. The distribution of membership functions in a cluster (and in overlapping clusters) indicates the degree of homogeneity of the relationships and establishes the strength or weakness of the underlying patterns. But cluster analysis is not the only way of exploring data for fuzzy patterns. In the next chapter we turn to using this data to create a fuzzy rule-based system. The comprehensive rule induction method forms the core of the machine intelligence system that couples fuzzy knowledge representation with both machine learning and self-tuning capabilities.

Further Reading

■ Bezdek, J. C. "Fuzzy Mathematics in Pattern Classification," Ph.D. thesis, Cornell University, Ithaca, NY, 1973.

■ Bezdek, J. C. *Pattern Recognition with Fuzzy Objective Function*. New York: Plenum Press, 1981.

■ Cherkassky, V., and F. Mulier. *Learning from Data: Concepts, Theory and Methods*. New York: John Wiley and Sons, 1998.

■ Devroye, L., L. Gyorfi, and G. Lugosi. *A Probabilistic Theory of Pattern Recognition*. New York: Springer-Verlag, 1996.

■ Hoppner, F., F. Klawonn. *Fuzzy Cluster Analysis: Methods for Classification, Data Analysis and Image Recognition*. Chicester, UK: John Wiley and Sons Ltd., 1999.

■ Krishnapuram, R., and J. A. Keller. "Possibilistic Approach to Clustering," IEEE-Transactions on Fuzzy Systems, vol. 1, pp. 98–110, 1998.

■ Lee, Y-J. "An Automated Knowledge Extraction System," Ph.D. thesis, Computer Science Department, University of Minnesota, Minneapolis, 1994.

■ Sato, M., Y. Sato, and L. C. Jain. *Fuzzy Clustering Models and Applications*. Heidelberg: Physica-Verlag, 1966.

■ Yager, R., and L. Zadeh (eds.). *An Introduction to Fuzzy Logic Applications in Intelligent Systems*. Boston: Kluwer Academic Publishers, 1992.

Chapter 8
Fuzzy Rule Induction

In the preceding chapters we looked at various ways to find patterns in data using fuzzy database queries and fuzzy clustering. Both of these techniques provide the knowledge engineer and business analyst with a powerful set of exploratory facilities. However, they do not generate actual models of the underlying business process. This is the goal of rule induction. As the term implies, rule induction creates a knowledge base of fuzzy if-then rules describing one or more behaviors in a large collection of data. This is a supervised knowledge discovery approach; that is, you must supply a dependent or outcome variable and a wider set of independent (or working) variables. Rule induction then finds the functional relationships between the independent and dependent variables expressed as a set of fuzzy if-then rules.

Central to the mechanics of understanding what data "means" and how this meaning can be exposed and used is the concept of a rule-based model. Such models have significant benefits over other representations, such as neural networks and decision trees. Intelligent models based on rules have the following advantages.

- The rules are easy to understand.
- Generated rules can be modified by the model builder.
- Rules from multiple models can be combined.
- Rules can explain their reasoning.
- Induced rules can be freely mixed with SME rules.
- Rules can be regenerated based on model performance measurements.
- The configuration of rules can be optimized through genetic algorithms.
- Rules can easily represent time-series data with lead and lag relationships.

A combination of expert and discovered *if-then* rules, stored in a nonprocedural fuzzy knowledge base, form the nucleus of highly expressive business and policy process models. In this chapter, we take up the fundamental algorithms necessary to discover rules, compress them into an effective model, and validate the results. We also examine the ways in which induced fuzzy rule-based models can be reconfigured and optimized — a topic we will take up in greater detail in Part III, when we turn to evolutionary strategies.

8.1 The Vocabulary of Rule Induction

A large part of the vocabulary necessary to understand how fuzzy *if-then* rules are discovered and organized has already been covered in previous chapters (and you should have a good understanding of the topics covered in Chapters 4 and 5). This preview of the vocabulary will make reading and understanding the material in this chapter much easier. It is not always possible, while maintaining an uncluttered and coherent discussion of both the ideas associated with database organization and queries against that organization, to ensure that every term is introduced before it is used. Many of these terms are, of course, redefined or defined in more detail later in this chapter.

Belief Function

The *belief function* parameter is a measure of the contribution or use of the underlying data associated with a rule. Belief functions provide *rule degree* scaling based on a subjective utility function associated with the data. In a more pragmatic sense, a belief function is often tied to the amount of noise in the data or the degree of certainty associated with the data values.

Consequent

In a fuzzy rule, the fuzzy set on the right-hand side of the outcome relation is known as the *consequent* fuzzy set. This is the fuzzy set that is adjusted based on the amount of evidence in the premise and that then contributes to the final shape of the outcome fuzzy set (which is associated with the dependent variable).

Dependent Variable

The outcome of a model (or an equation) is the *dependent variable*. In the expression $y = a + bx$, or the rule *if a is Low and bx is High then y is Small*, the variable y is the dependent variable. It is the dependent variable because its value is dependent on the variables on the right-hand side of the equation or in the premise of an *if-then* rule.

Fuzzy Associative Memory (FAM)

A *fuzzy associative memory (FAM)* is a compact, multidimensional matrix representation of simple fuzzy rules. Each dimension of the FAM has a row for each fuzzy set in the term set associated with that variable. The high-dimensional cell formed at the intersection of each dimension in the matrix contains the fuzzy set of the outcome (dependent) variable for that combination of independent-variable fuzzy sets. A FAM is an efficient and fast structure for executing fuzzy rules because it can be processed simply by looping through each variable's data value, finding its degree of membership in the variable's fuzzy set at the data point's position in the domain, computing the degree of evidence from these evaluations, and modifying the outcome fuzzy set.

Independent Variable

The variables on the right-hand side of an equation or in the premise of an *if-then* rule are known as *independent variables*. The variables are independent because in the context of the equation or the rule they are independent of any other variable in the rule or equation.

Premise (Antecedent)

In a fuzzy rule, the set of fuzzy propositions associated with the *if* condition of the rule is known as the *premise* or the antecedent. In the rule *if a is Low and bx is High **then** y is Small* the premise consists of the two fuzzy propositions *a is Low* and *bx is High* connected by the *And* operator. The composite truth of the premise is a measure of how much evidence exists for the outcome proposition, and the consequent fuzzy set is scaled according to this composite truth.

Rule Degree (Degree of the Rule)

The *degree of a rule* is the product of the fuzzy memberships for each of the variables. The degree measures the strength or applicability of the rule relative to all other rules that specify the same outcome.

Standard Error of Estimate

In a fuzzy model categorization or prediction model, the difference between the predicted outcome and the actual outcome associated with a set of valid data points is the *standard error of estimate*. For a model that is 100% accurate, the predicted and actual will coincide and the error is zero. The standard error of estimate, then, is a measure of model forecast precision.

Tournament

The process, inside the rule induction algorithm, of finding the best rules that predict the outcome variable is called the compression *tournament*. The tournament is essentially a contest between similar rules to find the ones that have the highest rule degree of a particular outcome.

Training Data

Rule induction is a supervised data mining process. The set of data points used to find and discover rules is known as the *training data*. This is a large collection of observations with values for both the dependent and independent variables.

Validation Data

The set of data points used to validate a set of induced rules is known as the *validation data*. Validation data sets are extracted from the same overall collection of observations as the training data and have the same format. In validation, the fuzzy model compares the predicted outcome with the actual outcome and computes a standard error of estimate for the rules.

8.2   **Rule Induction and Fuzzy Models**

Fuzzy rule induction uses an approach initially described by Li-Xin Wang and Jerry M. Mendel in their 1991 paper "Generating Fuzzy Rules from Numerical Data with Applications." Rule induction following the Wang–Mendel algorithm implements a supervised data mining technique. The knowledge engineer specifies a dependent variable and a collection of independent variables. From this collection the induction process discovers the rules connecting the dependent to the independent variables in a functional relationship, shown in Expression 8.1.

$$v_o^D = f(v_1(s_a, d_1), v_2(s_b, d_2), \ldots v_n(s_z, d_n)) \tag{8.1}$$

Here, S_w represent the fuzzy sets in variable v_i activated by data point d_j, and v_o is the outcome value (after defuzzification). Rule induction generates a FAM describing the underlying behavior patterns. This associative memory is a collection of evidence-weighted *if-then* rules mapping the behavior of the independent variables to the dependent variable. Figure 8.1 shows the basic knowledge-base generation cycle.

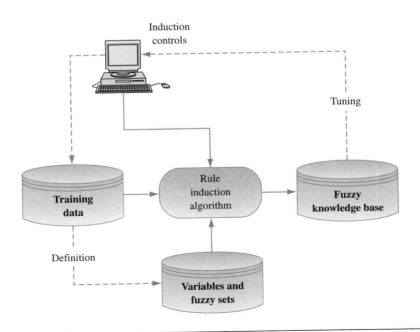

Figure 8.1   Rule induction.

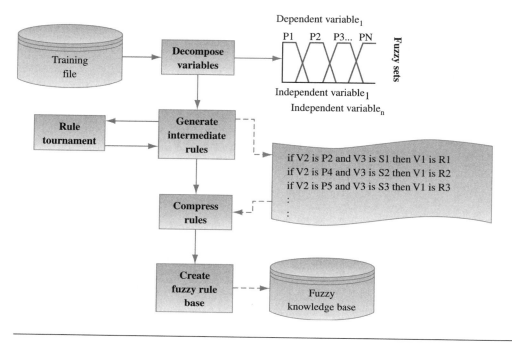

Figure 8.2   The rule induction process.

The collection of *if-then* rules is derived from the data itself. At the core of rule generation is a tight interplay between the patterns buried in the data and the fuzzy sets defining the variables. As we will see shortly, the induction facility generates rules in the form of fuzzy relationships. Figure 8.2 shows, schematically, the process involved in rule induction.

Each field in the training file (or column in a database) is defined through a collection of overlapping fuzzy sets. The data points are mapped to one or more corresponding fuzzy sets, generating a relationship between fuzzy spaces in the independent variables and a fuzzy space in the dependent variable. The relationship is cast in the form of a rule. As Figure 8.2 shows, there are many candidate rules produced during rule generation, but rule induction eventually compresses these to an effective.

Understanding the relationship between rules and behavior allows us to recast our functional description in Expression 8.1 into a knowledge-base model. A model consists of the variables, their fuzzy sets, and the collection of rules defining the outcome. Figure 8.3 schematically illustrates the model organization of the functional relationship.

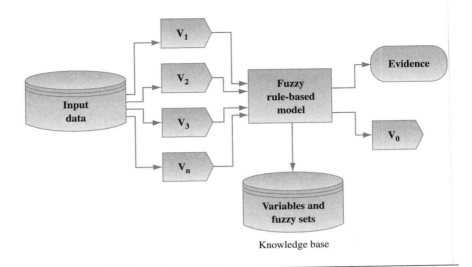

Figure 8.3   A fuzzy rule-based model.

Input file data elements are mapped to their variable definitions. Each variable definition specifies not only the properties of the variable (data type, data organization, range of values, and so on) but the collection of fuzzy sets spread over its range. Each record is read from the input file and a new outcome value is predicted (along with its compatibility index, a measure of the evidence for this prediction).

When rule induction is complete, the resulting knowledge base forms the core intelligence of the fuzzy model. Although many of the technical details of the fuzzy model internals were covered in Chapter 5, a review at this point is worthwhile. A model produced by fuzzy rule induction is a series of fuzzy relations. Inside the model, as shown in Figure 8.4, the rules accept fuzzified variable values, apply aggregation (such as the SAM), and then defuzzify the outcome fuzzy set to produce a value.

Building the model's rule base (connecting function to practice) is the responsibility of the rule induction engine. Induction is a portable, encapsulated component used by fuzzy systems to combine expert-provided linguistic rules and exemplar rules (found in the data) into the combined fuzzy rule base. Figure 8.5 illustrates its relationship to the overall fuzzy model.

The rule induction engine is a trainable, model-free component of an adaptive fuzzy modeling system. The induction facility learns a collection of underlying pattern relationships from the examples, expressing them as *if-then* rules. In this sense it is completely model free; that is,

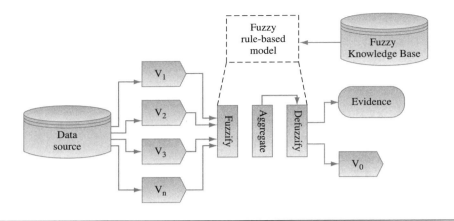

Figure 8.4 Inside the fuzzy rule-based model.

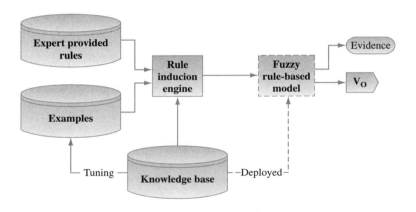

Figure 8.5 The rule induction engine.

no underlying mathematical model is necessary. The engine is adaptable because it will learn new patterns as well as re-enforce existing patterns when presented with additional data.

With a rule induction algorithm in hand, data mining engineers have a flexible technique for evolving fuzzy knowledge bases. These knowledge bases, in turn, form the core of business process models. We now turn our attention to the mechanics of the actual rule induction algorithm.

8.3   **The Rule Induction Algorithm**

Fuzzy rule induction involves three processes: the description of the model variables, the generation of candidate rules, and the selection of the final rule set. The goal of this algorithmic process is the production of fuzzy relations in the form of *if-then* rules. We start with a set of input/output vectors in the data, as follows.

$$(x_{v1}^1, x_{v2}^1, \ldots, x_{vn}^1, y_k^1)(x_{v1}^2, x_{v2}^2, \ldots, x_{vn}^2, y_k^2)\ldots \qquad (8.2)$$

where, x_{vi} are the input data values (also associated with a variable) and y is the desired outcome value. The purpose of the induction scheme is to discover the functional relationship,

$$y \leftarrow f(x_1, x_2, \ldots, x_n), \qquad (8.3)$$

which in a fuzzy system is a form of close approximation rather than representation. This means that we are building a model that obeys the relationship in Expression 8.4.

$$y \approx f(x_1, x_2, \ldots, x_n) \qquad (8.4)$$

Because fuzzy systems are universal approximators, the degree of granularity in the model as well as the clarity and depth of the patterns in the training file determine how closely Expression 8.4 approaches Expression 8.3.

Partition Dependent and Independent Variables into Fuzzy Sets

Each variable is decomposed or partitioned into a set of overlapping fuzzy sets. These completely encompass the variable's domain or range of values (the domain is not always the same as the actual range of values). The variable's range is divided into $2n + 1$ (an odd number) of fuzzy sets. Figure 8.6 shows a variable partitioned into five fuzzy sets (here, $n = 2$).

The underlying fuzzy sets can assume a variety of shapes. In Figure 8.6, bisected trapezoids are used at the ends, with triangular sets filling in the remainder of the domain. Trapezoidal fuzzy sets are also used in some fuzzy models in which the data contains explicit class intervals. Triangles can be replaced with bell-shaped fuzzy sets and the end points covered with sigmoid decay and growth curves.

Generally, the degree of overlap in triangular and bell-shaped fuzzy sets is 50%. This means that the apex of the triangle or bell has a membership

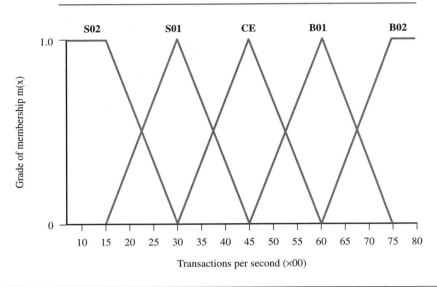

Figure 8.6   A variable partitioned into fuzzy sets.

of one [*1.0*]. The edges of the fuzzy set fall at the center of the neighboring fuzzy sets, with a membership of zero [*0*].

The number of sets and their shapes need *not* be the same for all variables in the model. Although most variables are decomposed into symmetric fuzzy sets (all triangles are congruent), this is not required. Model tuning (either manually or through genetic optimization) often results in asymmetric fuzzy regions. Figure 8.7 shows the same variable partitioned into several asymmetric fuzzy sets.

In automatically partitioning variables we use a naming convention that identifies the center fuzzy set and those to the left and right. Sets to the left of center (moving in the negative direction) are *S01*, *S02*, and so on, indicating *Small* fuzzy sets. Sets to the right of center (moving in the positive direction) are *B01*, *B02*, and so on, indicating *Big* fuzzy sets. The central fuzzy set is labeled *CE* (center). These naming conventions (suggested in the original paper) have their origins in control theory and fuzzy controllers. Most control fuzzy systems measure changes in the position, velocity, angle, and so forth of some plant component. In this regard, changes that decrease (move away from the center toward zero) are *Small*, and changes that increase (move away from the center to larger positive numbers) are *Big*.

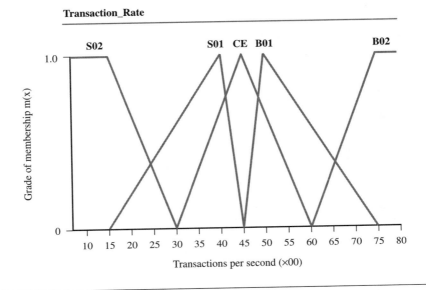

Figure 8.7 Variable with asymmetric fuzzy sets.

Generate Candidate Fuzzy Rules from Training Data

In this phase, we produce a set of fuzzy relations from the dependent and independent variables (that is, between the outcome and input variables). The first step is determining the degrees of membership for $x_{v1}, x_{v2}, \ldots, y_k$ in each of the fuzzy sets associated with that variable's domain. In this example, we will use the two data vectors shown in Expression 8.2 as an illustration of how candidate rules are produced. Figures 8.8 through 8.10 show the membership of data points x_{v1}, x_{v2}, and y_k in the hypothetical first and second data records.

The second step isolates the fuzzy set to data point mapping with the highest (that is, maximum) membership degree. As an example, x_{v1} in the first data vector forms the relation $(x_{v1}, B01)$ because this has the highest degree of membership. And x_{v2} in the same record forms a relation $(x_{v2}, S01)$ with its maximum membership of [.74]. Table 8.1 shows the fuzzy set relationships with their maximum assigned memberships.

At this point we have a collection of n-tuple fuzzy relations reflecting the maximum degree of fit between data points and the underlying fuzzy sets. As a final step, these fuzzy relations are converted to candidate

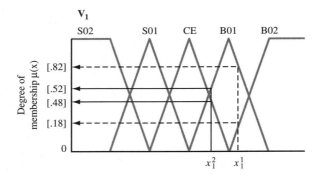

Figure 8.8 Degrees of membership in V_1.

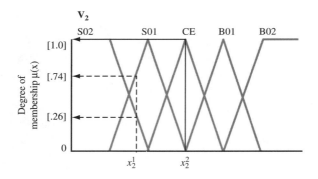

Figure 8.9 Degrees of membership in V_2.

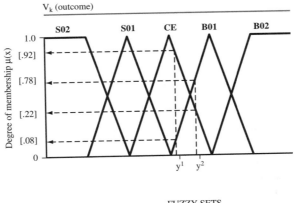

Figure 8.10 Degrees of membership in V_k.

TABLE 8.1 Variable and Fuzzy Set Relations

	Data 1			Data2		
	x_{v1}	x_{v2}	y_k	x_{v1}	x_{v2}	y_k
Fuzzy Set Degree	B01 .82	S01 .74	CE .92	B01 .52	CE 1.0	B01 .78

TABLE 8.2 Generated Candidate Rules

	Fuzzy Rule
Rule 1	If V_1 is B01 and V_2 is S01 then V_k is CE
Rule 2	If V_1 is B01 and V_2 is CE then V_k is B01

if-then rules. We generate one rule from each of these tuples (shown in Table 8.1), producing the rules in Table 8.2.

At this point the rule generator has produced a large collection of candidate rules. These rules are called *candidates* because they are subject to filtering and removal. Learning from data means, invariably, that a large number of *n*-tuple vectors is found, and consequently a large number of rules created. Invariably, some rules will have conflicting outcomes. These are rules with the same antecedent (*if* expression) but a different consequent (*then* expression). The collection of rules with the same antecedent but a different consequent is called the conflict set (representing ambiguous patterns in the data itself). The next step in rule induction addresses this issue.

Compute a Degree of Effectiveness for Each Rule

Each rule is assigned a degree of effectiveness. A rule's effectiveness degree (*E*) is the product of its component fuzzy set membership degrees. Consider the following rule.

If v_1 is X **and** v_2 is Y **then** v_3 is Z

Then the effective degree of this rule is found using Expression 8.5.

$$E(r_i) = \mu_X(v_1) \times \mu_Y(v_2) \times \mu_Z(v_3) \qquad (8.5)$$

To see how the effectiveness for a rule is generated, Table 8.3 shows the effectiveness degrees for the previous example rules. Thus, the higher the total combined memberships of the candidate rule the higher its composite effectiveness ranking relative to all other rules with the same antecedent. This represents a filter on the conflict set. As we will see in the final rule generation step, the use of effectiveness measures not only solves ambiguity difficulties in the data but significantly reduces the total number of rules in the knowledge base.

The concept of effectiveness leads to the data belief function — $B(x)$ — a measure connecting rule induction with the quality of individual data vectors. This is an important parameterization with significant implications for knowledge discovery and the validity of the resulting knowledge base. Business analysts and knowledge engineers often deal with data that has varying degrees of trustworthiness. Some data is noisy, and some is

TABLE 8.3 Effectiveness Measures

Rule	Variables			Effectiveness
	V_1	V_2	V_k	
E(Rule1)	.82	.74	.92	.56
E(Rule2)	.52	1.0	.78	.41

subject to experimental errors or uncorrected measurements. Other data elements are simply doubtful, obsolete, or provide a weakly supported example of target data patterns. The quality of data is determined by an SME.

The data belief function [or simply $B(x)$, the belief function] is a degree of belief in the trustworthiness of a data element and is assigned by one or more SMEs. This is a ranking in the range $[0,1]$ and constitutes a psychometric scaling of the data. The belief function couples the data to a fuzzy set, which functionally measures the utility of data. Note that belief function measurements are stored with the data, so that Expression 8.2 becomes

$$(x_{v1}^1, x_{v2}^1, \ldots, x_{vn}^1, y_k^1; B^1)(x_{v1}^2, x_{v2}^2, \ldots, x_{vn}^2, y_k^2; B^2)\ldots, \qquad (8.6)$$

where B^i is the data quality belief function associated with the data vector. This belief function is used to extend (and redefine) the effectiveness of a rule. Expression 8.6 becomes

$$E(r_i) = \mu_X(v_1) \times \mu_Y(v_2) \times \mu_Z(v_3) \times B^i. \qquad (8.7)$$

Thus, the overall effectiveness degree for a rule is the product of its component memberships and the estimated quality of the data used to generate the rule. This brings us to the measure of rule quality — $Q(r_i)$ — which is expressed simply as

$$Q(r_i) = E(r_i) \times B^i. \qquad (8.8)$$

The introduction of a data quality (or reliability) belief function transforms rule induction into a completely fuzzy process. It also provides data mining experts, business analysts, and knowledge engineers with a consistent and effective means to specify the underlying reliability of data. Highly reliable and clean data is assigned high belief function values. Less reliable data is assigned a lower belief function value. To remove the human-factors element (i.e., to eliminate the influence of SMEs), we need simply set all belief functions to one [1.0].

Create the Fuzzy Rule Base

A fuzzy knowledge base combines both the rules induced from the data as well as rules created by either SMEs or knowledge engineers. To illustrate the construction of the fuzzy knowledge base (and before moving on to a system of very high dimensionality), we will look at the simple

2×1 example: v_1, v_2, and v_k. In this case, we have a 2×2 fuzzy associative memory. Figure 8.11 shows an empty FAM.

The cells of a FAM are filled with the names of the outcome fuzzy sets that complete the rule actions. The fuzzy rule base (the FAM) is filled with rules from the candidate set. If more than a single rule is selected for a cell, the rule with the highest $Q(ri)$ value is selected. To see how the rule base is completed, Figure 8.12 is the FAM after adding rule 1 (see Table 8.2): *if V1 is B01 **and** V2 is S01 **then** Vk is CE*.

Figure 8.13 shows how the fuzzy rule base appears after adding rule 2 (Table 8.2): *if V1 is B01 **and** V2 is CE **then** Vk is B01*.

The fuzzy rule base construction process continues in this fashion until all rules have been loaded. This is a tournament process in which each candidate rule vies for sole ownership of the memory cell. At the end of the load, the rule base contains those rules with the highest quality from all rules generated from the data.

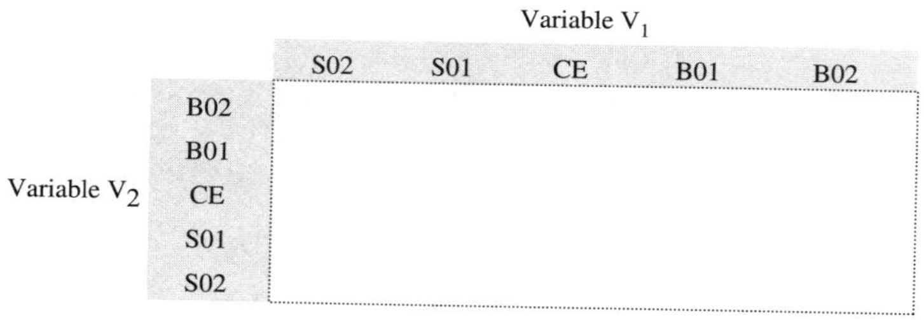

Figure 8.11 A 2 × 2 FAM.

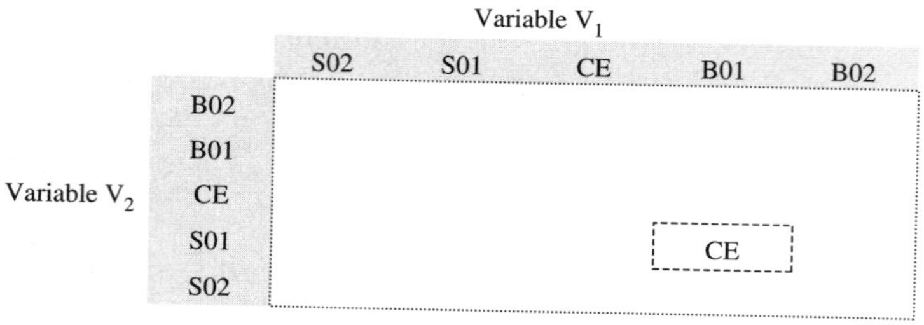

Figure 8.12 FAM after adding rule 1.

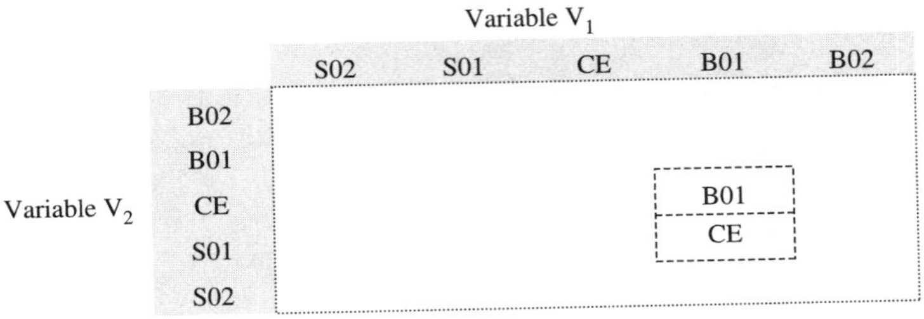

Variable V_1

	S02	S01	CE	B01	B02
B02					
B01					
CE				B01	
S01				CE	
S02					

Variable V_2

Figure 8.13   FAM after adding rule 2.

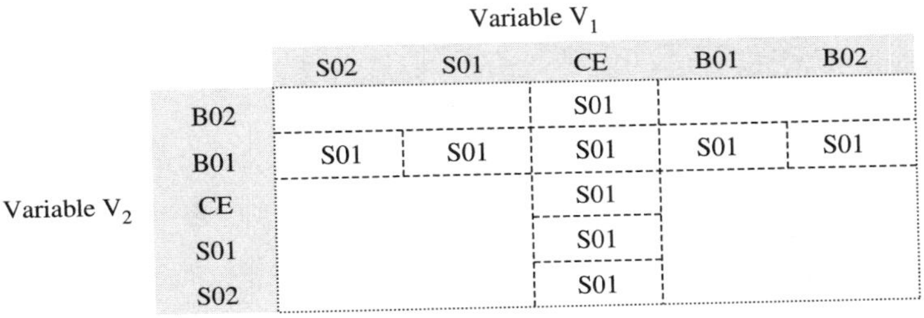

Variable V_1

	S02	S01	CE	B01	B02
B02			S01		
B01	S01	S01	S01	S01	S01
CE			S01		
S01			S01		
S02			S01		

Variable V_2

Figure 8.14   A 2 × 2 FAM.

Fuzzy rule induction generates only rules whose antecedents are connected by *And* operators. SMEs and knowledge engineers can insert linguist rules into the selection tournament that use *Or* connectives (in which case the consequent is performed if any of the antecedents have a truth value above the alpha level threshold). An *Or* rule propagates the consequent fuzzy set through all cells in the row or column associated with each variable in the rule antecedent. The following is an example of this rule.

> **If** *V1* is CE **or** *V2* is B01 **then** *Vk* is S01

Figure 8.14 shows the FAM filled out after adding this rule. The consequent (outcome) fuzzy set *S01* has been added to the row for *B01* and the columns for *CE*.

Rule quality measurements for *Or* rules are computed in the same way as regular *And* rules. The degree values of each cell in the fuzzy rule base are the same as the quality degree of the rule.

Run the Fuzzy Model

Executing a fuzzy model involves defining the methods for fuzzification, correlation, aggregation, and defuzzification. A form of the SAM is used. For a rule such as

if V_1 is *B01* **and** V_2 is *S01* **then** V_k is CE

fuzzification and correlation (as in all fuzzy models) involves finding the membership of x_{vi} in *B01* and x_{v2} in *S01* and using this to measure the degree of control exercised by the rule. This means that the control degree for a vector of input data points $x_{v1}, x_{v2}, x_{v3}, \dots x_{vi}$ is found by

$$d_o^i = \prod_{i=1}^{n} \mu_{A_i}(x_i) \tag{8.9}$$

As an illustration, the control degree for the previous rule is computed as

$$d_o^{r1} = \mu_{B01}(x_{v1}) \times \mu_{S01}(x_{v2}) \tag{8.10}$$

A control degree for each rule forms the scaling factor that correlates the degree of truth in the antecedent with the degree of strength (control) in the consequent (outcome). Our defuzzification strategy, shown in Expression 8.11, for the rule-induced model sums the scaled outcomes and divides by the sum of the scaling.

$$x_{v_o}^D = \frac{\sum_{i=1}^{n} d_o^i \times \hat{x}_{v_o}}{\sum_{i=1}^{n} d_o^i} \tag{8.11}$$

Here,

$x_{v_o}^D$ The defuzzified value of the outcome variable
$\hat{x}_{v_o}$ The center of the outcome fuzzy region

In other words, we treat the outcome fuzzy region (O_i) as a singleton [a line of a height of $max(O_i)$ and width of zero]. In this approach to defuzzification we do not actually form an outcome fuzzy set (you can only use this approach when the model does not contain unconditional fuzzy rules). Defuzzification produces a weighted average of the scaled outcomes.

8.4   **The Model Building Methodology**

In the next few sections the underlying temperature forecasting model is defined and then created using the rule induction engine. In constructing a model, we need to observe a regular process or methodology that addresses the nature of the data as well as the nature of the target model. As Figure 8.15 schematically illustrates, creating and verifying a fuzzy rule-based model from a training set of data involves a definite set of steps.

The overall model construction process is relatively straightforward. The individual steps, however, can be complicated and often time consuming (especially the process of cleaning, transforming, and organizing the data, discussed in some detail in material to follow). Each step fuses to form a uniform way of using data to build a rule-based model.

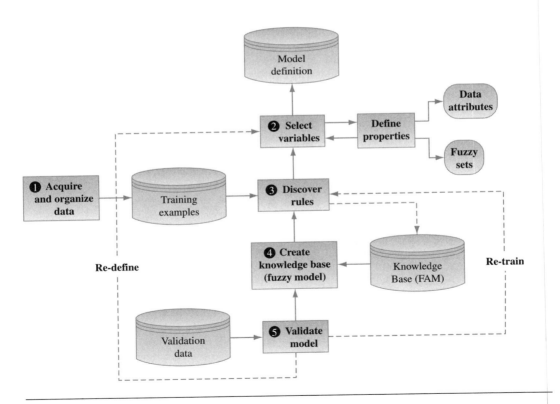

Figure 8.15   The model development methodology.

❶ Acquire, Clean, Transform, and Organize the Data

Building a model from historical information necessitates acquiring sufficient data to represent all underlying patterns. To predict monthly temperature variations, for example, a model needs at least one year of monthly data. Data must also be cleaned and often normalized. Cleaning is the process of removing obvious errors and extraneous outliers. Cleaning also involves identifying and correcting missing data. Data transformation for a time-series model, as we have previously discussed, involves transforming the data into an indexed representation. The *Year x Month* data matrix becomes the serial data file shown in Listing 8.1. Note that *Year* is not included in the data file because it is not an explicit variable. Rather, each year is represented by a repeating block of monthly temperatures.

```
Month,  Temperature
   1,      -1.9
   2,       2.2
   3,      12.2
   4,      13.7
   5,      16.1
   6,      21.3
   7,      25.2
   8,      25.4
   9,      20.9
  10,      14.4
  11,       7.7
  12,      -2
   1,       2.9
   2,      -2.1
   3,       2.7
   4,      13.1
   5,      17.7
   6,      22.8
   7,      24.9
   8,      29.7
   9,      22.2
  10,      19.3
  11,       8.2
  12,       3.7
```

Listing 8.1   The temperature data file.

After acquiring the data, it must be separated in training and validation sets. The temperature prediction model is a supervised knowledge discovery process. Supervision means that the rule discovery algorithm is fed examples of the (temperature, month) relationships and from these examples extracts the patterns in terms of an *if-then* rule base. These examples constitute a training set for the model. Another set of the same data is set aside for model validation (see "Validate Model" for details).

❷ Select Variables and Define Properties

Part of the model definition is the need to identify the dependent (outcome) variable and the set of independent (generally, input) variables. Each variable in a model has a variety of attributes or properties that affect the way it is used. In building the model we can consider such properties as the following.

- Data type (numeric, Boolean, or string)
- Data structure (continuous or discrete)
- Range of values (domain)
- Unit of measure
- Underlying division into fuzzy regions

Based on a preliminary statistical analysis, the modeling system provides defaults for each of these properties. A variable is usually considered continuous and numeric. The number and location of the underlying fuzzy sets are determined by the statistical properties of the data.

❸ Discover Rules

The core of the model constructor is the rule discovery (or induction) algorithm that reads the training file and finds the underlying rules relating the independent variables to the dependent variable. Rule discovery (or induction) generates the core collection of fuzzy *if-then* rules. Listing 8.2 illustrates a portion of the discovered rules. From the discovery process, the rules are numbered, assigned a weight reflecting their degree of evidence, and then expressed as a fuzzy relation in the form *variable fuzzy set variable fuzzy set*. These rules represent each of the unique fuzzy relationships between temperature and time embedded in the data.

```
001 1.023 Month Mon_06 Temperature Tem_09
002 1.042 Month Mon_07 Temperature Tem_09
003 1.049 Month Mon_09 Temperature Tem_05
004 1.030 Month Mon_10 Temperature Tem_03
005 1.023 Month Mon_02 Temperature Tem_02
006 1.068 Month Mon_05 Temperature Tem_08
007 1.072 Month Mon_01 Temperature Tem_01
008 1.015 Month Mon_03 Temperature Tem_06
009 1.038 Month Mon_09 Temperature Tem_06
010 1.049 Month Mon_02 Temperature Tem_03
011 1.053 Month Mon_04 Temperature Tem_07
012 1.019 Month Mon_05 Temperature Tem_09
013 1.019 Month Mon_03 Temperature Tem_04
014 1.049 Month Mon_11 Temperature Tem_01
015 1.004 Month Mon_01 Temperature Tem_03
```

Listing 8.2 Discovered temperature rules.

❹ Create the Fuzzy Knowledge Base

A knowledge base represents the final results of the rule discovery process and consists of the rules and variable definitions. It is the knowledge base that forms the actual mode that is effectively compiled and executed to run the temperature prediction system. Listing 8.3 shows a part of the knowledge base generated from the rule induction process.

```
[R001; Wgt=1.023]:
if Month is Mon_06
   then Temperature is Tem_09;

[R002; Wgt=1.042]:
if Month is Mon_07
   then Temperature is Tem_09;

[R003; Wgt=1.049]:
if Month is Mon_09
   then Temperature is Tem_05;

[R004; Wgt=1.030]:
if Month is Mon_10
   then Temperature is Tem_03;
```

Listing 8.3 Temperature prediction rules.

A knowledge base becomes a self-contained container of rules and variables that is opened and run by the fuzzy inference engine. In the temperature model, the knowledge base connects to an inference engine that reads a month and predicts a temperature for that month (along with the amount of evidence associated with that prediction).

❺ Validate the Model

Once a model's knowledge base has been generated, the model prediction effectiveness must be tested. The predictive precision of a model depends on a variety of factors, such as the following.

■   The amount and richness of the training data
■   The resolution granularity of the partitioning fuzzy sets
■   The generation parameters of the algorithm

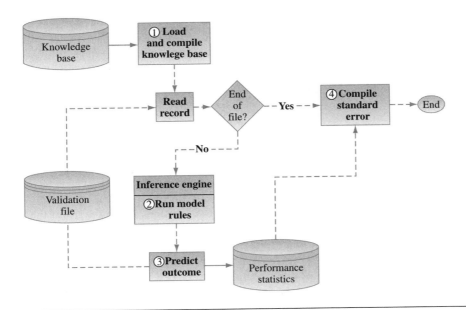

Figure 8.16   The model validation process.

As the name implies, the purpose of validation is to measure how well the model works — to validate its performance against new and untested data. A validation file is usually extracted from the pool of initially acquired, cleaned, and transformed data. The majority of the data, in the form of a training file, is fed to the rule discovery algorithm so that a broad spectrum of patterns is discovered and learned. A smaller but nevertheless broadly representative collection of data points are set aside in one or more validation files. Figure 8.16 schematically shows the validation process.

Validation parallels the execution of a deployed model except that validation data also contains the value of the outcome or dependent variable. After a knowledge base is loaded and compiled ①, data from the validation file is continuously read and passed to the active model ②. The model predicts a temperature and compares the predicted value with the actual value ③. The actual and the predicted values are stored in the performance statistics file. When all validation data has been processed ④, the performance statistics are used to compute an average standard error. The smaller the standard error the more precise and robust is the model.

If the average standard error associated with a model is not acceptable, the model must be recreated. A new model is generated by retraining or by redefinition or a combination of the these approaches. Retraining means increasing the amount and pattern richness of the training data. Redefinition means changing the parameters of the model itself (such as increasing or decreasing the independent variables or the number and shape of the underlying fuzzy sets for one or more of the variables).

In the next section we will follow the development of a rule-based model through model specification, rule generation, and validation.

8.5 A Rule Induction and Model Building Example

The rule induction process provides the core model building mechanism underlying a large family of usually nonlinear models. A typical nonlinear model involves discovering the trend behavior of time-series data. Time series regularly have significant periodicity cycles as well as a high level of ambient noise. Although polynomial regression techniques are available that do an excellent job of developing a time-series model, the fuzzy rule induction mechanism is also capable of modeling this type of nonlinearity. We turn our attention to building a time-series prediction model as an example of the nonlinear model as a general class.

A Nonlinear Time-Series Model

A time series, as the name implies, is a collection of data organized across time. It has the important characteristic of having one or more monotonic time axes. In general, each time axis is a finer-grained elaboration of a higher-level time perspective. In this model we are using 30 years of temperature data (see Table 8.4) from the Midwest (Kansas City).

TABLE 8.4 Annual Temperatures from 1945 to 1972

		Jan	Feb	Mar	Apr	May	Jun	Jul	Aug	Sep	Oct	Nov	Dec
	1945	−1.9	2.2	12.2	13.7	16.1	21.3	25.2	25.4	20.9	14.4	7.7	−2
	1946	2.9	−2.1	2.7	13.1	17.7	22.8	24.9	29.7	22.2	19.3	5.2	3.7
	1947	1.3	4.6	13.8	16	16.9	24.5	26.9	23	20.9	17.1	9.3	4.9
	1948	−3.1	1.4	6.6	15.4	18.4	24.1	26.1	26	22.4	13.8	8.9	3.7
	1949	0.6	2.7	6.7	12.3	20.6	25.3	27	25.5	18.4	15.9	9.4	4.9
	1950	3.4	2.8	5	10.6	20.1	23.6	24.6	22.7	19.7	18.3	3.9	−1.4
	1951	0.3	1.9	4.5	11.2	19.7	22.3	25.7	24.8	19.1	15.1	3.8	0.9
	1952	2.2	4.3	5.8	12.7	18.8	28.4	27.4	24.8	21.1	12.1	7.8	2.8
	1953	1.8	4.4	8.2	11.2	19.6	27.5	27.4	25.7	22.4	16.7	8.7	3.2
	1954	0.4	6.6	5.6	16.7	16.4	26.3	29.4	26.7	23.7	14.9	7.7	2.6
	1955	0.6	2.2	7.2	17.2	20.2	21.9	28.6	26.8	23.1	14.6	5.4	0.6
	1956	−1.6	2.7	7.3	11.9	19.9	24.6	25.4	26.3	21.6	18.1	7.2	3.6
	1957	−2.8	4.7	6.3	13.6	19	24.2	26.7	26.3	20.2	12.7	6.4	4.9
Year	1958	−0.4	−3.7	3.3	13.2	18.9	21.9	24.7	25.3	20.6	15.1	9.4	0
	1959	−3.2	2.1	7.6	13.8	20.9	24.7	25.6	27.1	21.8	13.9	3.9	4.1
	1960	0.8	−0.7	−0.9	14.9	17.1	23.3	24.6	26.2	23.4	15	8.1	−0.6
	1961	−2.1	2.2	7.5	10	14.6	21.2	24.5	24.1	21.7	15.1	6.7	0
	1962	−4.1	2.6	4.2	11.8	22.2	23.3	24.3	24.2	19.1	16.1	7.2	−0.4
	1963	−5.9	−1.9	9.3	14.6	17.7	24.1	25.2	23.8	20.3	19.4	7.6	−5.4
	1964	1.5	1.3	5.7	14.8	20.9	23.8	25.8	24.7	20.7	12.2	8.5	−0.1
	1965	−0.1	1	1.4	14.7	21.4	23.9	24.9	24.3	20.6	13.6	9.2	5.4
	1966	−3.9	0.1	8.2	10.9	16.5	23.2	28.3	23.4	18.7	12.3	8.4	1.6
	1967	1.5	−0.4	9.1	14.7	16	23.3	23.8	22.4	19.2	14.1	5.6	1.6
	1968	−0.1	−1.6	7.8	13.1	16.6	25	25.3	25.1	19.3	13.9	6.4	0.2
	1969	−1.6	1.8	3.2	13.8	18.7	22.5	26.9	25	20.7	13.4	6.3	0.1
	1970	−4	0.5	4.7	14.4	20.7	22.4	25.5	24.6	22.1	13.4	6.4	2.8
	1971	−2.6	1.1	5.4	13.3	16.8	26.1	24.1	24.3	22.5	17.6	7.8	4.8
	1972	−1.2	1.3	7.2	13.4	19.1	23	25.3	24.6	21.7	12.7	4.3	−0.9
	1973	0.3	1.4	10.5	12.1	16.5	23.7	25.9	24.9	21.1	15.9	8.3	−1.1
	1974	−1.2	2.3	8.9	14.2	18.3	20.8	26.6	23.6	16.8	14.3	6.7	1.1

Using this data, we use the rule induction methodology to create a model that predicts the temperature, given the month of the year. In more general terms, this means building a model that relates temperature to month in a functional manner, as shown in Expression 8.12.

$$T_t = f(M_t) \tag{8.12}$$

where,

T_t is the dependent variable and represents the temperature at time t.

M_t is the independent variable and represents the month at time t. The value for M_t is not the month but the time index value, discussed in the next section (on organizing time-series data).

The rule discovery process uses historical temperature data (see Table 8.1) to discover a set of association rules that makes this functional connection. These rules are in the form

if month is M **then** temperature is T,

where M is a fuzzy interval associated with the underlying monthly time frame and T is a fuzzy number created from the association rules. The model created by rule induction consists of a collection of fuzzy *if-then* rules. The rules are organized in a knowledge base and executed in parallel. Expression 8.13 illustrates this process.

$$\begin{bmatrix} R_1 \\ R_2 \\ \vdots \\ R_n \end{bmatrix} \Rightarrow T \Rightarrow d(T) \Rightarrow T_t \tag{8.13}$$

The outcome of the model is a fuzzy region T. When T is reduced or defuzzified (d(T)), the value is T_t, the predicted temperature for the month.

Organizing Time-Series Data

To model a time series with periodic cycles we need to convert the time axis into a set of repeating index values that represents these cycles. This allows the trend analysis system to learn the underlying periodicity patterns and match them to the indexing cycles. For example, Table 8.5 illustrates part of the temperature data with the month names replaced with period index values.

TABLE 8.5   Temperature Data with Month Index Values

		1	2	3	4	5	6	7	8	9	10	11	12
						Months							
	1945	−1.9	2.2	12.2	13.7	16.1	21.3	25.2	25.4	20.9	14.4	7.7	−2
	1946	2.9	−2.1	2.7	13.1	17.7	22.8	24.9	29.7	22.2	19.3	5.2	3.7
Year	1947	1.3	4.6	13.8	16	16.9	24.5	26.9	23	20.9	17.1	9.3	4.9
	1948	−3.1	1.4	6.6	15.4	18.4	24.1	26.1	26	22.4	13.8	8.9	3.7
	1949	0.6	2.7	6.7	12.3	20.6	25.3	27	25.5	18.4	15.9	9.4	4.9

TABLE 8.6   The Annual Temperature Data File

	Month	Temperature
Cycle 1	1	−1.9
	2	2.2
	3	12.2
	4	13.7
	5	16.1
	6	21.3
	7	25.2
	8	25.4
	9	20.9
	10	14.4
	11	7.7
	12	−2
Cycle 2	1	2.9
	2	−2.1
	3	2.7
	4	13.1
	5	17.7
	6	22.8
	7	24.9
	8	29.7
	9	22.2
	10	19.3
	11	5.2
	12	3.7

In this example, we have simply replaced the month names with the month number, but this number becomes the index into the period behavior of the data. This can be seen more clearly by examining Table 8.6, the actual data file generated from this transformation.

Each periodic cycle in a time series for which we want to learn and predict a value must be converted to an indexing scheme. The month index effectively converts the data into a series of separate vectors, one for each index. Thus, the learning mechanism resolves the patterns for the data along the index. For example, for a model that is interested in both monthly and quarterly temperature variations Table 8.7 shows how the underlying data would be indexed.

In Table 8.5 we have two interdependent cycles: months and quarters. With this decomposition, the rule induction process would learn two types of patterns: one for the monthly temperatures and one for the quarterly temperatures. Thus, we can look for patterns that repeat at greater or finer levels of granularity. Figure 8.17 illustrates how periodic cycles are represented and selected in the data and the model.

TABLE 8.7 Temperature Data with Month and Quarter Index Values

							Months and Quarters						
	Mnth	1	2	3	4	5	6	7	8	9	10	11	12
	Qtr	1	2	3	1	2	3	1	2	3	1	2	3
	1945	−1.9	2.2	12.2	13.7	16.1	21.3	25.2	25.4	20.9	14.4	7.7	−2
	1946	2.9	−2.1	2.7	13.1	17.7	22.8	24.9	29.7	22.2	19.3	5.2	3.7
Year	1947	1.3	4.6	13.8	16	16.9	24.5	26.9	23	20.9	17.1	9.3	4.9
	1948	−3.1	1.4	6.6	15.4	18.4	24.1	26.1	26	22.4	13.8	8.9	3.7
	1949	0.6	2.7	6.7	12.3	20.6	25.3	27	25.5	18.4	15.9	9.4	4.9

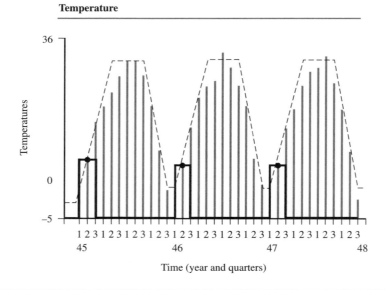

Figure 8.17 The periodicity of temperature data.

Figure 8.19 shows just one periodic cycle in the data: the second month in the first quarter of data in each year. However, of course, the actual periodic behavior is reflected in the repeating index values over the full year (and for each year in the available data). Table 8.8 illustrates how the data file for the month and quarter data would be constructed.

Quarterly cycles are independent of the monthly cycle because a quarter also breaks down the year into segments that logically subsume and define ongoing temperature changes. Often subcycles are not independent of other cycles in the data. For example, if the data file has daily temperatures the temperature cycles in a month $(1, 2, 3, \ldots, 30)$ only makes sense within the context of the month index itself. Table 8.9 shows the data broken down at the day level (which is then aggregated at the monthly and quarterly levels).

TABLE 8.8   The Annual Temperature Data File (Month and Quarter)

	Month		Quarter	Temperature
Cycle 1	1	Cycle 1	1	−1.9
	2		2	2.2
	3		3	12.2
	4	Cycle 2	1	13.7
	5		2	16.1
	6		3	21.3
	7	Cycle 3	1	25.2
	8		2	25.4
	9		3	20.9
	10	Cycle 4	1	14.4
	11		2	7.7
	12		3	−2
Cycle 2	1	Cycle 1	1	2.9
	2		2	−2.1
	3		3	2.7
	4	Cycle 2	1	13.1
	5		2	17.7
	6		3	22.8
	7	Cycle 3	1	24.9
	8		2	29.7
	9		3	22.2
	10	Cycle 4	1	19.3
	11		2	5.2
	12		3	3.7

TABLE 8.9   Temperature Data with Month, Quarter, and Daily Index Values

		Months and Quarters and Days										
	Mnth			1						2		
	Qtr			1						2		
	Days	1	2	3	4	.....	31	1	2	3	4	.....	28
	1945	−1.9	2.2	12.2	13.7	.....	21.3	25.2	25.4	20.9	14.4	.....	−2
	1946	2.9	−2.1	2.7	13.1	.....	22.8	24.9	29.7	22.2	19.3	.....	3.7
Year	1947	1.3	4.6	13.8	16	.....	24.5	26.9	23	20.9	17.1	.....	4.9
	1948	−3.1	1.4	6.6	15.4	.....	24.1	26.1	26	22.4	13.8	.....	3.7
	1949	0.6	2.7	6.7	12.3	.....	25.3	27	25.5	18.4	15.9	.....	4.9

The Importance of Periodicity (Separation of Recurring Patterns)

The implicit seasonal relationships in temperature across a year tend to obscure the real power of discovery in data, with many different types of patterns with various levels of granularity. Because temperatures become predictably warmer over the months from January through the end of the summer and then cooler as they approach the end of the year, the quarterly patterns do not repeat within the year. In many business, government, and scientific systems many types of periodicity cycles repeat at various levels of granularity. The following are examples.

- Annual sales by product line by division
- Annual highway traffic loads
- Project expenditures by department
- Inventory turnover by stock class
- Application server and database transaction rates
- Network node traffic by transaction type by node location
- Web traffic loads
- Container arrival volumes by port by geography

Modeling application transaction rates on a database server in order to understand capacity thresholds, performance bottlenecks, and resource collisions is a good example of a time-series system with many important

TABLE 8.10   Database Transactions by Type

		Month, Day of Month, Hour, Quarter Hour, Five Minutes									
	Mnth	1					1				
	Day	1					1				
	Hour	1					2				
	Qtr	1	2		4		1	2		4	
	5 Min	0005	0010	0015	0020	.....	0060	0005	0010	0015	0020	.....	0060
	T01	310	318	370	240	.....	280	310	318	370	240	.....	280
	T02	18	17	15	11	.....	19	14	17	22	16	.....	28
Type	T03	2310	3218	3370	2240	.....	2280	2310	3317	3270	2440	.....	2980
	T04	510	358	670	640	.....	580	518	313	571	644	.....	780
	T05	1311	1308	1320	1270	.....	1200	1311	1418	1390	1270	.....	1180

periodicity cycles. Many performance management tools collect transaction rates every five minutes. These sampled rates can be organized into time series with various degrees of granularity. Table 8.10 illustrates an example of transaction rates organized into multiple time series.

In the case of transaction analysis, understanding the periodicity of transactions over many different time frames is critical to understanding the behavior of application servers, databases, and the network. We know, for instance, that 10 a.m. Tuesday morning is different from 10 p.m. Tuesday night, and that the beginning of the month is different from the middle or end of the month. A decomposition of the transaction traffic into multiple time series with different periodic cycles provides the mechanism necessary to explore large-scale and fine-grain behaviors.

Rules with Multiple Time Index Values

The number of time index columns associated with the data determines the granularity and the scope of the model. In the temperature model, the functional relationship is relatively simple: one dependent variable (temperature) is related to one time index value (the month). In the server and database transaction model, predicting the transaction rate for a particular transaction type could involve learning the behavior associated with, for example, a composite time aggregate (month × day × hour). In this case, the functional relationship is a bit more complex, as shown in Expression 8.14.

$$R_t = f(M_t, D_t, H_t) \qquad (8.14)$$

where,

R_t is the dependent variable and represents the transaction rate at
time t

M_t represents the month at time t

D_t represents the day of the month at time t

H_t represents the hour of the day at time t

Exactly like the temperature model, the values for the independent variables are time index values. This functional relationship is discovered from the underlying data and is represented by a collection of *if-then* rules. These rules will qualify the outcome variable based on the fine detail of time indexes in the data. For example, a transaction rate rule might appear as follows.

Transaction Type T01:
if month is M
   and day is D
   and hour is H **then** rate is R

Here, M, D, and H are fuzzy intervals associated with the underlying monthly, day of month, and hour time frames (respectively), and R, the predicted rate, is a fuzzy number that is created from the association rules. Thus, this rule would predict the rate R at time t, where t is a 3-tuple value — such as $(8,16,22)$ — which would be the 16th of August at 10 p.m. This means, of course, that learning the transaction behavior at some set of time periods requires values for these time periods in order to execute the model. In dealing with data that has multiple time-series qualifiers, the degree to which you should include additional time index values should be predicated on the use and degree of resolution you need in the model. In many data collections, moving up the chain of detail will require producing new data collections with aggregated data. This is clearly the case with the transaction data. If we are only interested in hourly transaction rates, we need to create a new data file with the 12 five-minute sample values summed (or averaged) to a single hourly value.

Creating the Temperature Prediction Model

After covering the ways in which time-series data is represented in the data and the nature of the patterns expressed through this representation, we now turn to the specification of the actual model. This specification involves defining the properties of the dependent and independent variables. In building and validating the temperature forecasting model, examples from the Fuzzy Data Explorer, a graphical model building and data exploration system, are used.

The Temperature Properties

Temperature is the dependent variable; that is, the outcome of the model. A set of default data characteristics are supplied by the modeling system based on a preliminary statistical analysis. The way in which we use a variable and the nature of its underlying fuzzy partitions are based on how the variable is declared in the model. Figure 8.18 shows the nature of the temperature variable, including a compressed statistical frequency histogram of the underlying data.

Temperature is a continuous double-precision floating-point variable. Its UoD (or domain) is extended a small percentage beyond the minimum and maximum values (to accommodate both possible outliers in the validation set as well as the elastic boundaries of the underlying fuzzy sets). The actual data statistics are displayed at the bottom of the Variable Properties screen.

After a variable's data properties have been defined (or left to their defaults), its range of values must be partitioned into a collection of overlapping fuzzy sets. This partitioning can be done in one of three ways: (1) manually by defining the number, the position, and shape of the fuzzy sets, (2) automatically through a uniform placement of fuzzy sets

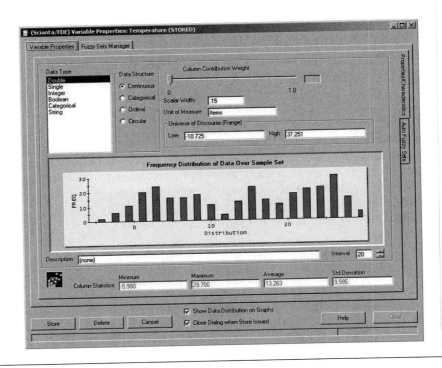

Figure 8.18 Statistical profile of temperature data.

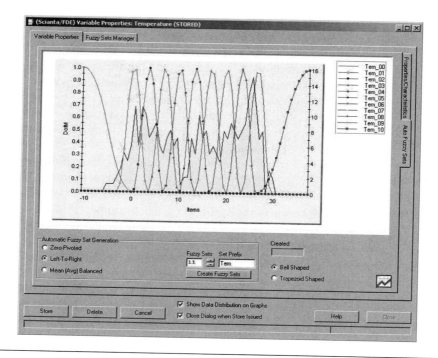

Figure 8.19 The fuzzy set partitioning for the *Temperature* variable.

over the domain, and (3) statistically according to the distribution of data across the domain. Figure 8.19 shows the fuzzy sets, generated through a statistical mechanism, arrayed along the *Temperature* variable's domain.

Figure 8.19 shows two properties: the collection of fuzzy sets and the distribution of the actual data (the gray area graph along the background). The left-hand vertical axis shows the degree of membership in the fuzzy sets. The right-hand vertical axis shows the frequency counts for the data. The statistical fuzzy set generator divides the variable range into a specified number of overlapping sets (in this case, 11 sets). Fuzzy sets are also named automatically left to right using the first three characters of the variable name.

The Month (Time Index) Properties

The month time index is the dependent variable, with a range from [*1*] (January) to [*12*] (December). Figure 8.20 shows the result of using a statistical approach to automatically decompose the *Month* variable into its fuzzy set partitions.

The level of granularity for the underlying fuzzy sets is closely tied to the number of index values. We are treating month as a continuous

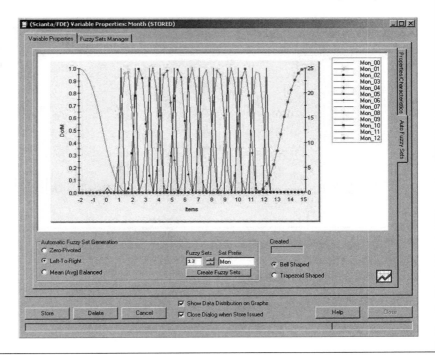

Figure 8.20   Month index decomposed into fuzzy sets.

number. However, it could also be viewed as integer-valued intervals or categorical data. The choice of representation is often dictated, especially in a fuzzy model, by the ease in treating the data as a continuous spectrum of values.

Discovering the Functional Rule Set

Rule discovery has two phases. This first phase runs the training file of exemplar cases through the rule induction engine to produce a collection of candidate rules. The second phase compresses the rules to generate the final knowledge base. Figure 8.21 shows the post-generation statistics.

The initial rule-evolver phases read 302 training exemplar cases from the training file, rejected 18, and stored 283 (about 94% of the total possible rules). The second phase, a compression process, conducts a tournament among rules, reads these 283 intermediate rules, and after eliminating and resolving ambiguities and rejecting 199 duplicates and updating 50 intermediate rules, creates a final knowledge base of 15 rules. Figure 8.22 shows a partial view of the rules in the evolver dialog window.

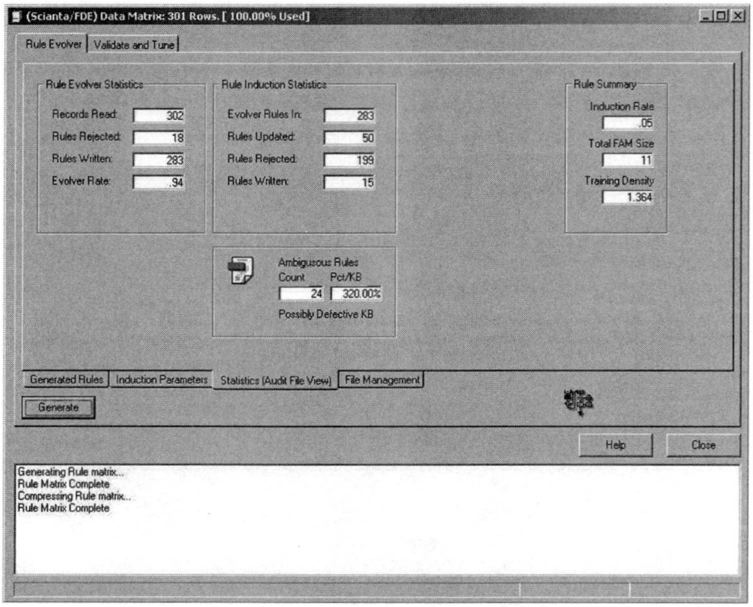

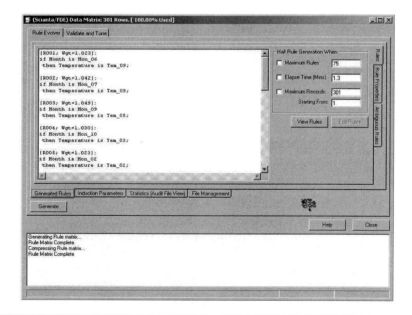

Figure 8.21 Rule discovery statistics.

Figure 8.22 Partial set of generated rules.

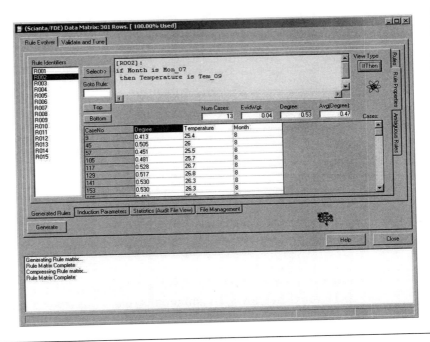

Figure 8.23   Case (exemplar) support for rule R002.

Rule Case Support

Every rule is produced from a set of exemplars or cases. Tracking these cases and evaluating their degree of evidence is an important factor in verifying the knowledge base as well as detecting any anomalous properties in the data (see also the ambiguous rule display). The case support for each rule is visible in the rule evolver dialog through the Rule Properties tab. Figure 8.23 shows the case support for the second rule.

The case support displays the actual records from the training file (*CaseNo* is the record number in the file), with the value of the variables used to generate the rule along with their quality degree (effectiveness times the data reliability belief function). In addition to the number of cases, we can see the evidence weight for the rule (discussed shortly), the rule's overall degree, and the average quality degree for the total collection of rules.

Ambiguity Detection and Resolution

An ambiguous rules indicator refers to the fact that some patterns in the data have associated rules with the same antecedent but different consequent (outcome) actions. This means that a possibly faulty knowledge

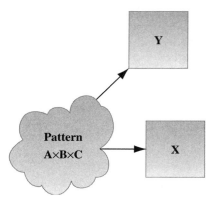

Figure 8.24 An ambiguous pattern.

base was evolved (ambiguous rules do not uniquely classify an outcome). As Figure 8.24 shows, an ambiguous rule set has two possibly equal ways of predicting or classifying the outcome of a rule.

Ambiguity always comes in sets. That is, at least two rules in the knowledge base share the same antecedent with different outcomes. The following two rules illustrate this type of ambiguity.

> If A and B and C, then X.
> If A and B and C, then Y.

The paired nature of ambiguous rules also explains the 320% of the rule base statistics. There were 24 ambiguous rules and 15 rules actually written to the knowledge base. This is 24/15, or 160%. Because the count of 24 represents two rules, the actual ambiguous-rule-to-final-rule percentage is twice this amount, or 320%. Ambiguous rules are stored with the knowledge base and, as shown in Figure 8.25, viewed in the rule evolver dialog.

Ambiguity arises in several places, and it is the responsibility of the data mining or knowledge engineer to determine its source. Conflicting patterns can be resident in the data. In this case, the historical record makes it difficult to induce effective rules because patterns exist that specify two different actions for the same source. The effectiveness ranking of rules and the tournament selection (considered next) will naturally weed out sparse and residual ambiguities of this nature. However, if a critical population of conflicting patterns exists they will persist and eventually be revealed as active rules. Ambiguity can also arise from the lack of resolution in the fuzzy sets associated with model variables. This type of ambiguity can often be tolerated in a model simply because of

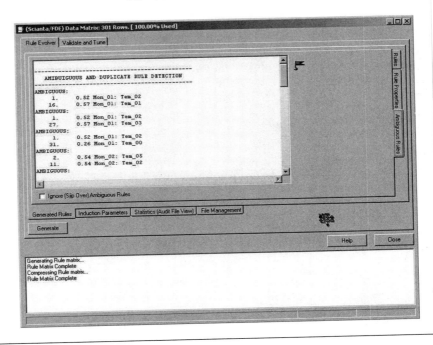

Figure 8.25 The ambiguous rules.

the noise tolerance of fuzzy models themselves. Knowledge engineers can reduce fuzzy-set-related ambiguity by slightly increasing the number of fuzzy sets or changing the membership function from bell-shaped to trapezoid-shaped surfaces.

Candidate Rule Induction

The preliminary rule evolution process generates a large population of candidate rules from the data. Many of these are duplicates, and some of these are ambiguous. Listing 8.4 shows a sample of the intermediate file of candidate rules. The intermediate rules file (created by the rule evolver) maintains the degree of membership that generated each rule component. Thus, *(ACCEL, S02, 0.5386)* indicates the date value *xi* for the *Acceleration* variable has a membership of *[0.54]* in the outcome fuzzy set *S02*. Finally, the candidate rule has its overall quality (or effectiveness) and its record number in the training file. This file (*kdrulmat*), the rule matrix, is read to create the first set of rules through a tournament process. Listing 8.5 shows the statistics issued by the rule evolver.

In the evolution phase, each data vector or record in the training file is used to generate a pattern relationship. If the pattern has sufficient

```
Temperature, Tem_02, 0.6172, Month, Mon_01, 0.5703, 0.3520,    3
Temperature, Tem_05, 0.7637, Month, Mon_02, 0.5408, 0.4130,    4
Temperature, Tem_05, 0.9737, Month, Mon_03, 0.6352, 0.6185,    5
Temperature, Tem_06, 0.9604, Month, Mon_04, 0.6080, 0.5840,    6
Temperature, Tem_07, 0.6699, Month, Mon_05, 0.5799, 0.3885,    7
Temperature, Tem_09, 0.6948, Month, Mon_06, 0.5507, 0.3827,    8
Temperature, Tem_09, 0.7778, Month, Mon_07, 0.5206, 0.4049,    9
Temperature, Tem_07, 0.8299, Month, Mon_09, 0.5104, 0.4235,   10
Temperature, Tem_05, 0.7637, Month, Mon_09, 0.5894, 0.4501,   11
Temperature, Tem_03, 0.8418, Month, Mon_10, 0.5605, 0.4719,   12
Temperature, Tem_02, 0.9132, Month, Mon_01, 0.4013, 0.3664,   14
Temperature, Tem_02, 0.8589, Month, Mon_02, 0.5408, 0.4645,   16
Temperature, Tem_05, 0.9934, Month, Mon_03, 0.6352, 0.6310,   17
Temperature, Tem_06, 0.7981, Month, Mon_04, 0.6080, 0.4853,   18
Temperature, Tem_08, 0.9633, Month, Mon_05, 0.5799, 0.5586,   19
Temperature, Tem_09, 0.5987, Month, Mon_06, 0.5507, 0.3297,   20
Temperature, Tem_08, 0.8111, Month, Mon_09, 0.5104, 0.4140,   22
Temperature, Tem_07, 0.9444, Month, Mon_09, 0.5894, 0.5566,   23
Temperature, Tem_02, 0.5408, Month, Mon_10, 0.5605, 0.3031,   24
Temperature, Tem_02, 0.9991, Month, Mon_11, 0.5308, 0.5303,   25
Temperature, Tem_01, 0.7778, Month, Mon_01, 0.4013, 0.3121,   26
Temperature, Tem_02, 0.8111, Month, Mon_01, 0.5703, 0.4626,   27
Temperature, Tem_05, 0.9737, Month, Mon_02, 0.5408, 0.5266,   28
Temperature, Tem_06, 0.9217, Month, Mon_03, 0.6352, 0.5854,   29
Temperature, Tem_06, 0.9843, Month, Mon_04, 0.6080, 0.5985,   30
Temperature, Tem_08, 0.7109, Month, Mon_05, 0.5799, 0.4122,   31
Temperature, Tem_09, 0.9688, Month, Mon_06, 0.5507, 0.5335,   32
Temperature, Tem_08, 0.9878, Month, Mon_07, 0.5206, 0.5143,   33
Temperature, Tem_07, 0.8299, Month, Mon_09, 0.5104, 0.4235,   34
Temperature, Tem_06, 0.9575, Month, Mon_09, 0.5894, 0.5643,   35
Temperature, Tem_04, 0.8644, Month, Mon_10, 0.5605, 0.4845,   36
Temperature, Tem_02, 0.6440, Month, Mon_11, 0.5308, 0.3418,   37
Temperature, Tem_01, 0.7778, Month, Mon_01, 0.5703, 0.4435,   39
Temperature, Tem_03, 0.9922, Month, Mon_02, 0.5408, 0.5366,   40
```

Listing 8.4   The candidate rules intermediate file.

strength, it is selected as a rule. In this example, these are two active filtering constraints.

- The membership of x_i in fuzzy set A_m must have a membership greater than [0.1], the data alpha threshold. A degree of membership below the data alpha threshold is set to zero. This, in turn, sets the entire rule degree to zero. Such a record will not be selected.

```
05/09/2004 8.41pm
RULE EVOLVER. MxN Rule Generation
Data File       : c:\annualtemps\temps.dat
Rule File       : c:\annualtemps\kdrulmat.fil
Data Alfa Threshold : 0.10
Belief Confidence   : 1.00
Rule Degree Limit   : 0.20
Degree Calculation  : Product
Number of Variables : 2

    Variable        Col  Type  Wght  Fuzzy Sets
    ----------      ---  ----  ----  ---------------------------------------------
1.  Temperature      1   IV    1.000 Tem_00,Tem_01,Tem_02,Tem_03,Tem_04,Tem_05,..
2.  Month            0   DV    1.000 Mon_00,Mon_01,Mon_02,Mon_03,Mon_04,Mon_05,..
RULE EVOLVER COMPLETE.
Records (In)    :  302
Rules   (Out)   :  283
Evolver Rate    : 0.94
```

Listing 8.5   The rule evolver phase.

- The rule's degree — $E(r_i)$ — must also be above [*0.20*], the rule degree limit. An $E(r_i)$ less than this is also set to zero, and the rule is not selected.

In this example, 19 records failed one or the other of these threshold constraints and were not selected as candidate rules. The remaining 283 candidate rules are used by the induction engine to produce the final knowledge base.

The Compression Tournament

Not all candidate rules will or can be used in the final model. Some method must be employed to select the most effective rules. The tournament selects a candidate rule, examines the virtual FAM, and implements one of the following actions.

- If the virtual FAM cell is empty, the rule is added (inserted) and its degree is also stored.
- If the virtual FAM cell is occupied, the two rules contend for a right to contribute their degree of effectiveness. The rule with the highest degree wins. If the incoming rule has a lower degree, it is rejected. If the incoming rule has a higher degree, the stored degree is updated to the incoming rule's degree.

In Listing 8.6 we can see the tournament held among all candidate rules to find the rules with the best goodness of fit. Only the count of rules with an *ADDED* action actually form part of the final knowledge base.

Tournament compression yields an 88% reduction in the number of rules. Rules can also be eliminated when they lack sufficient case or exemplar support in the data. A minimum case threshold can be established, either as an absolute value (a rule must have at least x number of exemplar cases) or as a percentage (the cases must represent x% of the data space). Although not used in this example, Listing 8.7 shows the same rule induction process with a 5% case threshold.

Finally, the compression process examines the knowledge base for ambiguous rules. These are removed, ignored, or reduced depending on the tournament controls. Ignoring the rules leaves them in the knowledge base, but marks each rule as inactive. Reducing the rules saves the rule with the highest effectiveness (and deletes all others with the same antecedent). In our example, we simply remove all ambiguous rules. Listing 8.8 shows the ambiguity resolution phase of rule induction.

At this point the collection of final rules has been selected and cast in *if-then* format. These rules now form the core intelligence of the derived business or policy model. Listing 8.9 shows these rules in their compact form. This display also includes the number of votes (cases) supporting the rule and the weight of evidence for the rule. The rules are stored in the knowledge base in the more conventional *if-then* format (just as they appear in Figure 8.22). Because the induced rules are stored as ASCII text strings, they can be modified through any text editor. New expert-based rules can also be added to the knowledge base in the same way. Thus, the integration of machine-derived and human-derived rules takes place at this point. Expert rules fused with machine-induced rules provide a broad base of intelligence for business process models.

Model Execution and Validation

Before a model is deployed it must be validated and tuned. This process involves executing the rule base against another file. During validation, the rule base is executed for each incoming record and a value for the dependent value is predicted. Because the validation file also contains the actual value of the outcome value, a validation manager can measure the distance between the actual value and the predicted value. This standard error is computed according to Expression 8.15.

$$e_s = \frac{\sum_{i=1}^{N} \| O_a - O_p \|}{N} \qquad (8.15)$$

```
05/09/2004 8.41pm
RULE INDUCTION. If-Then Rule Generation
Matrix File     :  c:\annualtemps\kdrulmat.fil
Rule File       :  c:\annualtemps\kdrulfam.fil
Tournament Strategy : (WTA) Winner Takes All
Compression Method  : Unique Antecedents
```

```
R U L E   C O M P R E S S I O N   T O U R N A M E N T
RecNo   Action    Degree              Rule
-----   ------    ------              --------------
  1.    ADDED     0.3514            Mon_01: Tem_02
  2.    ADDED     0.4203            Mon_02: Tem_05
  3.    ADDED     0.6170            Mon_03: Tem_05
  4.    ADDED     0.5899            Mon_04: Tem_06
  8.    ADDED     0.3876            Mon_05: Tem_07
  8.    ADDED     0.3839            Mon_06: Tem_09
  7.    ADDED     0.4134            Mon_07: Tem_09
  8.    ADDED     0.4238            Mon_09: Tem_07
  9.    ADDED     0.4563            Mon_09: Tem_05
 10.    ADDED     0.4706            Mon_10: Tem_03
 11.    UPDATES   0.3717            Mon_01: Tem_02
 12.    ADDED     0.4720            Mon_02: Tem_02
 13.    UPDATES   0.6295            Mon_03: Tem_05
 14.    REJECTED  0.5899>0.4896     Mon_04: Tem_06
 15.    ADDED     0.5540            Mon_05: Tem_08
 16.    REJECTED  0.3839>0.3304     Mon_06: Tem_09
 17.    ADDED     0.4118            Mon_09: Tem_08
 18.    UPDATES   0.5635            Mon_09: Tem_07
 19.    ADDED     0.3032            Mon_10: Tem_02
 20.    ADDED     0.5365            Mon_11: Tem_02
 21.    ADDED     0.3178            Mon_01: Tem_01
 22.    UPDATES   0.4646            Mon_01: Tem_02
 23.    UPDATES   0.5361            Mon_02: Tem_05
 24.    ADDED     0.5842            Mon_03: Tem_06
  :
  :
 36.    ADDED     0.3592            Mon_04: Tem_07
 37.    REJECTED  0.5540>0.4955     Mon_05: Tem_08
 38.    UPDATES   0.5422            Mon_06: Tem_09
 39.    UPDATES   0.5046            Mon_07: Tem_09
 40.    UPDATES   0.4446            Mon_09: Tem_08
```

Listing 8.6   The candidate rule tournament.

```
41.    UPDATES     0.5820           Mon_09:  Tem_05
42.    REJECTED    0.4824>0.4009    Mon_10:  Tem_04
43.    REJECTED    0.5365>0.5365    Mon_11:  Tem_02
44.    REJECTED    0.4459>0.3990    Mon_01:  Tem_01
45.    UPDATES     0.4902           Mon_01:  Tem_02
46.    REJECTED    0.5461>0.5461    Mon_02:  Tem_03
47.    REJECTED    0.6295>0.4838    Mon_03:  Tem_05
48.    UPDATES     0.5478           Mon_04:  Tem_07
49.    ADDED       0.4466           Mon_05:  Tem_09
50.    REJECTED    0.5422>0.5182    Mon_06:  Tem_09
51.    REJECTED    0.5046>0.4508    Mon_07:  Tem_09
52.    REJECTED    0.5635>0.2979    Mon_09:  Tem_07
53.    REJECTED    0.5721>0.5510    Mon_09:  Tem_06
54.    UPDATES     0.5122           Mon_10:  Tem_04
55.    REJECTED    0.5365>0.3468    Mon_11:  Tem_02
56.    REJECTED    0.4902>0.4064    Mon_01:  Tem_02
57.    UPDATES     0.5215           Mon_01:  Tem_02
58.    REJECTED    0.4720>0.3556    Mon_02:  Tem_02
59.    ADDED       0.6088           Mon_03:  Tem_04
60.    UPDATES     0.6096           Mon_04:  Tem_07
61.    REJECTED    0.5540>0.5500    Mon_05:  Tem_08
62.    ADDED       0.3438           Mon_06:  Tem_08
63.    REJECTED    0.5261>0.5128    Mon_07:  Tem_08
64.    REJECTED    0.5635>0.5062    Mon_09:  Tem_07
65.    REJECTED    0.5721>0.3104    Mon_09:  Tem_06
66.    UPDATES     0.5384           Mon_10:  Tem_02
67.    ADDED       0.2393           Mon_11:  Tem_01
68.    REJECTED    0.4459>0.4074    Mon_01:  Tem_01
69.    REJECTED    0.5215>0.2902    Mon_01:  Tem_02
70.    REJECTED    0.4720>0.4473    Mon_02:  Tem_02
71.    REJECTED    0.6088>0.4606    Mon_03:  Tem_04
72.    UPDATES     0.6104           Mon_04:  Tem_07
73.    REJECTED    0.5540>0.5026    Mon_05:  Tem_08
74.    REJECTED    0.5422>0.5007    Mon_06:  Tem_09
75.    REJECTED    0.5261>0.2736    Mon_07:  Tem_08
 :
 :
264.   REJECTED    0.6132>0.6132    Mon_04:  Tem_06
265.   REJECTED    0.5730>0.3430    Mon_05:  Tem_09
266.   REJECTED    0.5496>0.4302    Mon_06:  Tem_09
267.   REJECTED    0.5304>0.3690    Mon_07:  Tem_09
268.   REJECTED    0.5635>0.4801    Mon_09:  Tem_07
```

Listing 8.6 Continued.

```
269.    REJECTED    0.5937>0.5623    Mon_09: Tem_05
270.    REJECTED    0.5540>0.5422    Mon_10: Tem_03
271.    UPDATES     0.5368           Mon_11: Tem_01
272.    REJECTED    0.5662>0.3438    Mon_01: Tem_01
273.    REJECTED    0.5406>0.5406    Mon_02: Tem_02
274.    REJECTED    0.6295>0.6170    Mon_03: Tem_05
275.    REJECTED    0.6140>0.4713    Mon_04: Tem_07
276.    REJECTED    0.5743>0.5321    Mon_05: Tem_08
277.    REJECTED    0.5496>0.5376    Mon_06: Tem_09
278.    REJECTED    0.5304>0.3175    Mon_07: Tem_09
279.    REJECTED    0.5635>0.4542    Mon_09: Tem_07
280.    UPDATES     0.5977           Mon_09: Tem_05
281.    REJECTED    0.5540>0.5231    Mon_10: Tem_03
282.    REJECTED    0.5368>0.5318    Mon_11: Tem_01
283.    REJECTED    0.5368>0.5318    Mon_11: Tem_01
---------------------------------------------------

         COMPRESSION TOURNAMENT COMPLETED
---------------------------------------------------
Candidate Rules In : 283
Actual   Rules Out :  34
Percent(%)Rules    :  12.014
```

Listing 8.6 Continued.

Here,

e_s is absolute average standard error of estimate
N is the number of observations in the data file
O_a is the actual outcome
O_p is the predicted outcome

Obviously, if O_a equals O_p for all records in the validation file the cumulative standard error will be zero and the model is working perfectly. In the real world, all models have varying degrees of standard error. Figure 8.26 shows the predicted versus actual performance for the 25 induced rules across 86 records in the validation file.

With one or two under- or overfitting points, the model works fairly well. This model has a standard error of 2.71%, meaning that it fits the data well within 97%. From a fuzzy model perspective, an average compatibility index (CIX) measure of [.37] is also very good. The CIX measures the amount of evidence that went into the outcome prediction. For a series of model executions, the average value should be somewhere in the middle range (say from .30 to .70). Figure 8.27 shows a plot of the CIX values for

```
                RULES WITHOUT SUFFICIENT CASE SUPPORT
                Case Threshold :  8.00%
                Rule  (%)
                No.      Cases    Pct      Rule
                -----    -------  ------   --------------
                R0002     2 0.71  (0.54)   Mon_02:  Tem_05
                R0004     9 3.18  (0.61)   Mon_04:  Tem_06
                R0005     2 0.71  (0.39)   Mon_05:  Tem_07
                R0007    13 4.59  (0.53)   Mon_07:  Tem_09
                R0009    13 4.59  (0.60)   Mon_09:  Tem_05
                R0010    13 4.59  (0.55)   Mon_10:  Tem_03
                R0011     6 2.12  (0.54)   Mon_02:  Tem_02
                R0013     9 3.18  (0.51)   Mon_09:  Tem_08
                R0014     4 1.41  (0.55)   Mon_10:  Tem_02
                R0015    10 3.53  (0.54)   Mon_11:  Tem_02
                R0017     4 1.41  (0.63)   Mon_03:  Tem_06
                R0018    11 3.89  (0.53)   Mon_07:  Tem_08
                R0019    10 3.53  (0.60)   Mon_09:  Tem_06
                R0020     8 2.83  (0.51)   Mon_10:  Tem_04
                R0021    13 4.59  (0.55)   Mon_02:  Tem_03
                R0022    14 4.95  (0.61)   Mon_04:  Tem_07
                R0023     5 1.77  (0.57)   Mon_05:  Tem_09
                R0024     5 1.77  (0.63)   Mon_03:  Tem_04
                R0025     6 2.12  (0.51)   Mon_06:  Tem_08
                R0026    13 4.59  (0.54)   Mon_11:  Tem_01
                R0027     1 0.35  (0.57)   Mon_01:  Tem_03
                R0028     2 0.71  (0.43)   Mon_02:  Tem_01
                R0029     1 0.35  (0.42)   Mon_04:  Tem_05
                R0030     1 0.35  (0.50)   Mon_04:  Tem_08
                R0031     1 0.35  (0.26)   Mon_01:  Tem_00
                R0032     2 0.71  (0.48)   Mon_02:  Tem_04
                R0033     1 0.35  (0.29)   Mon_11:  Tem_00
                R0034     1 0.35  (0.36)   Mon_11:  Tem_03
                Rules In       :  34
                Rules Removed  :  28
                Rules Out      :   6
```

Listing 8.7 Insufficient case evidence filtering.

```
RULES WITHOUT SUFFICIENT CASE SUPPORT
Case Threshold :    0.00%
Rules In       :   34
Rules Removed  :    0
Rules Out      :   34


Evidence FKB Compression. Rules Out: 34
   1.    0.52 Mon_01: Tem_02
   1.    0.52 Mon_01: Tem_02
  31.    0.26 Mon_01: Tem_00
   2.    0.54 Mon_02: Tem_05
   2.    0.54 Mon_02: Tem_05
  28.    0.43 Mon_02: Tem_01
  32.    0.48 Mon_02: Tem_04
   3.    0.63 Mon_03: Tem_05
   3.    0.63 Mon_03: Tem_05
   4.    0.61 Mon_04: Tem_06
  29.    0.42 Mon_04: Tem_05
  30.    0.50 Mon_04: Tem_08
   8.    0.39 Mon_05: Tem_07
   8.    0.39 Mon_05: Tem_07
  25.    0.51 Mon_06: Tem_08
  18.    0.53 Mon_07: Tem_08
   8.    0.56 Mon_09: Tem_07
  13.    0.51 Mon_09: Tem_08
   8.    0.56 Mon_09: Tem_07
  14.    0.55 Mon_10: Tem_02
  20.    0.51 Mon_10: Tem_04
  15.    0.54 Mon_11: Tem_02
  33.    0.29 Mon_11: Tem_00
  34.    0.36 Mon_11: Tem_03

Ambiguity FKB Compression. Rules Out :   15
```

Listing 8.8   Compressing ambiguous rules.

each model execution cycle. The cycle at which the CIX drops close to zero often corresponds to weakly learned or poorly generalized patterns, and is consequently a point at which the prediction and the actual values do not match well.

Fundamentally, a model validation is the process of running a fuzzy model and checking the results. This involves the use of a fuzzy inference

```
                Evidence
        Rule    Votes    Weight      F U Z Z Y   R U L E
        ----    -----    ------      ------------------
         1.       6       0.02       Mon_06:  Tem_09
         2.      11       0.04       Mon_07:  Tem_09
         3.      13       0.05       Mon_09:  Tem_05
         4.       8       0.03       Mon_10:  Tem_03
         8.       6       0.02       Mon_02:  Tem_02
         8.      18       0.07       Mon_05:  Tem_08
         7.      19       0.07       Mon_01:  Tem_01
         8.       4       0.02       Mon_03:  Tem_06
         9.      10       0.04       Mon_09:  Tem_06
        10.      13       0.05       Mon_02:  Tem_03
        11.      14       0.05       Mon_04:  Tem_07
        12.       5       0.02       Mon_05:  Tem_09
        13.       5       0.02       Mon_03:  Tem_04
        14.      13       0.05       Mon_11:  Tem_01
        15.       1       0.00       Mon_01:  Tem_03


        RULE DISCOVERY.  FKB Generation Complete
        Total Rules       :       283
        Rules Used        :        15
        Rules Rejected    :       199
        Rules Updated     :        50
        Pct Rules Used    :         8.30
        Ambiguous Rules   :        24
        FKB Dimensions    :         1
        FKB Rule Space    :        11.000000
        FKB Utilization   :         1.364
```

Listing 8.9   The final knowledge base.

engine (to load and actually run the rules) and a results manager to compare the output of the inference engine with the outcome variable's value in the validation file.

8.6   **Measuring Model Robustness**

Robustness is how well a model performs over time. The initial robustness of a discovered rule set is determined by the average standard error

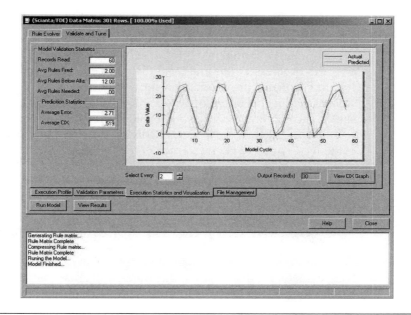

Figure 8.26 Model validation performance.

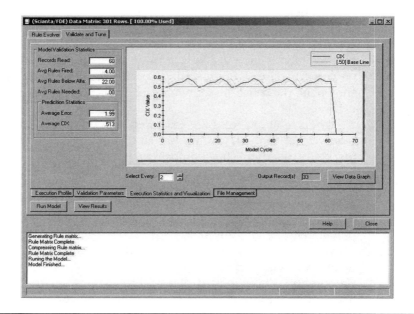

Figure 8.27 Model compatibility profile.

measurement when the validation sets are run through the rules. This is possible because we have the actual outcome and the predicted outcome values. When a model is deployed, however, we have as a general case only the predicted outcome from the rule set. Over time, the robustness (or precision) of the model can decay due to a variety of factors, such as changes in the range of data values. When the range of data values shifts, the mapping between the rules and their underlying fuzzy sets will also change. We can detect this shift by looking at the amount of evidence in model executions over time. This evidence is reflected in the compatibility index of the solution variable.

The Compatibility Index: A Measure of Evidence

The solution variable's compatibility index (CIX) is a measure of the underlying evidence in the solution. The index is the maximum membership (or truth) value in the composite fuzzy set associated with the solution variable. The greater the membership value the more truth in the combined rule predicates. For example, consider a one-rule system (from the pendulum balancing system). Figure 8.28 shows the height of the outcome fuzzy set when the rule executes.

The height of the outcome fuzzy set, [.48], represents the amount of evidence in the two predicate propositions. The outcome fuzzy set is adjusted (either scaled or truncated) by the truth of the predicate. If the amount of evidence in the rule predicate is reduced, the height of the outcome variable's fuzzy set is also reduced. For example, Figure 8.29 shows the outcome height when the predicate has a minimal amount of evidence.

When multiple rules are executed, the outcome fuzzy sets are combined either through a composite maximum technique or by adding the fuzzy sets together. The composite maximum approach continually combines the outcome fuzzy sets, maintaining the maximum of all adjusted solution fuzzy sets. The addition approach continually combines the outcome fuzzy sets by adding the adjusted fuzzy sets on a membership-by-membership basis. Figure 8.30 illustrates this process for three rules that generate a solution fuzzy set.

When all rules have been executed, the resulting solution fuzzy set's height will reflect the amount of evidence in all rules that contributed to the solution. On an individual model run, the compatibility index may or may not be important (its importance depends primarily on whether or not a significant loss of evidence or an abundance of evidence is critical in interpreting a specific outcome event).

if Theta is SP and DeltaTheta is ZE then Motorforce is SN

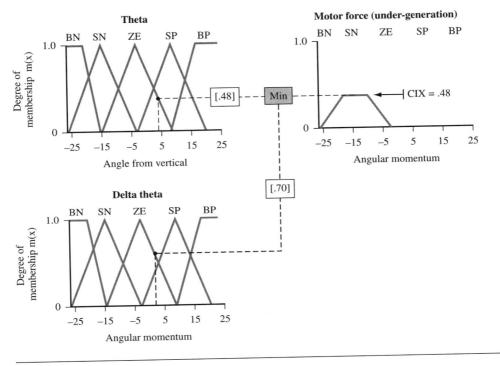

Figure 8.28 The compatibility index (example 1).

Assessing Robustness Using the Compatibility Index

Over the lifetime of a model, however, the CIX is a measure of a model's robustness and resilience. If the CIX is plotted over time, it should generally fluctuate in a general band just above the [.5] membership level. This band represents a well-formed fuzzy model with sufficient evidence to support the model's outcome conclusions. Figure 8.31 illustrates a typical distribution of compatibility index values over several execution periods.

The underlying evidence associated with an outcome provides a consistent and domain-free method of assessing the robustness of a model. As long as the CIX remains in a more or less straight line across the execution horizon, the amount of evidence in the outcome stays roughly constant. The outcome is therefore consistent with the design parameters of the

if Theta is SP and DeltaTheta is ZE then MotorForce is SN

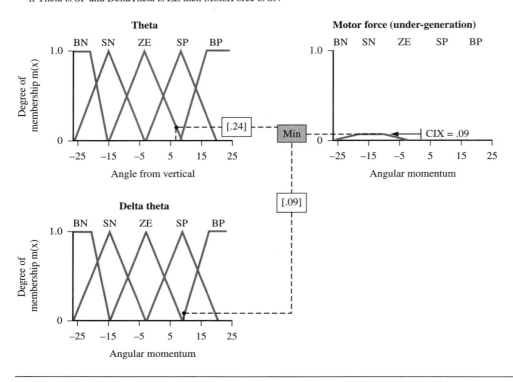

Figure 8.29   The compatibility index (example 2).

model (that is, the induced rules still reflect the underlying patterns in the data).

The relationship between a model's trustworthiness and the underlying evidence in the outcome variables provides a mechanism for measuring the stability and robustness of the model itself. Although individual CIX values tell us little about a model's long-term state, a change in the robustness or precision of the model can be detected by examining the slope of a regression line through the CIX values. As Figure 8.32 illustrates, a significant change in the trend line through the CIX history indicates a lack of predictive robustness in the model.

Why does a trend either up or down over time indicate a loss of model robustness? Oddly enough, due to the nature of fuzzy models even a trend line toward the [1.0] membership threshold is a cause of concern. The reason a movement in either direction is important is related to how the CIX is generated (see the previous section "The Compatibility Index: A Measure of Evidence"). A CIX value that is consistently close to [1.0]

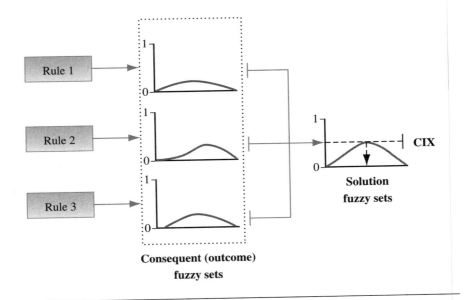

Figure 8.30   The compatibility index (example 3).

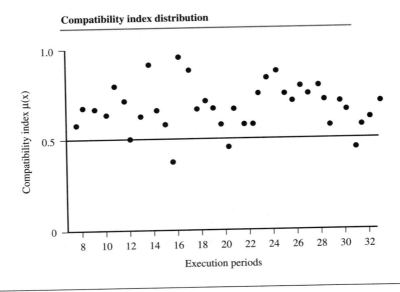

Figure 8.31   The typical distribution of CIX values.

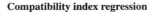

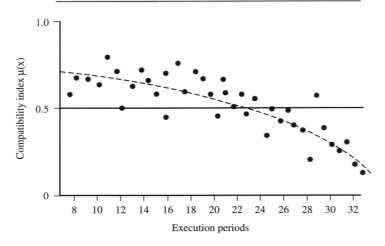

Figure 8.32 The CIX trend line.

means that the truth in all contributing rule predicates is very close to [*1.0*]. This, in turn, means that all the incoming model data points fall close to the upper (or lower) boundary of the underlying fuzzy sets. This also means that the active regions of the fuzzy sets defining the variables have become restricted to a small region of the data space. Hence, the data points are no longer positioned in the overlap of multiple fuzzy sets where they would naturally acquire and accumulate the semantics of multiple decision spaces. The model has thus become brittle and lacks robustness and flexibility.

Detecting and Correcting a Lack of Robustness

One way to measure the stability and robustness of a fuzzy model is to use another fuzzy model (a fuzzy expert system) to fit a polynomial regression line through a historical vector of CIX values and then measure the degree of significance in the slope of the trend line. Figure 8.33 illustrates the schematic organization of this arrangement.

An advantage of a fuzzy expert system in this situation is the control it brings to understanding the changes in the trend line from a semantic viewpoint. Although many possible organizations of the fuzzy sets are possible, a simple design involves just the degree of the slope and the corresponding criticality classification.

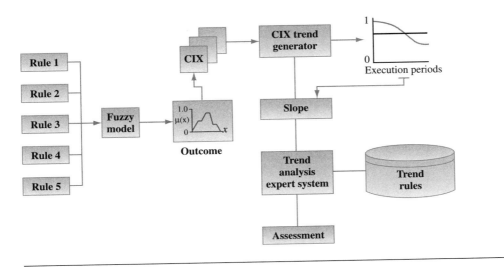

Figure 8.33   The self-monitoring fuzzy model architecture.

Fuzzy Set Decomposition and Rules

The slope of the trend line can be decomposed into a set of semantic fuzzy sets defining the nature of the slope relative to a straight line. Figure 8.34 shows one possible decomposition of the slope variable.

The trend line's slope is decomposed into three broad areas: a small up or down movement, a medium up or down movement, and a large up or down movement. Based on the angular change in the slope, the state of the trend line can be classified as *Normal*, *Caution*, or *Critical*. Figure 8.35 shows a possible decomposition for these outcome states.

The behaviors for this model are very simple. The trend condition is *Normal* to the degree to which the slope angle is small; the trend condition is *Caution* to the degree that the slope angle is medium; and the trend condition is *Critical* to the degree that the slope angle is large. Expressed as fuzzy rules, the behaviors appear as follows.

> If *DegreeOfSlope* is *Small* then *TrendCondition* is *Normal*.
> If *DegreeOfSlope* is *Medium* then *TrendCondition* is *Caution*.
> If *DegreeOfSlope* is *Large* then *TrendCondition* is *Critical*.

When these rules are executed, the slope angle will generate an outcome that combines the evidence for membership in one or more adjacent fuzzy regions and produces a scaled result in the range [0,100], indicating the

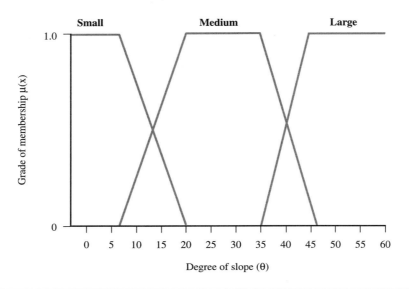

Figure 8.34 The fuzzy sets for the trend slope.

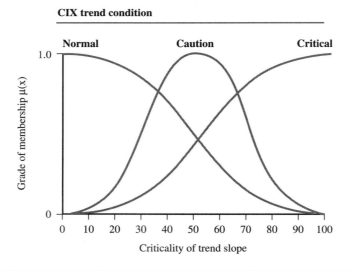

Figure 8.35 The fuzzy sets for the trend criticality condition.

degree to which the angle represents a significant and important change in the CIX trend line.

Methods for Correcting the Model

Once a shift in the CIX trend is detected, there are several broad methods of repairing the model, described in the following. Most of these methodologies are accomplished "off line"; that is, the model is reprocessed and a new model is created, validated, and redeployed. However, the use of adaptively selected rules is designed to work in real time with the execution of a deployed model.

- *Rediscover the rules and build a new model.* In this approach, all rules are discarded. New training and validation sets are produced using the same sampling techniques (generally) that produced the original training and validation sets. This approach often requires a redesign and analysis of the data, as well as a reengineering of the knowledge base. The approach, however, is fundamentally the same as the basic rule induction algorithm discussed in this chapter.

- *Dynamically regenerate rules and test them for effectiveness.* This approach forms the core of an adaptive system that uses the rule induction process as a form of machine learning. Instead of discarding the existing rule set, the model collects its own historical data from the current input. When sufficient history is collected, the rule induction process is called to produce a new set of rules. These rules are combined with the existing rules. Those rules, new or old, that are not executed with a minimum degree of frequency (or degree of evidence) are removed. Over time, this strategy will replenish the knowledge base with rules that automatically adapt themselves to changes in the data. Figure 8.36 is a high-altitude schematic of how a system incorporating dynamically regenerated rules might be designed.

    In this design, an ongoing data history for each variable is automatically maintained by the model. Whenever the assessment value from the trend analysis exceeds a specific threshold, the rule induction engine is started. Rule induction generates a new set of rules and inserts these into the current knowledge base. As the model executes the rules, a tournament facility evaluates each rule (new and old) for effectiveness. The most effective rules, based on the statistics of executing and amount of evidence (the CIX value), are kept in the model and the less effective rules are gradually removed.

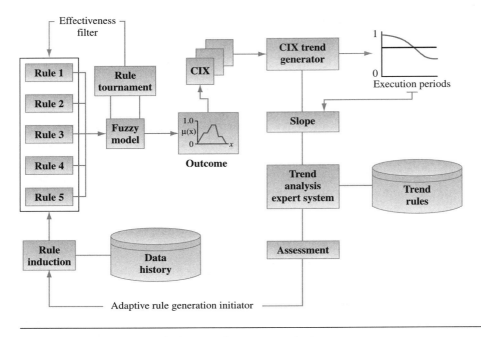

Figure 8.36 A system with dynamically regenerated rules.

■ *Retune the model's infrastructure configuration by adjusting the fuzzy sets for one or more variables.* If the underlying patterns in the data remain more or less constant but the data has been changing, the model can conceivably be corrected by changing the type, number, and overlap of the fuzzy sets underlying each variable. A multiobjective and multiconstraint genetic algorithm is used to generate, breed, and test a large population of new models. In this approach, new rules are not created (we are modifying the fuzzy decision space in the existing rules to accommodate new data ranges). Figure 8.37 shows a high-altitude schematic view of this genetic tuning.

In this design, like the rule regeneration, an ongoing data history for each variable is automatically maintained by the model (per the following).

① Whenever the assessment value from the trend analysis exceeds a specific threshold, the genetic fuzzy set optimizer engine is started. The underlying genetic algorithm uses the existing set of rules and generates a population of feasible models (the fixed set of rules), each with a random set of fuzzy sets for each dependent and independent variable.

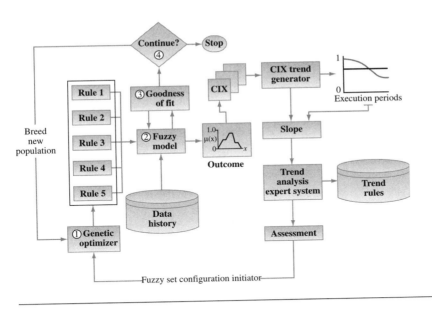

Figure 8.37   Genetically tuning the rule fuzzy sets.

② Each new fuzzy model in the current population of models is executed against the validation data.[1]

③ The standard error of estimate for the new model is used by the genetic algorithm as its goodness of fit. The GA attempts to minimize this standard error.

④ If we have found a minimal and stable standard error, the genetic tuner stops and the current rules with their fuzzy set organization are moved into production.

Otherwise, a new population of candidate models is created and the process of standard error minimization continues. This is, of course, the same process used to optimize a fuzzy model created by the initial rule induction algorithm.

8.7   **Technical Implementation**

The architecture of the rule induction engine and the surrounding business process modeling capabilities integrate several different data

---

[1] Note that we do not need a training set in this approach because we are using the existing rules that were initially generated from the original training set. We only need to use a validation set to measure how well a new model with its new fuzzy set organization predicts a correct response.

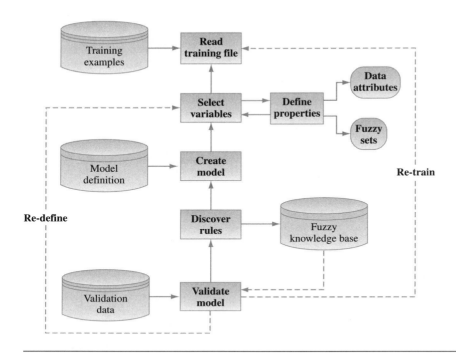

Figure 8.38 The rule induction and modeling process.

structures and code features. In this section we take up the issues associated with the actual implementation of a rule induction facility and a host modeling environment. This section can be bypassed for those not interested in the underlying code model.

Using the rule induction software requires an integration of several different technical engines: a variable properties manager, a model framework manager, the rule induction engine, and a fuzzy inference engine to run the rules. Figure 8.38 provides a high-altitude schematic of these functional parts.

The overall process is relatively straightforward. The training file of examples is read to pick up the column field names. These are the attributes of the model. A number of the fields are selected as attributes of the model (or are all selected). For each selected field, the model builder can define a set of data properties and a collection of underlying fuzzy sets (fuzzy set decomposition can be done automatically by the variable property manager). When all variable properties have been defined, an initial model is created. The model acts as a named repository for all of its components. After a model is created, the rule induction engine is used

TABLE 8.11   The Automobile Performance File

MPG,	CYLS,	DISP,	HP,	WGT,	ACCEL,	YR,	ORIGIN,	CAR_NAME
18.0	8	307.0	130.0	3504.	12.0	70	1	"chevrolet chevelle malibu"
15.0	8	350.0	165.0	3693.	11.5	70	1	"buick skylark 320"
18.0	8	318.0	150.0	3436.	11.0	70	1	"plymouth satellite"
16.0	8	304.0	150.0	3433.	12.0	70	1	"amc rebel sst"
17.0	8	302.0	140.0	3449.	10.5	70	1	"ford torino"
15.0	8	429.0	198.0	4341.	10.0	70	1	"ford galaxie 500"
14.0	8	454.0	220.0	4354.	9.0	70	1	"chevrolet impala"

to create the underlying rule (or knowledge) base. This knowledge base is used by the fuzzy inference engine to actually run the rules against the validation data file. Validation measures how well the model performs by keeping track of the average standard error as it predicts an outcome value for each incoming record. If the model does not perform well, you have two basic choices: retrain the model or redefine the model variables.

In practice, these functional parts are independent pieces of systems tied together through a common structural interface (such as the graphical user interface of the Fuzzy Data Explorer). However, the process remains essentially a cohesive iterative loop that converges on a working model. A file containing the training examples is identified. This is a flat, comma, tab, or space-delimited ASCII file. The first line of the file contains the name of the fields. These are the names that will be used throughout the modeling process. Table 8.11 shows part of the automobile performance file in this format. The file and variable handler reads the file to (1) acquire all column names, (2) find all the numeric columns, and (3) determine the file length (number of records in the file). At this point you must select a set of columns for the model. A model must have a dependent variable (the outcome) and at least one independent variable. Because this is a fuzzy model, all variables must have a numeric data type (either continuous or categorical). At this point we need to understand the basic control blocks that maintain all data elements, files, and parameter settings for the model and rule induction process.

8.8   **External Controls**

Control controls (or "control blocks") are external structures housed in the main code regions of the rule induction and modeling dynamic link library (DLL). The control blocks provide global access to the main data elements in the code without the cumbersome overhead of passing large structures or multiple arrays of variables as parameters. The rule induction

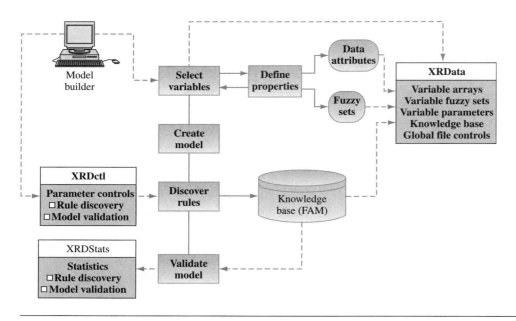

Figure 8.39 Use of control blocks.

software uses the control blocks to store all model variables and their properties, the currently active knowledge base, global file definitions, operating parameters, and post-mortem execution statistics. Figure 8.39 extends Figure 8.38 to show how the control blocks are connected to the processing architecture.

The actual model definition and associated controls are centralized in the *XRDData* external structure. The maximum number of variables and other properties (such as fuzzy sets) are controlled by symbolic variables (found in the *rdsyms.hpp* header file). Each variable property is stored in a parallel array indexed from zero to the current count of variables. When fuzzy sets are defined for a variable, they are also stored in an array of fuzzy set descriptor pointers. Figure 8.40 schematically illustrates the way the controls are organized.

A model variable is a name selected from one of the field names in the training file. Field names have only intrinsic or default properties (data type, for example), whereas model variable names have a large number of extended attributes. These include such properties as the following.

- Description
- Unit of measure

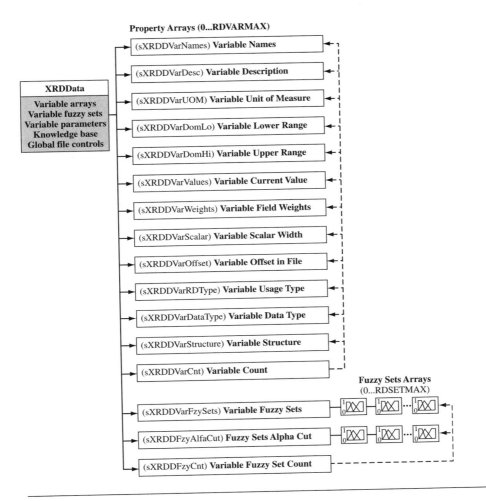

Figure 8.40 Variable properties in *XRDData*.

- Domain or permissible range of values
- Weight used to bias the rule generation
- Usage type (independent or dependent variable)
- Explicit data type (integer, float, double, Boolean, and so on)
- Organization structure (continuous, categorical, periodic)

Variables also have semantic properties: their underlying collection of fuzzy sets. These sets break down the domain of the variable into overlapping fuzzy regions. Every variable used by the rule induction engine must have its domain partitioned into fuzzy sets. A set of properties is defined when a variable is selected from the field name. The attributes are automatically updated from a graphical user interface (such as the Fuzzy Data Explorer's Property Manager) or are specified through the rule discovery system's Application Program Interface (API) services.

This control block also has a pointer to the active knowledge base (containing the rules either discovered in the current rule induction process or loaded into the knowledge base from a stored model). A principal use of the control block architecture is communication between the C/C++ code and rapid application development (RAD) environments.

Representation of Fuzzy Sets

A fuzzy set is defined and represented by an FDB (fuzzy set descriptor block) structure. These structures are allocated and controlled within the C/C++ code space and cannot be directly accessed by Visual Basic and other languages (such as Java) or by RAD environments (such as Delphi and Power Builder) except through the API services. Listing 8.10 shows the structure and content of the FDB. The symbolic constants defining the dimensions of the structure are found in *mssyms.hpp*.

In addition to a name and description, a fuzzy set description contains the type of curve (*FDBgentype*), the fuzzy set's domain (*FDBdomain[]*), the alpha cut threshold (*FDBalfacut*), and the parameters that

```
struct FDB
{
char     FDBid [IDENLEN+1],      // Identifier name of Fuzzyset
         FDBdesc[DESCLEN+1];     // Description of Fuzzyset
Ctlswitch  FDBgentype;          // Generator Set type
mbool    FDBempty;              // Is this a populated Fuzzyset?
int      FDBorder,              // Order of fuzzy set
         FDBparmcnt;            // Count of stored parms
double   FDBdomain[2],          // Lo and Hi edges of the set
         FDBparms[PARMMAX];     // Generation parameters
float    FDBalfacut,            // AlfaCut for this fuzzy set
         FDBvector[VECMAX];     // The fuzzy set truth vector
FDB      *FDBnext;              // Pointer to next fuzzyset
};
```

Listing 8.10 The FDB.

were used to create the fuzzy set (*FDBparms[]*). The core descriptive property of the fuzzy set, however, is its membership function (*FDBvector*[0 . . . VECMAX]), defining the actual shape of the fuzzy set's surface. Each cell in the *FDBvector[]* array represents a small region of values across the variable's domain. These numbers share the same membership and define the lower limits of resolution or granularity for a fuzzy set. Given a particular scalar number (*S*) and its domain of allowed values (*d_low* and *d_high*), from which we can calculate a range interval (*R*), we can find its membership in a fuzzy set by finding what cell contains this value. Expression 8.16 shows the equation for finding the cell.

$$cell_S = \left[\frac{s - d_{low}}{R} \right] \times VECMAX \qquad (8.16)$$

Then, of course, *FDBvector*[*cell_S*] is the degree of membership for this number. This scalar-to-cell relationship also means that given a cell number we can return the scalar representative of that cell (for details see *FzyGetScalar*). Finding the scalar value associated with a particular degree of membership is not quite as simple, in that no mapping of range to membership is maintained; that is, the degree of membership for a cell is not a linear relationship to a cell number (unlike numbers from the domain). Seeking a number in this manner requires an algorithmic approach (for details see *FzyEquivalentScalar*).

Representing the Rule Base

In our previous example of an FAM, the knowledge base was 2D (see Figure 8.15 for details). Handling this situation in program code is relatively straightforward. One possible declaration is shown in Figure 8.41, along with the table organization.

```
FDB *pVert_Var[MAXVERT],
*pHorz_Var[MAXHORZ],
*pFAM[MAXVERT][MAXHORZ];
```

where, *pVert_Var[]* contains the fuzzy sets for the variable on the vertical axis of the FAM, *pHorz_Var[]* contains the fuzzy sets for the variable on the horizontal axis of the FAM, and *pFAM[][]* contains the fuzzy sets associated with the dependent variable at each intersection. This is satisfactory for handling all systems with two antecedents and one consequent. However, for rules in the form

if x_{v1} is A **and** x_{v2} is B **and** x_{v3} is C **then** x_{v4} is Y

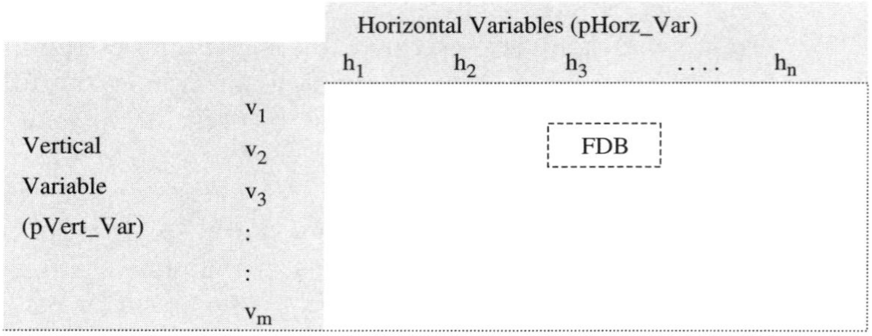

Figure 8.41   Code declaration for a 2 × 2 FAM.

a 3D array is needed (one axis for each independent variable). In real-world applications the number of variables in a fuzzy system can be quite large. A knowledge engineer cannot know a priori the required size of the fuzzy associative memory. The requirement, especially in a language such as C/C++, that dimensions be statically defined places a severe limitation on the flexibility of a rule induction tool with a fixed dimensioning scheme for its rule base. Not only does the changing of array dimensions in the code necessitate significant reprogramming of the control logic but it invariably introduces errors into code that would otherwise run cleanly. Further, a statically dimensioned FAM substantially restricts the type of model content optimization performed by such processes as factor analysis (adding new variables dynamically to the model becomes impossible).

Rather than allocate arrays of differing sizes in the code and reprogramming the inference engine for changes in the dimensionality of our model, we can define rules so that they carry their position in a virtual FAM (the knowledge base). Each rule maintains an array of indexes into the *XRDData* control block for each independent variable and a pointer to the rule's outcome fuzzy set (associated with the dependent variable). Listing 8.11 shows the organization and content of the rule description. This data structure couples the rule definition to the storage of fuzzy sets associated with the model variables and reduces the rule processing to a matter of indexing the fuzzy set arrays. Each rule also has a pointer to a working outcome fuzzy set (this fuzzy set is used when the aggregation fuzzy reasoning mode is used). Figure 8.42 shows the schematic relationships between the rule structure and the stored fuzzy sets.

The maximum dimensionality of a fuzzy model is determined by the *RDVARMAX* constant (in that each variable, excluding the dependent or outcome variable, creates one dimension in the knowledge base).

```
struct RDR
{
FDB     *pDVFDB;               //--Pointer to Outcome Fuzzy Set
int     iDVIdx;                //--Index to DV fuzzy set
float   fRuleDegree;           //--Degree for this rule
int     iRuleEvidence;         //--Evidence (Count of rule hits)
int     iFzySetIdx[RDVARMAX];  //--Indexes into IV Fuzzy Sets
RDR     *pNextRDR;             //--Pointer to next rule
};
//
```

Listing 8.11   The rule descriptor (RDR) structure.

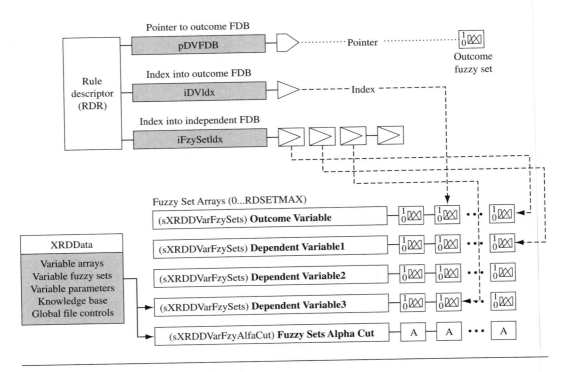

Figure 8.42   Rule and fuzzy set relationships.

The *iFzySetIdx* is the mapping between the rule and the virtual FAM. This arrangement has several important benefits.

- *Only actual rules consume space*. The index for an RDR structure defines its location in the virtual FAM space. Thus, the array *(2,8,4)* indicates the second fuzzy set for the first independent variable, the eighth fuzzy set for the second independent variable, and the fourth fuzzy set for the third independent variable. Only this space is occupied in the FAM matrix. Null pointers (usually 4 bytes each) are *not* kept for unused rules.

  In many rule discovery applications the rule base itself is quite sparse. This is a consequence of the dimensionality of the system against the set of all possible exemplars in the data itself. A fuzzy model, assuming each variable is decomposed into the same number of fuzzy sets, has a dimensional space (*d*) equal to

$$d = R^k, \tag{8.17}$$

  where R is the number of fuzzy sets per variable and k is the number of independent (input) variables. This means that a model with five variables and five fuzzy sets per variable will need a dimensional space of 3125 cells. Even smaller models require a significant amount of training exemplars to fully populate a model. A model with five variables, each decomposed into three fuzzy sets, still requites 3^5 (or 243) exemplars to put a rule into each cell. If we are using monthly data, this would require 20 years of exemplars to have one rule in each cell. With fewer than 20 years, the FAM becomes quite sparse.

- *Rules are stored serially in conventional array (see the FKB structure discussed in material to follow)*. As rules are added to the knowledge base, the only data structure required is either a simple linear array (a vector of rules) or a linked list. Access to the rules and processing of each rule is very easy. The serial architecture of rule storage means that various modifications to the inference engine can be made without deep and costly changes to the rule access and processing procedures.

- *Processing is high-speed*. The array organization of a rule means that rule evaluation requires simple indexing. Because the indexes represent an abstract dimensional space, only a single *for* loop is necessary. We thus, in effect, unroll the dimensional space of an FAM and reduce it to a single vector of offsets. Such unrolling significantly improves efficiency.

- *Representational flexibility and compactness are increased.* Because fuzzy sets are detached from the rule and the two are linked only through indexes into arrays, variables as well as fuzzy sets can be added and deleted easily. Up to the limit imposed by *RDVARMAX*, new variables can be added to rules or existing variables removed. Such expedients support genetic tuning and factor analysis. This works in two ways. New variables with their properties can be added to the *XRDData* control and then referenced by the rules. Alternatively, rules can ignore or select variables out of the *XRDData* control, thus searching the variable space for the best model. The same applies to fuzzy sets. Without changing the number of fuzzy sets, a model can explore the effects of shape and overlap changes on a model's performance. The number of fuzzy sets associated with a variable can also be easily changed. This flexibility in model organization allows various forms of factor analysis and model genetic tuning to work quickly and efficiently on the model's structure.

The RDR rule structure, similar to the FDB fuzzy set structure, contains a pointer to the next instance of itself. These pointers provide, at little space expense, a method of linking these objects into hash tables or linear lists. Unlike fuzzy sets, rules formed by the induction engine lack an identifier (other than their order in the knowledge base), and thus they would need a tag of some type before they could be inserted into a conventional hash table.

8.9 Organization of the Knowledge Base

The knowledge base organizes a collection of rules for execution. In a fuzzy model, all rules are run in parallel, and thus we need only a way of effectively accessing and evaluating the rules. Listing 8.12 shows the structure of the fuzzy knowledge base (FKB). A knowledge base provides a container for rules. They are organized in a vector and sorted by their independent variable index values (in increasing order). As Figure 8.43 illustrates, there are few important controls in the knowledge base: simply the count of independent variables (to speed up access) and the count of actual number of rules in the vector.

In this structure the knowledge base holds a maximum of *RDRULE-MAX* (found in the *rdsyms.hpp* header file). The knowledge base also maintains a list of active and inactive rules. This Boolean vector is used during the training and tuning phase to turn rules on and off. As a compact

```
struct FKB
{
int   iFKBIVCnt,               //--Independent var Count
      iFKBRuleCnt;             //--Total rule in KB
RDR   *pFKBRules [RDRULEMAX];  //--Vector of rules
mbool bFKBActive[RDRULEMAX];   //--Active rule indicator
FDB   *pDVFDB;                 //--Dependent var fuzzy set
};
```

Listing 8.12 The fuzzy knowledge base.

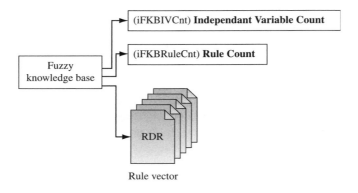

Figure 8.43 The rule induction knowledge base.

representation of the model rules, the knowledge base constructs a virtual FAM. These rules are executed for each record from the validation or the production database. Listing 8.13 shows the simple C/C++ routine that executes a single fuzzy rule.

There is a one-to-one correspondence between the index in the rule structure's *iFzySetIdx[]* array and the variables appearing in the *XRDData* control block. This allows us to invert the rule processing by looping across the variables and using the index in *iFzySetIdx[]* to find which of the fuzzy sets is needed. The current data value (*dColValue*) is used to find the degree of membership. This membership is for each variable used to compute a final membership product (which is the degree for this rule). If the rule's degree is above the alpha cut threshold, the rule fires. For each rule that fires, we pick up the sum of the degree and the sum of the scaled center of the outcome fuzzy set. These are used by the high-level model execution facilities to compute a model outcome value after all

```
void   mpExecuteRule(
RDR    *pRDR,
char   *sTokens[],
int    iTokCnt,
mbool  *bpRuleFired,
double *dpSum_of_Degrees,
double *dpSum_of_Centers,
float  *fpDegree,
int    *ipStatus)
/*-------------------------------------------------------------------*
 | This procedure actually executes a single rule in the linear     |
 | Fuzzy Knowledge Base. Executing a rule means evaluating all the  |
 | antecedents, calculating the predicate truth, and then updating  |
 | the sum of degrees and scaled values.                    |
 *-------------------------------------------------------------------*/
{
FDB    *pIVFDB;
int    i,
       iIdx,
       iDVIdx,
       iIVset,
       iCOffset;
float  fMemVal,
       fThisMemVal;
double dX,
       dColValue;

*ipStatus=0;
*bpRuleFired=mFALSE;
iDVIdx=1;
fMemVal=(float)1.0;
*fpDegree=(float)0;

for(i=0;i<XRDData.iXRDDVarCnt-1;i++)
   {
   iCOffset =XRDData.iXRDDVarOffset[iDVIdx];
   dColValue=atof(sTokens[iCOffset]);
   //
   //--Now see which fuzzy set is associated with the rule
   //
   iIVset=pRDR->iFzySetIdx[i];
   pIVFDB=XRDData.pXRDDVarFzySets[iDVIdx][iIVset];
```

Listing 8.13 The rule execution procedure.

```
      fThisMemVal=FzyGetMembership(pIVFDB,dColValue,&iIdx,ipStatus);
      if(bUseRuleWgts) fThisMemVal=fThisMemVal*pRDR->fRuleDegree;
      if(i==0) fMemVal=fThisMemVal;
      else    fMemVal=fMemVal*fThisMemVal;
      iDVIdx++;
      }
*fpDegree=fMemVal;
if(fMemVal>fRuleAlfa)
   {
      (*dpSum_of_Degrees)+=fMemVal;
      dX=mpMaximumValue(pOCFDB);
      (*dpSum_of_Centers)+=(dX*fMemVal);
      *bpRuleFired=mTRUE;
   }
   else
   iAvgRulesBelowAlfa++;
return;
```

Listing 8.13   Continued.

rules have been fired. The following code shows part of this high-level
manager (somewhat simplified).

```
          dSum_of_Degrees=0;
          dSum_of_Centers=0;
          for(i=0;i<pFKB->iFKBRuleCnt;i++)
              {
              mpExecuteRule(
                pFKB->pFKBRules[i],
                sTokens,
                iTokCnt,
                &bFired,
                &dSum_of_Degrees,
                &dSum_of_Centers,
                &fDegree,
                ipStatus);
              }
          if(iRulesFired==0)
              {
                  fCIX=(float)0;
                  dDVEstimate=(double)SOLUNDEFINED;
                  iAvgRulesNotFired++;
              }
```

If at least one rule was executed, the outcome value (*dDVEstimate*) is generated by defuzzification. The value is a weighted average computed by dividing the sum of the scaled center valued by the sum of the individual rule degrees. The compatibility index (degree of evidence in the model's solution) is calculated as the average degree.

```
if(iRulesFired>0)
{
    fCIX=(float)(dSum_of_Degrees/(double)iRulesFired);
     dDVEstimate=(dSum_of_Centers/dSum_of_Degrees);
    if(fCIX<fMinCIX)
        iAvgRsltBelowCIX++;
    fTotCIX+=fCIX;
}
```

The technical overview provides an introduction to the underlying data structures and code models used in the rule induction engine, although naturally it does not cover all procedures and structures.

8.10 **Review**

Rule discovery forms the core mechanism in the development of effective models as well as the implementation of adaptive, self-tuning systems. An adaptive model learns new rules and adjusts existing rules depending on changes in the data space. Regenerating rules is an effective strategy for maintaining a coherent and robust system responsive to shifts in the modeling environment. In this chapter we examined the fundamental rule induction mechanism and illustrated its potential for model nonlinear problems. You should now understand the general algorithm and be familiar with such concepts and ideas as the following.

- How data variables are partitioned into fuzzy sets
- The use of quality and belief measures during rule induction
- How rules are generated and compressed
- How to handle conflicting and ambiguous rules
- The use of training and validation data
- The techniques for measuring degrees of error in a generated model
- How to measure model robustness using the compatibility index
- Possible ways to restore robustness and precision to a fuzzy model

These are the basic features of the rule induction process. Working models that represent real-world problems, however, generally require some extensions to the rule discovery process, which include the ability to

- Discover and encode lead and lag relationships
- Incorporate crisp predicates and outcomes
- Track the effectiveness of discovered rules
- Tune themselves based on statistical changes in their measures of evidence

An implementation of these extensions is left to the reader. They are basically straightforward modifications to the underlying algorithms (although the discovery of lead-lag relationships and the tuning of a model based on evidence in the solution set is often best handled through a genetic algorithm).

Further Reading

■ Bennett, J. *Building Decision Support Systems*. Reading, MA: Addison-Wesley, 1983.

■ Berkan, R., and S. Trubatch. *Fuzzy System Design Principles: Building Fuzzy IF-THEN Rule Bases*. New York: IEEE Press, 1997.

■ Buchanan, B., and E. Shortliffe. *Rule-Based Expert Systems: The Mycin Experiments of the Stanford Heuristic Programming Project*. Reading, MA: Addison-Wesley, 1984.

■ Cox, E. *The Fuzzy Systems Handbook* (2d ed.). San Diego, CA: Academic Press Professional, 1999.

■ Goonatilake, S., and S. Khebbal (eds.). *Intelligent Hybrid Systems*. Chichester, UK: John Wiley and Sons, 1995.

■ Keen, P., and M. Morton. *Decision Support Systems: An Organizational Perspective*. Reading, MA: Addison-Wesley, 1978.

■ Kosko, B. *Neural Networks and Fuzzy Systems: A Dynamical Systems Approach to Machine Intelligence*. Englewood Cliffs, NJ: Prentice-Hall, 1991.

■ Martino, J. *Technological Forecasting for Decision Making* (3d ed.). New York: McGraw-Hill, 1993.

■ Rao, V., and H. Rao. *C++ Neural Networks and Fuzzy Logic* (2d ed.). New York: MIT Press, 1995.

■ Wang, L-X. *Adaptive Fuzzy Systems and Control, Design and Stability Analysis*. Englewood Cliffs, NJ: Prentice-Hall, 1994.

■ Wang, L-X., and Mendel, J. M. "Generating Fuzzy Rules from Numerical Data with Applications," USC-SIPI Report No. 169.

■ Welstead, S. *Neural Network and Fuzzy Logic Applications in C/C++*. New York: John Wiley and Sons, 1994.

Part III
Evolutionary Strategies

Contents

Chapter 9
Fundamental Concepts of Genetic Algorithms

Evolutionary strategies address highly complex optimization and search problems through an emulation of natural selection. They also incorporate a form of parallel processing to effectively evaluate a large population of possible solutions. Their ability to solve high-dimensional, highly complex problems that are often intractable, slow, brittle, or difficult to formulate with conventional analytical techniques has made genetic algorithms and evolutionary programming a critical component in intelligent systems that require adaptive behavior, systematic exploration of alternatives, and multiobjective and multiconstraint optimization. This chapter introduces the concepts underlying genetic algorithms and evolutionary programming. The concepts in this chapter are necessary in order to understand the nature of genetic algorithms and evolutionary programming in the context of fuzzy model tuning and in the context of advanced predictive and classification models (topics covered in the remaining chapters of Part III).

Although not the first to explore the idea of combining the mechanics of evolution and computer programming, the field of genetic and evolutionary algorithms can be traced back to John H. Holland's 1975 book *Adaptation in Natural and Artificial Systems: An Introductory Analysis with Applications to Biology, Control, and Artificial Intelligence* (see "Further Reading"). John Holland formalized the concepts underlying the genetic algorithm and provided the mathematical foundations for incrementally and formally improving their search techniques. Holland was primarily interested in the nature of adaptive systems. The adaptive nature of his genetic models provided the foundation for a broad and robust field of computer science that allows a handful of simple constructs to solve complex, highly nonlinear and often mathematically intractable problems. As we will see in this chapter and in the remainder of Part III, these evolutionary strategies allow model designers and data mining engineers to optimize their models, generate new and robust predictive models, and explore highly complex decision spaces.

9.1 **The Vocabulary of Genetic Algorithms**

Much of the literature in evolutionary strategies adopts its nomenclature from biological models. Thus, we speak of chromosomes, alleles, mutations, breeding, goodness of fit, and survival of the fittest. Before moving on with a complete and detailed analysis of the algorithm and how it works, we need to understand the principal nomenclatures and how they are related to the components of the algorithm. As we pointed out in our discussion of fuzzy logic, a preview of the vocabulary will make reading and understanding the material in this chapter much easier. It is not always possible, while maintaining an uncluttered and coherent discussion of the genetic process, to ensure that every term is introduced before it is used.

Allele

The value at a particular locus in the genome is called the *allele*. In a binary representation, this will be a one or a zero. In a real number representation, the allele will be an integer or floating-point number.

Annealing

Annealing (often called simulated annealing) is a process for disrupting the current state of a genetic algorithm to avoid premature convergence to a solution. In a genetic algorithm, this is accomplished through mutation, the random introduction of new individuals into a population, the retention of a few poor-performing individuals, and changes in the size and compactness of future populations.

Breeding

A new population of possible solutions to the current problem is primarily (but not completely) created through a process that resembles biological *breeding*. High-performance individuals (those with very good fitness values) are mated to produce offspring in a process somewhat analogous to sexual reproduction; that is, their genetic material is distributed to one or more offspring. Figure 9.1 illustrates how a crossover at a single point on the chromosome produces a new offspring from two parents.

In this breeding example a left-hand part of one parent's genome and a right-hand part of another parent's genome are exchanged to create a new individual with the combined genetic material from both parents.

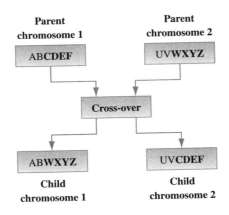

Figure 9.1 Breeding through a single-point crossover.

Chromosome (Individual)

A collection of genomes representing a potential solution to the problem is called a *chromosome*. This is the genetic material of the genetic algorithm. A chromosome may consist of multiple genomes, each expressing a feature of the target system that must be considered a constraint or an objective function. For example, a genetic algorithm that solves the traveling salesman problem (TSP)[1] would encode the order of cities in its chromosome. Figure 9.2 shows a collection of cities and one possible route between these cities.

There is a very large number of possible routes for even a small number of cities (in that the number of routes grows with the factorial of the number of cities). For eight cities, for example, the combinatorial complexity is 8! or over 40,000 possible routes. We can simplify the encoding of the chromosome by assigning each city an index number. Table 9.1 shows the index values for each table.

Using this encoding, the TSP is encoded in a chromosome by specifying a possible path. The path is the set of edges in the route graph. In this problem, we are always starting in Seattle. This becomes the start

---

[1] The objective of the traveling salesman problem (TSP) is to find the shortest route in time, capital, or distance between all cities without visiting any city twice. The general TSP problem has applicability in a wide range of configuration and design problems (such as the design and manufacture of microprocessor chips).

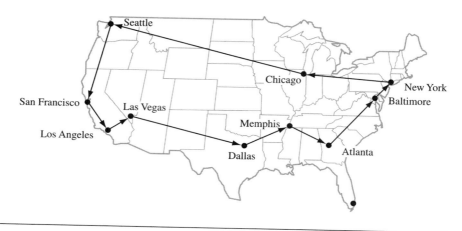

Figure 9.2 One possible solution to a TSP.

TABLE 9.1 The City Index Numbers

City	Index
Atlanta	1
Baltimore	2
Chicago	3
Dallas	4
Los Angeles	5
Las Vegas	6
Memphis	7
New York	8
San Francisco	9
Seattle	10

and end of the directed graph. Figure 9.5 shows the chromosome for the route shown in Figure 9.3.

The chromosome defines a directed graph with the edges *(10,9)*, *(9,5)*, *(5,6)*, and so forth. If the TSP problem can start at any city, the starting city can be encoded as part of the genome as a separate parameter. A potential solution can be created for a path by generating a set of unique

TSP Chromosome									
9	5	6	4	7	1	2	8	3	10

Figure 9.3   A chromosome expressing a TSP solution.

random numbers in the first nine positions within the range *[1,9]*, in that the last genome locus must return the path to the origin (in this case, Seattle).

Constraints

Constraints define the feasibility of a schedule. Objectives define the optimality of a schedule. Although objectives *should* be satisfied, constraints *must* be satisfied. In a crew-scheduling system, for example, the schedule might have three constraints: the precedence relationship between jobs, the availability of the crew at the time it is needed, and a match between the type of crew and the skills required for the job. These constraints must be obeyed and define the properties of a feasible and workable solution. (See "Feasible Solution" for additional details.)

Convergence

The process of breeding a genetic algorithm's population over a series of generations to arrive at the chromosome with the best fitness value is known as *convergence*. That is, the population converges on a solution. Convergence is controlled by the fitness function: fitter chromosomes survive to the next generation and breed new chromosomes that (hopefully) improve the average fitness of the population. This continues until the fitness does not improve; thus, it converges on a final value.

Crossover (Recombination)

The process of creating a new chromosome by combining or "mating" two or more high-performance chromosomes is known as *crossover*. In a crossover, the genetic material of one chromosome is swapped in some manner with the genetic material of another chromosome to produce one or more offspring. There are several techniques for combining the genetic material (genomes), such as one-point, two-point, and uniform crossover. These techniques are discussed in the detailed analysis of the algorithm.

Feasible Solution

A genetic algorithm must start with and always generate *feasible solutions*. Otherwise, the solution, even if its goodness of fit is the best, is useless. Feasible solutions must consider the nature of the objective function and constraints placed on the system. For example, consider the TSP. If a business constraint on the route plan specifies that the salesperson must visit all west coast cities before any other cities, a schedule that creates an initial route from Seattle to Chicago violates this constraint and is not a feasible solution. In a crew schedule, a solution that schedules a task when a critical and necessary piece of equipment is unavailable or that assigns a task to a crew that does not have the necessary skill set or cannot work in the task's geographic area is not a feasible solution.

Fitness Function

The *fitness function* is a measure associated with the collective objective functions that indicates the fitness of a particular chromosome (or the phenotype) in terms of a desired solution. A genetic algorithm is a directed search. This search is controlled by the fitness function. For minimization problems, the fitness function usually approaches zero as the optimal value. For maximization problems, the fitness function usually approaches some upper boundary threshold as its optimal value. For multiobjective functions, the fitness function often approaches some saddle point in the overall solution space. In the TSP, we want to minimize the distance, and thus we need a fitness function that approaches zero. One possible fitness function, shown in Expression 9.1, is fairly straightforward (it is 1 minus the inverse of the sum of the distances).

$$f = 1 - \frac{1}{\sum_{i=1}^{N-1} d(c_i, c_{i+1})} \tag{9.1}$$

For N cities, this function sums the distance between each successive city in the graph stored in the current chromosome. This fraction is subtracted from 1. Smaller distances will yield relatively larger fractions, thus driving the fitness function toward zero. When the entire population of potential paths has been evaluated, those with the smallest fitness will be the best solution found during that generation.

Generation

A genetic algorithm creates a new population of candidate solutions until a termination condition is reached. Each new population is known as a *generation*. A maximum number of generations is one of the termination conditions for a genetic algorithm.

Genome

A particular feature in the chromosome is represented by a *genome*. In many cases, a chromosome may consist of a single genome, but for multiobjective and multiconstraint problems a chromosome can consist of several genomes. The nature of a genome depends on the underlying data representation. For bit (or binary) representations, the genome is a series of bits. For a real number representation, the genome is an integer or floating-point number.

Genotype

The complete structure of a chromosome is often called the *genotype*. It is simply a handy way of referring to all genomes. The actual instance of a chromosome (the actual values of the genotype) is called the phenotype.

Goodness of Fit

The *goodness of fit* is a measure of how close the fitness function value is to the optimum value. A fitness function returns a goodness-of-fit value for each chromosome.

Locus

A *locus* in a chromosome is simply a position in the genome. In the TSP chromosome (see Figure 9.3), there are 10 node positions in the genome. Each of these values is a locus in the underlying chromosome.

Mutation

One of the ways in which a genetic algorithm attempts to improve the overall fitness of a population as it moves toward a final, optimal solution is by randomly changing the value of an allele. This process is called *mutation*. Mutation enriches the pool of phenotypes in the population, combats local minimum and maximum regions (and as such is a form of annealing), and ensures that new potential solutions, independent of the current set of chromosomes, will emerge in the population at large.

Objective Function

An *objective function* defines the purpose of the genetic algorithm and is the value that will be either minimized or maximized. Each genetic algorithm must have one or more objective functions. It is the objective function value that is measured by the fitness function and evaluated for its goodness of fit.

Performance

A general way of looking at the fitness of a chromosome is its *performance* in the population. Chromosomes with high goodness-of-fit values are considered high-performance segments of the population. Those chromosomes below some goodness-of-fit threshold are considered low-performance chromosomes.

Phenotype

The actual values of a genome (its position in the solution space) are called the *phenotype*. Whereas the genotype expresses the overall properties of the genetic algorithm by defining the nature of the chromosome, the phenotype represents an individual expression of the genome (or genotype). This is somewhat similar to the relationship between classes and objects in an object-oriented programming language: a class represents the definition of an object, whereas an object represents a concrete instantiation of a class.

Population

A collection of chromosomes with their values is a *population*. A genetic algorithm starts by creating a large population of potential solutions represented as chromosomes. As the algorithm continues, new populations of old and new chromosomes are created and processed. In some genetic algorithm implementations the total population size is fixed, whereas in others the population size can increase or decrease depending on the nature of the problem space.

Schema

Many of the mathematical foundations of genetic algorithms are built on the evaluation of emerging and transient bit patterns in the population. A pattern of bits that repeats through the high-performance region of the population provides a method of explaining how a genetic algorithm converges on a solution. In general practice, however, an understanding of *schema* patterns provides little, if any, benefit in the management of a genetic algorithm.

Selection

How individual chromosomes are chosen for crossover and mutation is based on the process of *selection*. Selection is used to pick the high-performance segment of the population for crossover breeding, to pick a few chromosomes for mutation, and in some problems to pick a few low-performance chromosomes for inclusion in the next generation (simply to ensure a mix of genetic material).

Survival of the Fittest

In a fashion similar to natural evolution, individuals in a genetic algorithm survive from one generation to the next based on their goodness-of-fit values. The fittest individuals are preserved and reproduce (see "Breeding"), which is referred to as *survival of the fittest*. In this way, the average goodness of fit of the entire population begins to converge on the best possible set of solutions.

System

A genetic algorithm is connected to an underlying *system*. The current phenotype values in the chromosome are the parameters used to run the system and evaluate the system's outcome in terms of goodness of fit. For example, a genetic algorithm that solves the TSP has chromosomes

TABLE 9.2 Inter-city Distances for TSP Route Analysis

From		1	2	3	4	5	6	7	8	9	10
							To				
Atlanta	1	0	600	900	1200	2900	1800	400	800	2800	2500
Baltimore	2	600	0	450	1150	2890	1940	510	200	2820	2470
Chicago	3	900	450	0	640	2100	1100	480	700	1950	2200
Dallas	4	1200	1150	640	0	1100	570	630	1020	1500	2050
Los Angeles	5	2900	2890	2100	1100	...					
Las Vegas	6	1800	1940	1100	570		...				
Memphis	7	400	510	480	630			...			
New York	8	800	200	700	1020				...		
San Francisco	9	2800	2820	1950	1500					...	
Seattle	10	2500	2470	2200	2050						...

containing possible paths between all cities. The system it calls is the graph analyzer that computes the total travel time for each chromosome. The graph analyzer generally contains an N × N table of the distances between each city. Table 9.2 shows part of this table of inter-city distances.

In this route table (routes *[10][10]*), any chromosome phenotype can be decoded though the following distance function.

```
Function real d(integer fromCity, integer toCity){
    return(routes[fromCity][toCity]);
}
```

(See the "Fitness Function" definition for the actual system fitness function that uses this route inter-city distance function.) Thus, the genetic algorithm sets up the population of candidate routes. Each chromosome is then made part of the parameters of the route analysis system, which computes and returns the fitness.

Termination Conditions

A genetic algorithm must be told when to stop searching for a solution. The criteria for stopping are called *termination conditions*. The criteria include the maximum number of generations having been reached, the amount of computer time having been exceeded, one or more individuals having fitness values that satisfy the objective function, or the best fitness function in successive generations having reached a plateau. A genetic algorithm can use one or more of these terminating conditions.

9.2 **Overview**

One of the principal uses of a genetic algorithm, and the use that will be the focus of most chapters in this part of the book, is optimization: the process of finding the best solution to a problem under a set of objectives and constraints. Finding the best solution usually, but not necessarily, means finding the maximum or minimum value for the variable representing the objective function. Because genetic algorithms can search very large, highly nonlinear, and often very noisy landscapes, they are ideal as solution engines for optimization problems involving a large number of constraints and many different (sometimes conflicting) objective functions. Some everyday examples include the following.

- Project, crew, and class scheduling; delivery and distribution routing (the TSP); container packing (the classical "knapsack" problem); timetabling; assembly line balancing; configuration management; and retail shelf-location planning
- Regression and trend curve fitting, automatic cluster detection, and route identification
- Process control, engineering structural design, integrated circuit design, urban planning, and highway capacity analysis
- Evolution of neural networks, optimization of fuzzy models, general function optimization, exploration of game theory scenarios, protein folding and related modeling of molecular systems, and high-throughput screening and drug discovery and design
- Capital budgeting, portfolio suitability, balancing, and mix analysis; sales, inventory, and consumption forecasting; new product pricing; and economic models
- Network topology configuration, server capacity planning, fault detection, application scheduling, web design, and database design

Genetic algorithms are also used in a wide spectrum of evolutionary programming systems. Evolutionary programs breed and mutate mathematical, logical, and fuzzy expressions to produce an optimal model. Not only are evolutionary programs another form of knowledge discovery (data mining) but they form an important class of solutions for rule-based and mathematics-based models.

Generate and Test

A genetic algorithm is an enhancement to one of the earliest approaches in machine problem solving. The approach is known as generate and test. Using this strategy, a new solution to the current problem state (which, of course, may be a partition of the final problem state) is generated and tested. If it satisfies the criteria for a solution, it is accepted;[2] otherwise, a new potential solution is generated and tested. Because the generate-and-test method is always guided by an allowable outcome, it is called a directed search. Figure 9.4 illustrates this process.

A generator, using a model of constraints, creates a possible solution case to the current problem. The testing program evaluates the solution according to the current problem state. If the solution solves the current

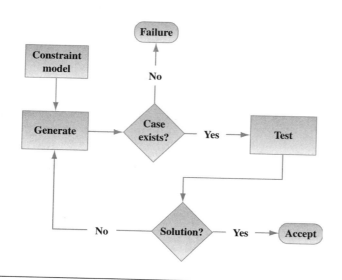

Figure 9.4 The generate-and-test process.

---

[2] In some cases a set of candidate solutions is collected from the generate-and-test process. These candidates are then ranked by additional evaluation criteria and the best of the potential solutions is selected.

problem state, it is accepted; otherwise, another potential solution is produced (or, if no other solutions are available, the process terminates with a failure). The core of the generate-and-test method is the ability of the generator to produce a set of well-formed nonredundant candidate solutions. The test process incorporates two capabilities: the ability to run the candidate solution against the target system and the ability to compare the results to a valid solution. It is the comparison between a potential solution and an acceptable solution that drives the generate-and-test methodology. Where the criteria for a successful solution can be specified, the generate-and-test approach has proven to be a very powerful tool and has been used in variety of difficult and computationally intensive problems in such areas as configuration, design, and graph generation.

The Genetic Algorithm

A genetic algorithm (GA) is a form of the generate-and-test paradigm. Like the generate-and-test method, it is also a directed search and works by generating a large number of possible solutions, testing each of these against an allowable outcome. The genetic algorithm, as the name implies, breeds a solution to complex optimization and search problems using techniques that simulate the processes of natural evolution. The genetic algorithm starts with a large population of potential (or feasible) solutions and through the application of recombination (also called crossover) and mutation evolves a solution that is better than any previous solution over the lifetime of the genetic analysis. Figure 9.5 shows the organization of a genetic algorithm.

The genetic algorithm works by creating an initial population of N possible solutions in the form of candidate chromosomes (or simply, individuals). Each of these individuals is a representation of the target system. The encoding of the target system's parameters in the individual is used to run the system and measure the outcome against an objective function. The objective function measures the goodness of fit of the individual. The better this goodness of fit the closer the individual is to representing a solution. After all individuals in the population have been evaluated for their goodness of fit, we decide whether to continue or to stop. If the terminating condition is not met, a new population is created by saving the top K best individuals, removing the bottom M poorly performing individuals, and replacing these with new individuals created by merging the parameters of the top best-performing individuals. New chromosomes are also created by randomly mutating the parameters in a few of the existing individuals.

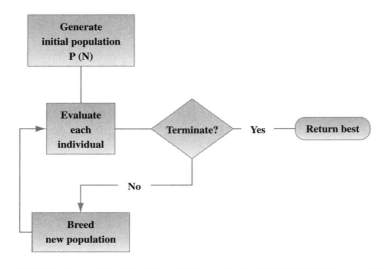

Figure 9.5 Organization of a genetic algorithm.

How a Genetic Algorithm Works

As the genetic algorithm creates and tests each population of chromosomes, it is searching for better and better solutions to the underlying problem. This search takes the form of a walkover of the underlying surface of the solution space. For example, consider Expression 9.2 and a genetic algorithm that seeks to maximize the variable z as a solution to the function in continuous variables x and y.

$$z = f(x, y) \qquad (9.2)$$

If we plot z over the possible values of x and y, we develop a terrain map of the solution surface for this function. Figure 9.6 shows a portion of the terrain map that we will use in the discussion of how the genetic algorithm works.

The genetic algorithm searches through this terrain to find the values of x and y that maximize z. This is essentially a process known as hill climbing. In hill climbing, the search mechanism explores the terrain around its current position looking for values in the independent variables that will increase the value of the target (or dependent) variable. It then moves in this direction (hence the analogy with climbing a hill). A major problem with hill climbing is its tendency to become stuck in a local maximum (or minimum, depending on the objective function). For example, Figure 9.7 shows a hill-climbing mechanism selecting a random position on the terrain.

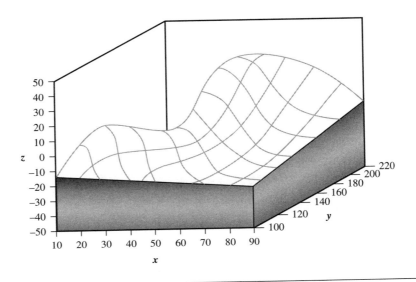

Figure 9.6   The solution space terrain for $z = f(x, y)$.

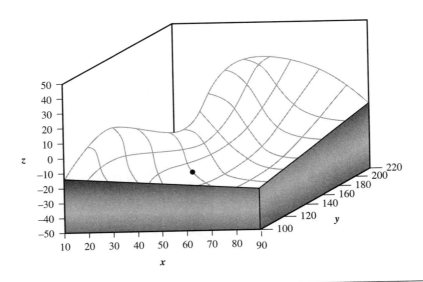

Figure 9.7   A random search point on the terrain.

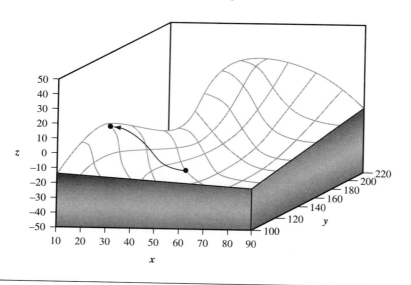

Figure 9.8 Hill climbing moving up a hill.

Examining the surrounding terrain, the hill-climbing mechanism moves to the left and up. Through a series of proximity tests, it works its way, as illustrated in Figure 9.8, to the top of the hill.

By generating a series of values for x and y, the search mechanism can work its way up the slope, always moving in the direction that gives a larger value of z. Eventually, as we can see in Figure 9.9, the search mechanism arrives at the top of the hill. There is no way to go except back down.

This hill-climbing example illustrates not only the way the search mechanism works but a significant weakness in the search methodology. Although we have arrived at the top of a hill, it is not the hill that maximizes the value of z (this hill lies off to the right). Once the hill-climbing mechanism starts up a slope, it has no way of going back down to find another, perhaps better, hill. Thus, hill climbing is always subject to finding local maximums (or minimums). We can compensate for this tendency to find local maximum or minimum regions through a process called simulated annealing. This approach saves the current maximum and then in effect "shakes" the surface to start the search point rolling around the terrain. It then starts the hill climbing from this new point. However, for any realistically large, complex, and often noncontiguous surface this approach is very inefficient. In real-world systems, the underlying terrain is often very hilly, with gaps, steep ravines, and long gullies.

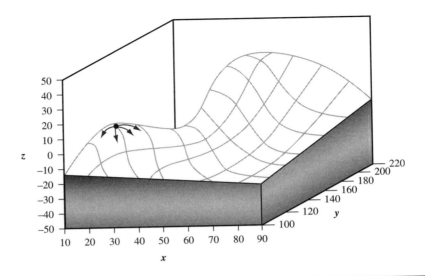

Figure 9.9   Arriving at the top of the hill.

Not only does a hill-climbing mechanism have little chance of finding a global maximum in such a surface but there is no way for the search mechanism to ensure that any maximum is in fact the global maximum (or minimum).

A genetic algorithm significantly improves the hill-climbing methodology of generate-and-test by selecting many possible maximums throughout the surface and then using the fitness function to breed better and better solutions as each of the randomly placed points moves up (or down) adjacent slopes. Figure 9.10 illustrates a population of potential solutions that would form the initial set of chromosomes for a genetic algorithm.

In Figure 9.10 we can see that the candidate solutions are scattered widely over the underlying terrain. Each point with an x, y coordinate value yields a value for z. Our fitness function is simply the value of z. The higher the value the better the goodness of fit. In the genetic algorithm, the initial population of solutions and each subsequent population are subjected to a set of transformations, as follows.

- A collection of the very best chromosomes (solutions) is retained.
- The bottommost poor solutions are removed.
- The members of a random set of the best solutions are "mated" to produce a set of children that shares the genetic material of their parents.

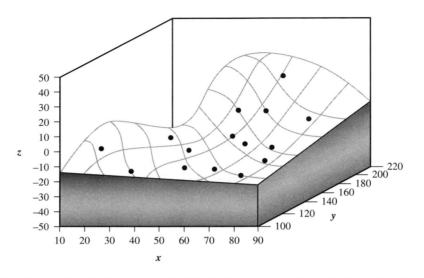

Figure 9.10   An initial population of possible solutions.

TABLE 9.3   Crossover Example

	Parent	Child
Genome N	(50,120)	(84,120)
Genome N+1	(84,173)	(50,173)

This is the process called crossover. For example, Table 9.3 shows a crossover for two genomes. In this case, the first locus (the *x* value) is swapped to generate two new children. The purpose of crossover is to increase variety and robustness in the population while preserving the genetic values of the best solutions.

■ Another random (but very sparse) set of the population is subjected to mutation. This involves randomly changing the value of a chromosome locus to a random but permissible value. Mutation is a form of annealing, which introduces new genetic material into the population.

■ Every so often a completely new chromosome is created and inserted into the population. This is also a form of annealing and, like mutation, introduces completely new genetic material into the population.

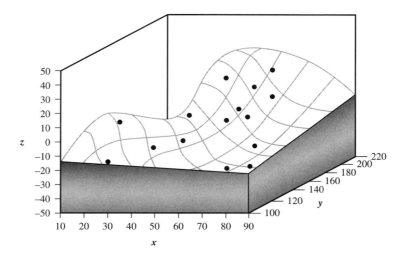

Figure 9.11   The solution population after several generations.

This process of breeding new solutions (creating a new population) by selecting the chromosomes with the largest fitness value and applying crossover and mutation continues for generation after generation. Figure 9.11 illustrates the population after a few generations.

Although there are still a few poor-performance chromosomes (due to the unpredictable random effects of individual crossovers and mutations), the average performance of all chromosomes has improved. Most of the solution points are beginning to move toward the global maximum. We also note that the points that have climbed the local maximum slopes are also being removed because their fitness function values are consistently less than the points that are moving toward the global maximum.

As we continue this process over a large number of generations, the ranking of chromosomes by their goodness of fit guides the search toward the global maximum. Figure 9.12 shows the result: the fitness function eventually finds the maximum (optimal) value of z.

In summary, genetic algorithms are a form of directed search. They work through the repetitive application of genetic operators and a fitness function to a population of potential solutions. The genetic operators breed new solutions. The fitness function selects the best of these new solutions. The genetic algorithm ranks the best solutions, applies the genetic operators to breed new solutions, and evaluates these against the fitness function. This process usually continues until no more improvement in a potential solution is found (or until another termination condition is reached).

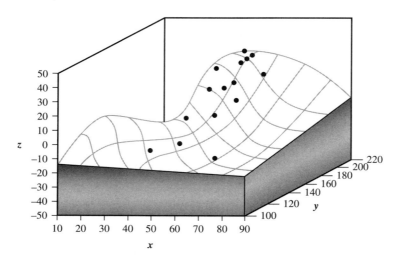

Figure 9.12 The maximum (optimal) value of z.

Strengths and Limitations

Although genetic algorithms are powerful tools for search and optimization they are not without their problems and limitations. Although many of the strengths and weaknesses of genetic algorithms will be explored later in Part III, in this section we review a few of their principal strong points and weak points.

■ *The ability to solve nonlinear, noisy, and discontinuous problems.* Although a genetic algorithm has many of the properties of a hill-climbing algorithm, it is actually a more sophisticated form of a stochastic search engine. The general capabilities of a stochastic search are more robust and broader than simple hill climbing. In particular, genetic algorithms are capable of solving highly nonlinear problems that involve discontinuous surfaces, noise, and internal dependencies (such as lead and lag relationships). Nonlinearity is a common property of most real-world problems, occurring in manufacturing, inventory management, portfolio mix optimization, construction, retailing, and a wide spectrum of other industries.

For example, in the normal course of running a production line the cost to assemble, paint, and ship 100 cars for the ABC Motor Company is $N. If $N = 20,000$, the cost per car is $200. What is the cost to assemble, paint, and ship a single car? What is the individual cost

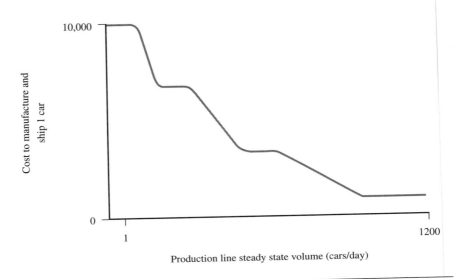

Figure 9.13 A nonlinear production cost curve.

to assemble, paint, and ship 1,000,000 cars? Both of these questions involve a nonlinear system. The cost of setup, labor, electricity, and other factors means that producing a single car (or any small number of cars) is far more expensive than a large number of cars in a production system. Figure 9.13 illustrates this nonlinear relationship between cost and production line volume.

The plateau regions in the function are generally related to the cost of energy and materials that often have quantity-based cost thresholds. On the other hand, the wear and tear on equipment alone means that the cost per car on a run of one million cars will steadily increase. The growth and decay curves in these examples are typical examples of nonlinear functions.

■ *The ability to solve complex optimization problems.* The genetic algorithm's ability to rapidly and thoroughly search a large, complex, and high-dimensional space allows it to solve multiobjective and multiconstraint optimization problems. In a multiple objective function schedule, the optimal solution often represents a saddle (or compromise) point in the solution space. Optimization in the presence of multiobjective functions usually means finding a way to rank the utility or importance of each objective and then finding a way to judge the optimality of a feasible solution based on the goodness of fit or rank of their optimality measures. As a rather simple example using a crew scheduler, if each objective function (*f*) returns a value between 0 and 100, indicating how close the schedule is to the optimal (0 = best, 100 = worst), we can find an optimality ranking for a multiobjective function schedule by evaluating Expression 9.3.

$$f_{ranked} = \frac{\sum_{i=1}^{N} f_i \times w_i}{\sum_{i=1}^{N} w_i} \tag{9.3}$$

where, N is the number of objective functions and w_i is the weight (or utility) value of that objective function. By selecting schedules with the smallest weighted average objective function, the feasible schedules with the closest optimality fit will continually percolate to the top. This form of evaluating a collection of objective functions makes it easy to combine both minimizing and maximizing objective functions in the same analysis (maximizing functions simply return the inverse of the fitness value).

■ *A complete dependence on the fitness function.* As a directed search technique, the fitness function evaluates each solution and ranks it according to a goodness of fit. If a fitness function cannot be defined, a genetic algorithm cannot be used to solve the problem. If a fitness function does not correctly define a separable universe of good and bad solutions (or if the fitness function is coded incorrectly), the genetic algorithm will behave according to the clarity and focus of the faulty fitness function and will fail to find the correct solution. And because a genetic algorithm is highly sensitive to the underlying gradient of the solution space, a fitness function must provide a way of guiding the search. The algorithm must be able to tell when it is moving in the right direction; that is, when in fact it is getting close to a solution.

Genetic algorithms are also sensitive to intelligent proximity and search capabilities built into the search methodology. This is both a strength and a weakness. The ability to encode intelligence into the fitness function so that degrees of fitness can be evaluated allows the genetic algorithm to rank chromosomes that are "close to" the main goodness-of-fit criteria. This process can help guide the search through a rough or chaotic solution space. At the same time, a lack of focus in the fitness function can spread the search over a larger segment of the population, slowing and often obscuring the optimization process. Finding a balance between the flexibility and brittleness of the fitness function is often a difficult task.

■ *A sensitivity to genetic algorithm parameters.* Genetic algorithms are intrinsically sensitive to the way in which new populations are generated; that is, they are sensitive to the way in which high-performance properties are inherited by future populations and the way in which new potential solutions emerge in future populations. Essentially, this means that the stability, coherence, and convergence of genetic algorithms depend on the rate of mutation and the crossover frequency. The higher the rate of the crossover and mutation properties the more variation appears in the population. This may initially provide a rich pool of possible solutions. However, as the frequency rates increase the continuity of high-performance individuals is lost among the resulting randomness. At some point, the algorithm becomes less and less stable and the genome itself becomes more and more random.

There are two significant problems associated with a lack of robustness in a genetic algorithm: premature convergence and delayed convergence. When the population size is too small or the genetic diversity is too small, a genetic algorithm can converge too quickly on a local optimum. On the other hand, if the population size is too large or the genetic diversity is too large an optimal solution may not emerge (due to the continual emergence of randomness in the genomes) or the convergence to a solution may take a very long time.

■ *A sensitivity to genome encoding.* Genetic algorithms are also responsive, but perhaps to a lesser degree, to the underlying coding scheme used to represent the genome. Traditional genome coding has been done through a bit string so that mutations can work in a way similar to random genetic miscoding in biological systems. Production genetic algorithms — those that have been deployed into regular use and are solving real-world problems, especially those used in complex, multi-objective business applications — commonly use real numbers as genomes. The use of numbers rather than bit strings provides not only higher evaluation performance but the ability to more easily control the underlying distribution (statistical) properties of the genome.

To summarize, genetic algorithms belong to a class of directed search methods that are be used for both solving optimization problems and modeling the core of evolutionary systems. They use a heuristic rather than analytical approach, and thus their solutions are not always exact and their ability to find a solution is often dependent on a proper and sometimes fragile specification of the problem representation and the parameters that drive the genetic algorithm.

9.3   **The Architecture of a Genetic Algorithm**

In the previous section we discussed the underlying concepts of the genetic algorithm and how the stochastic search and fitness functions work together to find a value for an objective function. We also reviewed some of the principal strengths and weaknesses of genetic algorithms. Now we turn to the actual mechanics of the genetic algorithm; how a genetic algorithm is designed, structured, and organized for a particular problem; the meaning and application of the algorithm parameters; and the specification of constraints, objectives, and fitness functions.

To illustrate the mechanics of a genetic algorithm and how the various algorithm parameters affect the search methods, we will use a very small, five-city TSP. In this problem, shown in Figure 9.14, we want to find the shortest complete path (or tour) between cities Able, Baker, Charlie, Delta, and Echo. To simplify the example, we are not attempting to find a circuit (that is, we need not return to the starting city).

To compute the path between the cities, we need to store the inter-city distances in a way that allows for a rapid evaluation of the path. The mileage between these cities, shown in Table 9.4, is maintained in a distance matrix (***D[][]***),

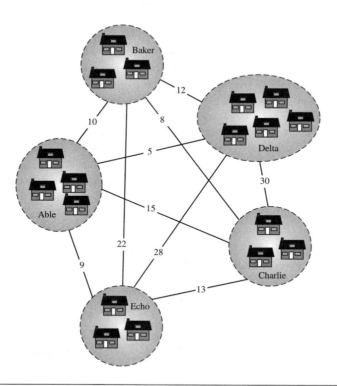

Figure 9.14 The five-city TSP.

TABLE 9.4   The Inter-city Distance Matrix

	Able	Baker	Charlie	Delta	Echo
Able	0	10	15	5	9
Baker	10	0	8	12	22
Charlie	15	8	0	30	13
Delta	5	12	30	0	28
Echo	9	22	13	28	0

TABLE 9.5   The City Coordinate Map

	Grid Coordinates	
	x	y
Able	3	3
Baker	5	1
Charlie	7	4
Delta	8	2
Echo	4	6

An alternative way of storing city-to-city distances, of course, is through a grid coordinate system. In this approach, each city is associated with an x-y coordinate in an N × M map. Table 9.5 shows a coordinate table for the five cities.

With a coordinate table, the distance between any two cities (C_n, C_m) is the Euclidean distance from the coordinates of C_n and C_m. Expression 9.4 is the distance metric.

$$d(C_n, C_m) = \sqrt{(x_m - x_n)^2 + (y_m - y_n)^2} \qquad (9.4)$$

The choice of representation depends to a large degree on how the distance metric is actually used. If the distance must be associated with road, rail, water, and other physical transportation systems, the inter-city distance map is the preferred representation method because it can capture the actual mileage between two cities based on actual driving or commuter rail distances (for example). Also, when the distance between cities are not symmetrical — that is, traveling from city C1 to city C2 is not the same as traveling from city C2 to city C1 — the inter-city matrix should be used. The Euclidean distance, on the other hand, is the straight-line mileage between two cities. In some problems, where the approximate distance is sufficient, the grid coordinate method can be used.

With five cities, there are 120 possible paths (because there are 5! possible combinations of cities). Our genetic algorithm will explore this space. Its objective is to minimize the transit length among the cities. With this in mind, we can turn to the internal workings of the genetic algorithm. Figure 9.15 shows the schematic flow of control and analysis in the genetic algorithm.

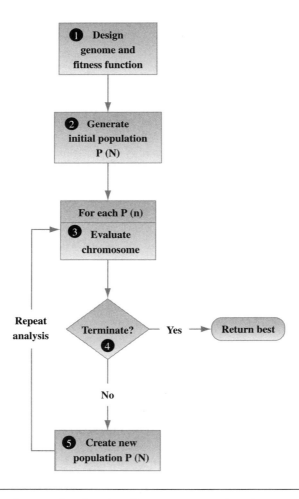

Figure 9.15 The control and analysis flow in a genetic algorithm.

❶ Design a genome representation and fitness function.

The efficiency and processing power of a genetic algorithm depend on the way the problem is expressed in a chromosome and the fitness function that evaluates the chromosome. This is the first step in using a genetic algorithm. The design of a chromosome or genome set to properly represent a problem is one of the crucial architectural decisions in the use of a genetic algorithm.

Genome Structural Design

A population consists of a collection of chromosomes. Each chromosome consists of one or more genomes. Every chromosome represents a possible solution. The way in which the chromosome is designed can, therefore, have a significant effect on processing speed, convergence, and the overall ease of crossover and mutation. It is important to understand that the values of a chromosome are the parameters of a solution and must always be associated with an evaluation system that can use the parameters to produce a state or outcome of the system. The degree to which this outcome is a better or worse solution, given the chromosome's parameter values, is measured by the fitness function (which is discussed in the next section).

In the TSP, an obvious chromosome representation is a genome with five loci, representing the order in which the cities are visited. The number in the locus is the city at the row location in the distance matrix (*D[][]*). Figure 9.16 shows a possible chromosome (a phenotype) for a route through five cities.

This chromosome describes a tour: start at Able, travel to Charlie, travel to Echo, travel to Delta, and then travel to Baker. A new chromosome can easily be developed using this presentation by generating five unique random numbers between 1 and 5. For a simple route through five cities, a chromosome that is a permutation of the cities is most likely the simplest and the best.

Chromosome design is, however, highly dependent on the problem. Consider a circuit through the same five cities. A circuit has the constraint

Locus (Allele) Positions				
1	2	3	4	5
1	3	5	4	2

Figure 9.16   A route chromosome in the TSP.

	Locus (Allele) Position				
1	2	3	4	5	6
1	3	5	4	2	1

Figure 9.17 A circuit chromosome in the TSP.

that we must return to the starting city. We can either modify the fitness function to consider the implicit loop or design a slightly different chromosome to make the circuit explicit and speed up fitness computation. An extra locus is added to the end of the chromosome. This site contains the city index of the first locus. Figure 9.17 shows a possible chromosome (a phenotype) for a circuit through the five cities.

In the circuit representation, however, the genetic algorithm is not free to perform crossover and mutate operations over the complete chromosome. Locus 5 completes the circuit and must always have the same value as the first locus. Thus, ease of representation increases complexity in the control strategies of the genetic algorithm.

Chromosomes can consist of more than single values. A chromosome locus can be a vector, a matrix, or a tree structure. The representation depends on the problem. As a simple example, suppose we change the objective of the five-city TSP to find the shortest route through the city considering traffic patterns during the day. Heavy traffic in city C_i effectively extends the distance between cities (C_i, C_j). We can represent this by a length multiplier associated with the *from* (or starting) city. Table 9.6 is a table of the effective lengths between cities — with the travel time between each city pair extended by the traffic multiplier.

For example, for the route segment Able to Baker (or to any other city) at 1615 (4:15 p.m.), the multiplier is 1.4, indicating, perhaps, moderately

TABLE 9.6 The City Traffic Multipliers

	From	Time of Day					
	From	0000	0531	0731	0931	1601	1901
	To	0530	0730	0930	1600	1900	2400
Able		1.0	1.2	1.4	1.1	1.4	1.2
Baker		1.0	1.2	1.3	1.3	1.2	1.1
Charlie		1.0	1.5	1.7	1.4	1.3	1.2
Delta		1.0	1.3	1.5	1.4	1.1	1.0
Echo		1.3	1.4	1.2	1.0	1.0	1.0

Locus Position

	1	2	3	4	5
City					
Time of Day					

Figure 9.18 The city route and time-of-day genome.

heavy rush-hour traffic. The distance from Able to Baker is 10 miles. The multiplier converts this to an effective distance of 14 miles (10 times 1.4). The chromosome representation now must consider two values: the city and the time of day of arrival at the city. Figure 9.18 shows the organization of the city and time-of-day genome.

Each genome locus in this representation consists of a 1×2 vector containing the city and the time of day. An initial population is generated by selecting a random permutation of cities and, for each city, a random arrival time.[3] The search process proceeds by breeding routes that minimize path length subject to the best time of day of city arrival times. More complex route scheduling problems can be solved in this manner. For example, city C_i may have N possible routes though the city. Baltimore, Maryland, for instance, has I-695 (the beltway), the harbor tunnel, the I-95 tunnel, and the Francis Scott Key bridge, each connecting cities south of Baltimore (such as Washington D.C.) to cities north of Baltimore (such as Wilmington and Philadelphia). Each route has its own length, or a traffic multiplier. A TSP algorithm could consider the order of the cities, the route through the city, and the time of arrival. Because every city has a different number of possible routes, the routing locus would be drawn from a different population of random highways associated with the city in the city locus of the genome.

The TSP illustrates one of the structural difficulties in designing a chromosome representation that is easy to use and amendable to genetic operators such as crossover and mutation. As we will see in the discussion of breeding techniques (see "Conventional Crossover (Breeding) Techniques"), a genome with a simple linear sequence of cities almost always produces an incorrect genome when subjected to conventional "cut-and-splice" crossover operations, as well as an incorrect

---

[3] Nothing in the genetic search process requires a uniform distribution of random times. For business trip schedules or crew scheduling, we might limit the random time to business hours, say 0630 to 1700 (or 1430 hours to allow end-of-day tear down and travel time). Naturally, as we will see in the discussion of fitness functions, we could also assign very large multipliers to non-work times to force the search mechanism to only schedule trips during a specific range of work hours.

Locus (Allele) Positions				
1	2	3	4	5
0001	0011	0101	0100	0010

Figure 9.19 The binary route chromosome in the TSP.

genome when subjected to conventional locus (site) mutation. Following the conventional crossover and mutation operations, we will take up more advanced issues in designing genomes for permutation and precedence-based (time-sequenced) problems.[4]

Genome Representations

In addition to the most effective and efficient way to encode parameters into chromosomes, the underlying form of the representation is also important. Historically, chromosomes have been encoded as bit strings. Figure 9.19 illustrates the bit (or binary) organization of the five-city TSP search.

Unlike the use of actual numbers, which use arrays or matrices for the genome, a binary representation uses a continuous string of 1 and 0 values. The chromosomes in Table 9.5 would be represented as *0001001100100100*. Bit strings provide several general benefits in genetic search.

- As a string of 1s and 0s they are a compact representation.

- Crossover operations are simplified. The mating process simply slices the bit string at some random point and appends the string fragments without regard to the actual values.

- Mutation is a simple matter of flipping a random bit in the string.

- Provide a pattern analysis space for the evaluation of schemata (patterns of high-performance genomes that move through the population). Whether or not schemata analysis contributes any significant control improvement to genetic algorithms is a matter of some debate. Most business genetic algorithms in scheduling, production management, logistics, data exploration, pricing, and similar areas evaluate the fitness function and the average fitness of the population without regard to the propagation of schemata patterns.

---

[4] Separating the discussion of genome design into two sections makes it much easier for readers unfamiliar with either genetic algorithm breeding operators or with scheduling, routing, covering, and TSPs to understand the fundamentals and then appreciate the difficulties in genomes that involve locus dependencies.

Binary representations, however, all have some significant problems.

- They must be converted to a real number for use as a parameter to the underlying system. This involves traversing the bit string from right to left, and for each non-zero position, computing the value (2^n, where n is the bit position) and adding it to the total of the under-generation value.
- They make feasibility and unique chromosome constraint checking very difficult (the requirements for feasibility and uniqueness are discussed in the section "Generate Initial Population").
- They make generating random values in a specific range a more tedious process.
- They are often a source of deep representation problems in genetic algorithms. Because we are (as a general rule) unaccustomed to working in base 2 arithmetic, debugging and tracing the operations of a genetic algorithm are often difficult, and are flawed by mistakes in either binary encoding or interpreting the output of the algorithm.
- They are (generally) unnecessary. Nearly all problems can be expressed with integer or floating-point numbers as the parameters. Using a variety of random number generators (uniform, Gaussian, binomial, and so forth), these parameters can be used in crossover and mutation operations in ways that are easy to understand, easy to implement, easy to constrain, and less prone to errors of encoding or interpretation.

All genetic and evolutionary programming problems discussed in this part of the book use real numbers as loci in their chromosomes. This has proven, in the problems designed and deployed by the author, to be an effective and robust means of genome representation. Although there are some debates in the literature about the performance of real numbers versus bit strings, in actual applications (many involving very large problem spaces and complex genomes) the difference in genome representation has been far outweighed by the efficiencies associated with ranking (sorting), selecting, and the evaluation of the fitness function in the target system.

Fitness Functions

In the TSP, we have a single objective function and a small set of constraints. Because we want to find the shortest route through the cities, the fitness function (shown in Expression 9.5) is the sum of the paths between the cities in the chromosome.

$$f = \sum_{i=1}^{N-1} d(c_i, c_{i+1}) \tag{9.5}$$

Here,

f is the fitness of the chromosome.

N is the number of cities in the chromosome (in this case, five cities).

c_i is the i-th city in the chromosome. This is the i-th locus in the genome and indexes the corresponding row in the distance matrix.

$d()$ is a function that returns the distance between two cities using their index values in the distance matrix.

Genetic algorithms can be used to solve multiobjective and multiconstraint problems. As a general practice, objective functions are encoded as a set of genomes, whereas hard constraints are part of the underlying system evaluation and affect the fitness function in terms of the feasibility of a solution. Soft constraints, on the other hand, are often encoded as penalty functions in the fitness evaluation.

For example, suppose the TSP had two objectives: find the shortest and least expensive route through the cites. The cost to travel from city C_i to city C_j can be encoded, as illustrated in Table 9.7, by adding a table of highway tolls to the problem.

Note that unlike distances the toll costs are sometimes different depending on whether the path is C_i, C_j or C_j, C_i, in that many toll roads charge for traffic moving in one direction but not in another. With the city distance and the toll costs matrices in hand, we can formulate a fitness function that looks for the minimum path length and the minimum cost. One simple way to design a fitness function, as illustrated

TABLE 9.7 The Inter-city Toll Matrix

	Able	Baker	Charlie	Delta	Echo
Able	0	2	0	3	0
Baker	2	0	4	0	2
Charlie	2	4	0	0	2
Delta	3	0	0	0	0
Echo	0	2	2	0	0

in Expression 9.6, is to take the sum of the path length and the toll costs.

$$f = \sum_{i=1}^{N-1} d(c_i, c_{i+1}) + t(c_i, c_{i+1}) \tag{9.6}$$

Here,

f is the fitness of the chromosome.

N is the number of cities in the chromosome (in this case, five cities).

c_i is the i-th city in the chromosome. This is the i-th locus in the genome and indexes the corresponding row in the distance matrix.

$d()$ is a function that returns the distance between two cities using their index values in the distance matrix.

$t()$ is a function that returns the toll costs between two cities using their index values in the toll matrix.

Thus, for equal path lengths paths with no tolls (or very small tolls) will have a better minimization fitness value than paths with larger tolls. We can also design a fitness function to seek for the shortest path *only* on toll roads. In this case, we want to penalize any solution that does not use a toll road. Expression 9.7 shows one possible way to encode a penalty into the fitness function.

$$f = \sum_{i=1}^{N-1} d(c_i, c_{i+1}) + \frac{1}{t(c_i, c_{i+1}) + 1} \tag{9.7}$$

In this case, when $t() = 0$ or near zero, the fraction is close to 1 and will increase the value of the fitness function. For all values of $t() >> 0$, the fraction becomes very small and contributes to the minimization of the solution. The fitness function minimizes route distance and maximizes toll costs. Thus, this fitness function will seek the shortest and most expensive route through the cities.

The idea of multiobjective and multiconstraint genetic searches can encompass a large number of possible objective functions. The fitness function determines the optimum balance between individual fitness and a composite solution. For problems that involve many objective functions, it is not generally possible to find a solution that is optimal for each objective function. In the previous example, there are two objective functions.

Minimize the total route distance between N cities.

Minimize (or maximize) the toll costs.

TABLE 9.8 The Inter-city Speed Limit Matrix

	Able	Baker	Charlie	Delta	Echo
Able	0	55	65	70	65
Baker	55	0	70	60	65
Charlie	65	70	0	70	70
Delta	70	60	70	0	65
Echo	65	65	70	65	0

We cannot simultaneously find the shortest route and the route with the least costs unless they just happen to coincide. In the real world, the solution with the minimum spanning route and the route that minimizes the toll costs will lie in a space somewhere between the two objectives. As the number of objective functions and penalty constraints increases, these saddle points become more and more difficult to define. For example, consider a slightly more complex genetic search system that incorporates, as shown in Table 9.8, a table of speed limits between cities.

The genetic algorithm now has three objective functions.

Minimize the total route distance between N cities.
Minimize the toll costs.
Minimize the time to travel the route.

Finding the optimal saddle point in the solution space that simultaneously satisfies all three constraints involves designing a fitness function that penalizes long routes, penalizes routes that involve toll roads, and penalizes route segments that have slow speed limits. Expression 9.8 shows one possible fitness function for this problem.

$$f = \sum_{i=1}^{N-1} d(c_i, c_{i+1}) + t(c_i, c_{i+1}) + (70 - s(c_i, c_{i+1})) \qquad (9.8)$$

Here,

f is the fitness of the chromosome.
N is the number of cities in the chromosome (in this case, five cities).
c_i is the i-th city in the chromosome. This is the i-th locus in the genome and indexes the corresponding row in the distance matrix.
$d()$ is a function that returns the distance between two cities using their index values in the distance matrix.

t()   is a function that returns the toll costs between two cities using their index values in the toll matrix.

s()   is a function that returns the speed limit between two cities using their index values in the speed limit matrix.

Knowing that the speed limit on interstate highways (which connect most of the cities) is between 65 and 70 mph, we subtract the inter-city speed limit from 70 (the maximum speed) to give a penalty weight to this part of the fitness function. The closer the city-to-city speed limit is to 70 mph the smaller the difference, and hence the smaller the contribution to the size of the fitness function (and thus, it contributes to minimizing the overall function). Naturally, other possible encoding forms that require no knowledge of the maximum speed limit exist, such as the inverse relationship we used to maximize the use of tolls (in that we are, in effect, maximizing the speed over the route). See Expression 9.5 for this use of the inverse (or fractional) weighting.

Multi-genome Fitness Functions

In the previous discussion, the fitness function was associated with a single route through the cities. Each chromosome represented a possible route and had its own fitness function. Every chromosome was also independent of every other chromosome in the population (at least in terms of fitness, although chromosomes are related to other individuals through a parent and child relationship generated by the crossover process). We now consider a slightly more complex version of the TSP — one associated with crew scheduling, project management, assembly line balancing, and similar operations. Instead of a single five-city path, the genetic algorithm is asked to schedule a set of N crews who must visit all five cities during the day. We have an electrical, a road repair, and a vehicle maintenance crew. Thus, $N = 3$. Figure 9.20 shows the organization of the crew trip-scheduling chromosome.

The objective of the genetic search is to find the crew trip schedule that minimizes the distance traveled by the three crews. One way to do this, as shown in Expression 9.9, is through a direct minimization fitness

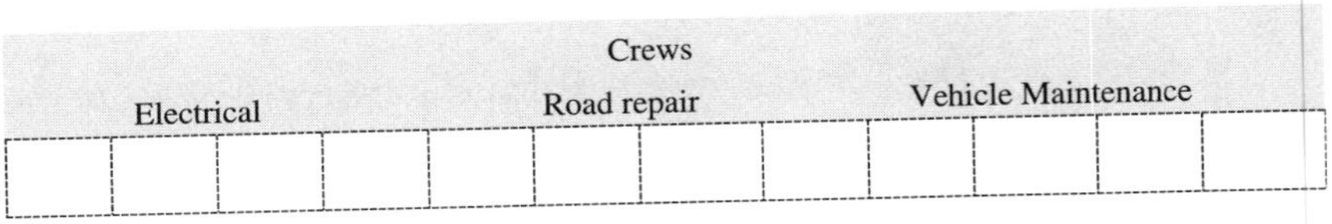

						Crews						
	Electrical					Road repair				Vehicle Maintenance		

Figure 9.20   The crew trip-scheduling chromosome.

378 of Chapter 9 Fundamental Concepts of Genetic Algorithms

function that simply sums the path length for the three crews.

$$f = f_e() + f_r() + f_v() \qquad (9.9)$$

Here,

f	is the fitness of the chromosome
$f_e()$	is the fitness of the electrical path
$f_r()$	is the fitness of the road repair crew path
$f_v()$	is the fitness of the vehicle maintenance crew

Another way to formulate a fitness function is to measure the fitness of a solution relative to the total distance traveled by any set of crews in a schedule. Thus, the best solution will be the smallest relative to the crews that took the longest path through the five cities. Expression 9.10 illustrates this type of fitness function.

$$f = 1 + \frac{d_i}{d_{max}} \qquad (9.10)$$

Here,

f	is the fitness of the chromosome.
d_i	is the total distance traveled by the three crews.
d_{max}	is the maximum distance traveled by any set of crews. This is discovered by iterating through the population and finding the crew schedule with the longest path length.

Basing a fitness function on factors spread over or intrinsic to the population is often used when the individual solutions have a high degree of variability. For example, consider a crew-scheduling system with the following characteristics.

- Crews are assigned pending jobs for the day.
- Depending on the distance to the jobs, crews may work on a variable number of jobs (that is, because a crew can only work eight hours, the mix of jobs and the distance to each job — from the main office or from a previous job — determines the number of jobs that can be done).
- The company wants as many jobs as possible completed each day.

In this case, we want to maximize jobs but minimize the travel time between jobs (in that long travel times incur elevated fuel costs, can lead to excessive wear and tear on equipment, and increase the probability that the previous job will be started late or remain incomplete for that day). A fitness function that only evaluates the schedule of a single chromosome independent of all other schedules cannot take into account the variability in the number of actual jobs scheduled coupled to the distance traveled to satisfy those jobs. Hence, a population-based fitness function is more appropriate. Expression 9.11 shows one possible fitness function.

$$f = (N - J_i) + \frac{d_i}{d_{max}} \qquad (9.11)$$

Here,

f is the fitness of the chromosome.

N is the total number of jobs being assigned to the crews on this day.

J_i is the number of jobs scheduled for the three crews.

d_i is the total distance traveled by the three crews.

d_{max} is the maximum distance traveled by any set of crews. This is discovered by iterating through the population and finding the crew schedule with the longest path length.

This is a minimization fitness function. The smaller the value the better the fitness. Thus, for two candidate schedules, s_1 and s_2, the one that schedules the most jobs is the best (as J_i approaches N, the value becomes smaller and smaller). If both schedules have the same number of planned jobs, the one with the smallest overall distance traveled is the best.

Designing the genome representation of the problem parameters and selecting a fitness function to measure each chromosome's goodness of fit is the first phase in using a genetic algorithm. We now turn to the actual mechanics of the algorithm, exploring the iterative process of breeding a solution.

❷ Generate Initial Population

A genetic algorithm begins with a population of potential solutions. These solutions are encoded in the chromosomes. An initial population of potential routes consists of randomly generated combinations of cities. Each genome site (locus) is the next city in the route. Thus, a genome of (3,2,4,1) would be a path from Charlie to Baker to Delta to Able. Table 9.9 is part of this population of N potential solutions.

There are two general performance objectives on the generation of all populations in a genetic algorithm (and they apply to initial populations as well as future populations that are bred from the initial population).

TABLE 9.9 A Population of TSP Solutions

Genome		Locus Values			
1	1	3	2	5	4
2	3	5	4	1	2
3	2	1	4	3	5
4	3	1	4	5	2
5	5	2	4	3	1
6	1	5	2	4	3
⋮	⋮				
N	1	4	5	3	2

■ First, each potential solution must be a feasible solution. Feasibility means that the solution obeys all hard constraints on the solution. If the TSP problem, for example, specifies a particular city as the starting point, randomly generated solutions that do not start with this city are not feasible solutions. It is often difficult in real-world problems to ensure that each solution is feasible, and this constraint often means that the mechanics of the genetic algorithm are intricately connected to the mechanics of the application.

■ Second, each potential solution must be a unique solution. This is a constraint on the population that is often overlooked in the literature on genetic algorithms, generally because most of the problems in the academic literature involve solving simple problems (such as this small TSP problem in which duplicate paths would not appreciably slow down the search process). Finding duplicate or nonunique solutions is often a difficult task because a duplicate genome is not always obvious. For example, if the direction of the path is immaterial the genome *(1,2,3,4)* is the same as *(4,3,2,1)* because both represent the same path.

In some applications, of course, one or both of these objectives cannot be met, either because knowing what is a feasible solution is impossible outside the internals of the application or because recognizing duplicates is either topologically impossible or would cost more in evaluation time than actually reevaluating a duplicate chromosome. The inability to recognize duplicate chromosomes is more often true in evolutionary programming models than in genetic algorithms.

Population Diversity

A critical factor that bears on the performance of a genetic algorithm is population diversity. Diversity is a measure of the robustness of chromosome representations; that is, how well they are distributed over the possible solution space. Early diversity is essential in the genetic algorithm, whereas later diversity indicates a problem with convergence. Diversity can be assessed in several ways, but there are two common methods.

■ *By computing the variation in the fitness values over a population.* This is essentially, as shown in Expression 9.12, the standard error of the fitness function (the degree of variation from the average fitness).

$$f^v = \frac{1}{N} \sum_{i=1}^{N} \sqrt{(f_a - f_i)^2} \tag{9.12}$$

Here,

f^v is the average variance of the population chromosomes as measured by the variance of their fitness values

N is the total number of chromosomes in the population

f_a is the average population fitness

f_i is fitness of the i-th chromosome

A large variance indicates a robust degree of variation in the fitness functions, whereas a small variance indicates a more compact and less varied population of fitness functions.

■ *By computing the average change in fitness between successive generations.* The idea behind a genetic algorithm is convergence, through selective breeding, on an optimal set of solutions. One way of examining diversity in the population is by computing the change in average fitness from one generation to the next. Expression 9.13 shows a simple method of tracking this change.

$$f_\Delta = \frac{1}{K} \sum_{n=2}^{K} \bar{f}_n - \bar{f}_{n-1} \tag{9.13}$$

Here,

f_Δ is the average change in the fitness from one generation to the next.

K is the total number of generations elapsed in the genetic search.

$\bar{f}_n - \bar{f}_{n-1}$ is the average fitness of the n-th generation.

Plotting the change in the average population fitness from one generation to the next is a key indicator of convergence. As new and better solutions are created, the difference between the average fitness in each successive generation should move toward zero.

Diversity measures the richness of the gene pool and plays an important part in the early stages of a genetic search. Creating an initial population with high diversity depends on a deep understanding of the problem space and the ability to create chromosomes that are scattered throughout the possible solution terrain. Maintaining genetic diversity through the search process rests on both the nature of the crossover operations as well as the rate of mutations and spontaneous birth in the overall population.

Population Size

Determining the size of the initial population is a difficult but crucial step in using a genetic algorithm. Each chromosome in the population represents a point somewhere in the solution terrain. When the population is too small, as illustrated in Figure 9.21, the genetic algorithm can only search a small region of the possible solution space.

When the population is very small in relation to the possible search space, a genetic algorithm will either take a very long time to find a reasonable solution or will wander around the terrain, often locking on a local minimum or maximum. On the other hand, a population that is too

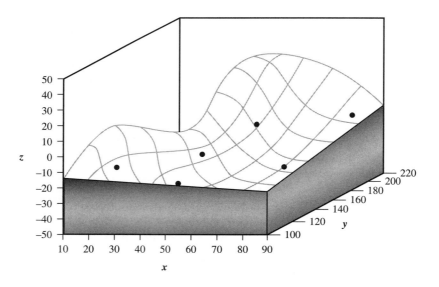

Figure 9.21   A small population spread over the solution space.

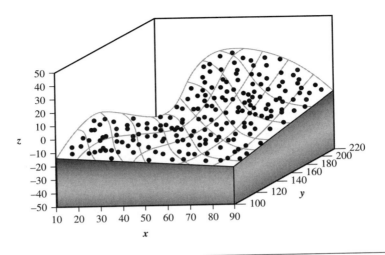

Figure 9.22   A large population spread over the solution space.

large, as shown in Figure 9.22, relative to the solution space covers too much of the underlying search space.

Such a very large population often lacks genetic diversity (because it covers so much terrain) and can require a very high number of generations to percolate high-performing chromosomes out of the large number of lower- or moderate-performing chromosomes.

An analysis of the optimal population size for many combinatorial and permutation problems in which the potential solution space becomes very large for even a small number of variables (such as the TSP) rests on the use of probability theory to judge the probability that an optimal solution lies within a population N chromosomes. These studies indicate that the performance of even large TSPs is not critically dependent on the population size if the population is reasonably large (144 chromosomes for a 30-city problem, and 409 chromosomes for a 75-city problem).

A good rule of thumb connects the initial population size to the number of variables in the algorithm (the number of loci in the chromosome) and the number of possible states in the solution space. An initial population, as shown in Expression 9.14, should be at least as large as five times the number of variables or about half the maxim number of possible states, whichever is smaller.

$$p = \min\left((5 \times v), \left(\frac{1}{2} \times s\right)\right) \qquad (9.14)$$

Here,

p is the population estimate
v is the total number of variables or chromosome loci
s is the number of possible states in the solution space

In a TSP, the maximum number of routes is n! (*1 × 2 × 3 × 4...× n*), meaning that the solution space has grown very large very fast. The five-city TSP, however, has only 120 possible routes. With this rule of thumb, the population size estimate is 25 individuals: the minimum of 25 (five times the five chromosome loci) and 60 (one-half the possible 120 states). Although the maximum number of states is small enough to include all possible solutions in the initial population, this would actually impede the genetic search. The genetic process of breeding and mutating new solutions in a population that as an initial condition already contains all possible solutions can easily result in a protracted search through the population, as the crossover process will simply produce duplicates that must be discarded.

❸ Evaluate the Chromosome

This is the core functional component of the genetic algorithm: evaluating a chromosome associates a goodness-of-fit or performance measure to each chromosome in the population. But assigning this goodness of fit is not necessarily a part of the genetic algorithm itself. In many large-scale business applications (such as those in inventory optimization, manufacturing assembly line balancing, and crew and project scheduling) the solution represents a configuration or a set of parameters that must be processed by the connected system. As illustrated schematically in Figure 9.23, the system generates an actual outcome whose degree of performance (or "goodness") is measured by the fitness function.

Figure 9.23 outlines the basics of the genetic algorithm's evaluation process. The iterative analysis of each chromosome creates a population of solutions ranked by their "goodness" as measured by the fitness function. The process is fairly straightforward.

① The evaluation process is applied to each chromosome (potential solution) in the current population. Much of the mechanism in a genetic algorithm is concerned with the production of this population of chromosomes.

② The next chromosome is selected from the population.

③ Use the solution configuration in the chromosome to execute the underlying system. In some cases, the system itself is embedded in the fitness function (as is the case with the TSP). In many other

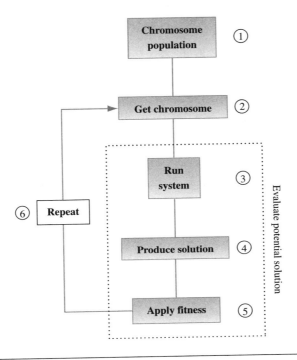

Figure 9.23   Evaluating a chromosome.

cases, the chromosome's values are passed to a larger system. For example, consider a genetic algorithm that performs trend fitting. The chromosome might contain the coefficients and powers of the equation terms. These values are passed to a regression engine that forms the equation, reads a file of data points, and computes the standard error from the differences between actuals and estimates. The regression engine is the "system" connected to the genetic algorithm.

④ From the chromosome configuration a solution is produced by the underlying system. In some cases, of course, the chromosome and the system are the same (as in the TSP model). In other cases, such as the trend-fitting model, the solution is the standard error of estimate produced from the equation described by the chromosome's coefficients and exponent values.

⑤ Apply a fitness function to the solution in order to assign a performance rank to the current chromosome. The fitness analysis actually changes the content of the chromosome by storing a goodness-of-fit measure.

⑥ Go back and get the next chromosome in the population. The evaluation process is repeated for each chromosome (unless some special application-specific control strategy interrupts this cycle).

Thus, in summary, a chromosome is a potential solution. The "system" is the process that creates an outcome state (a solution) based on the content of a chromosome. It is this outcome space that is evaluated by the genetic algorithm based on the fitness function. Because the evaluation process is the core of the genetic algorithm and because it is dependent completely on the fitness function, the genetic algorithm as a whole is critically dependent on a proper formulation of its fitness function.

❹ Terminate

Like biological evolution that goes on and on, a genetic algorithm continues to run, evolving solutions until explicitly terminated. After each population is evaluated, the algorithm checks a set of termination conditions. There are several common termination conditions used in genetic algorithms.

- The maximum number of generations has been reached.
- A maximum elapse (wall clock) time has been reached.
- A maximum amount of computer resources has been used.
- A chromosome with a particular fitness value emerges.
- The average (or best) fitness function value reaches a steady state over successive generations. Normally this is a tolerance comparison (for example, stop when the change in the fitness function is less than .001 over 100 generations).
- The average (or best) fitness function value oscillates over the generations.
- The average fitness reaches a very early steady state or begins to decay. A sudden or gradual lack of average fitness indicates a problem in the way high-performing chromosomes are bred and their offspring propagated into the next generation. This is sometimes caused by mutation rates that are too high.

These termination conditions are often used in combination. A genetic algorithm can be terminated after a certain number of generations, when a particular average fitness has been achieved, or when the fitness function does not change after a specific number of generations.

A genetic algorithm's termination conditions can also include a set of policy rules associated with the underlying application. These *if-then-else* rules are often invoked to check the way the search behavior is evolving, as well as to apply additional post-evaluation logic to the population.

❺ Create a New Population

Next to the evaluation of each chromosome's fitness, the techniques for breeding each succeeding generation of chromosomes are the most crucial component of a genetic algorithm. It is this phase that is intended to balance the dual and often conflicting objectives of increasing the average population fitness and increasing genetic diversity. Figure 9.24 outlines the step-by-step process of breeding a new generation from an old generation.

① The top *N* best (high-performance) chromosomes are retained. Some percentage of the chromosomes with the best fitness values is retained and moved to the next generation. These chromosomes will also form the core (but not complete) collection of chromosomes for the breeding (crossover) process that generates new child chromosomes.

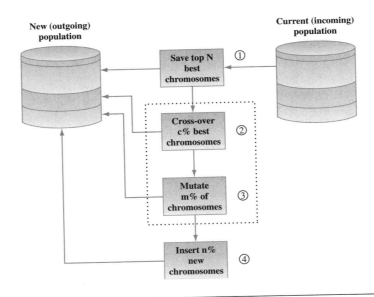

Figure 9.24   Breeding a new population of chromosomes.

② Of the fittest chromosomes, a percentage (*c%*) of these will become parents and generate one or more children in the new population. There are several stochastic-based techniques for selecting which pair of chromosomes will be mated, the most common being a form of roulette wheel that assigns a chromosome a chance of being selected based on its degree of fitness. These techniques are discussed in more detail later in this chapter.

③ After selecting the top-performing individuals and breeding new child chromosomes from the randomly chosen parents, a small number of chromosomes (*m%*) in the new population is subjected to mutation. Mutation increases genetic diversity by a process of selecting a random locus in the chromosome and changing its value to a random (but allowable) value.

④ Not a usual part of traditional genetic algorithms, inserting a small number (*n%*) of new chromosomes with randomly valued genomes can, along with mutation, increase genetic diversity in the population. Inserting new chromosomes often provides an effective form of simulated annealing when the mutation rate alone appears to be insufficient.

The idea behind breeding a new population is analogous to the evolution of fitter organisms in a biological population. Crossover (the equivalent of sexual reproduction) exchanges the genetic material of two parents and produces one or more offspring. If the genetics of the parents have a high degree of fitness, the crossover (or breeding) process is designed to produce children that also have genetics with an elevated degree of fitness, but due to the scrambling of the genomes their chromosomes will lie in a slightly different area of the solution terrain. Mutation, the equivalent of a fault in chromosome transcription during biological reproduction, is designed to introduce a small amount of genetic diversity in the population. Like biological mutation, some are advantageous and others are fatal (in terms of improving the fitness of the population). Although there is no direct biological counterpart to the insertion of new individuals into the population (aside from some ancient beliefs in spontaneous generation), one way of looking at the creation of new chromosomes is a localized form of complete genome mutation.

Strategies for Chromosome Selection

Which chromosomes in the current population do we select to become members of the next generation, to breed with another chromosome, or to have their existing genome changed through mutation? This is the process of selection. In many cases a different selection process is used for selecting the set of fittest individuals, for selecting parents for crossover, or for selecting chromosomes for mutation. Different selection techniques have differing access probabilities depending on how they are used in the genetic algorithm. We now turn to a discussion of several common techniques.

The Elitist Strategy

Using an elitist strategy, a percentage of the chromosomes with the best fitness function values are selected. Elitism is not only used to pick chromosomes for breeding but to directly copy chromosomes into the next generation. In many cases an elitist technique is used in combination with other selection methods to ensure that some of the strongest chromosomes always make it into successive generations. The elitist selection technique is implicit in the first step of the genetic algorithm mechanism shown in Figure 9.13.

Proportional Fitness

Using a proportional (or roulette wheel) fitness strategy, a wide spectrum of chromosomes with varying degrees of fitness are selected. The selection is biased toward chromosomes with best fitness values. Proportional fitness works in two steps: it first creates a conceptual roulette wheel weighted according to the best fitness function values, and then essentially spins the wheel and finds the chromosome that fits in the currently weighted slot. In a conventional approach to proportional selection, the ratio to of each unique fitness value and the sum of the total fitness values in the population is used to create the roulette wheel. For populations that contain repeating fitness functions, using a weighted frequency count of the fitness function provides a way of maintaining the same type of roulette wheel approach. Expression 9.15 shows how the wheel slice is calculated.

$$w = \frac{f_i}{\sum_{k=1}^{N} f_k} \tag{9.15}$$

Here,

   f_i is the fitness of the i-th chromosome
   f_k is the fitness of the k-th chromosome
   N is the number of chromosomes in the population

This expression works well for maximization functions because the larger the individual fitness value the larger its fraction of the sum of all fitness values and the larger its proportion of the wheel. For minimization functions, the magnitude of the numbers must be reversed. Expressions 9.16 and 9.17 show one possible way of reversing the magnitude of the fitness functions.

$$f^R = (f_{\max} - f_i) + 1 \tag{9.16}$$

$$w = \frac{f^R}{\sum_{k=1}^{N} f_k^R} \tag{9.17}$$

Here,

f^R is the reversed magnitude fitness function

f_i is the fitness of the i-th chromosome

$f_{\max}$ is the maximum fitness among all chromosomes in the population

f_k is the fitness of the k-th chromosome

N is the number of chromosomes in the population

Examining a small portion of the TSP population illustrates how the weighted roulette wheel is created from the fitness value. Because we are attempting to minimize the route through the five cities, the wedge expression from Expression 9.17 is used. Table 9.10 shows the fitness (path length) values for a set of city routes, their adjusted fitness values, and their proportion of the fitness roulette.

The ratio (w) derived from the total sum of adjusted fitness values in the population specifies the weighted slot in the underlying roulette wheel. Figure 9.25 shows this roulette wheel (not exactly to scale) proportioned according to the magnitude of the adjusted fitness values.

The actual proportional fitness algorithm is rather easy to understand and implement. Listing 9.1 shows the basic logic. This code computes a random fitness level (*max_fitness*) from the sum of the population's individual fitness values. The algorithm then loops through the population,

TABLE 9.10 The TSP fitness and fitness ratios

	Tour	Raw Fitness	Magnitude Adjusted	w
1	Able, Baker, Echo, Delta, Charlie	90	1	.007
2	Able, Echo, Charlie, Baker, Delta	34	57	.387
3	Able, Echo, Delta, Baker, Charlie	57	34	.232
4	Able, Baker, Charlie, Echo, Delta	59	32	.217
5	Able, Charlie, Echo, Delta, Baker	68	23	.156
	Sum	308	147	1.000

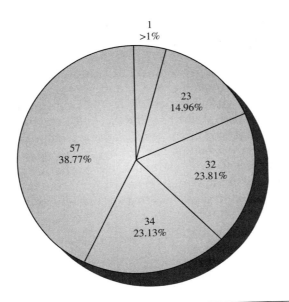

Figure 9.25   The proportional fitness roulette wheel.

```
Proportional Selection:
   For each chromosome (i)
         total_fitness = total_fitness + chromosome(i).fitness
   End for each

   max_fitness = total_fitness * random()
   cumm_fitness=0
   for each chromosome(i)
      cumm_fitness = cum_fitness + chromosome(i).fitness
      If chromosome(i).fitness > max_fitness
         Then select(chromosome(i))
   end for each
```

Listing 9.1   The proportional fitness approach.

summing each chromosome's fitness (into *cumm_fitness*). When the algorithm encounters a chromosome with a fitness greater than or equal to the *max_fitness* value, that chromosome is selected. Note that it is important that the population not be sorted by fitness. Otherwise, the selection process is significantly biased (and will simply function as a slightly more complicated form of elitism).

Proportional fitness selection suffers from two general problems. This first has already been directly encountered: it is difficult to use on minimization problems. Often, the fitness function for minimization must be converted to a maximization function. Although to some degree this solves the selection problem, it introduces semantic confusion into the problem (the best chromosome in the TSP problem, for instance, will continually be assigned a fitness value that is the maximum of all other fitness functions, and thus we are seeking the minimum tour but the fitness maximizes the fitness value). The second problem is directly related to how the roulette wheel is constructed. The proportional fitness selection will fail (it will drive the population to early convergence) if some of the chromosomes have fitness values that are very much larger than all other fitness values.

Ranking

Using a linear ranking strategy, an ordered population of chromosomes is assigned fitness values based on their position or rank within the population. There are many mathematical means of converting a rank into a relative or subjective fitness.

$$f_i = \frac{(N - r) \times \left(f_{\max}^u - f_{\min}^u\right)}{N - 1} + f_{\min}^u \tag{9.18}$$

Here,

N is the number of chromosomes in the population (the population count, obviously, must be greater than 1).

r is the current rank of the chromosome. In most cases (but not necessarily all) for the i-th chromosome $r = i$.

f_i is the fitness assigned to the i-th chromosome.

$f_{\max}^u$ is the maximum user fitness that should be assigned to the best-performing individual.

$f_{\min}^u$ is the minimum user fitness that should be assigned to the worst-performing individual.

The ranking strategy prevents extremely fit individuals from dominating the population during the early generations of the search process. Thus, the ranking technique can be very effective in maintaining diversity and inhibiting convergence. The outcome of ranking can be used with an elitist selection or with other selection approaches (such as proportional fitness). One constraint on the use of ranking is the requirement that the population be reordered and reranked for each generation.

Tournament

Generally used for large diverse populations, this approach is somewhat akin to the divide-and-conquer strategy in search and sorting. In a tournament selection, a set of k chromosomes is selected randomly from the population (where $k = 2$ is the usual size). From the set of k chromosomes the individual with the best fitness is selected. For example, using the TSP chromosomes in Table 9.10, the tournament strategy could select genomes 2 (Able, Echo, Charlie, Baker, Delta) and 4 (Able, Baker, Charlie, Echo, Delta). Chromosome 2 would be selected over 4 because 2 has a better raw fitness function (34 miles instead of 59 miles). This process of selecting a group and picking the best (fittest) chromosome is continued as long as a selection process is needed.

Tournament differs from proportional fitness because it is indifferent to the relative frequency or range of fitness values. It is only sensitive to the fitness ranking within the population. Because it is essentially probing the population in blocks of k chromosomes (with replacement, so that chromosomes may participate in multiple tournaments), the tournament approach can select a wider spectrum of chromosomes with varying degrees of fitness.

Random

Using a random strategy, a random chromosome in the population is selected. Random selection is used to pick chromosomes for breeding and to directly copy chromosomes into the next generation. In hybrid algorithms, a random strategy is used in combination with other selection methods to ensure that a mix of chromosomes with a wide spectrum of fitness values always makes it into successive generations.

Selection strategies are malleable; that is, a genetic algorithm can switch from one strategy to the next during the search. An example is using an elitist strategy for a few generations to quickly increase the average fitness and then switching to proportional fitness to ensure some continued measure of fitness diversity in the population. In the next section we will discuss the actual process of breeding new chromosomes. The breeding mechanism is tightly coupled to the selection strategy.

Conventional Crossover (Breeding) Techniques

A genetic algorithm derives its name from the way in which potential solutions are developed. They are bred from existing solutions using a process with analogies to sexual reproduction in biological organisms. The process of mating and reproduction in a genetic algorithm is called crossover.

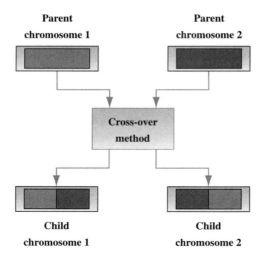

Figure 9.26 Mating and breeding of chromosomes.

This name follows from the way in which genetic material is exchanged. Pieces of the genetic material from two parents are exchanged by extracting a set of loci from one parent and a set of loci from another parent and appending or inserting them in the corresponding position in each other's genome. Thus, they move in an X pattern as the genome segments cross over each other. Figure 9.26 illustrates the way two chromosomes mate and breed two offspring.

Like biological reproduction, reproduction in genetic algorithms is intended to create better chromosomes from already highly performing parents while at the same time adding genetic diversity to the gene pool (the population of chromosomes in the current generation). Philosophically, a genetic algorithm is a directed eugenics program designed to breed better and better individuals. This section examines the principal methods of crossover and explains how they work in the search algorithm's breeding program. As discussed in the section on genome design (see "Genome Structural Design"), conventional crossover cannot be used for the TSP. Breeding and mutation techniques for the TSP and similar connectionist problems are discussed in the section "Advanced Crossover and Mutation Techniques."

A Crew Scheduling Cost Model

To illustrate crossover (and mutation, in the next section), we will explore a small and quite simple cost modeling system for crew-to-job assignments.

TABLE 9.11   Job ID and Duration and Crew ID and Rate

Job ID	Duration		Crew ID	Rate
J1	6		C1	10
J2	5		C2	15
J3	9		C3	20
J4	8			
J5	3			

The model contains two tables: an $N \times M$ matrix of jobs and their duration times and an $N \times M$ matrix of crews and their daily charge rates. Table 9.11 shows the job and crew schedules.

This is a cost minimization problem. We want to assign the crews to the jobs in order to find the minimum cost schedule. There are fewer crews than jobs, and thus some crews will be assigned to multiple jobs. The total cost for a schedule is shown in Expression 9.19 (which is also the fitness function).

$$f = \sum_{i=1}^{K} d(i) \times r(c(i)) \qquad (9.19)$$

Here,

K is the number of jobs. In this case, there are five jobs.
f is the total cost of the job assignments and is the fitness assigned to the i-th job-to-crew chromosome.
$d()$ is duration of the i-th job (chromosome locus).
$r()$ is the rate of the crew assigned to the i-th job.
$c()$ is the crew found in the i-th genome locus.

Because the number of jobs is static, the genome representation can be very straightforward: five locus sites. Each locus contains the crew assigned to the job (that is, it contains the index to Table 9.11, the crew table). Figure 9.27 is a schematic of the job-to-crew costing chromosome.

The genetic search mechanism generates a population of candidate cost plans by assigning crews randomly to the five jobs. Our only constraint is that every crew must be used at least once. Table 9.12 shows a small part of the initial population.

This small job-cost planning model now provides the background needed to explore the various types of conventional crossover techniques. These techniques are used to breed new cost models based on the genetic

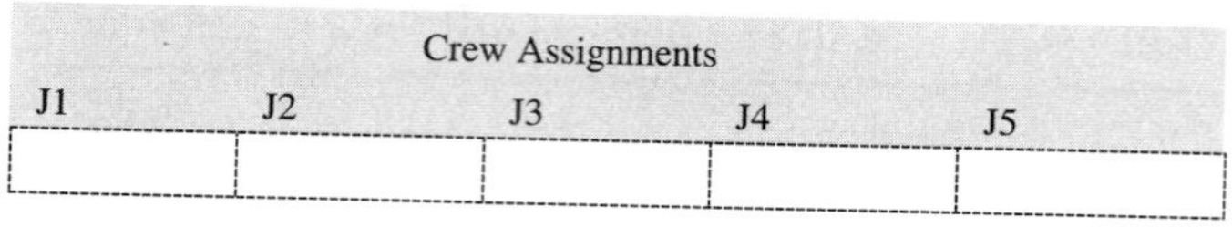

Crew Assignments				
J1	J2	J3	J4	J5

Figure 9.27 The job-to-crew assignment genome.

TABLE 9.12 Initial Population of Job Cost Genomes

	Jobs with Crew Assignment				
	J1	J2	J3	J4	J5
1	C1	C3	C3	C2	C3
2	C2	C3	C1	C1	C1
3	C2	C1	C2	C3	C3
4	C3	C1	C2	C2	C1
5	C2	C2	C2	C1	C3
6	C3	C2	C2	C1	C3

material in parents (ultimately chosen through one of the selection strategies). The next section explores the single-point crossover in some detail. The remaining crossover patterns are extensions of this basic concept.

Single-point Crossover

In single-point crossover a single point along the genome is selected. Two parent chromosomes are selected from the population. A crossover point is chosen at random. The genome segments to the right (or left) of the point are swapped, creating two new chromosomes (the children). Figure 9.28 schematically illustrates the crossover process that produces new children from the genetic material of the parents. The single-point crossover is immediately after the second locus in the chromosome.

In this example, the children inherit the first two loci from the parents. Child 1 inherits the right-hand genetic material from parent 2, whereas child 2 inherits the right-hand genetic material from parent 1. The children are usually inserted into the new population, displacing either the parents or two chromosomes whose fitness values are less than the parents' fitness value. Table 9.13 shows the small job assignment population with each chromosome's fitness (cost) and the average population fitness.

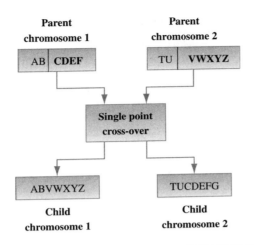

Figure 9.28 The single-point crossover process.

TABLE 9.13 Job Cost Genomes with Fitness Values (Costs)

	Jobs with Crew Assignments					Cost
	J1	J2	J3	J4	J5	
1	C1	C3	C3	C2	C3	520.00
2	C2	C3	C1	C1	C1	318.00
3	C2	C1	C2	C3	C3	495.00
4	C3	C1	C2	C2	C1	455.00
5	C2	C2	C2	C1	C3	440.00
6	C3	C2	C2	C1	C3	470.00
					Average Fitness	449.66

Through some selection process, individuals 2 and 4 are chosen as parents. The single-point crossover is at the second locus (at job *J2*). As Table 9.14 shows, the crossover generates two new chromosomes (c_1 and c_2). Both have fitness values less than the maximum fitness of the two parents. Even without removing two lower-performing chromosomes, this average population is improved (a change of 16.91).

If the genetic algorithm maintains a steady population size (as is conventional in most but not all situations), the two new children replace poorer-performing genomes. In this case, chromosomes 1 and 4 are

TABLE 9.14 Job Cost Genomes with Fitness Values (Costs)

| | Jobs with Crew Assignments | | | | | |
	J1	J2	J3	J4	J5	Cost
1	C1	C3	C3	C2	C3	520.00
2	**C2**	**C3**	**C1**	**C1**	**C1**	**318.00**
3	C2	C1	C2	C3	C3	495.00
4	**C3**	**C1**	**C2**	**C2**	**C1**	**455.00**
c_1	**C2**	**C3**	**C2**	**C2**	**C1**	**370.00**
c_2	**C3**	**C1**	**C1**	**C1**	**C1**	**394.00**
5	C2	C2	C2	C1	C3	440.00
6	C3	C2	C2	C1	C3	470.00
					Average Fitness	**432.75**

TABLE 9.15 Job Cost Genomes with Fitness Values (Costs)

| | Jobs with Crew Assignments | | | | | |
	J1	J2	J3	J4	J5	Cost
1	C2	C3	C2	C2	C1	370.00
2	C2	C3	C1	C1	C1	318.00
3	C3	C1	C1	C1	C1	394.00
4	C3	C1	C2	C2	C1	455.00
5	C2	C2	C2	C1	C3	440.00
6	C3	C2	C2	C1	C3	470.00
					Average Fitness	**407.83**

removed and the new children take their place. Table 9.15 shows both the new population with the children of 2 and 4 and the significant increase in the average population fitness.

Not every crossover will improve the fitness of the population. In fact, in addition to the goal of finding better and better chromosomes, breeding has the goal of increasing genetic diversity in the population. Only through genetic diversity can a genetic algorithm economically and effectively explore a sufficient portion of the solution terrain. The other forms of crossover provide different approaches to breeding new offspring. Each technique has its own place in attempts to gain better (fitter) individuals.

Double-point Crossover

In double-point crossover two points along the genome are selected at random. The genome segment to the left of the rightmost point is swapped with the genome to the right of the leftmost point, creating two new children. Figure 9.29 schematically illustrates the crossover process that produces new children from the genetic material of the parents. The crossover points are immediately after the second locus and immediately before the last locus in the chromosome.

In terms of exchanging genetic material and how it is used, the double-point process is almost exactly like the single-point: the children inherit the loci to the right of the rightmost point and to the left of the leftmost point. The genetic material to be swapped is bounded by the two random point values. Child 1 inherits bounded genetic material from parent 2, whereas child 2 inherits the bounded genetic material from parent 1. The advantage of the double-point crossover is its inherent ability to introduce a higher degree of variability (randomness) into the selection of genetic material.

Uniform Crossover

Uniform crossover works at the individual locus level rather than with segments of the genome. Loci positions are picked at random from the genomes and exchanged. Figure 9.30 schematically illustrates the

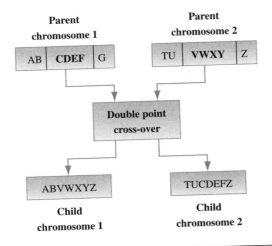

Figure 9.29 The double-point crossover process.

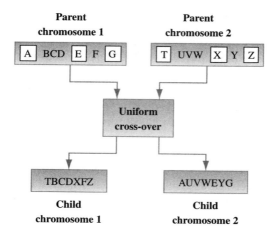

Figure 9.30 The uniform crossover process.

crossover process that produces new children from the genetic material of parents.

The probability of selecting a locus for exchange, called the *mixing rate*, can be very low or very high. A mixing rate of .5, for example, means that any locus in the genome has a 50% chance of being selected for exchange. The mixing rate acts like a variable rheostat, increasing or decreasing the probability that the *n*-th locus on the genome in parent 1 will exchange its value with the *n*-th locus on the genome in parent 2. Although uniform crossover has the advantage of precisely controlling the amount of genetic variability in the population, it also has two significant disadvantages. First, because the crossover is done at the individual gene (locus) level rather with sets or patterns of genes, behavior that evolves as patterns in the population will not normally be preserved. Second, if the mix rate is too high, too much genetic diversity (that is, noise) emerges in each successive population and the search mechanism cannot find an accurate solution. On the other hand, if the mix rate is too low not enough genetic diversity will emerge and the search mechanism cannot efficiently spread over the solution terrain.

Weighted (Arithmetic) Crossover

Weighted (or arithmetic) crossover is unlike the other crossover operations. Weighted crossover modifies rather than exchanges genetic material and works at the complete genome level rather than with segments of the genome. The crossover appears in the way a weighting factor is used. A weighting factor (w) in the range *[0,1]* is selected before each crossover. Loci are picked at random from the genomes and exchanged. Expression 9.20 is the crossover process that produces new children from the genetic material of the parents.

$$c_1 = (w \times p_1) + ((1 - w) \times p_2)$$
$$c_2 = ((1 - w) \times p_1) + (w \times p_2)$$

(9.20)

Here,

c_1 is child 1 from the crossover operation
c_2 is child 2 from the crossover operation
p_1 is the first selected parent
p_2 is the second selected parent
w is the weighing factor in the range *[0,1]*

The weight values act like scaling factors over the range of the chromosome. The values are rescaled (from $0 \ldots n$, where n is the value of the genome at that locus). Table 9.16 illustrates the creation of child c_1 from two parents when the scaling weight is .4 (see Table 9.13 for the underlying chromosomes).

Arithmetic scaling mathematically distorts the genome values in a predictable manner, but it does not rely on the mixing of genetic materials. From the author's experience in production models, weighted crossover (unless the weight is carefully adjusted) tends to produce lower average population fitness than the single- or double-point crossover. Table 9.17 (based on the data in Table 9.13) shows the result of applying weighted crossover to individuals *(2,4)*.

In this instance, the average fitness of the population is reduced by the crossover. Naturally, the same decrease in fitness can result from any of the other crossover techniques. This example simply illustrates that different crossover methods yield different fitness values (as you would

TABLE 9.16   Creating Child c_1 from Parents *(2,4)*, where $w = (.4)$

	J1	J2	J3	J4	J5
P_1	90.00	100.00	90.00	80.00	30.00
P_2	120.00	50.00	135.00	120.00	30.00
P_1*w	36.00	40.00	36.00	48.00	12.00
$P_2*(1-w)$	72.00	30.00	81.00	72.00	18.00
Total	**108.00**	**70.00**	**117.00**	**120.00**	**30.00**

TABLE 9.17 Job Cost Genomes with Fitness Values (Costs)

| | Jobs with Crew Assignments | | | | | |
	J1	J2	J3	J4	J5	Cost
1	C1	C3	C3	C2	C3	520.00
2	90.00	100.00	90.00	80.00	30.00	318.00
3	C2	C1	C2	C3	C3	495.00
4	120.00	50.00	135.00	120.00	30.00	455.00
c_1	108.00	70.00	117.00	120.00	30.00	445.00
c_2	173.60	80.00	75.60	76.60	30.00	435.80
5	C2	C2	C2	C1	C3	440.00
6	C3	C2	C2	C1	C3	470.00
					Average Fitness	**596.46**

expect) and, in this case, the single-point crossover for these two parents results in a better set of offspring.

Analytical Crossover

The analytical crossover method is a final crossover technique that like the weighted approach works at the complete chromosome level. This technique is somewhat iterative, and like tournament selection considers the best and worst fitness of two selected parents.

$$c_1 = p_b + s \times (p_b - p_w)$$
$$c_2 = p_b \tag{9.21}$$

Here,

c_1 is child 1 from the crossover operation
c_2 is child 2 from the crossover operation
p_b is the parent with the best fitness
p_w is the parent with the worst fitness
s is a scaling factor in the range [0,1]

The scaling factor is a random number that changes the range of the difference between each of the parent genome sites. This can sometimes lead to infeasible solutions because the scaled value is unallowable. As a consequence, analytical crossover generally has a search parameter, k, that attempts to find a new value of s that will produce a feasible solution. After the number of searches exceeds k, $s = 0$, so that the best-fit parent is also returned as the first child. Other modifications to this technique are also implemented, such as searching through the population for acceptable parents instead of changing the scaling factor.

Breeding techniques create new chromosomes in the population. By breeding individuals with a high fitness ranking the genetic search process hopes to introduce new individuals that are slightly superior to some other chromosomes in the population. These fitter chromosomes, over generations, place selective pressure on the population and slowly replace less fit individuals. Breeding alone, however, is insufficient in many cases. genetic algorithms can become locked in a local region of the solution space due to a general lack of diversity in the current gene pool. The next section takes up issues and techniques related to one of the conventional methods for recovering genetic diversity.

Conventional Mutation (Diversity) Techniques

Genetic algorithms are very sensitive to genetic diversity. In some cases, the diversity introduced by crossover breeding is insufficient to explore the underlying solution space. The population becomes confined to a small region of the solution space. Breeding simply moves the search around and around this region. Figure 9.31 illustrates this problem. Each point represents the average fitness of the entire population.

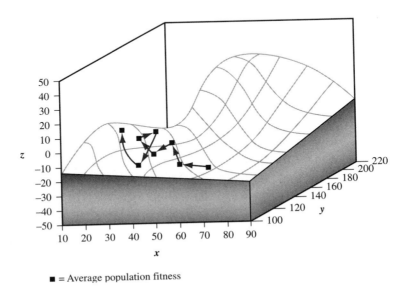

■ = Average population fitness

Figure 9.31   A population without sufficient genetic diversity.

In this figure, the genetic algorithm is wandering around a small region of the potential solution space. Any combination of the current genetic material is insufficient to produce individuals that move outside this region. To solve this problem, genetic algorithms use the concept of mutation. Mutation, as the name implies, randomly changes the value of a genome locus. Through mutation, genetic diversity can be maintained or reintroduced into the population. Figure 9.32 illustrates the locked population in Figure 9.31 with a few mutations in one of the generations.

Mutation operators must be applied carefully and sparingly to the population. Too much mutation and the genome loses its ability to retain any pattern, and although the population may be scattered over a wide region of the solution terrain the search mechanism has no way of improving its performance. Only a very small number of individuals should be subject to mutation during a generation. In many genetic algorithms, a parameter of the search system itself determines whether or not a mutation is applied to any chromosomes during the current generation. In this section, the various types of conventional mutation operators are discussed. With the exception of the binary inversion technique, these mutation operators are designed to work on integer and real-number genomes. A knowledge of

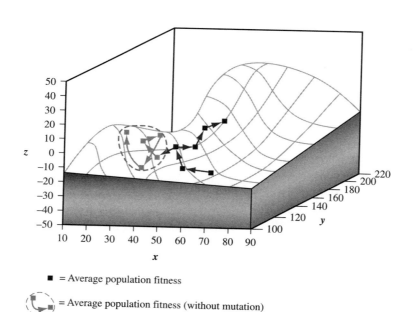

■ = Average population fitness

= Average population fitness (without mutation)

Figure 9.32 Genetic diversity through mutation.

the loci allowed range of values is necessary for each operator that works on numbers instead of bit strings.

Binary (Bit) Inversion

For genomes represented by binary (bit) strings, the inversion operator simply flips the value of a randomly chosen bit. A 1-bit becomes zero, and a 0-bit becomes one. Due to the nature of binary chromosomes, this is the primary and often principal mutation operator used in classical (binary-represented) genetic algorithms.

Uniform Replacement

Uniform mutation replaces a randomly selected gene (locus) with a value chosen from a uniform random distribution between the upper and lower domain bounds for the gene. This is the most frequently used mutation operator because it requires only the range of allowed values for the gene.

Distribution-based Replacement

Instead of a value uniformly drawn from the domain of the gene, this operator updates the gene position with a statistical value drawn from some probability distribution. Normally, a Gaussian distribution is used (and the value is truncated or regenerated if it lies outside the allowable range for the gene). However, a binomial (Poisson or other type) of distribution can also be used.

Central-and-Limits Replacement

The central-and-limits mutation replaces the gene value with one of three randomly chosen values: the upper boundary value from the gene's domain, the lower boundary value from the gene's domain, or the value from the center of the domain *(upper-lower)/2)*. Generally, the mutation operator has differing probabilities for each assignment: a high probability for boundary values and a smaller probability for the center of distribution value. The central-and-limits mutation operator often provides a way of introducing a significant amount of genetic diversity into the population and is useful in the early stages of evolution. The sharp three-step process of assigning the minimum, maximum, or middle domain values "shakes" the genome in a way similar to simulated annealing.

Nonuniform Decay

The nonuniform decay operator is designed to slowly reduce genetic diversity caused by mutation as the number of generations increases. The operation begins to drive the probability of a mutation toward zero as the number of generations increases. Expression 9.22 shows one possible representation for the decay mutation operator.

$$p_m = p_m \times \min\left(\frac{l}{g^c}, 1\right) \tag{9.22}$$

Here,

p_m is the current probability that a gene will mutate.

l is the switchover limit. When $l = 1$, the decay begins right after the first generation. When $l > 1$, the mutation probability stays at its initial value until $g^c = l$, after which time it begins to fall.

g^c is the current generation count $(1, 2, 3, \ldots, n)$.

The nonuniform decay operator keeps genetic diversity relatively high during the early generations of the search but slowly eliminates mutation as the search mechanism begins to evolve toward the target solution. In many cases, a form of decay mutation is switched on by the search mechanism if it determines that convergence is being inhibited (possibly by too much mutation).

Advanced Crossover and Mutation Techniques

Breeding approaches that use the conventional crossover and mutation methods discussed in the previous section will not work for a large family of problems involving structural, time, and flow dependencies between genes. Typical examples include the following.

- Resource-constrained project, crew, and machine (job shop) scheduling
- Packing and containerization problems in logistics
- Transportation route scheduling (such as the TSP family of problems)
- Configuration planning

These problems are encountered frequently in the real worlds of business, industry, and government. They all share a common property: the sequence of genome values represents a collection of discrete objects that

TABLE 9.18   Invalid Conventional Crossover for the TSP

	City Tour				
P_1	Charlie	Baker	Charlie	Able	Echo
P_2	Baker	Able	Echo	Delta	Charlie
c_1	Charlie	Baker	Echo	Delta	Charlie
c_2	Baker	Able	Charlie	Able	Echo

are being arranged in a particular order. It is the attributes of the objects that determine the goodness of fit, not the value of the object itself. For example, returning to the TSP, consider the single-point crossover operation (at the second locus) shown in Table 9.18.

The crossover operators generate tours with duplicate cities (Charlie in child 1 and Able in child 2). Conventional mutation operators also generate duplicate tours (because a tour includes all cities, mutating any of the five cities to another city will automatically create a duplicate city in the tour). To address these problems, a large number of alternate crossover and mutation techniques have been developed. This section discusses a few of the more common and easy-to-implement methods, addressing crossover issues first and then mutation techniques.

Greedy Crossover

The greedy crossover approach (also called the nearest-neighbor crossover) was first formalized by Grefenstette in 1985 (see "Further Reading"). The algorithm assembles offspring tours in a small but effective number of steps.

Let t be the current tour
Let c_i be the current city

Select one parent as the base
The first city in the parent is chosen as the starting node.
    This is the current city (c_i)
    t = c_i
Repeat:
    Examine the connecting edges leaving c_i in both parents.
    Make a list of all cities on the connecting edges
    Remove any cities already in the tour

If the list is empty exit repeat
The edge with the shorter duration is used as the next city in the tour.
Set this next city as c_i
  t = append(c_i)
End repeat
For each unused city (c_u)
  t = append(c_u)
End for each
child = t

The idea of crossover occurs as the algorithm searches for the next segment in a tour by comparing the length of the next edge in the tour. The algorithm is repeated for each parent to produce two children. In this section we examine, for compactness, the generation of one child from the two candidate parents. Figure 9.33 shows the two tours defined by the distance measurements in Table 9.4. The numbers on the edges are the distances between the connected cities.

Using these two tours, the greedy crossover works in the following steps to produce one of two possible children.

1. Select a parent as the base. In this example, we choose the second parent. This starts the template for constructing a child. The template now appears as follows.

Baker	?	?	?	?

2. Find the edges in both parents from Baker to the next city. These are *(Baker,Able)* in parent 2 and *(Baker,Charlie)* in parent 1. Choose the edge that has the shortest distance. This edge becomes the next segment in the tour. The shortest edge is *(Baker,Charlie)* in parent 2, with a length of 8 miles. The template now appears as follows.

Baker	Charlie	?	?	?

3. Find the edges in both parents from Charlie to the next city. These are *(Charlie,Echo)* in parent 2 and *(Charlie,Able)* in parent 1. The shortest edge is *(Charlie,Echo)* in parent 2, with a length of 13 miles. This becomes the next edge and the template now appears as follows.

Baker	Charlie	Echo	?	?

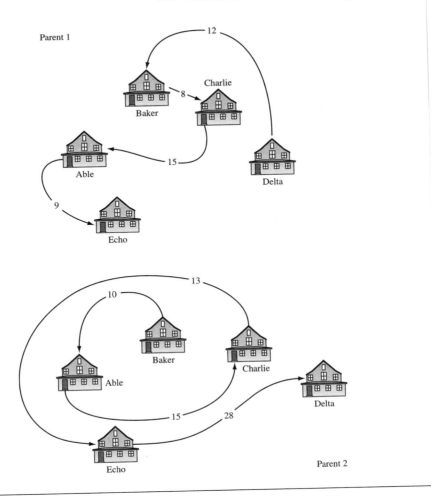

Parent 1

Figure 9.33 Two five-city tours.

4. Find the edges in both parents from Echo out to the next city. These are *(Echo,Delta)* and *(Echo,<terminate>)*. Thus, *Delta* is selected as the next city node, as follows.

Baker	Charlie	Echo	Delta	?

5. Find the edges in both parents from *Delta* out to the next city. These are *(Delta,Baker)* in parent 1 and *(Delta,<terminate>)* in parent 2. *Baker* has already been used in the tour and is removed from the candidate list. *Delta* is a terminal city in the parent 2 tour

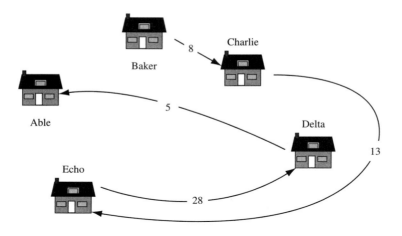

Figure 9.34   The child tour from greedy crossover.

and is removed. We now complete the tour by adding *Able*, the only unused city, as follows.

Baker	Charlie	Echo	Delta	Able

Figure 9.34 shows the tour created by the greedy crossover, using parent 2 as the starting point (the template basis).

The greedy algorithm has created a valid tour with a length of 54 miles (8 + 13 + 28 + 5). This is about midway between the lengths of the incoming parents, which have tour length of 44 and 66, respectively. A second child is created by selecting the remaining parent (parent 1) as the base and reapplying the algorithm.

The greedy (or nearest-neighbor) crossover approach produces feasible offspring tours with a minimum of exception processing. This is a byproduct of its reliance on graph theory to drive the generation of a tour based on edges. To complete this section on advanced crossover techniques, we examine two methods that are modeled after the conventional single-point crossover. Both of these generate infeasible solutions and must employ exception handling to compensate for duplicate and missing cities.

City Pivot Crossover

The city pivot approach selects a city in the tour at random. This city becomes the crossover point in the same manner as conventional

TABLE 9.19 City Pivot Crossover on *Baker*

	City Tour				
P_1	Delta	**Baker**	Charlie	Echo	Able
P_2	Able	Echo	Delta	**Baker**	Charlie
c_1	Delta	Baker	Able	Echo	Charlie

single-point crossover except that (1) the crossover position is not the same for both chromosomes but is relative to the location of the city in each tour and (2) a compression technique must be used to ensure that duplicate cities do not appear in the offspring chromosomes. Table 9.19 illustrates how a child chromosome is produced from the city pivot crossover when *Baker* is selected as the crossover city.

In the crossover at *Baker*, we have two tour segments sliced by *Baker*: *(Delta, Baker)* in parent 1 and *(Able,Echo,Delta)* in parent 2. *Delta* is a duplicate and is removed from the second segment. When they are spliced together, the offspring *(Delta,Baker, Able,Echo,Charlie)* form a valid tour.

Position Pivot Crossover

The position pivot crossover approach, shown in Table 9.20, is very similar to the conventional single-point crossover discussed previously. In this method, a crossover position is selected at random along the length of the tour. The child chromosome consists of the tour in parent 1 on the left and parent 2 on the right. However, this crossover approach must also ensure that (1) any duplicate cities (those that appear, for instance, to the left of the crossover point) are not included in the final tour and (2) any missing cities (those that for example appear to the left of the crossover but are not included in the left-hand chromosome) are included in the final chromosome.

TABLE 9.20 Position Pivot Crossover on Locus 2

	City Tour				
P_1	Delta	Baker	Charlie	Echo	Able
P_2	Able	Echo	Delta	Baker	Charlie
c_1	Delta	Baker	Able	Baker	Charlie

In the crossover at locus 2, we have two tour segments: *(Charlie, Echo, Able)* in parent 1 and *(Delta, Baker, Charlie)* in parent 2. *Delta* is a duplicate and is removed from the second segment. *Able* is missing from the offspring when the left-hand set of *p1 (Delta, Baker)* is crossed with the right-hand side of *p2 (Delta, Baker, Charlie)*. We now delete *Delta* and push *Able* onto the tour. When they are spliced together, the offspring *(Delta, Baker, Able, Baker, Charlie)* form a valid tour.

In the next section the various types of genome mutations are discussed. For chromosomes in which relationships are defined as connected edges, these mutation operators change the chromosome structure instead of changing the value of a single gene.

Random Swap Mutation

In random swap, two loci (chosen at random) have their values swapped. As illustrated in Table 9.21, this results in a valid tour.

Move-and-Insert Gene Mutation

Using move-and-insert, a genome locus (chosen at random) is moved before or after another randomly chosen locus in the genome. Table 9.22 shows the offspring when *Baker* is selected as an insert before a point and *Echo* is selected as the city node to move.

TABLE 9.21   The Random Swap Mutation

	City Tour				
p₁ (before)	Delta	**Baker**	Charlie	Echo	**Able**
p₁ (after)	Delta	Able	Charlie	Echo	Baker

TABLE 9.22   The Move-and-Insert Gene Mutation

	City Tour				
p₁ (before)	Delta	**Baker**	Charlie	**Echo**	Able
p₁ (after)	Delta	Echo	Baker	Charlie	Able

TABLE 9.23 The Move-and-insert Gene Mutation

City Tour					
p₁ (before)	Delta	**Baker**	**Charlie**	**Echo**	**Able**
p₁ (after)	Delta	Charlie	Echo	Able	Baker

TABLE 9.24 The Order Reversal Mutation

City Tour					
p₁ (before)	Delta	**Baker**	**Charlie**	**Echo**	Able
p₁ (after)	Delta	Echo	Charlie	Baker	Able

Move-and-Insert Sequence Mutation

Sequence mutation is very similar to the gene move-and-insert but instead of a single locus a sequence of loci are moved and inserted. Table 9.23 shows the offspring when *Baker* is selected as an insert before a point and the gene sequence *(Charlie, Echo, Able)* is selected as the set of nodes to move.

Order Reversal Mutation

With order reversal, a series of the genome loci (chosen at random) have their values reversed. As illustrated in Table 9.24, this results in a valid tour. Although treated here as important mechanisms for modifying the organization of a schedule, configuration, or route, they can also be used with conventional genetic algorithms (with varying degrees of effect on the population diversity).

9.4 Practical Issues in Using a Genetic Algorithm

To use a genetic algorithm you must generally have the ability to perform the following.

■ Generate possible solutions to a problem
■ Set the properties of the genetic algorithm so that it can converge on a solution

- Measure the goodness of those solutions in terms of the outcome from the underlying model

- Change the system if the solutions are not very good

The practical issues confronted with analysts in using a genetic algorithm usually fall within two areas: properly setting the population, breeding, and mutation properties of the genetic algorithm and finding ways to model large, highly complex systems without executing the real-world model itself. In the next section we address the last two of these issues.

Execution Times for Real-world Systems

In many cases, the execution time is fairly straightforward; that is, the fitness function and the system that processes the potential solution are essentially the same. Finding the maximum value for a function, the shortest circuit through a set of cities, the least cost to assemble a piece of equipment, or the maximum carrying capacity of a road system are straightforward applications of mathematical models. That is, a genetic algorithm does not need to depend on dispatching a fleet of vehicles to follow a potential tour and then actually clocking their time between cities spread over several states to find the shortest route. A road atlas and a table of inter-city distances from the atlas are sufficient to build a credible and accurate TSP model. On the other hand, this disconnect between physical reality and the genetic model does not always exist. In such cases, a genetic algorithm may be difficult or impossible to use. This brings us to a set of issues associated with applying genetic algorithms to complex, large-scale, real-world models.

This disconnect is not universal. Some genetic algorithms are attached to complex business, industrial, and government policy models. In these cases, running one generation of 50 chromosomes could take anywhere from several hours to several days. For example, suppose we want a genetic algorithm to optimize (that is, minimize) point-of-sales transaction throughput time in a commercial relational database. Unless we have a reliable mathematical model of how the database performs under specific loads with a specific set of configuration parameters, the genetic algorithm must run its evaluation against a working relational database. Our genetic algorithm can generate configuration parameters for the relational database, feed in a very large collection of transactions, and measure the throughput time. The same set of transactions is used over and over to measure the change in processing and total throughput times. Some combination of virtual-memory-swap area size, disk space, table page size, transaction (or job) queue length, number of page buffers, and column indexing will produce the best database configuration. However, the time to reconfigure a dedicated relational database with a new page size, buffer count, and different column indexing could take anywhere from four to five minutes. Processing all transactions (say a mix of 150,000 query and update transactions, with a reasonable amount of noise such as bad SKU numbers, invalid quantities, out of stock responses, and so on) might take an additional three minutes. Thus, Expression 9.23 is the time per chromosome.

$$c_t = t_t + t_r + t_p \tag{9.23}$$

Here,

c_t is the current chromosome evaluation elapse time
t_t is the tear-down and setup time for each evaluation
t_r is the runtime to evaluate the chromosome
t_p is the inter-generation processing time

As a result, the total time to optimize the database, shown in Expression 9.24, is the sum of the individual chromosome evaluation times the number of chromosomes in the population times the total number of generations used to evolve the solution.

$$E_t \approx N \times \sum_{i=1}^{P} (c_t)_i \tag{9.24}$$

Here,

E_t is the total evolution elapse time
N is the total number of generations
P is the number of chromosomes in the population
g_t is generation elapse time (see previous expression)
t_r is the runtime
t_p is the inter-generation processing time

When c_t is eight (8) minutes, then for 50 chromosomes a database-tuning generation will take 400 minutes or 6.6 hours (a bit less than a full work day of processing). For 20 generations, the total optimization time is 132 hours (or 5.5 full days). This time frame is not the norm, but it can be typical for many real-world applications that involve large-scale complex systems.

Setting Process Parameters

Translating the concepts of a genetic algorithm into a working engine involves not only designing ways to represent the basic data structures but ways of setting the principal properties or parameters of the genetic algorithm. Most commercial or off-the-shelf genetic algorithms provide default values for these parameters, but a brief review of the typical values for each major parameter also provides a check list for the control properties necessary in a genetic algorithm.

Population Size

The initial number of chromosomes in the population depends on the number of variables in the search. For a "typical" problem of moderate complexity, a population of 50 chromosomes is often a good starting point. In many genetic algorithms the population size remains the same from generation to generation. In others, the population size can expand or contract depending on the degree of genetic diversity, the rate of convergence, or other factors in the search process.

Population Generation

There are generally two types of population management techniques in a genetic algorithm. In the steady-state model, a single population is constantly updated. In the dynamic-state model, a new population is created form the old population of each generation. As a general guideline, dynamic populations are often easier to maintain and usually provide a higher intrinsic degree of diversity.

Maximum Number of Generations

One of the primary termination conditions is a limitation on the maximum number of generations. The default value for this parameter is difficult to set independently of the number of variables and the number of objective functions. However, a default of 2.5 times the population size is often a good maximum generation count estimate.

Type of Crossover

The type of crossover used in breeding depends on the nature of the chromosome; that is, whether it is a binary or real number representation, the length of the chromosome, the possible number of states that can exist, and the amount of genetic diversity needed in the search model. A relatively good choice is double-point crossover during the early generations of the model, converting to single-point crossover in later generations. For scheduling, configuration, and other dependency problems, the greedy (or nearest-neighbor) algorithm is almost always the best choice.

Type of Mutation

The type of permissible mutation depends on the genome representation. The bit inversion technique is used for binary chromosomes, whereas a wider range of mutation options is available for real-number representations. For real numbers the uniform replacement is an excellent default mutation type (and for scheduling and network or dependency problems, random swap is a good default mutation technique).

Retention Rate

The retention rate is a percentage of the population and determines how many of the top-performing chromosomes in a ranked (sorted) population will be selected and copied into the next generation (or for steady-state modes which will remain in the existing population). A default value of 10 to 15% is a good estimate.

Breeding Rate

Whether or not a chromosome is selected for breeding (crossover) is often determined by a probability tied to its fitness relative to all other fit chromosomes in the population (this is the case with proportional fitness). In many cases, however, the algorithm selects the first $2n + 1$ chromosomes in the population and breeds these (subject to the crossover rate) in order to create the next generation of offspring. The quantity n is tied to the breeding rate, which is expressed as a percentage of the population.

Crossover Rate

The crossover rate is a probability that a chromosome will be selected for breeding. This is used when the search algorithm uses a breeding rate to pick chromosomes for crossover. A default value between *[.5]* and *[.9]* (say .66) is a good default estimate for the crossover rate. In some genetic searches, the crossover rate can begin low and increase if the average fitness of the population does not significantly improve over a specified number of generations.

Mutation Rate

The mutation rate determines the probability that a chromosome will have one of its genes changed through a mutation technique. In general, mutation rates should be very low, in order to sustain genetic diversity but not overwhelm the population with too much noise. Expression 9.25 shows a good default mutation probability rate.

$$m_r = \max\left(.01, \frac{1}{N}\right)$$ (9.25)

Here,

m_r is the current probability of mutation
N is the population size

The mutation rate is inversely proportional to the population size, but not less than .001 is a good default value. For a population of 125 chromosomes, this is max(.01,.008), or [.01].

New Individual Rate

In some genetic algorithms new individuals are introduced into the next generation. These individuals have randomly valued genes (created in the same way as the genetic algorithm's initial population). New individuals can significantly increase genetic diversity but can also have an adverse effect on convergence if overused. As a rule of thumb, if new individuals are introduced into the population the probability should be half the mutation rate (.5*m_r).

9.5 Review

Genetic algorithms form a family of directed optimization and search techniques that can solve highly complex and often highly nonlinear problems. They can be used to explore very large problem spaces and find the best solution based on multiobjective functions under a collection of multiple constraints. In this chapter we examined the fundamental nature of genetic algorithms, how they work, and how they evolve or breed solutions to problems. You should now understand the principal nature of the genetic algorithm and be familiar with such concepts and ideas as the following.

- The types of problems solved by genetic algorithms
- The organization and flow of control in a genetic algorithm
- How a problem solution is encoded in a chromosome
- The design and use of a fitness function

- How to introduce and limit diversity in a population
- How to measure and control convergence in a population
- How to select the correct crossover and mutation types and rates
- How to set the process parameters for a genetic algorithm
- The strengths and weaknesses of genetic algorithms

Genetic algorithms play an important role in tuning, optimizing, and measuring the performance of adaptive models. They can be instrumental in evolving parameters that keep models responsive to many external stresses. In this part of the book we continued our exploration of genetic algorithms and evolutionary strategies. In the next chapter we examine a simplified (but still rather complex) crew-scheduling system. This is followed by a chapter on the genetic tuning of fuzzy models and the genetic discovery of linear and nonlinear regression equations.

Further Reading

■ Goldberg, D. E. "A Note on Boltzmann Tournament Selection for Genetic Algorithms and Population-Oriented Simulated Annealing," in *Complex Systems, Volume 4*, pp. 445–460, Complex Systems Publications, 1990.

■ Goldberg, D. E. *Genetic Algorithms in Search, Optimization, and Machine Learning*. Reading, MA: Addison-Wesley, 1989.

■ Goldberg, D. E. "Real-coded Genetic Algorithms, Virtual Alphabets, and Blocking," in *Complex Systems, Volume 5*, pp. 139–167, Complex Systems Publications, 1991.

■ Goldberg, D. E., and K. Deb. "A Comparative Analysis of Selection Schemes Used in Genetic Algorithms," in *Foundations of Genetic Algorithms*, G. J. E. Rawlins (ed.), pp. 69–93, San Mateo, CA: Morgan Kaufmann Publishers, 1991.

■ Goldberg, D. E., and J. Richardson. "Genetic Algorithms with Sharing for Multimodal Function Optimization," in *Genetic Algorithms and Their Applications: Proceedings of the Second International Conference on Genetic Algorithms*, pp. 41–49, 1987.

■ Goldberg, D. E., K. Deb, and J. H. Clark. "Genetic Algorithms, Noise, and the Sizing of Populations," in *Complex Systems, Volume 6*, pp. 333–362, Complex Systems Publications, 1992.

■ Grefenstette, J., R. Gopal, R. Rosmaita, and D. Gucht. "Genetic Algorithms for the Traveling Salesman Problem," in *Proceedings of the Second International*

Conference on Genetic Algorithms, Mahwah, NJ: Lawrence Erlbaum Associates, 1985.

■ Holland, J. H. *Adaptation in Natural and Artificial Systems: An Introductory Analysis with Applications to Biology, Control, and Artificial Intelligence*, 1975.

■ Krishnakumar, K. "Micro-Genetic Algorithms for Stationary and Non-Stationary Function Optimization," *SPIE: Intelligent Control and Adaptive Systems*, vol. 1196, Philadelphia, PA, 1989.

■ Syswerda, G. "Uniform Crossover in Genetic Algorithms," in *Proceedings of the Third International Conference on Genetic Algorithms*, J. Schaffer (ed.), pp. 2–9, Los Altos, CA: Morgan Kaufmann Publishers, 1989.

Chapter 10
Genetic Resource Scheduling Optimization

In Chapter 9 we explored the nature, organization, and function of GAs. These search and optimization mechanisms not only play an important part in effectively deriving fuzzy models but provide advanced optimization, exploration, and analysis features that play an important role in many applications in such varied fields as logistics, transportation, financial services, retailing, manufacturing, and project management. In this chapter we focus on solidifying our understanding of how GAs work. We do this by examining a small but nevertheless complex crew-scheduling system. Crew scheduling brings together the multiple objective and multiple constraint optimization capabilities of GAs in a way that illustrates how a GA connects to and works with the underlying application (in this case, a resource-constrained scheduling system). We begin our study of the genetic scheduler by examining the architecture of a fully robust scheduler and then explore a real scheduler with a small number of constraints.

10.1 **The Vocabulary of Resource-constrained Scheduling**

Most of the underlying terminology associated with genetic scheduling should already be familiar from the previous chapter on GAs. A review of some vocabulary terms that are used in ordinary resource-constrained scheduling, however, will make reading and understanding the material in this chapter somewhat easier. It is not always possible, while maintaining an uncluttered and coherent discussion of the clustering process, to ensure that every term is introduced before it is used. This preview of vocabulary is primarily concerned with the crew scheduler discussed in this chapter. For some exceptions to or elaboration on these definitions see "Some Terminology Issues" following the definitions.

Availability

Availability specifies the amount of resource supply available per unit time. For example, an individual could have available eight hours per day for work. A crew, regardless of the number of individuals in the crew, also has for the purpose of scheduling eight hours per day. Availability is a hard constraint on producing a feasible schedule.

Calendar

A *calendar* is a component of the scheduler that indicates the distribution of a resource's availability. A calendar of a crew or an individual indicates which days of the year are working days and which hours of the day are working hours. Each individual resource has its own calendar, allowing specification of different work days, holidays, working cycles, and so forth.

Crew

A *crew* is a composite resource used in scheduling. A crew is the unit of resource availability that is assigned to a job. A crew normally has its own availability, but can also have an availability that is the composite of its underlying members (although we do not consider this advanced type of resource constraint in this chapter).

Duration

The *duration* is the elapse time of a task (or job) specified in the units of the associated resource (or expressed in some multiple of the resource). Hence, jobs are specified in duration times of minutes, whereas crews are specified with an availability in hours per day. The combination of duration and availability created the underlying supply-and-demand model, which is the basic mechanism that drives all resource-constrained schedulers.

Early Start

An *early start* is the earliest possible start for a job. This time is assigned by the crew dispatcher and is the time the crew is scheduled to be on site. In real-world schedules this is the time the service department has promised the customer that the crews (or customer service engineer) will be at the customer's site.

Execution Window

Each job has an *execution window*. This is the time between the early start and the latest finish date. The execution window implicitly indicates the amount of elasticity in the job's start.

Feasible Schedule

For each job, a feasible schedule (or solution) has (1) a crew with the required skills, (2) a time frame that corresponds to a time when the crew is available, (3) all the necessary supporting resources, and (4) a start time that is after all its predecessor jobs have been completed. Feasibility is the highest integrity constraint on a schedule. Every potential schedule must be a feasible solution.

Float

The job *float* is the amount of surplus time in the execution window. This is the length of the execution window minus the length of the job. Thus, float is the number of days the job can be delayed without exceeding the latest finish date.

Job

A demand on crew time is a *job* (or a service order in the argot of crew scheduling). In crew scheduling, jobs have several important properties: an initially fixed window in time, an estimated duration, a set of required skills, a priority, and a planned or expected start and finish time. The core idea behind crew scheduling is to assign, from a pool of many possible crews, a crew to each job that produces a feasible schedule with the minimum possible span of time.

Latest Finish

Latest finish is the latest possible completion time for a job. This can be either a hard or a soft constraint. When the latest finish is a soft constraint, the date is relaxed and the job is scheduled to complete regardless of the planned finish date. When the latest finish is a hard constraint and a job is scheduled fully or partially outside its execution window, the job must remain unscheduled. Although we do not deal with unscheduled jobs in this chapter (in that [in that?]the latest finish is a soft constraint), the fitness function assigns a very large penalty value to unscheduled jobs.

Network

The complete collection of precedence-connected jobs is called the *network*. This is a term drawn from graph theory that specifies a collection of nodes connected by edges.

Precedence Relationship

The time dependency relationship between two nodes in a network (such as two or more jobs) is called a *precedence relationship*. If job B cannot start until job A completes, a precedence relationship exists between the two jobs. In this case, job A is the predecessor to job B and job B is the successor to job A.

Precedence Strategy

The way in which precedence relationships connect two nodes (such a jobs) is the dependency or *precedence strategy*. The normal strategy is finish to start (job B cannot start until job A is finished). But there are many other strategies, such as finish to finish, start to start, and so forth. Precedence strategies also involve lead and lag weights that specify lead or lag time delays between jobs.

Renewable and Nonrenewable Resources

A resource that, once consumed, is no longer available is called a *nonrenewable resource*. An allocated budget is nonrenewable. On a daily basis, crews are nonrenewable (one a crew's time is consumed for the day, no more crew time is available), although on a day-by-day basis they represent a *renewable resource* (the next day the full crew time is available for assignment).

Resource

A source of supply is called a *resource*. In general, when we want to construct a feasible schedule that can be implemented in the real world each task in the schedule must be associated with some type of resource.

Span Time

The total elapsed time for a schedule from the start of the earliest task to the completion of the latest task is known as the *span time*. The objective function of the crew schedule is designed to minimize span time.

Supply-and-Demand Model

A model that is constrained by resource availability is, in general terms, known as a *supply-and-demand model*. Supply-and-demand models have long been known as a regular feature in economics (where they are subject to many forms of dynamic equilibrium analysis). All scheduling systems (crew schedulers, project management systems, machine shop schedulers) are forms of supply-and-demand models.

10.2   Some Terminology Issues

Crew scheduling and general project management are related disciplines but with different meanings associated with some of their terms. These differences arise primarily in crew-scheduling plans (such as that discussed in this chapter) that do not involve precedence relationships. In the analysis of a project schedule, the project is given a start date and each task is assigned a duration. From these two values (resource availability and precedence relationships) the network analysis computes the early and late start and finish dates, as well as the amount of float for each task. In the crew schedule, each task (or job) is assigned an early start date and latest allowed finish date. The difference between these two dates less the actual duration of the job is the amount of float in the job. Many real-world crew-scheduling plans are constructed in this fashion (most major electric and water utilities and cable television companies schedule their repair and service crews in this fashion).

10.3   **Fundamentals**

The genetic-based crew scheduler finds an optimal solution to the problem of assigning crews to outstanding jobs (service orders) consistent with crew availability and the required completion dates of each job. The task is complicated by both the constraints imposed on a feasible solution and the combinatorial complexity of even a simple crew-scheduling problem. We start our exploration of crew scheduling with the very simple example illustrated in Figure 10.1. We have a problem of three crews and five jobs.

If a job can be handled by any crew, there are 3^5 or 243 possible schedules (combinations), and each of these schedules, lacking any additional constraints, would be just as good as any other. This perspective constitutes the assignment problem in crew scheduling.

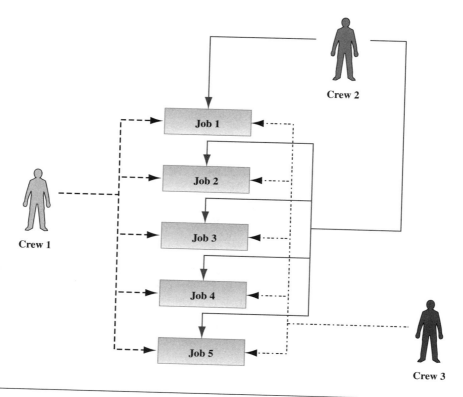

Figure 10.1   A 3 × 5 crew-scheduling problem.

The Crew-scheduling Problem

So, if all choices of crew assignments are equally good, why is there a problem? There is a problem because real-world scheduling involves more than parceling out work to a set of waiting crews. Even if the crews are interchangeable in terms of skills, some crews may have properties that make them a better choice for a particular assignment to a particular job at a particular time. If, for example, crews have varying availabilities or crews must contend for limited and shared equipment assets (or if we take the locality of a crew's preceding job into account, or take the size or experience of a crew's members into account, thus accounting for risk factors), the complexity of the assignment problem is increased significantly.

Feasible Solutions: An Example

Let's examine the way this crew-scheduling problem can be resolved. Our objective is to assign a job to a crew and then schedule each job so that it is completed within as few days as possible. First, we need to know the time required by each job. Table 10.1 shows the duration, in hours, for each of the jobs.

The simplest way of solving this problem is to start with the first crew and begin making assignments, starting with the first job. If the daily availability of a crew is eight hours, Figure 10.2 shows a solution to this problem.

This is a feasible schedule (that is, a workable schedule that does not violate any constraints and meets our basic objective of completing all work on the first day). If the schedule is satisfactory, our work is complete and we can stop. On the other hand, we might have imposed a few other objectives for our schedule: that each job is completed as soon as possible within the day, that travel time between jobs is minimized, and that whenever possible all available crews are used. A simple rearrangement of jobs can help us meet our first objective (minimizing

TABLE 10.1 Job Duration Times

Job	Duration (Hours)
JOB1	3.0
JOB2	4.0
JOB3	2.0
JOB4	3.5
JOB5	2.0
Total	14.5

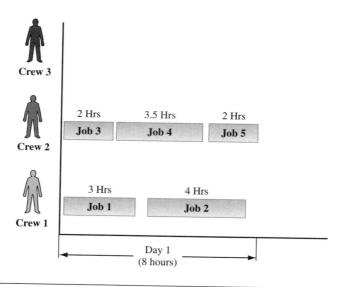

Figure 10.2 A feasible crew schedule.

job completion times). Figure 10.3 shows a schedule in which completion times are minimized relative to the initial schedule.

A particular crew-scheduling problem often has several equally feasible (and occasionally equally optimal) solutions. For example, Figure 10.4 illustrates another feasible solution to the assignment of these five jobs across three crews.

This is the nature of crew scheduling: assigning jobs to crews so that each job is completed consistent with any constraints (see the section "Objective Functions and Constraints"). As the number of jobs increases and the number of crews increases, the assignment process becomes increasingly difficult. Finding a solution that meets the minimum requirements (all work is done within its allowable time frame) as well as respects all constraints on the schedule (such as minimizing the completion time or assigning crews to minimize travel time) can be a computationally intensive task. This computational burden evolves not just from the number of jobs and crews in the schedule but from the objectives and constraints placed on the schedule.

10.4 **Objective Functions and Constraints**

Objective functions (or simply, objectives) and constraints are developed as part of the problem specification. Constraints define the feasibility

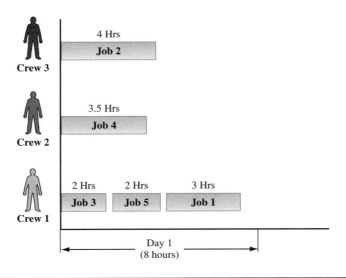

Figure 10.3   A schedule with minimized completion times.

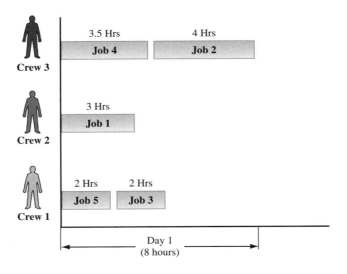

Figure 10.4   An alternative feasible solution.

of a schedule. Objectives define the optimality of a schedule. Although objectives *should* be satisfied, constraints *must* be satisfied. We now turn to a discussion of these issues.

Constraints

Returning to the simple crew schedule shown in Figure 10.1, because there are a few hundred possible schedules and our only criterion is that each job must be paired with an available crew, we can select any of these as our working schedule. In the real world of crew scheduling, however, the choice among feasible, acceptable, and optimal schedules[1] is narrowed considerably. This narrowing process is driven by the constraints imposed by both the schedule user and the schedule developer (human or machine). These constraints are in the form of objective functions and solution constraints. Constraints impose restrictions on the overall nature of the schedule and may be in conflict with one or more objective functions.

Thus, in real-world crew scheduling we have restricted degrees of freedom in constructing a workable or feasible schedule. Although these objective functions and constraints may reduce the total possible number of schedules, finding a feasible (not to mention optimal) schedule in the restricted space can be a very difficult and time-consuming process. To list just a few constraints, a feasible solution must match a job's

- Skill and asset requirements
- Degree of difficulty
- Work site (customer identification)
- Geographic location relative to related jobs
- Predecessor relationship with other jobs
- Customer priority
- Estimated duration (time demand)
- Earliest possible start time
- Latest permissible finish time

---

[1] A *feasible* schedule can be actually implemented. It does not violate start date constraints (the start must be after or on today's date), resource availability, job precedence relationships, or crew-to-job skill requirements. It *may* violate objective functions or the latest permissible finish date of a job. An *acceptable* schedule is both feasible and close to optimal (a "very good" schedule). An *optimal* schedule is one in which no other schedule is objectively (but sometimes subjectively) better. There may be more than one optimal schedule.

and a crew's

- Skill proficiencies
- Job performance history
- Available (remaining) time
- Charge rate
- Renewable and nonrenewable asset rates
- Access to limited asset resources
- Inter-job travel time
- Geographic work restrictions

These factors establish constraints on the form of a final schedule. They are an intrinsic part of the relationships among crews, assets, and jobs. As such, they are implicit in the nature of any schedule and form the kernel constraint criteria for any feasible solution. A few of the constraints implied by even this relatively small list of job and crew properties include the following.

- The matching of a job's required skills and the skill proficiencies of a crew means that jobs cannot be randomly assigned to crews but must be assigned to crews that have the proper skills.
- Some jobs are inherently more difficult than others, and some crews have greater or lesser proficiencies in particular skills. This implies a relationship between crew assignments and risk of meeting a completion date. Thus, high-priority, high-visibility, or rescheduled jobs should be assigned to crews with the highest possible proficiency in the required skills.
- A crew's daily availability coupled with a job's estimated duration (earliest start date and its latest permissible finish date) means that a crew can only work on a certain number of jobs each day (that is, the total estimated time for all jobs cannot exceed the daily availability of the crew).
- A crew's geographic work restriction. In a statewide crew schedule, for example, crews might be restricted to particular counties. In any case, some crews have restrictions on their general work areas. These restrictions are on the same constraint level as the crew's skill and overall availability.
- The travel time between jobs means that the total daily availability of a crew is not actually available to work on a set of candidate jobs. This

"dead time" must be factored into the schedule. And, of course, some crews must share critically limited assets, and thus the availability of the asset must be considered when scheduling the crew.

■ The fact that some jobs are dependent on the start or completion of other jobs means that we must consider the precedence relationships between jobs in devising a schedule. It also means that if a scheduled completion date of a job exceeds its latest permissible date the start or allowed finish dates of successor jobs must be adjusted.

Not all constraints implicit in the properties of crews, jobs, and assets are implemented in a scheduling system, but the constraints we chose will impose a limitation on the number of feasible solutions that can be constructed. Thus, as previously mentioned, all constraints imposed on a schedule must be obeyed.

As a matter of fundamental principles in scheduling there are, generally, only two types of constraints that must always be considered. The first is the predecessor and successor relationships between jobs. Satisfying this constraint produces a *time-feasible* schedule. The second is the availability of resources to actually perform the work (crews, money, tools, machines, and so on). Satisfying this constraint produces a *resource-feasible* schedule. Because jobs must be properly sequenced in time in order to determine resource availability, a resource-feasible schedule is always a time-feasible schedule. The purpose behind a resource-constrained scheduler is to produce a set of resource-feasible schedules.

Objectives

The set of feasible solutions satisfies all constraints imposed on a valid schedule. An optimal schedule, often thought of as the best schedule, not only satisfies all the constraints but is at least as good as any other feasible solution. This quality of goodness is defined by the objective functions. Objective functions characterize the critical nature of the schedule itself — an attempt to minimize or maximize a measure of goodness in the schedule. Some of the objective functions include the following.

■ Minimize the scheduled completion time of each job
■ Maximize the number of jobs done in a particular time period
■ Minimize overall costs
■ Maximize resource (crew) utilization

- Minimize risk
- Minimize slippage
- Maximize crew efficiency
- Minimize travel time

Crew scheduling typically minimizes the scheduled completion times for each job as its primary objective. A schedule, however, can have multiple objective functions. These objective functions are often in conflict with each other. We can, for example, minimize the cost of jobs by assigning less experienced crews or scheduling jobs when less expensive resources become available. However, this might conflict with the completion date minimization or risk minimization objective functions.

Evaluating Objective Functions

In a multiobjective function schedule, the optimal solution often represents a saddle (or compromise) point in the solution space. Optimization in the presence of multiobjective functions usually means finding a way to rank the utility or importance of each objective and then finding a way to judge the optimality of a feasible solution based on the goodness of fit or rank of their optimality measures. As a rather simple example, if each objective function (f) returns a value between 0 and 100 indicating how close the schedule is to the optimal (0 = best, 100 = worst), we can find an optimality ranking for a multiobjective function schedule by evaluating

$$f_{\text{ranked}} = \frac{\sum_{i=1}^{N} f_i \times w_i}{\sum_{i=1}^{N} w_i}, \qquad (10.1)$$

where

f_{ranked} is the ranked fitness from all individual fitness functions
f_i is the fitness of the i-th objective function
N is the number of objective functions in an individual chromosome
w_i is the contribution weight for the i-th objective function

By selecting schedules with the smallest weighted average objective function, the feasible schedules with the closest optimality fit will continually percolate to the top. This form of evaluating a collection of objective functions makes it easy to combine both minimizing and maximizing objective functions in the same analysis (maximizing functions simply return the inverse of the fitness value).

10.5 **Bringing It All Together: Constraint Scheduling**

There are a wide variety of possible and actual constraint factors in a real crew schedule. These constraints, as we saw earlier, affect the solution space of a feasible schedule. There are, however, three principal constraints that must be satisfied before any schedule is considered for other constraints. These involve matching jobs to allowable crews and then accounting for the availability of crews and other related resources. In this section we will look at these two issues and see how they affect the schedule. Allowable crew determination involves two restrictions: a crew's geographic range and a crew's set of skills.

Operating Area-constrained Crew Assignments

If we consider the crew-scheduling process to encompass a set of widely dispersed crews that operate in restricted geographic regions,[2] the naive schedules in Figures 10.2 through 10.4 fail to account for this feature of a feasible schedule. We can plan for the matching of crews to jobs with a site restriction by visualizing customer sites placed on a very fine grid. Figure 10.5 illustrates this concept.

Our crews then have restricted operating limits. These limits are often placed on political as well as economic considerations (some examples include: road crews are restricted to a particular county, crews cannot travel more than X miles from their home base, some crews can only service residential customers and others only business customers). As Figure 10.6 illustrates, we have a set of crews that operate within a particular physical or logical territory.

In many cases the grid contains the degree to which a crew can operate within the territory or adjacent territories. If the partitioning into territories is hard, the degree will be zero or one. If the partitioning is relatively soft, the degree along the edges of territories will be a number in the interval *[0,1]*. This acts as a form of topology or hurdle function, ensuring that a crew from one territory is only scheduled into another territory when no other satisfactory solution is available.

---

[2] We use geographic constraints as a common example. However, this type of operating constraint could just as easily be based on similar restrictions, such as sales territory (customer assignments), seasonal or shift constraints, department or organizational function, and so on. The territory grid (or grids), of course, need not be rectangular. Any arbitrarily nonuniform shape can be used.

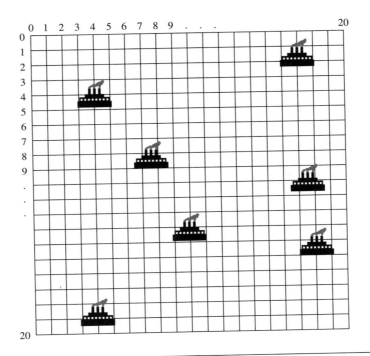

Figure 10.5 Customer sites on the location grid.

Skill-constrained Crew Assignments

The schedules illustrated in Figures 10.2 through 10.4 also omit a critical constraint on the feasibility of a schedule: the matching of jobs with the correct crew. This correctness is a function of the skill set required by the job and the skill set of one or more crews. This means that the first constraint in producing a schedule, as illustrated in Figure 10.7, is a match between a job and the crews that have the skills to perform that job.

Thus, the first step in formulating a feasible solution is the matching of jobs to the crews with the correct skills. This matching process is complicated by several considerations.

- Crews can have multiple skills. They can also have varying degrees of proficiencies in each of their skills. For example, a telecommunications-placing crew might have skills in both copper and optical fiber land lines. However, due to the composition of the crew it has a high degree of proficiency (or experience) in copper lines and a low degree of proficiency in optical fiber lines.

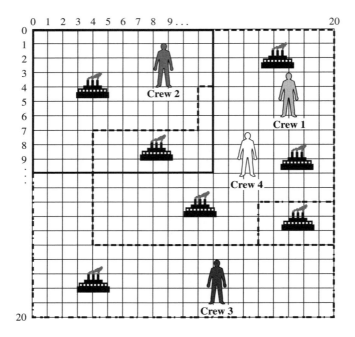

Figure 10.6   Territory crew restrictions.

■ Jobs can also have multiple skill requirements. A single job might require, for example, expertise in electrical work, in construction, and in ground excavation work.

This multiple-skills-to-multiple-skills relationship means that we have two distinct options in satisfying the crew-to-job constraint. To illustrate these options, consider a job that requires welding and electrical skills. A schedule generator can perform the following.

■ Find a single crew that has both *Welding* and *Electrical* in its skill set. In this case, the assignment problem is reduced to the ordinary crew assignment.

■ Find a collection of crews that has *Welding* and *Electrical* in their skill sets. In this case, each crew is assigned the same job. The scheduler must then ensure that both crews are scheduled together so that they are at the job site at the same time to complete the task

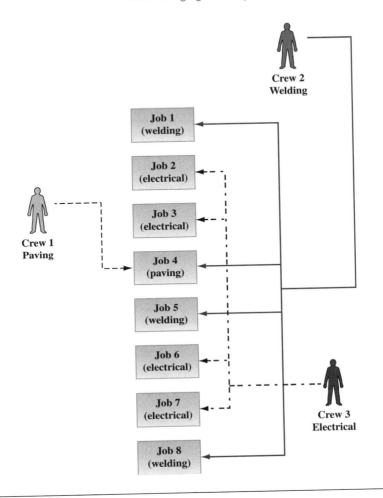

Figure 10.7 Aligning crews and jobs based on skills.

(or are scheduled according to the permissible predecessor relationships associated with the underlying work).

The process of merging crews and jobs with multiple skills is further
complicated by a need to consider the proficiency or experience of a
crew relative to the complexity, priority, duration, location, or customer
satisfaction criteria associated with the job. This type of extended matching between jobs and crews is critical under certain objectives (such as
minimizing risk or minimizing slippage).

Resource-constrained Scheduling

A pervasive and persistent constraint in real-world scheduling is a respect for resource availability. The basic resource in a crew-scheduling problem is the crew. However, crews can be composed of individuals (with their own available times, rates, skills, and proficiencies). A crew can also be dependent on other scarce or costly nonrenewable and renewable resources (collectively known as assets). In matters of generating a feasible solution, the complications arising from limited resource availability combined with the cost, quantity on hand, and the renewable or nonrenewable properties of a resource must be taken into consideration. Nonrenewable and fixed-quantity resources are depleted as they are used or distributed. Ordinary nonrenewable resources include the following.

- Supplies
- Raw materials
- Capital

Fixed-quantity resources include assets such as shared machinery. For example, a long-lines placing or splicing crew may contend with other crews for a limited number of cherry pickers. A feasible schedule depends not only on the availability of the crew but on the availability of the cherry pickers. Such nonrenewable resources often have a rate as well as a penalty for use. Renewable resources are generally refreshed in each time period. Crew availability or equipment availability is an example of a renewable resource.[3] When we combine resource constraints with the job pools, as illustrated in Figure 10.8, the result is a resource-feasible schedule that respects crew assignments (based on skills).

Let's see how this works in practice. At its simplest level, crew scheduling must respect the daily availability of each crew. If we assume that each crew is available eight hours a day (ignoring break and lunch times), Figure 10.9 illustrates a feasible schedule that considers resource constraints.

Crew 1 (paving) has a single job during day 1. Crew 2 (welding) is scheduled to work on jobs 1, 3, and 5 on day 1. Although two hours time

---

[3] A renewable resource may have a renewable pattern that is (1) not aligned with the period availability of the crews and (2) not regular. For example, there are N special band saws available to X carpenter crews. Crew X_i checks out a band saw and keeps it for M days (knowing that they will need it for three upcoming job assignments). Thus, crew X_i has exclusive use of this resource (it has a periodic renewable behavior as perceived by crew X_i) while it is unavailable to all the other crews during this period.

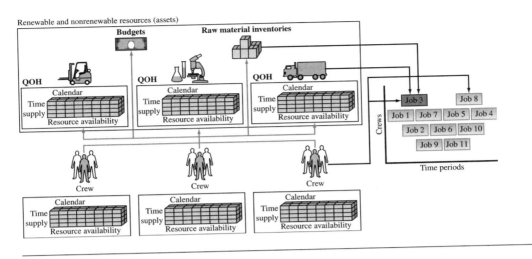

Figure 10.8 Factors in resource-constrained scheduling.

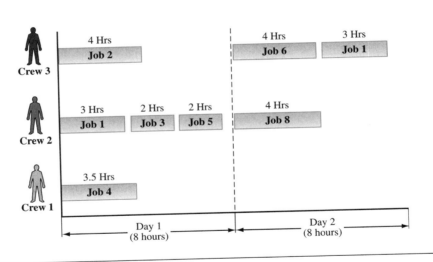

Figure 10.9 A resource-feasible schedule.

remains on day 1, job 8 must be moved to the next day because it requires eight hours of crew time. Crew 3 (electrical) is scheduled to work on job 2 during day 1. But the travel time to both job 6 and job 3 is two hours, and thus neither can be scheduled on day 1 and must be moved to day 2. Unlike our simple examples in the overview section, we are unable to move jobs delayed by resource constraints to other crews because they are matched to crews by their skill requirements.

- *Topology:* Defines the network of predecessor and successor jobs in the master schedule. The topology network is actually constructed from the predecessor relationships defined in the master plan jobs.

❷ The Job Sequencer

The first step in sense preparing a crew schedule is the job sequencer. This facility is used to order jobs that have predecessor relationships. The sequencer works in a fashion similar to a critical path analysis in traditional project management: by using the earliest permissible start date in a chain of jobs and by applying the duration of each job, it orders the jobs across time and thus provides an initial time-feasible schedule (but not yet resource feasible).

❸ The Crew Scheduler

The crew scheduler is the top-level controller for the scheduling framework. The crew scheduler manages the various elements in the schedule, monitors the convergence of the GA toward an optimal solution, and notifies the application framework when the final schedule is available. The crew scheduler also manages all constraint conditions and objective functions for the current schedule process. The crew scheduler is responsible for decomposing large multidimensional schedules into linearly separable pieces for stepwise resolution.

❹ The Genetic Optimizer

The genetic optimizer solves the underlying multiconstraint, multiobjective schedule through the parallel exploration of and convergence through a large *n*-dimensional space of candidate schedules. The genetic optimizer explores this space by creating a random set of crew-feasible and time-feasible schedules. These are then sent to the resource-constrained scheduler, where they are turned into working, resource-feasible schedules. Each feasible schedule is measured against the objective functions and ranked according to their particular goodness of fit. The optimizer continues to breed better and better schedules from the fittest schedules found in each analysis cycle.

❺ **The Resource-constrained Scheduler**

The resource-constrained scheduler generates a complete feasible schedule. This component takes a candidate-time and crew-feasible schedule and turns it into a working schedule by attempting to start each job at its earliest possible time. If the associated crew does not have sufficient availability, the job is moved forward until a day and time of day are found where it can be scheduled. The resource-constrained scheduler also uses the precedence analyzer to adjust any successor jobs when due to resource availability constraints the current job slips past its target date. The resource-constrained scheduler also couples the current job schedule to the availability of any limited asset requirements (thus, a job must be scheduled into a time frame consistent with both the crew availability and the availability of all other limited assets).

❻ **The Precedence Analyzer**

A precedence analyzer manages the topological relationships among the various jobs. It is used by the job sequencer to initially order jobs that do not have a specified start and finish date. The resource-constrained scheduler uses the precedence analyzer to adjust the start and likely completion times for successor jobs when a predecessor job slips beyond its target completion time.

❼ **The Auditing Facility**

Integrated into the scheduling framework is a comprehensive, multilevel auditing facility that allows the analyst or developer to expose a considerable amount of the fine-grain details in all scheduling components. The auditing levels range from *OFF*, through *LOW, MEDIUM, HIGH*, and *MAXIMUM*. Each level exposes more detail than the one below it.

❽ **The Crew Schedules**

The crew scheduler automatically produces two schedules: one ordered by job and one by crew. However, the GA sometimes finds and ranks several optimal schedules. These are available to the application framework as alternative schedules.

10.7 **Implementing and Executing the Crew Scheduler**

In this section we examine the structure and processing of the resource-constrained crew scheduler. This Java implementation is less robust and extensive than the architecture discussed in the previous chapter. It is concerned only with a single objective function (minimizing completion time) and a single resource constraint (crew availability).

Objective Functions and Constraints

The objective function for the resource-constrained crew scheduler is simple: minimize job completion time. Each job has an estimated duration (measured in hours) and an allowed window of execution (see the discussion of master file content). The scheduler attempts to complete each job as early as possible within this window of execution consistent with the availability of the assigned crew. The fitness of a schedule is determined by Expression 10.2.

$$f = \sum_{i=1}^{N} (s_i^a - s_i^e) + ((c_i^a - c_i^l)^2 \times (c_i^a > c_i^l)) \tag{10.2}$$

Here,

f is the fitness of the current schedule
N is the number of jobs in the schedule

Each of the following expression variables represents the *i*-th job in the schedule defined by the current chromosome.

s_i^a is the actual start date of the job
s_i^e is the earliest permitted start in the execution window
c_i^a is the actual completion date of the job
c_i^l is the latest permitted finish in the execution window

The fitness function computes the degree of early start fitness for the current schedule. The goodness of fit sums the difference between the earliest possible start for a job and its actual (scheduled) start. The more jobs scheduled close to or on their earliest possible time the smaller the delta. If all jobs finish as soon as possible, the total fitness function will be zero. The fitness function also includes a penalty for completing a job after its latest permitted finish. We also sum, for all jobs that were scheduled late, the square of the delta between the scheduled date and latest allowable date. This is added to the fitness function (and thus biases the fitness toward solutions in which all jobs complete at the earliest possible time).

Constraints establish the boundaries for a feasible solution. Hard constraints are imposed by the actual scheduling system, whereas soft constraints are imposed as penalties in the fitness function. There are several hard and soft constraints embedded in the scheduling system.

- (Hard) A job can only be assigned to a crew that has the necessary skills
- (Hard) A job cannot start before its earliest start time
- (Soft) A job should complete before its latest completion time
- (Hard) A job must be scheduled in a contiguous time frame (that is, for this scheduler a job cannot be interrupted)
- (Hard) A job cannot be scheduled unless the assigned crew has sufficient available time

The constraints fall generally into two classes: resource availability restrictions and time-to-schedule restrictions. The resource constraints ensure that the proper crew resource is assigned to a job and that the job is performed when the crew has available time. The time-to-schedule constraint ensures that a job does not start early, but allows a job to be scheduled anytime after its earliest start date (although late finishes are penalized by the fitness function; see Expression 10.2).

The Genome Structure

A genome in the scheduler represents a complete schedule. The structure is relatively simple, allowing very rapid access and evaluation of each scheduled job. As Figure 10.11 illustrates, in addition to the fitness function value the chromosome consists of an array of N cells or objects, where N is the number of jobs.

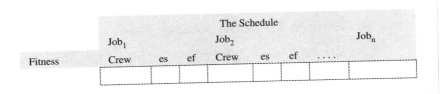

Figure 10.11 The scheduling genome structure.

In this chromosome, the *i*-th array (or vector) position corresponds to the *i*-th job in the table of jobs for this schedule (see Listing 10.3). At this location is the assigned crew (also an index into the table of available crews for this schedule; see Listing 10.3) and the early start (*es*) and the early finish (*ef*) calculated by the underlying resource-constrained scheduler. Thus, the chromosome consists of an array of three values (*C, s, f*; crew, start, and finish).

In this exploration of resource-constrained crew scheduling the jobs are located in a fixed order, left to right across the chromosome. The scheduler also supports a priority attribute on a job (see Listing 10.1). When prioritization is used, the jobs are sorted in descending order by priority (the lower the number the higher the priority) and a different chromosome structure is used: the genome is an ordered array of four values (*J, C, s, f*; job, crew, start, and finish). When all priorities are the same, this is essentially equivalent to the chromosome structure we use in this chapter. Note also that this chromosome organization is also necessary when precedence relationship constraints are used.

The Genetic Scheduler Process

The object design and control structures in the crew scheduler generally follow the overall architecture of the general scheduler discussed in the previous section (see Figure 10.10). The chief difference is in the restricted set of scheduling objects and the lack of precedence or topology management in the current scheduler. Figure 10.12 is a schematic overview of the scheduler with the principal object classes.

❶ Assign Log and Audit Files

Audit and error logging files are attached to the system as one of the first activities. Any number of different audit files (both formatted and unformatted) can be attached. The listings in this section are all derived from an audit file (somewhat modified to remove date and time stamps, class name signatures, and other forms of clutter).

❷ Compile Schedule Master Plan

Although numerous methods exist for fetching the schedule components from diverse sources (such as corporate databases), a basic master plan compiler provides a simple and straightforward way of stating a crew-scheduling problem. Listing 10.1 is the master plan for the example in this chapter.

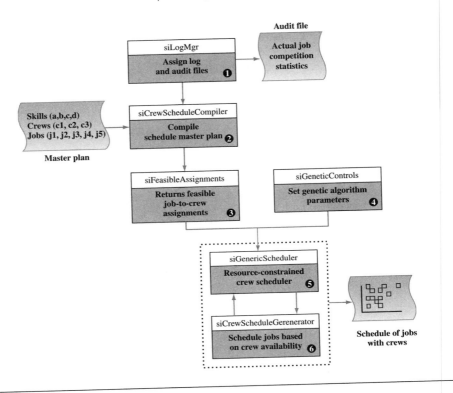

Figure 10.12   The Java implementation of the crew scheduler.

The master plan layout specifies a collection of skills (indicated by the *skill* keyword). One or more of these skills is associated with a crew in the section that lists all crews with their daily availability (a crew is specified with the *crew* keyword). The jobs to be scheduled are specified after the crews. Each job (indicated by the *job* keyword) has a name, a priority (unused in this example), a time requirement in minutes, a required early start, a late finish, and a list of skills required to perform this job. In this example, to reduce complexity each job has a single required skill.

Note that the required start and finish dates in this example are expressed as offsets from the current date (in that a job cannot, in all likelihood, start on the date that the schedule is actually produced, the earliest start date is tomorrow, which has an offset of 1). In a real-world implementation of the crew scheduler the actual calendar dates supplied for the start and finish dates are converted to Java date values so that we can do date arithmetic in the same way as the these integer offsets.

```
            schedule;
            skill   welding;
            skill   welding;
            skill   electrician;
            skill   splicer;
            skill   placer;
            skill   builder;
            #
            #_____name__supply___skills
            crew   C1   8     welding;
            crew   C2   9     splicer;
            crew   C3   8     welding electrician;
            crew   C4   8     placer builder;
            crew   C5   8     welding;
            crew   C6   8     electrician;
            #
            #------name--priority-time-------es---ef--skill
            job   J01  5      50    1  20 welding;
            job   J02  5      75    1  10 electrician;
            job   J03  5      58    1  35 placer;
            job   J04  5      96    1  40 welding;
            job   J05  5     209    1  16 electrician;
            job   J06  5      50    1  20 welding;
            job   J07  5      95    1  10 electrician;
            job   J08  5     158    1  35 placer;
            job   J09  5      96    1  40 welding;
            job   J10  5     209    1  16 electrician;
            job   J11  5      50    1  20 welding;
            job   J12  5     375    1  10 electrician;
            job   J13  5     158    1  35 placer;
            job   J14  5     296    1  40 welding;
            job   J15  5     279    1  16 electrician;
            #
            end;
```

Listing 10.1   The crew schedule master plan.

❸ Return Feasible Job to Crew Assignments

The crew schedule compiler builds a number of important tables (the list of jobs and properties and the list of crews and their properties). The compiler also creates an important $M \times N$ matrix of all jobs, their required skills, and the list of crews that can be assigned to this job. This matrix, shown in Listing 10.2, shows all feasible assignments.

```
Feasible Assignments (Jobs-->Crews)

                  Required
   Service Order   Skill      Feasible Crew Assignments
   -------------  ----------  -------------------------
      J01         welding         C1  C3  C5
      J02         electrician     C3  C6
      J03         placer          C4
      J04         welding         C1  C3  C5
      J05         electrician     C3  C6
      J06         welding         C1  C3  C5
      J07         electrician     C3  C6
      J08         placer          C4
      J09         welding         C1  C3  C5
      J10         electrician     C3  C6
      J11         welding         C1  C3  C5
      J12         electrician     C3  C6
      J13         placer          C4
      J14         welding         C1  C3  C5
      J15         electrician     C3  C6

   Compile Time: 31 milliseconds.
```

Listing 10.2 The feasible assignments.

The *Feasible Assignments* class fuses the active crews and the active service orders (jobs) based on their skill requirements to generate a matrix of jobs and the set of crews that could feasibly be assigned to the job. The feasible assignments matrix is the core data control mechanism in the genetic scheduler. It specifies the elements that can constitute a valid (that is, feasible) schedule. The GA works by creating an initial random schedule from this set of feasible assignments. The algorithm randomly selects crews from the feasible set and then generates a schedule (consistent with crew resource availability). Crossover and mutations act on the index values into the crew array by breeding good schedules. Mutation occurs by randomly picking one of the crews in the feasible set and assigning it randomly to one of the other legal assignments.

❹ Set Genetic Algorithm Parameters

A relatively large number of parameters control the operation of a GA. These are collected in a single class. Within the controls object you can set such parameters and attributes as the maximum number of generations, the type and frequency of crossover, the type and frequency of mutations, the termination conditions, convergence tolerance, the size of the initial population, and the population breeder type of the GA (steady state or dynamic; see Chapter 9 for details on population management).

❺ Execute the Resource-constrained Scheduler

The scheduler consists of two main class components: the GA that creates and breeds possible schedules and the resource-constrained scheduler itself, which implements a schedule, develops the start and finish times, and measures its goodness of fit. The constructor[4] for the schedule takes two parameters: the feasible assignments and the GA parameters. Listing 10.3 is the Java application interface that creates and runs the sample crew schedule.

A schedule is actually initiated by the *solve()* method in the *aiGeneticScheduler* class (see Listing 10.3, where the *solve* method starts the scheduler for an initial population of 135 chromosomes). Listing 10.4 shows the scheduler front end with the principal GA properties and the underlying crew and job tables.

The default calendar for each crew allocates six hours of work time (one hour for lunch and one hour for combined travel to and from jobs). Because the job times are specified in minutes, the scheduler also converts the crew availability to minutes (as shown in the crew table). From the feasible assignments matrix, the GA creates a population of potential schedules. Each chromosome in the population represents a schedule (see Figure 10.11) with a crew, selected from the job's feasible assignments, randomly selected for each job. Listing 10.5 shows part of an initial schedule (truncated both vertically and horizontally).

There are 135 chromosomes in this population, numbered at the left-hand side of the initial population listing. As Listing 10.4 illustrates, an initial schedule is simply a random assignment of crews to jobs. There is no fitness measure for any of the chromosomes.

❻ Schedule Jobs Based on Crew Availability

To convert the assignments into an actual schedule and measure its fitness, we need to pass each chromosome, in turn, to the actual

---

[4] A constructor in an object-oriented system is a special class method that actually allocates memory and initializes an instance of the object associated with the class. In this example, an *siGeneticScheduler* object is created from the *siFeasibleAssignments* and *siGeneticProperties* objects.

```
package com.scianta.schedulers;

import java.io.IOException;
import java.util.Vector;
import com.scianta.tools.*;
import com.scianta.acm.*;
import com.scianta.common.*;
import com.scianta.audit.aiAuditMgr;
import com.scianta.audit.aiLogMgr;
import com.scianta.crewscheduler.objects.*;
import com.scianta.crewscheduler.utilities.*;
import com.scianta.crewscheduler.compiler.*;
import com.scianta.crewscheduler.scheduler.*;

public class SampleCrewScheduler {
  public static void main(String args[]) {
    // Configure the Log File System
    siLogMgr.initLog("scianta", "c:/scianta/", "sciantalog.fil");

    siAuditMgr.initAudit(siCrewScheduleStrategy.CLASSNAME,
      true,false,aiAuditMgr.MAXIMUM,"schedules",
        "c:/sciantalog/","audit.fil");
    siCSLogger.putHeader();
    siCSLogger.msg(" ");

    System.out.println(" 1--compile the schedule definition.");
    siCrewScheduleCompiler compiler = new siCrewScheduleCompiler();
    System.out.println(" 2--run the scheduler.");
    try
      {
      siCrewScheduleStrategy strategy=
        compiler.compile("c:/schedules/example01.mplan");
      siFeasibleAssignments fa = strategy.getAssignments();
      siGeneticControls gc = new siGeneticControls();
      gc.setMaximumGenerations(50);
      gc.setRemoveDuplicates(true);
      siGeneticScheduler gs = new siGeneticScheduler(gc,fa);
      gs.solve(135);
      }
    catch(Exception e) {
      System.out.println(" ERROR----> exception thrown.");
    }
  }
}
```

Listing 10.3   Running the crew scheduler (main class).

```
Crew Scheduling Generator
Maximum Duration (days): 40


=========================================================
G E N E T I C   C R E W   S C H E D U L I N G
=========================================================
GENETIC ALGORITHM PARAMETERS
   Genome Length    : 15
   Population Size  : 135
   Maximum Cycles   : 50
   Cross Over Rate  : 0.6
   Mutation  Rate   : 0.05
   Selection Type   : Strong Tournament
   Cross-Over Type  : One Point Cross-Over
   Breeder Type     : Steady-State Breeder
```

Crew Name	Supply	Associated Skill Capabilities
C1	480.00	welding
C2	540.00	splicer
C3	480.00	electrician welding
C4	480.00	builder placer
C5	480.00	welding
C6	480.00	electrician

Job Name	Pri	Earliest Time	Latest Start	Finish	Required Skills
J01	5	50	1	20	welding
J02	5	75	1	10	electrician
J03	5	58	1	35	placer
J04	5	96	1	40	welding
J05	5	209	1	16	electrician
J06	5	50	1	20	welding
J07	5	95	1	10	electrician
J08	5	158	1	35	placer
J09	5	96	1	40	welding
J10	5	209	1	16	electrician
J11	5	50	1	20	welding
J12	5	375	1	10	electrician
J13	5	158	1	35	placer
J14	5	296	1	40	welding
J15	5	279	1	16	electrician

Listing 10.4   Initial scheduling parameters.

```
Initial (Random) Schedules
Population size: 135


   Fitness   (Job,Crew)
   --------  ----------------------------------------------------------------
   1. (none) (J01,C5) (J02,C6) (J03,C4) (J04,C1) (J05,C6) ... (J15,C3)
   2. (none) (J01,C3) (J02,C3) (J03,C4) (J04,C1) (J05,C3) ... (J15,C6)
   3. (none) (J01,C3) (J02,C6) (J03,C4) (J04,C1) (J05,C3) ... (J15,C3)
   4. (none) (J01,C5) (J02,C3) (J03,C4) (J04,C3) (J05,C3) ... (J15,C3)
   5. (none) (J01,C1) (J02,C6) (J03,C4) (J04,C3) (J05,C3) ... (J15,C3)
   6. (none) (J01,C1) (J02,C3) (J03,C4) (J04,C3) (J05,C6) ... (J15,C6)
   7. (none) (J01,C1) (J02,C6) (J03,C4) (J04,C3) (J05,C3) ... (J15,C3)
   8. (none) (J01,C1) (J02,C3) (J03,C4) (J04,C1) (J05,C3) ... (J15,C3)
   9. (none) (J01,C1) (J02,C3) (J03,C4) (J04,C1) (J05,C6) ... (J15,C6)
  10. (none) (J01,C3) (J02,C3) (J03,C4) (J04,C5) (J05,C6) ... (J15,C3)
   :
   :
 130. (none) (J01,C3) (J02,C6) (J03,C4) (J04,C5) (J05,C6) ... (J15,C6)
 131. (none) (J01,C5) (J02,C6) (J03,C4) (J04,C1) (J05,C6) ... (J15,C6)
 132. (none) (J01,C5) (J02,C3) (J03,C4) (J04,C1) (J05,C6) ... (J15,C3)
 133. (none) (J01,C1) (J02,C6) (J03,C4) (J04,C5) (J05,C3) ... (J15,C6)
 134. (none) (J01,C3) (J02,C6) (J03,C4) (J04,C1) (J05,C3) ... (J15,C6)
 135. (none) (J01,C3) (J02,C6) (J03,C4) (J04,C5) (J05,C6) ... (J15,C3)
```

Listing 10.5 The initial job-to-crew population (extract).

resource-constrained scheduler. Jobs within a chromosome, however, are not processed in left-to-right order. If there are n jobs in the chromosome, they are selected randomly until all n jobs have been scheduled. Listing 10.6 illustrates this with a small section of Java code from the scheduler.

The method creates a bit (Boolean) array the same size as the number of jobs in the genome (say, n). When the scheduler selects the next job to schedule, it generates a random number between $[0,n-1]$, picks that job, and sets the bit array position to "true," indicating that that job has already been scheduled. This is repeated for each of the jobs in the chromosome.

The scheduler takes a selected job, finds its early start date, and attempts to schedule the job on that day. If insufficient time exists to schedule the entire job on that day (one of the hard constraints requires each job to be contiguously scheduled), it is moved to the next day and an attempt is again made to schedule the job. This is repeated until the job is eventually scheduled. Listing 10.7 is the result of the result-constrained scheduler applied to the first generation of chromosomes.

```
boolean[] numberUsed = new boolean[genomes.length];
for(int k=0;k<genomes.length;k++) numberUsed[k]=false;

for(int g=0;g<genomes.length;g++)
  {
    int i=0;

    getNewJob:
    while(true)
    {
      i=randomNumbers.nextInt(genomes.length);
      if(!numberUsed[i])
      {
        numberUsed[i]=true;
        break getNewJob;
      }
    }
  }
}
```

Listing 10.6   Selecting random jobs from the schedule chromosome.

Upon returning from the resource-constrained scheduler, each job has a start day and a time of day (expressed as the start minute in the day). Each job is scheduled in the order it was randomly selected. Table 10.2 shows, in job order, the complete schedule for the first chromosome in the schedule.

Ordering Table 10.2 by start time within day by crew reveals the actual schedule. For example, crew 4 begins with job J08 at time zero (at start of day), and then 158 minutes later begins job J13. At this point, as shown in Table 10.3, 316 minutes (158 + 158) of its 480-minute daily availability have been used. Job J03 is now scheduled at time offset 316.

After each schedule is generated, a fitness function value is produced (see Expression 10.2). The fitness function measures the goodness of the schedule relative to the objective function (which in this case is the minimization of the completion times for all jobs). In this initial schedule, the fitness value has a wide spectrum of values, from a minimum of 2 through a maximum of 13, and an average of 4.5.

When each schedule has been evaluated, every chromosome in the population will have a fitness value. The steady-state breeder operation now randomly breeds, saves the top few best-performing chromosomes, and then breeds (applies a crossover operator) and applies the mutation operator to the remainder. Listing 10.8 shows a small extract of the new population.

```
Generation: 1: Schedule Populations


 Fitness (Job,Crew,StartDate,StartTime)
 _____ _____
 1.    4.0000 (J01,C5,1,50)   (J02,C6,1,375) (J03,C4,1,316) (J04,C1,1,146) ... (J15,C3,1,0)
 2.    6.0000 (J01,C3,1,100) (J02,C3,2,209) (J03,C4,1,316) (J04,C1,1,0)   ... (J15,C6,2,0)
 3.    3.0000 (J01,C3,1,375) (J02,C6,1,0)   (J03,C4,1,316) (J04,C1,1,346) ... (J15,C3,3,0)
 4.    5.0000 (J01,C5,1,146) (J02,C3,2,209) (J03,C4,1,316)(J04,C3,1,375)  ... (J15,C3,3,0)
 5.    7.0000 (J01,C1,1,50)  (J02,C6,1,0)   (J03,C4,1,316) (J04,C3,2,0) ...(J15,C3,3,0)
 6.    4.0000 (J01,C1,1,96)  (J02,C3,2,0)   (J03,C4,1,316) (J04,C3,1,375)... (J15,C6,2,0)
 7.    4.0000 (J01,C1,1,96)  (J02,C6,1,0)   (J03,C4,1,316) (J04,C3,2,0) ...(J15,C3,3,0)
 8.    4.0000 (J01,C1,1,146) (J02,C3,1,259) (J03,C4,1,316)(J04,C1,1,196) ... (J15,C3,2,0)
 9.    5.0000 (J01,C1,1,50)  (J02,C3,1,96)  (J03,C4,1,316) (J04,C1,2,0)  ... (J15,C6,3,0)
 10.   3.0000 (J01,C3,1,146) (J02,C3,2,0)   (J03,C4,1,316) (J04,C5,1,296) ... (J15,C3,1,196)
 11.   3.0000 (J01,C1,1,0)   (J02,C3,1,279) (J03,C4,1,0) (J04,C1,1,346)  ... (J15,C3,1,0)
 12.   5.0000 (J01,C3,1,209) (J02,C3,1,259) (J03,C4,1,0) (J04,C3,1,334)  ... (J15,C6,2,0)
 13.   3.0000 (J01,C3,1,209) (J02,C3,1,309) (J03,C4,1,0) (J04,C5,1,50)   ... (J15,C6,2,0)
 14.   3.0000 (J01,C1,1,0)   (J02,C6,1,375) (J03,C4,1,0) (J04,C1,1,346)  ... (J15,C3,1,50)
 15.   5.0000 (J01,C3,1,259) (J02,C6,1,375) (J03,C4,1,0) (J04,C5,1,0)    ... (J15,C6,2,0)
  :

  :
 130.  4.0000 (J01,C3,1,0) (J02,C6,1,279) (J03,C4,1,0) (J04,C5,1,296) ... (J15,C6,1,0)
 131.  2.0000 (J01,C5,1,0) (J02,C6,1,374) (J03,C4,1,0) (J04,C1,1,296) ... (J15,C6,1,0)
 132.  4.0000 (J01,C5,1,0) (J02,C3,1,374) (J03,C4,1,0) (J04,C1,1,96) ... (J15,C3,1,0)
 133.  4.0000 (J01,C1,1,0) (J02,C6,1,374) (J03,C4,1,0) (J04,C5,1,0) ... (J15,C6,1,0)
 134.  4.0000 (J01,C3,1,0) (J02,C6,1,279) (J03,C4,1,0) (J04,C1,2,0) ... (J15,C6,1,0)
 135.  6.0000 (J01,C3,1,279) (J02,C6,2,95) (J03,C4,1,0) (J04,C5,1,0) ... (J15,C3,1,0)


 Generation: 1
 Current Convergence Statistics
   Minimum Fitness (Best)  : 2.0000
   Maximum Fitness (Worse) : 13.000
   Average Fitness         : 4.5185
```

Listing 10.7   Generation 1 of the genetic scheduler (extract).

Newly created chromosomes and those with mutated genomes have their fitness values removed (as shown at the bottom of Listing 10.6). This initial population forms the population for the next generation of schedules. The process of creating potential schedules, scheduling each potential schedule based on resource availability and time constraints, and evaluating each schedule for its goodness of fit continues generation after generation. Listing 10.9 shows the population after 48 generations.

By the end of the genetic search (48 out of 50 generations), the population has converged toward a large number of high-performance schedules.

```
Generation: 48: Schedule Populations

  Fitness (Job,Crew,StartDate,StartTime)
  ------- --------------------------------------------------------------------
  1.    1.0000 (J01,C5,1,0)   (J02,C6,1,374) (J03,C4,1,158) (J04,C1,1,96)  ... (J15,C6,1,0)
  2.    1.0000 (J01,C5,1,96)  (J02,C6,1,95)  (J03,C4,1,316) (J04,C5,1,0)   ... (J15,C6,1,170)
  3.    1.0000 (J01,C3,1,0)   (J02,C6,1,374) (J03,C4,1,158) (J04,C5,1,50)  ... (J15,C6,1,95)
  4.    1.0000 (J01,C1,1,0)   (J02,C6,1,375) (J03,C4,1,0)   (J04,C5,1,346) ... (J15,C6,2,0)
  5.    1.0000 (J01,C1,1,96)  (J02,C6,1,304) (J03,C4,1,158) (J04,C3,1,375) ... (J15,C6,2,0)
  6.    1.0000 (J01,C1,1,96)  (J02,C3,1,405) (J03,C4,1,158) (J04,C3,1,259) ... (J15,C3,2,0)
  7.    2.0000 (J01,C1,1,392) (J02,C6,1,375) (J03,C4,1,316) (J04,C5,1,50)  ... (J15,C3,1,0)
  8.    2.0000 (J01,C5,1,0)   (J02,C3,1,146) (J03,C4,1,316) (J04,C5,1,50)  ... (J15,C3,2,0)
  9.    2.0000 (J01,C5,1,50)  (J02,C3,1,0)   (J03,C4,1,316) (J04,C5,1,100) ... (J15,C6,1,0)
 10.    2.0000 (J01,C1,1,0)   (J02,C3,1,96)  (J03,C4,1,316) (J04,C1,1,50)  ... (J15,C6,1,0)
 11.    2.0000 (J01,C3,1,0)   (J02,C6,1,374) (J03,C4,1,0)   (J04,C1,1,296) ... (J15,C6,1,0)
 12.    2.0000 (J01,C5,1,0)   (J02,C3,1,374) (J03,C4,1,0)   (J04,C5,1,146) ... (J15,C3,1,0)
  :
  :
133.    3.0000 (J01,C5,1,146) (J02,C6,1,0)   (J03,C4,1,158) (J04,C5,1,0)   ... (J15,C6,1,75)
134.    4.0000 (J01,C3,1,424) (J02,C6,1,0)   (J03,C4,1,158) (J04,C5,1,0)   ... (J15,C3,1,50)
135.    4.0000 (J01,C3,1,424) (J02,C6,1,0)   (J03,C4,1,158) (J04,C5,1,0)   ... (J15,C3,1,50)

Generation: 48
Current Convergence Statistics
  Minimum Fitness (Best)  : 1.0000
  Maximum Fitness (Worse) : 4.0000
  Average Fitness         : 2.4592
```

Listing 10.9 Generation 48 of crew scheduler (extract).

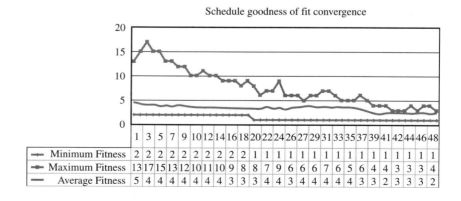

Figure 10.13 The goodness-of-fit convergence.

```
BEST SCHEDULE CONFIGURATION
Order: Service Order (Job) Name
Service Order   Duration Crew   Day Time
-------------   -------------   --------
 1. J01            50 C5         1 0800
 2. J02            75 C6         1 1414
 3. J03            58 C4         1 1038
 4. J04            96 C1         1 0936
 5. J05           209 C3         1 0850
 6. J06            50 C3         1 0800
 7. J07            95 C6         1 1239
 8. J08           158 C4         1 0800
 9. J09            96 C1         1 0800
10. J10           209 C3         1 1219
11. J11            50 C1         1 1112
12. J12           375 C3         2 0800
13. J13           158 C4         1 1136
14. J14           296 C5         1 0850
15. J15           279 C6         1 0800


------------------------------------------------------------


BEST SCHEDULE CONFIGURATION
Order: Crew Assignment/Date and Time of Day
Service Order   Duration Crew   Day Time
-------------   -------------   --------
 1. J09            96 C1         1 0800
 2. J04            96 C1         1 0936
 3. J11            50 C1         1 1112
 4. J06            50 C3         1 0800
 5. J05           209 C3         1 0850
 6. J10           209 C3         1 1219
 7. J12           375 C3         2 0800
 8. J08           158 C4         1 0800
 9. J03            58 C4         1 1038
10. J13           158 C4         1 1136
11. J01            50 C5         1 0800
12. J14           296 C5         1 0850
13. J15           279 C6         1 0800
14. J07            95 C6         1 1239
15. J02            75 C6         1 1414
```

Listing 10.10 The best resource-constrained crew schedule.

10.8 **Topology Constraint Algorithms and Techniques**

The crew scheduler is representative of a broad class of problems that are strictly (or mostly) concerned with placing objects in time subject only to resource availability. None of the jobs has a time dependency on any of the other jobs in the schedule. That is, any job can move backward or forward in time without directly affecting[5] the scheduled start or completion time of any other job. When two (or more) jobs are dependent on each other, they have a precedence relationship with each other. These dependencies form a graph. Before taking up the issues associated with predecessor-successor constraints in a genetic scheduling system, we review some basic principles in graph theory.

A Brief Introduction to Graph Theory

Scheduling is predicated on a branch of mathematics known as graph theory. Graphs are collections of "things" connected in some fashion. Generally speaking, a graph and a network are equivalent and we use the terms somewhat interchangeably. This introduction is intended to be just that: a high-altitude and rather superficial discussion of the way graphs are assembled, what they can represent, and how they become concrete representations instead of arbitrary abstractions.

Nodes and Edges: Basic Terminology

The basic principles and terminology of a graph are fairly easy to understand. Essentially, a graph consists of two components: *nodes* and *edges*. Nodes are connected by edges. Figure 10.14 shows the organization of a simple graph.[6]

This graph has four nodes (A, B, C, and D) and five edges (e1, e2, e3, e4, and e5). Note that a node is an object or thing in the network and the edge is the relationship that establishes the connection between two

---

[5] Even without explicit precedence relationships, the slippage of job A can affect the start or completion of job B if they share the same crew or if they both need, for example, a piece of equipment that has limited availability.

[6] Although graphs and networks share a common topology (shape), they differ in a technical way. Graphs are homogeneous: all of their nodes are the same. Networks, on the other hand, are heterogeneous. That is, their nodes can be different types of things. For example, a network of computers can have nodes that are application and web servers, mainframes, desktop computers, load balancers, and other devices.

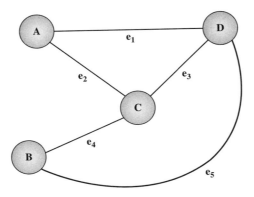

Figure 10.14 The organization of a simple graph.

nodes. It is common practice in graph theory to refer to a unique edge by the two nodes it connects (thus, edge e1 is *A,D*, or simply *AD*). Both nodes and edges can have a wide assortment of properties. Some of these properties are associated with the nature of the node, whereas others are associated with the organization, semantics, and characteristics of the graph itself.

Connectivity

If you can navigate from any node in a graph to any other node in the graph, the graph has the important property of being fully connected. The way you get from node X to node Y is called a *path* (which represents a list of all edges in the order that they must be traveled). In most graphs, the path from one node to another is not unique. Thus, for the network shown in Figure 10.14 the path from B to D could be any of the following.

	Path
1	(B, C)(C, D)
2	(B, D)
3	(B, C)(C, A)(A, D)

Because a graph is an abstraction, the number of edges in a path does not necessarily reflect the length of the route. The length depends, usually, on some value of the edge (the value being measured). For example, suppose Figure 10.15 represents the highway distances (or traveling times) on the roads that connect four neighboring cities in the Midwest.

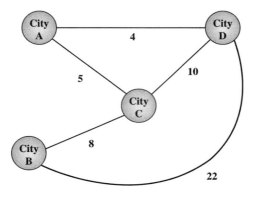

Figure 10.15   Highway travel distances between cities.

In this case, the direct path from city B to city D is 22 miles, but the shortest path is through city C and then through city A and on to city D (for a total of 17 miles). In the travel graph shown in Figure 10.15, the edges contain the distances between cities and the nodes are the cities themselves. Nodes and edges can have rather complex properties. As an uncomplicated example, the city node might also contain the average travel time through the city. The edge could contain the distance in miles as well as the average speed limit,[7] any toll charges, the amount of highway construction arrayed by month and time of day, the average number of speeding tickets given to in-state and out-of-state drivers over the past 12 months (by month), and the driving conditions (snowfall, rain, and so on) by time of year. With these properties a network analysis could arrive at many driving solutions between these cities, such as the least cost, least time (independent of risk), least time (weighted by risk and best time to travel), worse time to travel, and so forth.

Direction and Cycles

Graphs come in a variety of flavors: cyclical and acyclical, as well as directed and undirected. These two concepts are very closely related. A directed graph means that node-to-node movement is restricted to a specific direction (such as left to right or top to bottom). A cyclical graph allows loops and generally means that the graph is undirected. In Figure 10.15, for example, a driver can go from city B to city D and then

---

[7] Hence, a short path that has several edges at a low speed limit might take longer to travel than a longer path with most or all edges having a high speed limit.

drive back from city D to city B. The graph does not specify a direction of process flow. A driver can also drive from city C to city D to city A and back to city C (thus making a loop within the graph).

Although graphs in a large number of applications are loop tolerant, most scheduling applications (such as project management and crew scheduling) require a directed, acyclical graph. A crew schedule is directed in time. It cannot contain any loops (which are considered errors in the network graph, because following a loop would mean going back in time and would introduce dependency errors in the network). Each node represents a job and specifies the associated resource and time requirements. The edges not only connect the nodes in precedence order but allow for overlaps in the way successor nodes can start.

Scheduling Network Dependency Issues

The precedence relationship enforces a time constraint. If job A must occur before job B, a slip in the completion of job A might mean a slip in the start of job B. These types of dependencies are common in most scheduling and configuration problems. For example, Figure 10.16 is a small critical path precedence network in a project-scheduling system.

In a more practical and real-world crew-scheduling system, this independence from precedence constraints seldom exists. If a crew is scheduled to work on job A and then work on job B, job B cannot be wholly independent from the completion of job A. The network of interconnected jobs forms the topology of the schedule. This topology places a hard constraint on the feasibility of a schedule. How a network places a constraint, however, depends on the nature of the precedence relationship. Figure 10.17 illustrates a small portion of a crew schedule with a set of jobs, their assigned crews, and their precedence relationships.

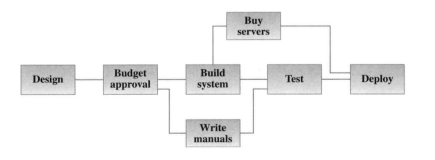

Figure 10.16 A project critical path network.

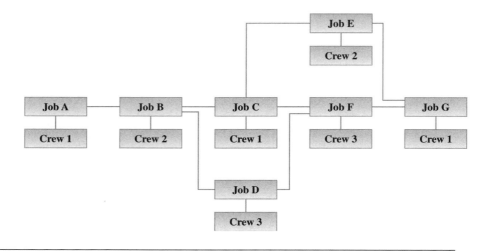

Figure 10.17   A crew schedule with precedence-connected jobs.

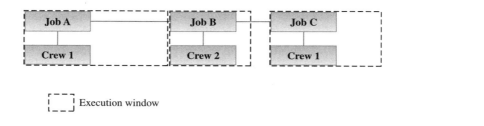

Figure 10.18   The execution windows for jobs A, B, and C.

The nature of the precedence relationships determines how tightly a schedule is constrained. For example, from Figure 10.15 suppose job A slips. What impact will this have on job B? This depends to a large extent on the size of job A's permissible execution window. Figure 10.18 examines the schedule in finer detail, showing the execution windows for jobs A, B, and C.

If job A's actual completion time falls within the execution window, job B can still start on its scheduled (earliest) start time. Job B, on the other hand, has a very narrow execution window, and thus even a small amount of slippage will have an effect on the scheduled start time of job C. In crew schedules that use execution windows, the overall effect is a network that is very similar to a critical path project network with built-in float.

Types of Dependency Relationships

The network constraints discussed so far have been finish-to-start (FS) relationships. These are the most common, but a complex crew, project, configuration, or loading schedule can be constrained by many other types of relationships. Each network relationship is a dependency strategy. The strategy can also have an associated weight, the meaning of which depends on the associated strategy. A scheduling (or any other type of general network) can support the followings types of precedence relationships.

- Finish-to-finish (FF). An activity cannot finish until its predecessor event is also complete. The weight value entered with the strategy indicates a lag time between the completion of the predecessor and the completion of the successor. Figure 10.19 illustrates a finish-to-finish relationship.

- Finish-to-start (FS). An activity cannot start until its predecessor event is complete. This is generally the default precedence relationship in a network. The weight is entered with the strategy, indicating a lag time between finish of the predecessor activity and the start of the successor activity. Figure 10.20 illustrates a finish-to-start relationship.

- Start-to-finish (SF). An activity cannot complete until its predecessor event starts. The weight entered with the strategy indicates an overlap

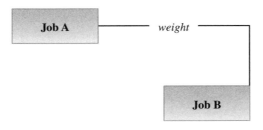

Figure 10.19   The finish-to-finish strategy.

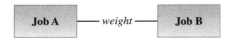

Figure 10.20   The finish-to-start strategy.

of lead times between the predecessor and successor events. Figure 10.21 illustrates a start-to-finish relationship.

■ Start-to-start (SS). An activity cannot start until its predecessor activity also starts. The weight entered with the strategy indicates an overlap of the starting times for the predecessor and successor activity. Figure 10.22 illustrate a start-to-start relationship.

In crew scheduling, the lag value on the finish-to-start relationship (the most common strategy) can be used to specify the travel time between jobs. For example, in Figure 10.23 consider the finish-to-start precedence relationship.

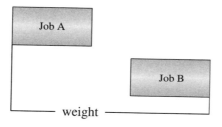

Figure 10.21 The start-to-finish strategy.

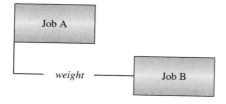

Figure 10.22 The start-to-start strategy.

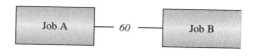

Figure 10.23 A delay relationship between activities.

When job A is complete, 60 minutes must elapse before job B can start. This reflects the travel time from the site of job A to the site of job B. An important enhancement to crew-scheduling systems involves learning the optimal travel time weight for a job that occurs in the neighborhood of site X and is followed by a job occurring in the neighborhood of site Y. Using the actual values form the completed work order forms, a real-time, long-range GA can, for example, explore the effects of generating travel times for future schedules that slightly extend or slightly contract the travel times — depending on whether the jobs in the *(SiteX,Site Y)* relation in the previous schedule experienced a slippage or completed on time (or completed early).

Representing Dependency Graphs

There are several compact ways to represent a precedence graph. Perhaps the best and the easiest to use is the dependency matrix. This approach not only provides simple methods for traversing the graph but incorporates robust and flexible methods of specifying and managing the properties of both nodes and edges. To see how the dependency (sometimes called an adjacency) matrix is used consider the simple scheduling network shown in Figure 10.17. The dependency graph is an $N \times N$ square matrix. For nodes N_1, N_2, N_3, and N_k, rows R_i and column C_i correspond to node N_i. The rows (vertical nodes) are the *FROM* nodes, and the columns (horizontal nodes) are the *TO* nodes. In its simplest form, the dependency matrix is Boolean. We place a "1" (or true) value in any *(row,column)* intersection when there is an edge between the *FROM* node and the *TO* node. To see how this works, consider the crew schedule network shown in Figure 10.15. The corresponding dependency matrix[8] is shown in Figure 10.24.

This matrix representation lacks ambiguity and is essentially direction free as long we are consistent in the way we specify the topology of the network. The choice of representation is, of course, somewhat arbitrary. In Figure 10.22 we listed the nodes in left-to-right order (the way we visualize them in a time-ordered crew schedule). We could also enter the nodes in top-to-bottom order or any order that records each unique edge only once in the network. In this way, dependency matrices can represent any arbitrarily complex graph (such as a tree of class inheritances).

---

[8] The zero (Boolean *false*) values have been omitted for clarity.

$$\begin{array}{c} \\ \\ FROM\text{-}Node \end{array} \begin{array}{c} TO\text{-}Node \\ \begin{array}{ccccccc} A & B & C & D & E & F & G \end{array} \\ \begin{array}{c} A \\ B \\ C \\ D \\ E \\ F \\ G \end{array} \left[\begin{array}{ccccccc} & 1 & & & & & \\ & & 1 & 1 & & & \\ & & & & 1 & 1 & \\ & & & & & 1 & \\ & & & & & & 1 \\ & & & & & & 1 \\ & & & & & & \end{array} \right] \end{array}$$

Figure 10.24 The job schedule dependency matrix.

Implementing Edge Properties

How do we incorporate node and edge properties into the dependency matrix? One of the significant advantages of the matrix approach is the ease with which we can specify edge and node properties. We simply replace the Boolean value in the row and column intersection with a reference to an edge property object. When the intersection is *NULL* (or empty), we know that no edge exists (equivalent to the Boolean *false*). Otherwise, we examine the edge object to determine the properties of this particular edge. Because nodes are only implied in the matrix, we create an ordered array of node identifiers and an associated node property object (these need not, of course, be two distinct objects). Figure 10.25 shows a schematic of how this might appear.

The node array provides a clean and rapid correlation between any row or column in the matrix and its corresponding node (thus, the node for Row_i is simply $Node_i$ in the array). This data structure allows us to robustly and efficiently handle node and edge properties. It also provides both the key mechanism for traversing the graph and connecting multiple graphs into a heterogeneous network.

Sparse Matrix Representations

A significant drawback to the dependency matrix representation is its storage requirements. The computer memory needed to store the matrix grows exponentially as the square of the number of nodes. Furthermore,

TO - Node

FROM - Node	A	B	C	D	E	F	G
A		e_1^p					
B			e_2^p	e_3^p			
C					e_4^p	e_5^p	
D						e_6^p	
E							e_7^p
F							e_8^p
G							

$\rightarrow$

Node	Properties
A	$(p_1, p_2, ..., p_n)$
B	$(p_1, p_2, ..., p_n)$
C	$(p_1, p_2, ..., p_n)$
D	$(p_1, p_2, ..., p_n)$
E	$(p_1, p_2, ..., p_n)$
F	$(p_1, p_2, ..., p_n)$
G	$(p_1, p_2, ..., p_n)$

Figure 10.25   Adding node and edge properties to the matrix.

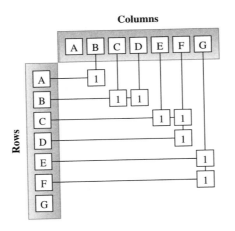

Figure 10.26   A sparse matrix representation.

the actual network itself is almost always represented by just a small number of non-zero cells (relative to the very large size of the matrix). This means that the matrix is very sparse. Fortunately, efficient and very robust space matrix algorithms exist that can represent extremely large matrices in a small amount of actual storage. As Figure 10.26 illustrates, a sparse matrix only stores the non-zero (or nonempty) cells.

In this example (using the graph in Figure 10.22), only nine out of a possible 81 cells are stored, meaning that only 11% of the matrix actually exists in computer memory. Sparse matrix representations allow scheduling, configuration, and routing models to form very large multinetwork graphs and perform high-speed data access and analysis without loss of generality or extensive modifications to existing analysis algorithms.

Graph Traversal Algorithms

To move forward in the matrix (from left to right for the graph in Figure 10.22) along the first available path, we follow the chains implicit in the matrix rows. This is expressed in the following algorithm.

Let $D(n,n)$ be the dependency matrix of n nodes
Let $N(n)$ be the ordered set of node identifiers
Let $P(n)$ be the ordered path found by this algorithm
Let S be the current node identifier

```
Traversal:
P() ← empty
S ← a Node Identifier
P(1) ← S
Walk_Forward:
   k = location of S in N()
   for j=1 to n
      if D(k,j) not NULL then
         insert N(j) into P()
         S ← N(j)
         Goto Walk_Forward
      End if
      Exit Traversal
   End for
```

Note that this algorithm returns the path associated with the first node in each row. Thus, starting with node A the algorithm finds B as the first node identifier. It then stores (A,B), sets the current node to B, and searches across the row associated with node B. It will then find node C, and store (B,C). This continues until it finds an empty row or column. Any number of recursive or stack-based extensions to this algorithm would allow it to search through all paths from the starting node identifier to the end of the graph.

To move backward in the matrix (from right to left for the graph in Figure 10.22) along the first available path, we follow the chains implicit in the matrix columns. This is really a trivial modification to the algorithm (essentially reversing the subscripts in testing for an empty $D()$ matrix position), which for completeness is expressed in the following algorithm.

Let   D(n,n) be the dependency matrix of n nodes
Let   N(n) be the ordered set of node identifiers
Let   P(n) be the ordered path found by this algorithm
Let   S be the current node identifier

```
Traversal:
P() ← empty
S ← a Node Identifier
P(1) ← S
Walk_Backward:
   k = location of S in N()
   for j=1 to n
      if D(j,k) not NULL then
         insert N(j) into P()
         S ← N(j)
         Goto Walk_backward
      End if
      Exit Traversal
   End for
```

These simple graph-traversal algorithms provide the core mechanism for incorporating all node and edge property capabilities (although this description has excluded, as overly detailed, the necessary table lookup routines, the associated node identifier tables, and the exact nature of the node and edge objects). This extensibility and robustness in design allow the easy development of much more advanced families of graph exploration algorithms.

Topological Sorts

A topological sort places the nodes of a network in their dependency order. The algorithm is used to create a working list of nodes for subsequent processing and to detect loops in the network. The algorithm is relatively straightforward.

```
while not done
   if the graph is empty, then we're done
      exit the loop
   pick a node with no predecessors
   if no such node exists
      send message "the graph has a loop"
      exit the sort
   output that node (number that node)
   delete that node from the graph
end while
```

For example, a topological sort applied to the crew-scheduling schedule shown in Figure 10.17 creates a linear, ordered array of the job nodes. Listing 10.11 shows a small Java program that creates the job schedule network, prints out the topology in backward and forward order, performs a topological sort, and displays the results.

This small Java driver for the topology display facilities creates a network (an instance of the topology manager) and populates it with the job network (shown in Figure 10.17). It then creates an instance of the topological sort for this network and displays the results. Listing 10.12 is the audit log from this program, with the topological sort output shown at the bottom.

A topological sort guarantees that the identifiers will be in precedence order. This means that when we select Job_n for processing we are certain that all predecessors for Job_n are in the list from Job_1 to Job_{n-1}. The topological sort does not necessarily place them in the best possible order. In the topological sort order in Listing 10.11, perhaps a better organization would have placed *Job-D* immediately before *Job-F*.

The topological sort is also an important network validation tool because it can check for loops in an acyclical directed graph — exactly the type of graph we use in crew scheduling. If we change the network construction to connect job F back to job A (thus forming a loop in the network), the outcome of the topology driver (Listing 10.13) now appears with a loop error.

Understanding the nature of precedence networks and how they are constructed and used is crucial in designing advanced genetic scheduling, configuration, planning, and transportation systems. Network topology constraints must be considered in the design of the genome, in the methods of creating an initial population, in techniques for crossover breeding, and in the allowable forms of genome mutation. The idea of a feasible schedule in complex genetic scheduling systems must consistently involve a topological analysis of the network.

```
public class JobTopoSort{

public static void main(String args[]) {

//--Configure the Log File System
aiLogMgr.initLog("crews", "c:/jobs/", "joblog.fil");
aiAuditMgr.initAudit(aiModelManager.CLASSNAME,
   true,false,aiAuditMgr.MAXIMUM,"crews","c:/jobs/","audit.fil");

System.out.println(" 1--creating an empty network.");
aiTopologyManager network = new aiTopologyManager("mynetwork");
try
  {
  System.out.println(" 2--adding the job nodes");
  network.connect("Job-A","Job-B");
  network.connect("Job-B","Job-C");
  network.connect("Job-B","Job-D");
  network.connect("Job-C","Job-E");
  network.connect("Job-C","Job-F");
  network.connect("Job-E","Job-G");
  network.connect("Job-F","Job-G");
  System.out.println(" 3--nodes have been added.");
  System.out.println(" 4--network structure reports.");
  aiModelLogger.msg("Unique Network Node Identifiers:");
  String[] keys = network.getIdentifiers();
  for(int i=0;i<keys.length;i++)
    aiModelLogger.msg(keys[i]);

  aiModelLogger.msg(" ");
  network.setTraverseDirection(aiModelConstants.FORWARD);
  network.printNetwork("The forward network topology");
  network.setTraverseDirection(aiModelConstants.BACKWARD);
  network.printNetwork("The backward network topology");

  System.out.println(" 5--calling topological sort.");
  aiModelLogger.msg("Performing topological sort");
  aiTopologicalSort tsort = new aiTopologicalSort(network);
  Vector orderedKeys = tsort.order();
  System.out.println(" 6--topological sort is complete.");

  aiModelLogger.msg("Topological Order:");
  for(int i=0;i<orderedKeys.size();i++)
    aiModelLogger.msg((String)orderedKeys.get(i));
  return;
  }
catch(Exception e) {
    System.out.println("ERROR. " + e.getMessage());
    }
  }

}
```

Listing 10.11 The Java topological sort program.

```
Audit Level   : MAXIMUM
Debug         : On

Unique Network Node Identifiers:
Job-A
Job-B
Job-C
Job-D
Job-E
Job-F
Job-G


The forward network topology
   The Network nodes
   From-Node   Edges    To-Node
   ---------   -----    -------
1.             Job-F   1 Job-G
2.             Job-E   1 Job-G
3.             Job-C   2 Job-E Job-F
4.             Job-B   2 Job-C Job-D
5.             Job-A   1 Job-B

The backward network topology
   The Network nodes
   To-Node   Edges    From-Node
   -------   -----    ---------
1.           Job-G   2 Job-E Job-F
2.           Job-F   1 Job-C
3.           Job-E   1 Job-C
4.           Job-D   1 Job-B
5.           Job-C   1 Job-B
6.           Job-B   1 Job-A

Performing topological sort
Topological Order:
Job-A
Job-B
Job-D
Job-C
Job-F
Job-E
Job-G
```

Listing 10.12 Topology operations and sort on job schedule.

```
1--creating an empty network.
2--adding the job nodes
3--nodes have been added.
4--network structure reports.
5--calling topological sort.
ERROR. [ID: com.scianta.model.topology.aiTopologicalSort-0003]
   [Severity: 05]=> Unable to place network into topological order.
    ::[ID: com.scianta.model.topology.aiTopologicalSort-0005]
      [Severity: 01]=> Unable to order. Loop exists in topology.
      Probable Loop: Job-A to Job-F
```

Listing 10.13 Topological sort with a loop error.

10.9 **Adaptive Parameter Optimization**

A schedule relies on the accuracy of its constraints and its parameters. Many of the parameters in a schedule are often difficult to predict and establish with a high degree of certainty. Yet, the relative precision of parameter values affects not only the outcome of the schedule but the way in which optimization is achieved. There are several critical factors (or parameters) that are especially important in evolving a workable and effective crew schedule. These include the following.

- *Job duration times:* The actual time necessary to complete a job given the type, location, intrinsic difficulty, site work constraints, crew assignment, and other variables associated with the job itself. This is often quite different from the "standard" time associated with a particular type of job. Job duration times are often time-of-day dependent.

- *Crew efficiencies:* The actual productivity or effective skill efficiency of one crew versus another crew with the same skills in the same geographic or demographic region. Crew effectiveness is a critical measure in managing the assignment of crews to high-priority, high-cost, or high-risk jobs.

- *Travel times between sites:* The actual elapse time necessary for a crew to travel from site X to site Y. Learning the time-of-day variations or the travel constraint properties of certain sites allows the scheduler to fine tune the actual travel times between customer sites, thus providing a more robust and realistic schedule.

- *Available crew times:* Each crew has a calendar that specifies its total daily availability and its time-of-day intervals that are open for work. Actual available times are often different from the theoretical (calendar-based) times. Learning to estimate the effective available supply of a crew as well as its effective available time intervals significantly improves scheduling performance.

- *Crew size or crew composition:* The organization or size of a crew often has a direct bearing on its effectiveness, adaptability, and travel time. Crew size is also a factor in setup and tear-down times for jobs.

- *Job prioritization:* How to effectively prioritize jobs based on past customer experiences, risk assessment, travel time, and other factors provides an important ordering element that can be critical in satisfying one class of jobs over another.

The first three of these factors (duration times, crew efficiency, and travel times) are part of the standard machine learning facilities in the crew scheduler. This machine learning approach uses an adaptive feedback mechanism to learn the actual properties of these parameters. This is accomplished by comparing the estimated or standard values for parameters (such as the normal or standard duration time for a particular type of job) with the actual value for the parameter. In this way, the system evolves a set of crew-to-job performance metrics. Figure 10.27 illustrates schematically how the best values for a schedule are developed by an adaptive learning technique.

The optimization of scheduling parameters involves two principal components: a mechanism that learns the behavior of crews "in the field" and compares this behavior to the parameters that generated the current schedule, and an adaptive feedback loop that adjusts the set of parameters for the next schedule.

❶ The Current Schedule

The current schedule is generated from the mixture of crews and jobs based on the set of constraint parameters, such as estimated job duration times, travel times, crew availability, and crew skill effectiveness. This schedule is the currently fielded and operational plan.

❷ The Actual Completion Statistics

A learning mechanism needs to know how the scheduled jobs were actually completed. This is a measure of how well the schedule matched

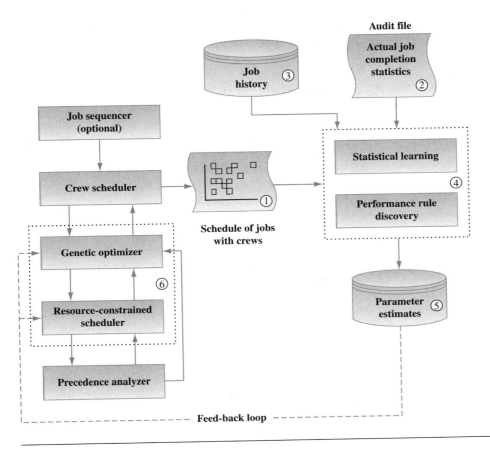

Figure 10.27   The adaptive schedule parameter optimization.

reality. In most cases the acquisition of job completion statistics is fairly straightforward and is derived form the field service report associated with the job. The fundamental properties the scheduler needs to extract from the actual completion data are the differences between the times specified in the current schedule and the times actually recorded by the crew.

❸ The Job History Repository

The scheduler maintains a comprehensive repository of past job completion statistics. The history provides the foundation for learning about the past and predicting the future. Each current schedule is transformed into a set of descriptive statistics that is used by the learning mechanism.

❹ The Machine Learning System

The machine learning facilities are the core of parameter optimization. The first component of this system is based on statistical learning theory and extracts, from the historical database and from the differences between the planned and actual schedules (the value for each parameter over time). As Figure 10.28 illustrates, these values are discovered at various levels of granularity. The granularities constitute various types of periodic cycles across time.

The second component of the machine learning system is a very advanced and very deep pattern-recognition processor. Using a form of knowledge discovery (also known as data mining), this process extracts behavior rules in the form of fuzzy logic from the historical database. These rules are stored in a knowledge base and are used to make fine-grain classification and categorization decisions. As Figure 10.29 illustrates, the combination leads to better and better values for critical scheduling parameters.

As the learning progresses, the parameters converge on a small optimal range of values consistent with the properties of the associated feature. Learning is a continuous process that provides constant reinforcement so that values change as the scheduling environment changes.

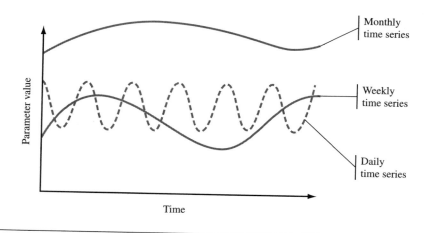

Figure 10.28 The periodic behavior of parameters.

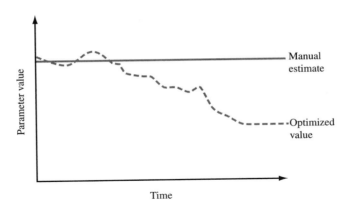

Figure 10.29   Estimated versus optimized parameters.

❺ **Parameter Estimates**

This is the result of the statistical learning and rule extraction — a collection of estimates for each of the underlying parameters associated with the schedule. The parameter estimates are designed to coincide with the actual schedule parameters. This means that duration time estimates, for example, are computed for individual job classes (such as jobs of the same type, at the same site location, and falling within the same periodicity).

❻ **The Feedback Loop**

The current generation of parameter estimates is fed back into the genetic scheduler and the resource constraint scheduler to produce the next-generation schedule. The actual completion statistics for this schedule are then used to compute or refine the parameters, thus completing the feedback loop.

   Adaptive optimization of the underlying scheduling parameters allows the scheduler to respond dynamically and continuously to the actual performance of crews, as well as to the actual estimates for job time duration. This dual approach to optimality provides unequaled power and flexibility.

10.10   **Review**

Multiobjective and multiconstraint scheduling problems are members of a larger class of computationally intensive and computationally difficult problems. These problems take many forms and appear in various guises in a broad spectrum of industries, as well as in policy formulation and military strategic decision making. Examples include route planning, production and materials requirement scheduling, integrated circuit fabrication design, network topology optimization, and containerization and packing. The resource-constrained crew scheduling application in this chapter illustrates many of the important features and capabilities of evolutionary systems — features that when combined with fuzzy system modeling allow system architects and designs to build robust, flexible, adaptive components to corporate and agency applications. From this chapter you should now be familiar with the following.

- The concepts behind resource-constrained scheduling
- How to represent schedules in a varying-length genome
- How to organize and implement objective functions as well as hard and soft constraints
- The way a genetic system is partitioned into two major object components: the GA and the underlying scheduler (or other complex allocation, scheduling, or configuration system)
- How to measure fitness, convergence, and the effect of constraints on the problem as the genetic search engine works toward a solution
- Techniques and algorithms for implementing precedence and other topology constraints
- How to apply the basic principles of the crew scheduler to a broad family of similar problems to solve similar objectives

The core technologies and methods used in the crew scheduler are found throughout the modern enterprise, government agencies, and the military. This chapter has provided a way of examining the application of GAs in a structured problem domain in much the same way that the fuzzy SQL application provides a way of examining the use of fuzzy logic in a well-focused, structured domain (see Chapter 6).

Further Reading

■   Goldberg, D. E. "A Note on Boltzmann Tournament Selection for Genetic Algorithms and Population-Oriented Simulated Annealing," in *Complex Systems*, *Volume 4*, pp. 445–460, Complex Systems Publications, 1990.

■ Goldberg, D. E. *Genetic Algorithms in Search, Optimization, and Machine Learning*. Reading, MA: Addison-Wesley, 1989.

■ Goldberg, D. E. "Real-coded Genetic Algorithms, Virtual Alphabets, and Blocking," in *Complex Systems, Volume 5*, pp. 139–167, Complex Systems Publications, 1991.

■ Goldberg, D. E., and K. Deb. "A Comparative Analysis of Selection Schemes Used in Genetic Algorithms," in *Foundations of Genetic Algorithms*, G. J. E. Rawlins (ed.), pp. 69–93, San Mateo, CA: Morgan Kaufmann Publishers, 1991.

■ Goldberg, D. E., and J. Richardson. Genetic Algorithms with Sharing for Multimodal Function Optimization," in *Genetic Algorithms and their Applications: Proceedings of the Second International Conference on Genetic Algorithms*, pp. 41–49, 1987.

■ Goldberg, D. E., K. Deb, and J. H. Clark. "Genetic Algorithms, Noise, and the Sizing of Populations," in: *Complex Systems, Vol. 6*, pp. 333–362, Complex Systems Publications, Inc., 1992.

■ Krishnakumar, K., "Micro-Genetic Algorithms for Stationary and Non-Stationary Function Optimization," *SPIE: Intelligent Control and Adaptive Systems*, Vol. 1196, Philadelphia, PA, 1989.

■ Syswerda, G., "Uniform Crossover in Genetic Algorithms," in: *Proceedings of the Third International Conference on Genetic Algorithms*, J. Schaffer, (Ed.), pp. 2–9, Los Altos, CA: Morgan Kaufmann Publishers, Los Altos, CA, 1989.

Chapter 11
Genetic Tuning of Fuzzy Models

Fuzzy models come in two broad flavors: those in which the underlying fuzzy sets represent the semantics of the model and those in which the underlying fuzzy sets represent a somewhat arbitrary partitioning of the data space in each variable. The pricing model (see Chapter 5) is an example of a semantic-based fuzzy model. The fuzzy models generated by the rule induction process (see Chapter 8) represent the latter class of fuzzy models. Fuzzy control systems represent models that straddle the two extremes. Because fuzzy models are highly dependent on the term sets underlying each variable and on the method of aggregation and defuzzification, they are often difficult to design and tune. In this chapter we examine the ways in which a genetic tuner can optimize the architecture of a fuzzy model created through the rule induction process.

11.1 The Genetic Tuner Process

The genetic tuner optimizes the architecture of a fuzzy model by creating a population of new parameter specifications for the rule induction process. The parameters are encoded in the chromosome as real numbers representing the controls for the rule induction mechanism. Each chromosome represents the definition of a complete fuzzy system. Figure 11.1 schematically illustrates the overall flow and control mechanism for the genetic tuner.

❶ Generate and Initialize the Genetic Algorithm

The initial phase of the genetic tuner involves the design and implementation of a chromosome population to represent a set of parameters for inducing, executing, and evaluating a collection of rules (the fuzzy KB). For example, a fuzzy model that predicts investment risk from a

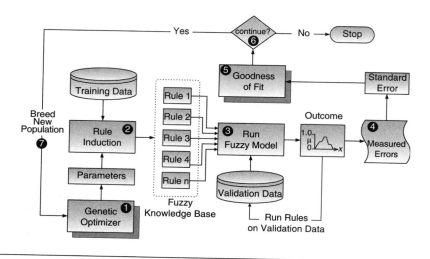

Figure 11.1 The fuzzy model genetic tuner.

Rule Induction Parameters Chromosome								
Client_Age			Client_Income			Investment_Risk		
#Sets	Shape	%Overlap	#Sets	Shape	%Overlap	#Sets	Shape	%Overlap

Figure 11.2 A simple rule induction chromosome.

client's age and income has three variables (*Client_Age, Client_Income,* and *Investment_Risk*). Figure 11.2 shows how a chromosome in the parameter population might appear.

This chromosome specifies for each variable the number of fuzzy sets (*#Sets*), the shape of the fuzzy set (triangular, trapezoidal, bell-shaped, and so forth, encoded as an enumerated value), and the percentage of overlap on each fuzzy set.[1] From this chromosome structure a random population of possible values is created, producing the initial population of fuzzy system models. At the same time, of course, a set of constraints must be developed. General constraints include not only restrictions on the fuzzy set shape values (the random number must be in the interval *[1 ... n],*

---

[1] Naturally, a more complex genome structure is possible (see the following section on Objective Function).

where *n* is the number of possible fuzzy set shapes), but constraints (for example) on the number of fuzzy sets and the amount of overlap. The minimum number of fuzzy sets might be held to three, and the maximum perhaps to some number that reflects the magnitude of the underlying domain. The overlap percentage should be constrained to the interval *[10,80]*.

In the case of a simple performance optimization model, the objective function is easy to specify. The model must minimize the standard error of estimate for the model's outcome variable (see "Evaluate Goodness of Fit"). Although accuracy is the primary objective of any tuning process, other contingent objective functions are possible (such as minimizing the number of fuzzy sets or minimizing the number of variables).[2]

❷ **Rule Induction**

Each chromosome defines a way of inducing rules from the data. Rule induction reads the associated training data file and, using the parameters in the current chromosome, creates the fuzzy KB. In the simplest case, the parameters define the number and shape of fuzzy sets in each variable's term set. This KB contains the *if-then* rules derived from the underlying data.

❸ **Run the Fuzzy Model**

Once the fuzzy KB has been created through rule induction, the rules are executed against the validation data file. The validation file compares the outcome generated by the rules against the actual value for each observation (record) in the validation file. The difference is the degree of error in the estimate.

❹ **Accumulate Measured Errors for Each Instance**

In this step the tuner measures the degree of error between the estimated and the actual values for each record or instance in the validation file. The standard error of estimate is used to find the accuracy of the current model.

---

[2] A genetic tuner can also provide variable selection or principal component analysis for an outcome variable by randomly selecting a collection of independent variables from the complete population of possible independent variables. The combination of variable with the minimum standard error of estimate is the best model.

Expression 11.1 defines this measure.

$$e_{\text{est}} = \sqrt{\frac{\sum_{i=1}^{N} (x_i^a - x_i^e)^2}{N}} \qquad (11.1)$$

Here,

e	is the error of estimate for the current model
N	is the total number of observations in the validation file
x^a	is actual value of outcome for the i-th observation
x^e	is estimated value of outcome for the i-th observation

When the estimate is close to the actual, the variance will be small. Thus, a small standard error in the model indicates a fuzzy system configuration with good predictive power.

❺ Evaluate Goodness of Fit

The standard error is a measure of how well a particular fuzzy model performs in predicting an outcome value. The smaller the standard error the better the model. In most instances this is sufficient to assign a goodness-of-fit value to a chromosome. After a fuzzy model, generated from a chromosome's parameters, has computed the standard error from the validation data file, this standard error is stored in the chromosome as the genome's goodness of fit.

❻ Decide Whether to Evolve More Models

When the current population of chromosomes has been evaluated, each chromosome will have a goodness-of-fit value indicating how well the model performed. Now some exit condition must be evaluated. This can be a maximum number of generations, but is more often a measure of the improvement in the overall population. This improvement, shown in Expression 11.2, is based on the average fitness in the population.

$$f_a = \frac{1}{N} \sum_{i=1}^{N} f_i \qquad (11.2)$$

Here,

f_a	is the average population fitness
N	is the total number of chromosomes in the population
f_i	is the fitness of the i-th chromosome

The average fitness is a measure of convergence in the population. If the genetic tuner is working correctly, the average should improve over time (the average standard error should approach zero). We can then decide to terminate the genetic tuner when there is no more improvement in the average chromosome fitness. That is, we can terminate when the GA has reached a steady state. Expression 11.3 shows how a termination condition can be established.

$$f_d = \frac{1}{N} \left(\sum_{i=1}^{N-1} (f_i^a - f_{i+1}^a) \right)$$

$$f_d \approx M$$

(11.3)

Here,

f_d is the average change in the population fitness

f_a is the average fitness of a population for the specified generation

N is the number of generations over which to compute the change in the average fitness

M is the change tolerance (a value, such as .005, indicating that if the difference in average population fitness over the previous N generations is not greater than M then the population has reached a steady state)

For a reasonably well-designed and reasonably performing GA, a measure of convergence toward a single value is preferable to terminating the algorithm after a specific number of generations. A maximum generation threshold, however, should almost always be a fail-safe condition on the genetic tuner.

❼ Breed a New Population of Fuzzy Model Configurations

If a termination condition is not satisfied, a new population of fuzzy model configuration parameters is created from the current population. Some portion of the best chromosomes is retained, some of the chromosomes are bred through crossover to produce new chromosomes, and a few chromosome genomes are randomly mutated to produce new varieties of models in the population. This is the core of the genetic tuning process.

11.2 **Configuration Parameters**

A configuration parameter tells the rule induction mechanism how to decompose variables into fuzzy sets, how to evolve the rules, and how to execute the rules. Tuning is the process of finding the set of configuration parameters that will create the best fuzzy model (one that has the highest degree of predictive accuracy). Tuning is, however, interpreted differently for different types of fuzzy systems. For semantic models, the tuning options are somewhat restricted and at a basic level include the following.

- Adjustments to the shape of fuzzy sets
- The degree of overlap in adjoining fuzzy sets
- The method of correlation and aggregation
- The defuzzification technique

The options are restricted to a large extent because the underlying fuzzy sets in semantic models represent the knowledge of SMEs and have been created by knowledge engineers to reflect this knowledge. Thus, we cannot arbitrarily add or remove fuzzy sets, change the overall shape of a fuzzy set, or change the degree of overlap between semantically related fuzzy concepts without altering the semantics and therefore the operation of the system.

The tuning aspects are particularly important and more varied in fuzzy models that are used to discover patterns in data and convert these into rules. This is due to the number of principal architecture components controlling the system's performance. These components include the following.

- The number of fuzzy sets
- The shape of the fuzzy sets
- The overlap of fuzzy sets
- The skew (asymmetry) of fuzzy sets
- The compactness (or range) of the fuzzy sets
- The method of correlation and aggregation
- The defuzzification technique

Each of these components has a significant effect on the performance of the fuzzy system. By changing the organization of the fuzzy sets underlying the independent and dependent (solution) variables, we can find a combination that provides the correct amount of decomposition or granularity and the correct shape for the component fuzzy sets.

Fuzzy Set Granularity

Figure 11.3 shows one possible representation of the variable *Client_Age* in a portfolio risk model automatically broken down into a number of equally spaced fuzzy sets.

This type of fuzzy set representation corresponds to the default decomposition method used in the Wang-Mendel fuzzy rule induction algorithm. The number of fuzzy sets specified for each variable determines the fine-grain resolution of the rules. Rules are induced from the intersection of the fuzzy sets underlying each variable. How much of the decision terrain is effectively mapped by each rule depends on how precisely each rule maps the relations between variables. For example, a rule induced from investment portfolios that gained or lost value might be represented as follows.

If Client_Age is A03
   And Client_Income is I03
      Then Investment_Risk is R15

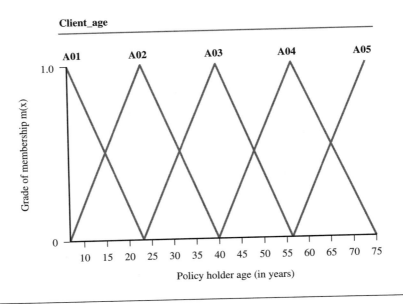

Figure 11.3 The decomposition of *Client_Age*.

Then, the degree to which a client age data value belongs to the *A03* fuzzy set and the degree to which a client income data value belongs to the *I03* fuzzy set indicates the degree to which *Investment_Risk* is a member of the *R15* fuzzy set. These form a patch of fuzzy regions representing the actual fuzzy rules. Figure 11.4 illustrates the fuzzy relationships for this rule.

As Figure 11.4 illustrates, the region over the variable's domain subtended by the fuzzy set directly affects the specificity of the rule. If fuzzy sets span large portions of the domain, the rules are less responsive to patterns that fall within these regions. We can see this by examining the same relationships with a less fine-grain set of fuzzy sets. As Figure 11.5 illustrates, the region covered by the intersection of *A03* and *I03* is much larger.

The size of the fuzzy region is the resolving power of the rules. Large regions are more likely to obscure patterns because they will be lost in the intrinsic noise associated with the span of data points underlying each fuzzy set. As we increase the number of fuzzy sets, the resolving power increases, but only to a certain limit. If the granularity is too fine, as illustrated in Figure 11.6, the rule induction process will miss larger patterns and find only random noise.

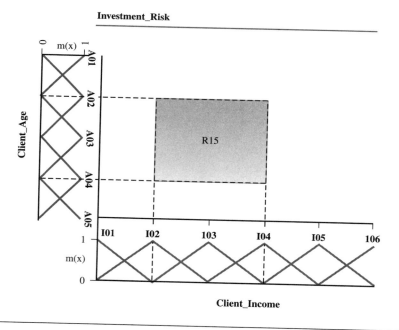

Figure 11.4 A rule as fuzzy relationships.

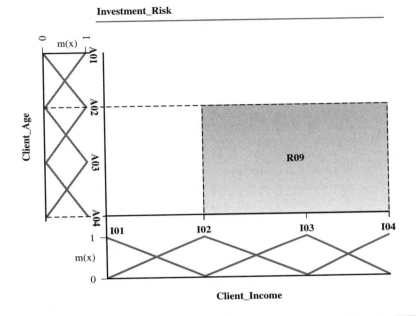

Figure 11.5   A rule with insufficient fuzzy relationships.

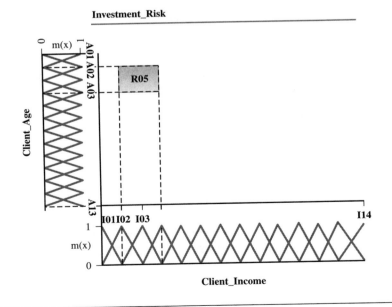

Figure 11.6   A rule with too many fuzzy relationships.

Finding the proper level of granularity or decomposition is one of the principal objective functions in tuning a fuzzy model. The genetic tuner creates a random number of fuzzy sets placed equidistantly across the variable's UoD. In fact, this will be the objective of the fuzzy system tuning example in this chapter.

Fuzzy Set Compactness and Skew

Compactness and skew are connected properties and are related to the distribution of fuzzy sets across the domain of the variable. In the ordinary way of decomposing a variable into fuzzy sets, a uniform partitioning of the variable's range is used to create N symmetric fuzzy sets, arbitrarily named and spaced from left to right. Yet in many models some parts of the range of values require a finer granularity than other parts (for example, a fuzzy model that evaluates health care requirements might need to have a higher distribution of fuzzy sets around the middle-aged and senior range of values in order to discriminate among various types of risks or services). Figure 11.7 illustrates an example of a patient's age variable with a change in fuzzy set compactness.

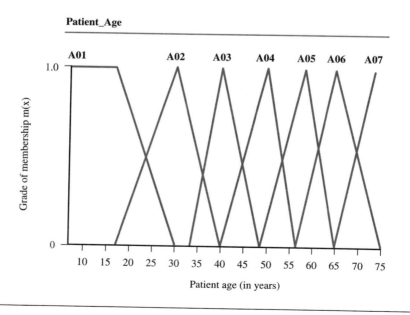

Figure 11.7   A variable with varying fuzzy set compactness.

Related to compactness is the concept of fuzzy set skew or asymmetry. One or more fuzzy sets must be asymmetric in order to create a variable term set with differing degrees of compactness (as you can see with fuzzy sets *A01* and *A02* in Figure 11.7). In some models, an even higher degree of skew is necessary to properly represent the patterns in the underlying data. Figure 11.8 illustrates the patient age variable decomposed into asymmetric fuzzy sets with a general focus around middle-aged values.

Changing the distribution of fuzzy sets across the domain of a variable is often a powerful pattern-discovery mechanism and should be one of the secondary parameter controls in the rule induction engine. Combining the number of fuzzy sets with the idea of compactness and skew, however, requires a significant and somewhat complex change in the way automatic fuzzy set partitioning is accomplished.

Fuzzy Set Shape

With the exception of the number of fuzzy sets, no other parameter has such a direct impact on model performance as the shape of the underlying fuzzy sets. Traditional control theory applications generally use triangular fuzzy sets due to their ease of construction and evaluation.

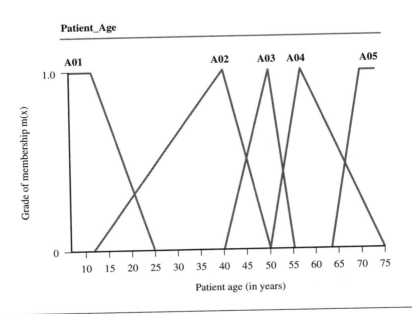

Figure 11.8 A variable with highly skewed fuzzy sets.

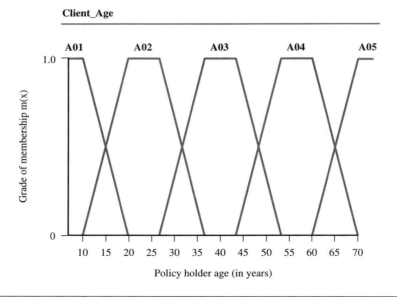

Client_Age

Figure 11.9 The trapezoid decomposition of *Client_Age*.

Business, industry, and policy fuzzy systems generally use bell-shaped or trapezoidal fuzzy sets. But the nature of how a variable is decomposed into fuzzy partitions depends on a fuller understanding of how the data is being used and the types of fuzzy relationships (or rules) we hope to induce from the data. Figure 11.9 shows the *Client-Age* variable decomposed into a collection of trapezoid fuzzy sets.

Although bell-shaped fuzzy sets provide a smoother and more robust partitioning than triangular sets, trapezoid fuzzy sets are often used when the model has (or the knowledge engineer expects that it will have) classes of values rather than continuous values across the domain. The use of trapezoids can force a subset of values in the domain to become clustered in plateaus and thus act as classes (so that, for example, all ages close to 40 years old will have the same membership value, which forms a class and causes rules to treat all of these values as essentially the same value).

11.3 **Implementing and Running the Genetic Tuner**

A genetic tuner must be connected to the both rule discovery mechanism and the fuzzy model execution engine in such a way that it can repetitively generate new systems and determine their level of performance. In this chapter we briefly examine a tuner that is connected to a fuzzy data mining and modeling tool. A tuning mechanism can be used to adjust the performance of any fuzzy model, including those based solely on semantic fuzzy sets derived by SMEs. A genetic tuner connected to a rule discovery facility provides a powerful mechanism for evolving fuzzy models with a diverse range of objective functions. In this section we examine a single objective: to find the best decomposition of variables into fuzzy sets.

The Temperature Prediction Model

The genetic tuner will optimize the temperature prediction model discussed in Chapter 8. As a review, the model learns the seasonal variations in annual temperatures in the Midwest of the United States from several years of data. The model then predicts the average temperature for a given month. Expression 11.4 shows this as a functional relationship.

$$t_m = f(m_i) \tag{11.4}$$

Here,

t_m is the average temperature for the specified month
m_i is a month index in the range $1 \ldots 12$
$f()$ is a function that maps the month index to a temperature

The idea behind rule induction is to evolve or discover this functional relationship. The relationship in the fuzzy temperature prediction model is expressed through a series of rules that defines regions on the underlying solution surface. Each region is defined by a fuzzy *if-then* rule. Figure 11.10 illustrates how the temperature and month fuzzy sets decompose the variables so that the seasonal periodicity of the temperature trend line can be defined (and later discovered).

As Figure 11.10 illustrates, as the temperature and time axes are decomposed into fuzzy sets a collection of "patches" emerges that defines the underlying function. In this case, the fuzzy relation *(T05,M05)* represents a region on the function in the area bounded by the domain of the temperature fuzzy set *T05* and the domain of the month fuzzy set *M05*. The number of fuzzy sets along the two axes determines the fine-grain detail of the function. Figure 11.11 illustrates this schematically by overlaying the implicit month-to-temperature function with a small set of overlapping fuzzy regions.

Each patch on the function line represents a potential rule. Whether a rule appears for the patch depends on whether a data point exists in the

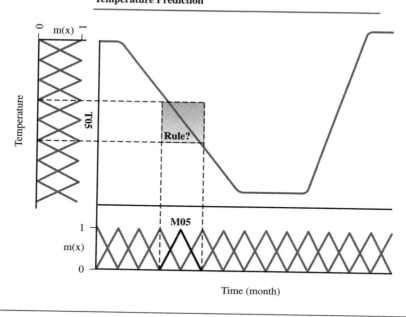

Figure 11.10 Fuzzy representation of the $t = f(m)$ function.

training data for the patch (fuzzy relationship). Whether a data point generates a fuzzy relationship depends on the number of observations in the training data corresponding to the fine-grain granularity of the variables. Unlike the rectangular rule space of a conventional FAM, which produces an implicit rule for each combination of fuzzy sets in the variables, the rule induction process generates rules from the training data, thus producing highly effective rules only in those regions of the problem space that have representative data. Figure 11.12 illustrates the connection between rule induction and the target fuzzy model.

In Figure 11.6, the data points aligned with the month-to-temperature function provide the exemplars for each generated rule. Note that the region specified by the relation (T06,M07) lacks any data points. No rule is generated for this point. If we increase the width of the time fuzzy sets, relations (T06,M06) and (T06,M07) could be merged and would have data points to generate a rule. However, the specificity in this case would be reduced.

The objective of a fuzzy tuning mechanism, then, is to find the granularity of fuzzy sets that corresponds to the data and at the same time to provide the highest degree of generality and specificity (often conflicting

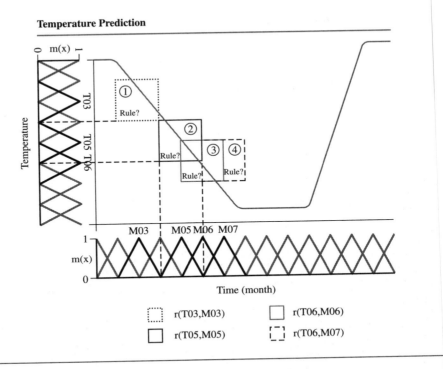

Figure 11.11 Fuzzy patches overlaying the month-to-temperature function.

objectives). In this genetic tuning example, we are concerned with only the second objective: reducing the standard error or estimate by finding the rules with highest degree of specificity.

Because the temperature prediction model itself is relatively simple, it makes it rather easy to explore the ways in which random fuzzy systems are created, processed, and evaluated to find this functional relationship. This section builds on three previous ideas: fuzzy systems, rule induction, and GAs.

The Parameter Chromosome

The genome structure for the genetic tuner consists of a single value for each variable: the number of fuzzy sets. Because this is a simple GA with an equally simple objective function (minimize the standard error of prediction), the tuner uses a binary (bit) encoding for the number. Figure 11.13 shows the structure of the chromosome.

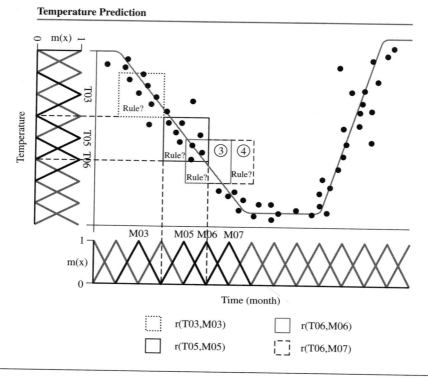

Figure 11.12   Data points on the function surface.

	Chromosome	
Fitness	Temperature	Month

Figure 11.13   The genetic tuner chromosome.

The genome locus for each fuzzy set count consists of 5 bits, giving a possible value of $(2^5) - 1$ or 31 fuzzy sets per variable. The fitness is stored as a real number. Each chromosome represents the term set size for the associated variables. The rule induction system will decompose the variables into this specified number of 50% overlapping triangular fuzzy sets. A collection of rules is derived from this configuration. Figure 11.14 is an example of the initial genome population for the tuner.

	Chromosome	
	Fitness	Fuzzy Set Counts
1		0011100010
2		1010000001
3		1000100110
4		0111110010
5		0101011101
6		0101111010
7		0010111110
8		0011111110
9		1001101110
10		1011111101

Figure 11.14 An initial population of genes.

Each bit string genome encodes the count of fuzzy sets for the model variables. In the first chromosomes, for example, *[11100]* (or 7) is the number of fuzzy sets in the temperature's term set, whereas *[01000]* (or 2) is the number of fuzzy sets in the month's term set. Each value is decoded using a simple power-of-2 accumulator to retrieve the decimal value. Listing 11.1 is the algorithm for making this binary to decimal conversion.

```
Let bits = incoming chromosome bit string
Let value = Returned decimal value

set value      = 0
set N          = length of(bits)
set powerOf2   = 1
set i          = 0

repeat while(i < N)
   if bits[i] = "1"
      set value = value + powerOf2
   powerOf2 = powerOf2 * 2
i= i + i
End repeat
Return(value)
```

Listing 11.1 Decoding a chromosome bit string.

The bit length of the chromosome automatically provides a constraint on the maximum number of fuzzy sets we can assign to any variable, thus maintaining an upward limit on the degree of granularity. This model does not ensure that the minimum number of chromosomes is greater than 1 (or some other small number), but this would be a reasonable constraint on the tuning algorithm.

Setting Up Initial Genetic Parameters

We start the tuning or optimization of the temperature model by specifying a population size (the number of initial chromosomes) and the maximum number of generations. A general control panel, shown in Figure 11.15, handles all high-level parameters for the tuner.

The control mechanism for genetic tuning also establishes several operating characteristics for the GA. These include a measure of the difference between one degree of fitness and the next (the sensitivity to changes in the standard error of estimate), the crossover probability rate,

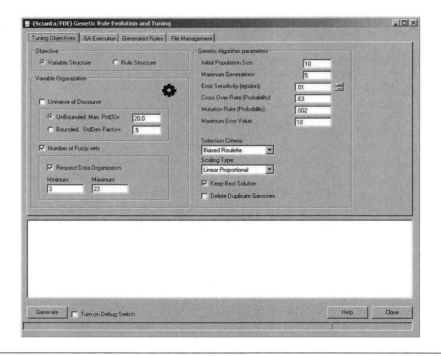

Figure 11.15 The genetic tuning parameters screen.

and the mutation probability rate. The type of selection strategy and the type of population scaling are also specified on this control screen.

Understanding the Objective Function

The GA now attempts to minimize the standard error of estimate by generating a series of fuzzy systems with the month and temperature variables partitioned into differing numbers of fuzzy sets. The number of fuzzy sets associated with a variable determines the number of possible rules. The number of rules, as discussed earlier, determines the level of granularity, which in turn determines broadly the number of rules that can be discovered. The GA uses the standard error of estimate as its goodness-of-fit measure and attempts to find the balance of fuzzy sets in the variables that minimizes the error. Examining the outcome of the genetic tuner for a few genomes in one generation illustrates this point. Listing 11.2 is part of the audit log from a tuning run.

The standard error for this model is relatively low due to the coverage of fuzzy sets over the problem space. Figure 11.16 takes the configuration represented by this model and illustrates its features in terms of fuzzy relationships. Each connection between a month and a temperature represents a possible rule.

At the same time, a less dense representation of the problem space (in terms of fuzzy set coverage) means that fewer rules can be discovered. Each rule covers a broader region of the problem space and has less specificity. Listing 11.3 is another chromosome from a tuning run with a smaller, randomly selected, number of fuzzy sets for each variable.

```
GENERATION: 1

GENOME: 1
GA--Gen: 1 RUN FUZZY SYSTEM...
GA--[01] Clear Fuzzy System
GA--[02] Create Fuzzy System (Genome=1101110110 )
    Temperature 11101---Term Set: 23
    Month    10110---Term Set: 13
GA--[02-1] END--Create Fuzzy System
GA--[03] Evolve IF-THEN Rules
GA--[03-1] END--Evolve IF-THEN Rules. Rule Count= 293
GA--[04] Execute Fuzzy System
GA--[04-1] END--Execute Fuzzy System. Std Error= 0.128
```

Listing 11.2 An extract from a genetic tuning audit log.

Temperature Prediction

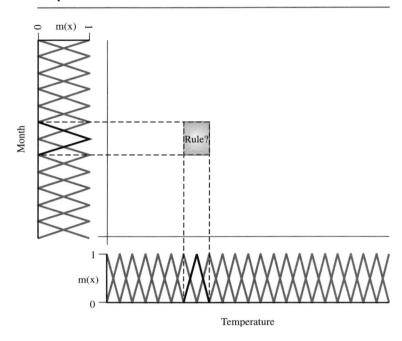

Figure 11.16   A dense fuzzy representation of the problem space.

```
GENOME: 2
GA--Gen: 1 RUN FUZZY SYSTEM...
GA--[01] Clear Fuzzy System
GA--[02] Create Fuzzy System (Genome=1111010100 )
   Temperature 11110---Term Set: 15
   Month     10100---Term Set:  5
GA--[02-1] END--Create Fuzzy System
GA--[03] Evolve IF-THEN Rules
GA--[03-1] END--Evolve IF-THEN Rules. Rule Count= 38
GA--[04] Execute Fuzzy System
GA--[04-1] END--Execute Fuzzy System. Std Error=4.405
```

Listing 11.3   An extract from a genetic tuning audit log.

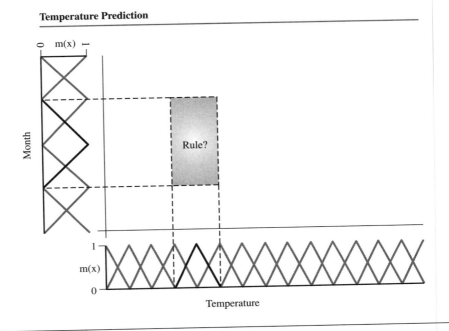

Figure 11.17 A sparse fuzzy representation of the problem space.

The standard error for this model is large due to the sparse coverage of fuzzy sets over the problem space. Figure 11.17 takes the configuration represented by this model and illustrates its features in terms of fuzzy relationships. Again, each connection between a month and a temperature represents a possible rule.

The GA generates many possible configurations, with many degrees of granularity in the underlying fuzzy sets. It is guided toward the correct balance by a simple objective function: minimize the standard error of estimate (the difference between the actual outcome and predicted outcome in the validation data file).

Executing the Genetic Tuner

Figure 11.18 shows the steady decrease in the average standard error as the algorithm converges on a proper number of fuzzy sets for each variable.

Without increasing genetic diversity in a small number of chromosomes over a relatively small number of generations, the optimal

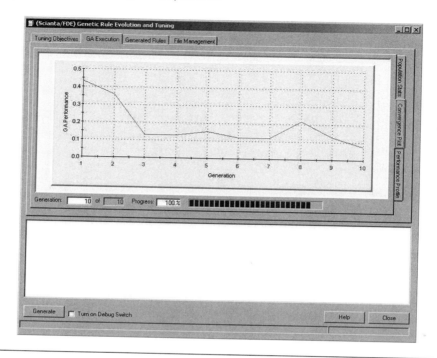

Figure 11.18 The standard error (performance) trace.

configuration can be missed. This means that the amount of variability in the genome drives the average standard error close to a single value too quickly over a small number of generations. Figure 11.19 shows an example of this situation.

In Figure 11.19, the standard error of estimate began at a larger value (the "luck of the draw" in a GA, presumably a fuzzy system configuration with fewer fuzzy sets than required for a higher degree of precision). In a small number of generations, the average fitness drops quickly to roughly 4.5, and remains steady at this value for the remainder of the generations. Without increasing genetic diversity in a small number of chromosomes over a relatively small number of generations, the convergence can be accelerated but the optimal configuration can be missed. This means, as reflected in Figure 11.19, that the amount of variability in the genome keeps the average standard error close to a single value over a small number of generations.

A genetic tuner provides a fast and flexible method of partitioning variables into a collection of fuzzy sets so that a balance is achieved between generality and specificity. By seeking to minimize the standard error of estimate, a genetic tuner can quickly find the best partitioning for fuzzy

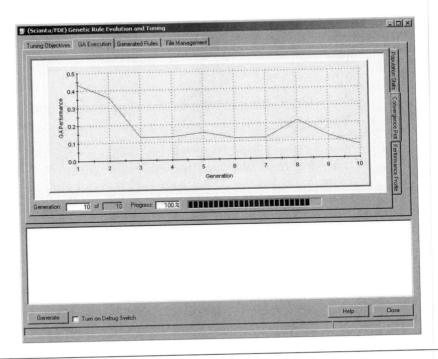

Figure 11.19   Early convergence with higher genetic variability.

models with even a large number of variables. In this example, we have explored the partitioning of the temperature prediction model because it provides a tight coupling between the issues covered in the rule induction chapter and the ideas covered in this chapter on the optimization of fuzzy systems. A GA, however, can provide a search and optimization mechanism to find the best architecture for systems under a variety of complex constraints.

11.4   **Advanced Genetic Tuning Issues**

Tuning or optimization provides a sophisticated tool for exploring the architecture, processing, and adaptive response of a model. Although finding the optimal partitioning of variables in a rule induction engine is an important capability, the same type of genetic optimization can also easily find a broad spectrum of configuration parameters (see "Configuration Parameters" at the start of this chapter). These configuration parameters are focused primarily on the nature of the fuzzy sets associated with a variable. That is, they address the configuration of the variable's term set. But more advanced optimization and search techniques can be used to tune a larger spectrum of model properties.

Principal Component Analysis and Variable Selection

In many large knowledge discovery (or data mining) projects the choice of independent variables (and sometimes the choice of a dependent variable) must be made from a very large collection of possible variables. A rule induction engine connected to a variable selection GA can search through a large number of variables attempting to find those that minimize the standard error of estimate. Figure 11.20 illustrates a possible architecture for a variable selector.

❶ Generate and Initialize the Genetic Algorithm

The initial phase of the genetic variable selector involves the design and implementation of a chromosome population to represent the set

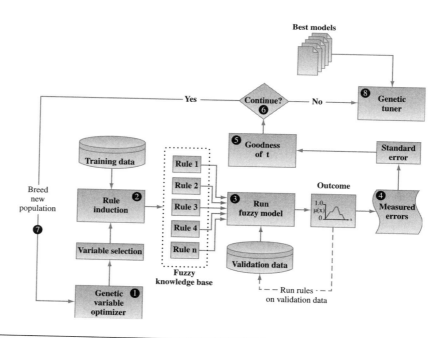

Figure 11.20   A variable selection genetic optimizer.

	Fitness	Chromosome					
		Variables					
1		3	8	17			
2		2	23				
3		7	12	17	21	34	
4		5	8	13	19		
⋮							
n		2	3	5	11	35	48

Figure 11.21   Chromosome design for variable selection.

of possible independent variables. Perhaps the easiest complement is a varying-length vector or linked list containing index values into an array of all possible names. Figure 11.21 illustrates one possible design for the chromosome.

This has the advantage of simplicity as well as extensibility, allowing the variable selector to more or less easily select modification operators for the variables. This provides a selection capability somewhat similar to evolutionary programming, providing the ability to pick *log(x)*, *sqr(x)*, *power(x,y)*, and similar transformational operators.

❷ Run the Rule Induction Engine

Each genome in the population represents a potential model. Assuming y is the dependent (outcome) variable, the first chromosome in the population (see Figure 11.21) represents the possible model shown in Expression 11.5.

$$y = f(v_3, v_8, v_{17}) \tag{11.5}$$

Here,

y is the dependent or outcome variable
v_i is an independent variable in the range $1 \ldots n$, where n is the maximum number of candidate independent variables
$f()$ is a function that maps y to the set of independent variables

From these independent and dependent variables the rule induction process generates a set of rules in the form

if $v_3 = x_i$ and $v_8 = y_i$ and $v_{17} = z_i$ **then** y, where x_i, y_i, and z_i are fuzzy sets drawn from the variable's corresponding term set. The term set is created automatically for each variable from the default parameters of the rule induction engine (which are based on a statistical analysis of a randomly selected subset of the data). At this phase of the process the engine is concerned with deriving a set of operationally effective rules, not with ensuring that the fuzzy set partitioning is optimal.

➌ Run the Fuzzy Model

Once the fuzzy KB has been created through rule induction, the rules are executed against the validation data file. The validation file compares the outcome generated by the rules against the actual value for each observation (record) in the validation file. The difference is the degree of error in the estimate.

➍ Accumulate Measured Errors for Each Instance

In this step the variable selection mechanism measures the degree of error between the estimated and the actual values for each record or instance in the validation file. The standard error of estimate is used to find the accuracy of the current model (see Expression 11.1 for a definition of this measure). We should expect that a rule with insufficient variable support will have a very high standard error of estimate. The objective function for variable selection, however, involves two conditions.

- Minimize the standard error of estimate
- Minimize the number of selected variables

That is, the GA searches for the rule set that has the smallest standard error with the minimum number of variables. Expression 11.6 is a simple weighted average objective function to drive the algorithm.

$$f_i = \frac{1}{w_1 + w_2} \left[\left(w_1 \times e_{\text{est}(i)} \right) + \left(w_2 \times \frac{v_i}{N} \right) \right] \qquad (11.6)$$

Here,

f_i is fitness for the i-th chromosome

w_1 is the weight associated with the standard error of estimate value

w_2 is the weight associated with the number of variables used

$e_{est(i)}$ is the standard error of estimate for the i-th chromosome (see Expression 11.1 for a definition of the standard error used in this context)

v_i is a count of the number of variables used in this model

N is the total number of variables in the selection pool

With $w_1 = 1$ and $w_2 = 1$, this is the average of the standard error and the ratio of the variables used to the total possible used. Changing the weight can bias the fitness function toward the standard error or toward the number of variables. In any case, for models with the same standard error of estimate the one with the smaller number of variables will be preferred.

❺ Evaluate Goodness of Fit

The multiobjective fitness function is a measure of how well a particular fuzzy model configuration performs in predicting the outcome values in the validation file. The smaller the fitness function the better the overall model configuration. After a fuzzy model, generated from a chromosome's variable selection, has computed the average standard error from the validation data file, this value is stored in the chromosome as the genome's goodness of fit.

❻ Decide Whether to Evolve More Models

When the current population of chromosomes has been evaluated, each will have a goodness-of-fit value indicating how well the model performed with a particular number of variables. Now some exit condition must be evaluated. This can be a maximum number of generations, but is more often a measure of the improvement in the overall population. This improvement (see Expression 11.2 and surrounding text for a more detailed discussion) is usually based on the average fitness in the population.

❼ Breed a New Population of Fuzzy Model Configurations

If a termination condition is not satisfied, a new population of variable configurations is created from the current population. Some portion of the best chromosomes is retained, some of the chromosomes are bred through crossover to produce new chromosomes, and a few chromosome genomes are randomly mutated to produce new varieties of models in the population.

❽ Optimize Fuzzy Set Partitioning for Set of Best Models

When the variable configuration GA is terminated, the population contains the models with the smallest possible number of variables and the best (minimum) standard error of estimate. These models were found because they had the best predictive ability based on the default (statistical-based) fuzzy set partitioning. In order to select the model with the best functional or predictive generality, the top N% of the models are selected for fuzzy set partitioning optimization.

Searching for an Optimal Choice of Model Parameters

Even in semantic models in which the fuzzy sets are derived from expert knowledge, the parameters associated with the type and size of fuzzy sets as well as measures of performance are often estimates. These estimates can, in many instances, be optimized through a genetic search process that measures the overall performance of the model against one or more calibration or global performance metrics. In Chapter 5, we discussed the competitive pricing model. This model, shown in Listing 11.4, has four principal rules.

Unlike most of the models discussed in previous chapters, the pricing model was not derived from data and as a result does not have a training and validation set. Its price prediction must "make sense" based on the expert pricing knowledge of the experts who built the model.

Search the Problem Landscape

The goal of this model is to find a price that satisfies a set of default boundary constraints (specified by a set of unconditional rules) and to balance the price subject to its relationship to the competition price. That is, as long as the competition price is not considered very high our price should be near the competition. Otherwise, our price should be constrained in

```
our price must be High
our price must be Low
our price must be around 2*MfgCosts
if the competition_price is not very High
   then our price should be near the competition_price
```

Listing 11.4   The fuzzy pricing model.

the space bounded by *Low*, *High*, and twice the manufacturing costs. Figure 11.22 illustrates the movement of price relative to the increase in competition price and subject to manufacturing costs.

The outcome price essentially follows the competition price until the competition price begins to be *very High*, at which point the price falls away and is constrained by the manufacturing costs. The central dashed area represents the region over the solution surface at which the landscape falls off as the competition price increases relative to the *very High* concept.

The Expectancy of Fuzzy Numbers

In this type of model we cannot arbitrarily generate fuzzy sets for *High* and *Low* (in the context of *price* and *competition_price*) because they have shapes that reflect a specific meaning in the model. We can, however, attempt to find the optimal expectancy (*e*) for the fuzzy numbers *2*MfgCosts* and *near competition_price*. Expectancy is the amount of tolerance or elasticity that exists in a fuzzy number and is generally measured as the distance from the center of the fuzzy number out to the edge of the number (the point where the membership value falls to either zero or below the alpha cut threshold). Figure 11.23 illustrates several different expectancies for twice the manufacturing costs.

As a percentage of the value, an expectancy has a broad range of values, from *e* = *0* (in which case the fuzzy number is equivalent to an

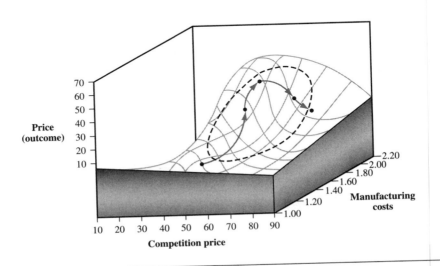

Figure 11.22 The movement of price in the fuzzy pricing model.

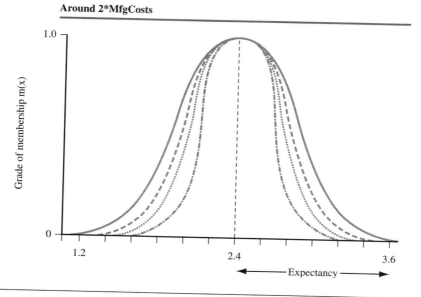

Around 2*MfgCosts

Figure 11.23 Different expectancy values for *2*MfgCosts*.

ordinary crisp number) to *e >> 100*, in which case the fuzzy number is spread out over a very large space. Normal expectancies are between 10 and 50% of the number's value.

The Performance Fitness System

The pricing model parameter optimization system is a form of adaptive feedback in that the outcome price is dependent on the expectancy measures of the manufacturing costs and the competition price, which in turn are modified by the value of the outcome price. Figure 11.24 is a schematic representation of the genetic system designed to discover the best expectancy values for the pricing model.

❶ Generate and Initialize the Genetic Algorithm

The initial phase of the genetic parameter optimizer involves the design and implementation of a chromosome population to represent the set of possible expectancy values for the *around* and *near* hedges (expressed as a percentage of the current value of the target variable). Given a static

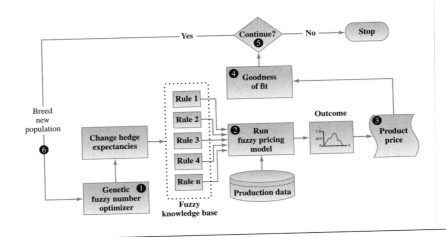

Figure 11.24 The fuzzy number (expectancy) optimization system.

	Chromosome	
	Expectancy (Percentages)	
Fitness	Around	Near
1	5	9
2	11	3
3	8	21
⋮		
n	13	7

Figure 11.25 Chromosome design for fuzzy numbers.

competition price and a manufacturing cost,[3] the chromosome for the problem (illustrated in Figure 11.25) involves the expectancy values for the *around* and the *near* hedges that convert the manufacturing costs and the competition costs into bell-shaped fuzzy numbers.

We generate a random population of expectancies between 5 and 50%, which is generally a reasonable range.

---

[3] This constraint is introduced to simplify the discussion. Production pricing models often involve price optimization against varying competition and manufacturing costs.

❷ Run the Fuzzy Pricing Model

Each chromosome in the population represents a pricing model with a different expectancy for the manufacturing costs and the *competition_price* variables.

❸ Find the Product Price Recommendation

The fuzzy pricing model fuses the conditional and unconditional rules to generate a recommended price. The outcome price is not only dependent in the model's concepts of *High* and *Low* pricing but the tolerances for being around twice the manufacturing costs and near the competition price. Changes in these tolerances move the recommended cost over the solution space.

❹ Compute and Evaluate Goodness of Fit

The GA minimizes the difference between the competition price and the recommended price consistent with the constraint that they cannot be the same. Model optimality is based on minimizing the simple objective function shown in Expression 11.7.

$$f_i = \|p_i - c\| > 0 \qquad (11.7)$$

Here,

f_i is fitness for the i-th chromosome
p_i is the outcome price for the model, for the i-th chromosome
c is the competition price

Thus, we are minimizing the difference between the predicted product price and the value of the competition price subject to the constraint that the difference must be greater than zero (our price cannot be the same as the competition). The recommended price must lie just above or just below the competition (we could preserve the sign of the difference and thus ensure that the recommended price moves toward but always stays just below the competition price).

❺ Decide Whether to Evolve More Models

In an analysis of the hedge expectancy parameters, we can terminate the GA based on the usual conditions (number of generations, steady state of hedge expectancy values, and so forth), but we can also impose a convergence tolerance on the recommended price. The tolerance stops the search when the price approaches the competition price and meets a specific price point value.

⊚ Breed a New Population of Hedge Expectancy Configurations

If a termination condition is not satisfied, a new population of hedge expectancy configurations is created from the current population. Some portion of the best chromosomes is retained, some of the chromosomes are bred through crossover to produce new chromosomes, and a few chromosome genomes are randomly mutated to produce new varieties of models in the population.

11.5 Review

This chapter extends the evolutionary strategy concepts introduced in the previous chapter by focusing on the optimal tuning or reconfiguration of a fuzzy system created through the rule induction algorithm. The technique highlights one of the important optimization capabilities of GAs: the ability to search through a high number of complex configurations to find an optimal or near-optimal solution. The chapter has also explored the general idea of optimizing the performance of any fuzzy system through a multiobjective and multiconstraint GA. You should now be familiar with the following.

- The way fuzzy systems are configured for optimization
- The possible objective functions used in tuning and reconfiguration
- How the number, shapes, and overlap of fuzzy sets influence the performance of a fuzzy system
- How tuning is balanced between generality and specificity
- The ways in which semantic fuzzy models can be tuned or reconfigured using GAs
- How evolutionary strategies can be used to perform variable-selection-related forms of principal component analysis

The use of GAs to create, tune, and reconfigure fuzzy models provides a powerful and flexible mechanism for building and deploying self-analyzing and self-modifying systems. The adaptive feedback capabilities supported by genetic programming allow models to adjust their internal controls and operating parameters in response to changes in data.

Further Reading

■   Cherkassky, V., and F. Mulier. *Learning from Data: Concepts, Theory and Methods*. New York: John Wiley and Sons, 1998.

Index